Whenever a student, client, or journalist asks for literature on pedophilia or online sexual offending against children, I always recommend the first edition of this book by Michael Seto—it's truly my favorite. The writing is clear and pedagogical, providing an authoritative overview of all the relevant information and scientific facts. Being a world-leading expert in the field, Michael Seto offers a profound, humanistic understanding of these complex issues. I'm thrilled that there is now a second edition!

—**Christoffer Rahm, MD, PhD,** specialist in psychiatry and Associate Professor at Karolinska Institutet, Stockholm, Sweden; Principal Investigator of several clinical trials directed to individuals with sexual interest in children

Why do people use the internet to cause sexual harm? What can we do about it? This book provides the best available account of this rapidly changing field: thoughtful, evidence-based, and practical.

—**R. Karl Hanson, PhD, C Psych,** Adjunct Professor, Carleton University, Ottawa, ON, Canada; President, SAARNA: the Society for the Advancement of Actuarial Risk Need Assessment

This book is a must-read for professionals seeking to understand and prevent online sexual offending. Dr. Michael Seto is the foremost authority on online sexual abuse and this second edition provides readers with the most current research on the assessment, treatment, and prevention of online sexual abuse.

—**Elizabeth L. Jeglic, PhD,** Professor, John Jay College of Criminal Justice, New York, NY, United States

Michael Seto's *Online Sexual Offending: Theory, Practice, and Policy* (2nd edition) addresses significant changes in the technological and political landscapes since its original 2013 publication (published as *Internet Sex Offenders*). It focuses on current and future trends in online sexual offending, including acts that may not yet be criminal in some judicial areas. The book is a valuable and original resource for both researchers and practitioners, especially concerning risk management and prevention. It adopts a public health framework and emphasizes evidence-based practices, making it an essential reference in the field.

—**Ethel Quayle, CBE,** Professor of Forensic Clinical Psychology, COPINE Research, Clinical & Health Psychology School of Health in Social Science, University of Edinburgh, Edinburgh, Scotland

Seto is the authoritative source on online offending, and this prodigious overview of the evidence is the go-to resource for everyone wanting to check on what the current state of knowledge is.

—David Finkelhor, PhD, Crimes Against Children Research Center, Family Research Laboratory, Department of Sociology, University of New Hampshire, Durham, NH, United States

This book is a must-read for trust and safety practitioners and scholars, discussing cutting-edge research on child exploitation in an accessible manner. Seto covers a range of topics, from how perpetrators use online services to exploit children to research on factors associated with these behaviors.

—Shelby Grossman, PhD, Research Scholar, Stanford Internet Observatory, Stanford, CA, United States

Online Sexual Offending
Second Edition

Online
Sexual Offending
Second Edition

Theory, Practice, and Policy

Michael C. Seto

 AMERICAN PSYCHOLOGICAL ASSOCIATION

Copyright © 2025 by the American Psychological Association. All rights, including for text and data mining, AI training, and similar technologies, are reserved. Except as permitted under the United States Copyright Act of 1976, no part of this publication may be reproduced or distributed in any form or by any means, including, but not limited to, the process of scanning and digitization, or stored in a database or retrieval system, without the prior written permission of the publisher.

The opinions and statements published are the responsibility of the author, and such opinions and statements do not necessarily represent the policies of the American Psychological Association.

Published by
American Psychological Association
750 First Street, NE
Washington, DC 20002
https://www.apa.org

Order Department
https://www.apa.org/pubs/books
order@apa.org

Typeset in Meridien and Ortodoxa by Circle Graphics, Inc., Reisterstown, MD

Printer: Gasch Printing, Odenton, MD
Cover Designer: Anthony Paular Design, Newbury Park, CA
Cover Art: Carolin Thiergart and Codioful (Formerly Gradienta) on Unsplash

Library of Congress Cataloging-in-Publication Data

Names: Seto, Michael C., author.
Title: Online sexual offending : theory, practice, and policy / Michael C. Seto.
Description: Washington, DC : American Psychological Association, [2025] |
  Includes bibliographical references and index.
Identifiers: LCCN 2024020486 (print) | LCCN 2024020487 (ebook) |
  ISBN 9781433839481 (paperback) | ISBN 9781433839498 (ebook)
Subjects: LCSH: Online sexual predators. | Sex offenders. | Child sexual
  abuse--Prevention. | Sex crimes--Prevention. | BISAC: PSYCHOLOGY /
  Psychopathology / General | PSYCHOLOGY / Forensic Psychology
Classification: LCC HV6773.15.O58 S483 2025 (print) | LCC HV6773.15.O58
  (ebook) | DDC 362.76--dc23/eng/20240820
LC record available at https://lccn.loc.gov/2024020486
LC ebook record available at https://lccn.loc.gov/2024020487

https://doi.org/10.1037/0000428-000

Printed in the United States of America

10 9 8 7 6 5 4 3 2

CONTENTS

Preface: Declaration of Personal and Professional Interests   vii
Acknowledgments   xi

    Introduction: The Growing Problem of Online Sexual Offending   3

1. **Prevalence and Characteristics of Online Sexual Offending**   13
2. **Child Sexual Exploitation Material**   31
3. **Sexual Solicitation of Minors**   67
4. **Other Online Sexual Offending**   89
5. **The Etiology of Online Sexual Offending and the Motivation–Facilitation Model**   109
6. **Risk and Other Clinical Assessment of Online Sexual Offending Perpetrators**   137
7. **Treatment of Online Sexual Offending Perpetrators**   183
8. **Prevention of Online Sexual Offenses**   203
9. **Conclusions and Future Directions: Understanding and Preventing Online Sexual Offending**   233

Appendix: Child Pornography Offender Risk Tool (CPORT) and Correlates of Admission of Sexual Interest in Children Scale (CASIC) Scoring Guidelines   243
References   249
Index   287
About the Author   293

PREFACE: DECLARATION OF PERSONAL AND PROFESSIONAL INTERESTS

I was trained and practiced as a clinical and forensic psychologist who realized that the scope of online sexual offending exceeded what could be addressed within the clinical and criminal justice systems. My first clinical and research interests were triggered by questions from colleagues in the early 2000s about the risk of reoffending and the treatment needs of individuals who had committed child sexual exploitation material (CSEM) offenses. The clinic I was affiliated with at that time—the Sexual Behaviours Clinic at the Centre for Addiction and Mental Health in Toronto, Canada—saw a dramatic increase in referrals for CSEM cases, from a small number of cases a year to one in six referrals when I left in 2008 to join The Royal, my current affiliation.

Some of my thinking about online sexual offending has been influenced by my identities as an Asian-Canadian, cisgender, heterosexual man who grew up in a working-class family and was a first-generation university graduate. As a result of my personal experiences, I hope I am more sensitive to the WEIRDness[1] of the research reported in this book, the exceptionalism of American policies and practices, the impact of environmental and systemic factors in addition to personal factors, and the implicit and sometimes explicit assumptions about whether the models, assessment tools, and interventions carried out with men in WEIRD countries will generalize across cultures or to women, nonbinary persons, or juveniles.

---

[1] WEIRD refers to Western, educated, industrialized, rich, and democratic, a term created by Henrich et al. (2010) to point out that most social science research has been conducted in a small set of countries such as Canada, the United States, the United Kingdom, and countries in Western Europe. Most people do not live in WEIRD countries, and whether the results of WEIRD research generalize is an empirical question.

In the first edition, I listed all my editorial board memberships and many professional and scholarly involvements in declaring my interests, but here, I focus only on those involving leadership. I have served as the editor-in-chief of *Sexual Abuse* since 2015; my second and final term ended in December 2023. Articles published in this journal are cited often in this book because its aims and scope closely correspond to the purpose of this book: understanding the etiology, assessment, and intervention of people who have committed sexual exploitation or abuse offenses. Articles in *Sexual Abuse* are not cited to pump up the impact factor of the journal, though they might contribute to citations for recent articles. The online sexual offending field is relatively small, so I cite friends and colleagues often. I also cite my own work a lot because it is relevant, but I am mindful that excessive self-citation is undignified.

I have received federal and provincial funding in Canada for research I describe in this book, including grants from the Social Sciences and Humanities Research Council and the Ontario Mental Health Foundation. These grants involved police partnerships and resulted in co-development of the Child Pornography Offender Risk Tool (CPORT) and the Correlates of Admission of Sexual Interest in Children Scale (CASIC) with Angela Eke of the Ontario Provincial Police (see Chapters 1 and 5). I received major funding from the Oak Foundation, with my coprincipal investigator, Elizabeth Letourneau (Johns Hopkins University), to advance perpetration prevention (see Chapters 6 and 7). I am part of an international consortium that received funding from the European Commission to translate and culturally adapt an online intervention for people who experience sexual urges regarding children that may lead to CSEM offending, online sexual solicitations, or other sexual offenses involving children (see Chapter 7). I received a grant from the Tiny Foundation for the social support study by Roche et al. (2022). I am part of the Correctional Services Accreditation and Advisory Panel that reviewed and accredited the iHorizon online sexual offending treatment program described in Chapter 6, and I continue to serve on this panel—funded by the United Kingdom's Ministry of Justice—for sexual offending programming.

I have served as a pro bono advisor for the Thorn Foundation, which is mentioned in multiple places in this book. The Thorn Foundation is a nonprofit organization dedicated to the elimination of online child sexual exploitation and abuse. Thorn has funded several research studies that are cited in this book, including an analysis of data from the National Center for Missing and Exploited Children on identified CSEM victims (see Chapter 1), an online survey of youth regarding self-generated CSEM (see Chapter 1), and sexual solicitation experiences (cited in Chapter 2). Through the Thorn Foundation, I became involved in the Technology Coalition, a nonprofit consortium of major tech companies, and in activities involving Thorn or Technology Coalition partners such as the WeProtect Global Alliance and End Violence Against Children.

I have been a paid consultant for Facebook (2019–2021), Google (2019–2023), and Apple (2021–2022) about child user safety, offering my knowledge as a clinician and scientist with extensive experience on the topics of offline and online sexual offending involving children. I signed nondisclosure agreements because these consultations involved access to internal data or processes, so I cannot discuss the specific consultations in this book. Broadly, my contributions included presenting to trust and safety professionals, reviewing proposed policies and procedures, and answering questions about perpetration and other online sexual offending research.

I helped develop several measures that are discussed in detail in this book. I have intentionally provided these measures—CPORT and CASIC and the Screening Scale for Pedophilic Interests (2nd ed.; see Chapter 6, this volume)—using Creative Commons licensing so they are noncommercially available and free to use, with attribution. Manuals, FAQs, and other documents about the CPORT and CASIC are provided freely on the ResearchGate platform. Readers can also contact me directly by email or social media. I sometimes indirectly make money from these tools by providing training workshops, but none of the measures require formal training, and I am not the only person who can provide this kind of training.

I have intentionally never testified in a court matter in the United States in the belief that this makes me more credible, so my research is not perceived as influenced by whether I tend to testify for the prosecution or defense. I still have no idea if this makes any difference! I have not testified in Canada in many years for the same reason. I did testify as an expert witness on CSEM offending before the United States Sentencing Commission in 2011, and I participated in an amicus brief to the California Supreme Court regarding a 2014 law mandating therapists to report if clients were viewing CSEM, a revision of an existing law that mandated reporting if someone was creating or distributing CSEM.

I was part of the *Diagnostic and Statistical Manual of Mental Disorders* (5th ed., text rev.; American Psychiatric Association, 2022) workgroup that provided text revisions regarding the paraphilic disorders. Almost all my contributions were for the text regarding pedophilia and pedophilic disorder. I argued for the inclusion of CSEM as a key indicator of sexual interest in children (Criterion A) successfully but was not successful in making the case that it is relevant behavior for Criterion B, which specifies distress or impairment sufficient to justify the diagnosis. I argued that CSEM use that resulted in social or legal repercussions is evidence of impairment (see Seto, 2022).

ACKNOWLEDGMENTS

I was able to complete this book because I had the support of Florence Dzierszinski and the University of Ottawa's Institute of Mental Health Research at The Royal for a writing leave when I was able to reduce some of my administrative duties for 6 months. As before, I was lucky to have excellent support from The Royal's librarians, particularly Susan Bottiglia, who puts up with my frequent and sometimes quite unusual requests for books and other resources.

I would like to thank Carissa Augustyn, Kelly Babchishin, Susan Curry, Angela Eke, Sacha Maimone, Lyne Piché, Kailey Roche, and Anton Schweighofer for their insightful and extremely valuable comments on draft chapters of this book. I also want to give extra special thanks to Carissa, Susan, Sacha, Lyne, and Kailey for reading the whole thing. I am also grateful to Kailey for creating the motivation–facilitation model and case formulation model figures in Chapter 4 and for helping to reformat tables and other elements.

I want to thank Susan Reynolds for her long-term and steady support of my books for the American Psychological Association (APA). This edition will be the fourth volume I have published with APA. I benefitted greatly from and am grateful for the editorship of David Becker through the production of this book from the first submitted draft, peer reviews, and revisions. The two peer reviewers gave excellent feedback, and I know this book is better as a result of their insightful comments.

I want to acknowledge the sacrifices and commitment of my parents, Ellen Shuet Ying Seto (1938–2019) and John Siu Hung Seto (1937–2024), who made it possible for me to live and work in Canada and pursue my interests in psychology and then research as a first-generation undergraduate and graduate student. I don't know if they ever fully understood what I do, but I know they realized what it meant to me and what it has meant to others.

This book is dedicated to Meredith and Oliver. Forever and always.

Online
Sexual Offending
Second Edition

Introduction

The Growing Problem of Online Sexual Offending

More and more people are online, and more and more people are using internet technologies to carry out their daily activities, including school, work, entertainment, news, community, and government services. Internet access rates are approaching a ceiling in the most economically developed countries—where the tiny fraction of those who do not use the internet are making this choice or do not have the resources due to poverty—and are rapidly increasing in less economically developed countries in Asia, Africa, and Central and South America (Our World in Data, 2023).

More internet access means more opportunities to engage in online sexual offending. Most of the attention so far has been on the problem of accessing and distributing child sexual exploitation material (CSEM, which is defined later in this chapter; see also Chapter 2) using internet technologies, followed by sexual solicitations of children that may involve demands for self-generation of child pornography, sexual messages, sending pornography, and in some cases, attempting to meet in real life where contact sexual offending may occur. As we will see in later chapters in this book, though, there are other ways that online technologies can be used to facilitate sexual offenses, including other kinds of offenses involving children, such as sextortion and sexual trafficking, sexual assaults of adults, digital exhibitionism and voyeurism, and other image-based offending.

My goal is for this book to be an authoritative source on the psychology of online sexual offending, with practical implications for researchers, clinicians, law enforcement, and policymakers. I combine both an applied and social

https://doi.org/10.1037/0000428-001
Online Sexual Offending: Theory, Practice, and Policy, Second Edition, by M. C. Seto
Copyright © 2025 by the American Psychological Association. All rights reserved.

science perspective, reflecting my career as a clinician–scientist. I am not aware of another book that covers the same ground. Though I have written this book to be published by the American Psychological Association (APA), I do not have only a clinical, counseling, and forensic psychology audience in mind. I believe this book is also of value to professionals in other health and social services, criminal justice, and the technology industry, which increasingly (if belatedly) recognizes its responsibility to provide safer products. Online sexual offending sits at the intersection of trends in technology, law, crime, psychology, public policy, child welfare, and human rights. This is probably why I have continued to be active as a clinician, consultant, and scientist in this area—because these intersections are complex, challenging, and fascinating.

I draw from diverse lines of scholarship but do not consider myself even close to being an expert on technology, law, public policy, or human rights. I do have substantial clinical and research experience in the psychology of crime, particularly online sexual offending and sexual offending against children. This book builds on my knowledge and experience as a clinical and forensic psychologist who has practiced, consulted, and conducted research on online sexual offending since the early 2000s, including the first recidivism study (Seto & Eke, 2005), meta-analysis of recidivism studies (Seto et al., 2011), and development of an offense-specific risk assessment tool (Seto & Eke, 2015). I have also trained and consulted in this area with clinicians, law enforcement, and child safety staff at major tech companies (see Preface for disclosures).

CHANGES FROM THE FIRST EDITION

I am grateful to have an opportunity to substantially revise and update this book, which first appeared in 2013 and was later published in an abridged Italian translation in 2017. There have been many developments in research, policy, and practice since the first edition, and I continue to be actively involved in this work. As I note several times in this book, technology continues to evolve rapidly, so some of the findings and conclusions I highlight may soon be outdated. At the same time, there has been an accumulation of evidence on some topics that gives me confidence that other conclusions will be robust. This includes what we have learned about the motivations of individuals who have committed online sexual offenses and the factors that increase their risk of committing such offenses.

As I recounted in the preface of the first edition, I was originally inspired to write a book on online sexual offending by positive feedback after I gave a plenary talk at the 2009 conference of the Association for the Treatment of Sexual Abusers (now the Association for the Treatment and Prevention of Sexual Abuse). This feedback indicated there was a lot of demand for an authoritative review and synthesis of the literature on online sexual offending. I believe that is just as true more than a decade later, with much more policy and public attention to the risks that internet technologies can pose for sexual harm, particularly to children. This includes the use of these technologies to facilitate the access and distribution of CSEM, online sexual solicitations, and other forms of sexual harassment and abuse, as well as belated recognition of the ways these technologies can be used to harm adults. This increasing attention has resulted in an amazing proliferation of scholarship on online sexual offending in the years since the first edition. A basic search of the APA's PsycInfo database, for example, shows there have been over 600 peer-reviewed articles and hundreds of books, chapters, or theses on CSEM offending since 2013 (see Chapter 2), with additional—though fewer—publications on sexual solicitation (see Chapter 3) and image-based abuse, including nonconsensual resharing of images and sextortion (see Chapter 4). Indeed, there has been enough scientific research to produce multiple meta-analyses and reviews of this literature since the first edition (Babchishin et al., 2015, 2018; Broome et al., 2018; Helmus, Eke, & Seto, 2024; Henshaw et al., 2017).

The scientific and political environments have changed a great deal since the first edition as well. As I am revising this Introduction, big technology companies are facing intense scrutiny regarding their policies and practices in online safety, including concerns about the scale of content moderation and reporting and evidence of negative effects of online behavior on mental health, user privacy, and misinformation. In addition to revising and updating the ideas and scientific knowledge for this edition, I made the following major changes:

- I go into much less detail about the history of the internet and CSEM offending because this was already covered in the first edition, and it is not essential for understanding the current and future problems created by online sexual offending because people are much more familiar with internet technologies and the impacts of different technologies on online sexual offending, particularly CSEM offending. I instead devote more space to discussing the general and specific affordances provided by internet technologies that can facilitate or deter online sexual offending in the hope that this leads to changes that increase online safety (see Technological Affordances That Can Facilitate Online Offending in Chapter 1).

- I aspire to use person-first language, inspired by an editorial by Willis and Letourneau (2018), guidelines I introduced as editor-in-chief of *Sexual Abuse*, a prominent journal outlet for research on online sexual offending, and the APA's (2023) guidance on bias-free and person-first language. Nonetheless, for ease of writing and reading, I still often refer to "perpetrators" as a shorthand for individuals who commit online sexual offenses, recognizing this is not person-first language.

- I cover more forms of online sexual exploitation and abuse, including some behaviors that are not (yet) criminal offenses in many jurisdictions because they are emerging and there are plans to criminalize them in other countries (e.g., nonconsensual sharing of sexual images). Other forms of online offending have received some attention, though not much (e.g., upskirting; see Chapter 4).

- I have a lot more to say about clinical and risk assessment because of advances in this literature (see Chapter 6). It is still the case that most of the assessment research has been on CSEM offending, but we do have more online solicitation research and emerging research on the factors associated with new forms of online sexual offending, such as nonconsensual resharing and other image-based offending.

- I say much more about primary and secondary prevention of online sexual offending instead of focusing on tertiary prevention, where interventions respond to offenses that have already occurred. I have shifted over time to a more global and public health perspective, which is also reflected in my career (collaborations that are more international and foundation-funded work on perpetration prevalence, risk and protective factors, and perpetration prevention). Therefore, I devote an entire new chapter to different prevention approaches and the challenges of online perpetration prevention (see Chapter 8).

TERMINOLOGY

What do I mean by "online"? I am referring specifically to the use of internet technologies—which can include messaging apps, social media apps or platforms, gaming platforms, and online forums—to facilitate sexual offending. This could be extended to mobile-to-mobile communications, though, technically, phone calls and texts using SMS do not directly involve internet technologies. In this book, I focus on sexual offending where internet technologies play a central role in the commission of these acts, such as in seeking illegal images of children online or engaging in sexual communications with children online. I use *sexual offending* to refer to sexually motivated behavior that violates criminal law and thus puts the actor at risk of prosecution, conviction, and punishment. I push this definition in this book, however, because I also review research on sexually motivated behavior that is rarely, if ever, prosecuted (e.g., use of illegal pornography depicting sexual violence toward adults or bestiality), behavior that is illegal in only a few jurisdictions so far (e.g., nonconsensual sharing of sexually explicit images of adults), or behavior that may become criminalized soon because of perceived harms (e.g., creating and sharing so-called deepfake images of real people; see Textbox 1.2).

In this book, I intentionally exclude some illegal behavior even though it would count as online sexual offending. For example, any minor self-generating content or sending it to a peer (self-generated CSEM or sexting; see Chapter 2) would be engaging in criminal behavior that could be charged as production or distribution of CSEM. Some jurisdictions are decriminalizing this behavior or using prosecutorial discretion, but it still meets the legal definitions. I discuss self-generated content in this book as risky behavior that can place a young person at risk of nonconsensual sharing (and thus becoming new CSEM content) and sextortion. Another exception in my coverage is the use of online technologies to facilitate sex work by adults. Again, this is illegal in many jurisdictions, but I do not include it in this book because it does not involve minors or coercion. Some advocates suggest all sex work is exploitative and coercive, but others argue that sex work is work and sex workers, therefore, deserve worker rights (e.g., Mgbako, 2020).

I frequently refer to *child sexual exploitation material* (CSEM) in this book, which is also sometimes referred to as *child sexual abuse material* (CSAM) in the literature. I use CSEM to refer to sexual content depicting minors, also referred to as "child pornography," which is the widespread, international legal term for sexually explicit content depicting minors (International Center for Missing and Exploited Children, 2023). Many scholars, clinicians, advocates, and victims are moving away from using the legal term because it can be seen as minimizing the seriousness and harm involved in the production and/or distribution of this content. Whatever one thinks of adult pornography, this content is produced with adults who must prove their age and identity and consent to be recorded. Child content, in contrast, involves children who cannot legally consent, is obviously unregulated in its conduct and, in many cases, are recordings of sexual abuse, as when someone records their sexual offenses against children.

Under Canadian and American law, CSEM encompasses sexually explicit visual depictions of a real minor. Sexually explicit depictions can include suggestive posing, a focus on the genitals in the recording, or depictions of sexual activity; nudity on its own may not meet this legal threshold. Canadian law differs from American law by including nonvisual depictions, such as audio recordings, as well as content depicting fictional minors, such as drawings, entirely computer-generated images, and stories (see Virtual CSEM and Child Sex Dolls section in Chapter 2). The International Center for Missing and Exploited Children (2023) surveyed laws across the globe and found commonalities across most countries that have CSEM laws or enforce prosecutions against CSEM under existing obscenity laws. The most common elements involve visual depictions, sexually explicit content, and a defined age range for minors, though sometimes set at different ages. As discussed in Chapter 2, content that would meet the legal criteria of CSEM that is produced by or exchanged between teen minors may be effectively decriminalized by police or prosecutor discretion, in recognition that this behavior is common and different in criminal intent than for adults engaging with CSEM (e.g., if produced and shared with a partner without coercion, not reshared without permission, or used for extortion; see Dodge & Spencer, 2018). However, it is still a concern because of the risk of nonconsensual sharing or sextortion in the future, as when an ex-partner decides to use the images to harm the person depicted in the images.

In this book, and in my previous writing about sexual offenses involving online sexual interactions between adults and children, I refer to *sexual solicitation* instead of luring, enticement, or grooming, which tend to be the terms used in laws and policies regarding this behavior (see Chapter 3). I prefer solicitation as a label because luring or enticement implies the use of incentives, which is not always the case, and grooming implies gradual, typically prolonged interactions that shift from seemingly innocuous to explicit sexual requests, often involving manipulation or deceit. However, these kinds of online sexual interactions are sometimes immediately coercive and direct. Sexual solicitation does not imply anything about tactics or sequence of interactions, only that an actor is soliciting some kind of sexual interaction from a target, whether that involves sexual chat, sexual images, online sexual behavior (e.g., live streaming while undressing or masturbating), or arranging to meet in person where sexual contact may take place. Most of the attention has focused on adult men sexually soliciting minors, particularly younger children, but sexual solicitations can also be directed at adults and can be perpetrated by women or older juveniles.

A. Powell et al. (2019) defined image-based sexual abuse as "the taking, distributing, and/or making of threats to distribute a nude or sexual image without a person's consent. Some definitions focus on distribution or threat—and not taking—however, resulting in a narrower focus on so-called 'revenge pornography'" (p. 393), where images may have been taken or shared consensually but then resharing is not consensual (e.g., Pacheco et al., 2019).

I refer to *image-based sexual abuse* when talking about nonconsensual image-related behavior involving adults; CSEM could also be considered a form of image-based abuse involving minors, as in the case of self-generated content that is shared without consent or used to blackmail the content creator. I prefer this term because it encompasses different forms of offending behavior, including *digital exhibitionism* (e.g., sending unsolicited "dick pics"), *digital voyeurism* (invading someone's privacy by recording them without their consent while they are nude, seminude, or engaged in normally private behavior), and *nonconsensual sharing* of sexually suggestive or explicit images. This last form of behavior is often colloquially referred to as "revenge porn," but this, in turn, is a misnomer because there are motivations other than revenge and, again, the word "porn" discounts the nonconsensual and distressing impact of the behavior (see Chapter 4). McGlynn et al. (2017) suggested there is a continuum of image-based abuse that includes digital voyeurism, nonconsensual resharing, and sextortion, as well as other ways of using images to potentially harm others, such as using photo manipulation software to create new images, as in the emergence of *deepfake* technology, where someone's face could be digitally integrated with existing pornographic images or video to create new content (see Deepfakes section in Chapter 2).

I use *sextortion* to refer to threats to release a sexually explicit message or image to coerce someone into further behavior, including sending more sexually explicit content or engaging in physical sexual activity. Sextortion can be committed by strangers who somehow obtain sexually explicit content, whether through hacking or online sexual solicitation, or it can involve threats to nonconsensually share sexual content such as messages or images by an intended recipient, as when a partner or ex-partner threatens to post nudes publicly. Sextortion can also involve demands to involve others in sexual exploitation or abuse, as when a sextortion victim is coerced into creating new CSEM with other minors, such as a younger sibling. In this case, the sextortion could be described as *multiplied sextortion*, where a single act involves multiple victims.

I use *technology-facilitated sexual assault* to refer to sexual assaults of adults that are directly linked to the use of technology, as when men intentionally use dating apps or platforms to find potential partners they intend to coerce into sex, either through intoxication, verbal pressure, or physical force. In other words, I am not considering cases where potential or current dating partners may communicate using messaging apps or where someone initially met the person they victimized online. I am restricting my focus on technology-facilitated sexual assault to those cases where individuals use technology to increase their reach in searching for targets. Similarly, I focus on sexual solicitation offending, where someone intentionally uses technology to sexually solicit a minor, and not cases where the perpetrator and target already knew each other and incidentally communicated sometimes online.

Sexual trafficking of children refers to the commercial sexual exploitation of minors by others, particularly adults who control the young person's activities, which can include family members or partners. Under American law, any commercial sexual exploitation of minors is de facto trafficking because the young person cannot consent to engage in sex work, unlike an adult who might choose to engage in sex work. Sexual trafficking of children is related to another form of technology-facilitated sexual offending involving children, which I refer to in this book as *child sexual abuse tourism*. Child sexual abuse tourism involves the cross-border movement of individuals to jurisdictions where child sexual abuse can occur more readily, for example, because of corruption, lax or unenforced laws regarding sexual activities involving children, or differences in the legal age of consent for sex. Both sexual trafficking of children and child sexual abuse tourism are forms of *commercial sexual exploitation of minors*. The focus of public policy and (limited) research on child sexual abuse tourism has been transnational offending, where someone goes to another country for this purpose, but child sexual abuse tourism could also involve movement between regions of the same country. Merdian et al. (2019) defined transnational child sexual abuse as "(a) offenders, including those with a criminal history, travelling to a different jurisdiction and engaging in the sexual abuse of children; (b) offenders who intentionally reside abroad for offending purposes (semi-permanent or permanent residence)" (p. 2). Merdian et al. also included cases where perpetrators engaged with children living abroad through live streaming, but I would count this instead as an example of online sexual solicitation (if the child is live streaming of their own accord) or online sexual trafficking of children because live streaming is often facilitated by adults who profit from these interactions. Online technologies can also be used to facilitate the sexual trafficking of adults, where adults are tricked, manipulated, or forced to engage in sex work against their will, and to facilitate sexual assaults of adults.

I discuss a number of different paraphilias in this book as potential motivations for different forms of online sexual offending. As explained in the *Diagnostic and Statistical Manual of Mental Disorders* (5th ed., text rev.; *DSM-5-TR*;

American Psychiatric Association, 2022), paraphilias are recurrent and intense sexual interests in atypical sexual targets or activities that manifest in sexual thoughts, fantasies, urges, sexual arousal or behavior for a period of 6 or more months. The most commonly discussed paraphilias in this book are *pedophilia* and *hebephilia*, referring to sexual interest in prepubescent or pubescent children, respectively. These and other age-related paraphilias are further analyzed in Seto (2017b). In this book, I often refer to *pedohebephilia*, given evidence these two paraphilias are closely associated (Stephens et al., 2019).

Other relevant paraphilias for this book are *exhibitionism*, where someone is sexually aroused by the idea of exposing their genitals to an unsuspecting person; *voyeurism*, where someone is sexually aroused by the idea of observing an unsuspecting person engaged in a normally private activity, such as undressing, bathing, or masturbating; *biastophilia*, where someone is sexually aroused by making someone engage in sexual activities without consent; and *sexual sadism*, where someone is sexually aroused by causing someone pain or suffering. In the *DSM-5-TR*, these paraphilias can be diagnosed as paraphilic disorders if they are accompanied by significant distress and/or impairment as a result of the sexual interest. The *International Statistical Classification of Diseases and Related Health Problems* (11th ed.; *ICD-11*; World Health Organization, 2019) refers to coercive sexual sadism disorder to capture the elements of coercion and causing pain or suffering. The *ICD-11* also includes a new diagnostic category, compulsive sexual behavior disorder, that has a high level of conceptual overlap with what I describe as *hypersexuality* in this book.

OVERVIEW OF THE BOOK'S CONTENT

In Chapter 1, I discuss the context in which online sexual offending occurs, focusing in particular on the expanding reach of internet access and how technology features (affordances) can facilitate online sexual offending. I anchor my subsequent reviews of online sexual offending by describing what we know about the harms of these crimes on victims. Because almost all online sexual offending research has been conducted in a handful of countries, with a focus on men, I discuss the limits of generalizing from this knowledge.

In Chapter 2, I summarize what we know about CSEM offending, beginning with prevalence and perpetrator characteristics and then the clinical and forensic significance of CSEM content, CSEM production, and dual offending (committing both CSEM and contact sexual offenses). I also discuss new challenges and debates in this area, including the technological arms race in how CSEM is accessed and distributed, AI-generated content, virtual CSEM, and other illegal sexual content (e.g., depicting sexual violence or bestiality).

In Chapter 3, I discuss sexual solicitation offending, again beginning with what we know about prevalence and perpetrator characteristics. I point out that there are different types of sexual solicitation and that this form of offending can overlap with CSEM offending when the perpetrator solicits sexual images of minors or sends CSEM as a way of grooming or manipulating targets.

In Chapter 4, I cover multiple forms of online sexual offending because there is much less research about image-based sexual abuse (including digital exhibitionism, digital voyeurism, and sextortion), technology-facilitated sexual assault of adults, and the use of online technologies to facilitate the commercial sexual exploitation of children through trafficking of minors and child sexual abuse tourism.

In Chapter 5, I describe the motivation–facilitation model of sexual offending (Seto, 2019) as a framework for considering the factors that motivate different forms of online sexual offending and the factors that facilitate acting on these motivations. The motivation–facilitation model is one way of engaging in case formulation that can drive risk and other clinical assessment (described in Chapter 6) and treatment (described in Chapter 7).

Chapter 8 is a new chapter that focuses on the prevention of online sexual offending as a proactive rather than reactive approach to this problem. The final chapter (Chapter 9) summarizes the key conclusions to be drawn from this book-length overview of what we know about online sexual offending, with a focus on future directions for research, policy implications, and practice implications.

CASE EXAMPLES LATER IN THIS BOOK

Brief, recurring hypothetical case examples were created for Chapters 2 to 8, appearing at the end of each of these chapters, to illustrate the range of individuals who might be seen by clinical or criminal justice professionals because they have committed online sexual offenses. They are necessarily short but include many elements of cases I am familiar with. These examples categorize perpetrators as "lower risk" or "higher risk." I recognize there are problems with using unanchored descriptions like these, but I also recognize this language is easily understood and is often used by police, the courts, and the public. Keep these examples in mind as you read Chapters 2 to 4 regarding CSEM offending, sexual solicitation offending, and other forms of online sexual offending. It will also be helpful to return to these cases in Chapter 5, where I present a theoretical model for considering the psychological factors that can motivate or facilitate online sexual offending, and the applied chapters regarding risk and clinical assessment (Chapter 6), treatment (Chapter 7), and prevention (Chapter 8).

1

Prevalence and Characteristics of Online Sexual Offending

A good source of information on the share of the population using the internet comes from Our World in Data (https://ourworldindata.org). In 2020, approximately 60% of people had access to the internet, representing a huge pool of potential perpetrators and potential victims (Our World in Data, 2022). However, this access is not uniform; it is available to 92% of people in North America; approximately 80% of people in Europe, Central Asia, the Middle East, and Northern Africa; and majorities in East Asia and Latin America, but it is available to less than half of the populations in South Asia and sub-Saharan Africa (though these latter rates had doubled in only 5 years). The rapid pace of growth in internet access, particularly using mobile devices, suggests that most people who want internet access will have it in the near future.

In some ways, the distinctions between online and offline behavior are becoming thinner and fuzzier because online technologies have permeated modern life. Internet technologies are regularly used for education and work, government interactions, information, entertainment, banking, dating, and so on for billions of people. The distinction between online and offline offending is likely to blur further as our digital and physical lives become even more intertwined and digital natives become adults and then older adults. There are still older adults, as I am revising this text in 2023, who do not use computers and are never online or are infrequent or limited users. However, many younger adults do everything online. It is conceivable that, eventually, most offline sexual offending against children will be facilitated by the use of internet technologies. This may include using internet technologies to record

https://doi.org/10.1037/0000428-002
Online Sexual Offending: Theory, Practice, and Policy, Second Edition, by M. C. Seto
Copyright © 2025 by the American Psychological Association. All rights reserved.

and store child sexual exploitation material (CSEM), sexually communicate with known or stranger targets, and engage in the commercial sexual exploitation of children.

Despite this blurring, however, I believe there will still be online-exclusive offending and offline-exclusive offending for those who eschew internet technologies or believe trace digital evidence can be incriminating. Online-exclusive offending is most likely to involve CSEM possession and distribution and solicitation offending that focuses on online sexual interactions only (see Chapter 3). At the same time, some forms of online offending necessarily involve in-person behavior, including the technology-facilitated sexual assault of adults, sexual trafficking of minors, and child abuse tourism.

The demand for CSEM is high for several reasons. First, up to 1% of men have pedophilia or hebephilia and thus may be motivated to seek content that matches their sexual interest in prepubescent or pubescent children (Seto, 2018). Next, men who are attracted primarily to adult women may still show a substantial sexual response to postpubescent adolescents and even some sexual response to prepubescent and pubescent children. One of the clearest demonstrations of this sexual response gradient was reported by Lykins et al. (2010). In this study, a community sample of heterosexual men who denied any sexual interest in children and who had no self-reported or official history of CSEM use or sexual offending against children showed the most genital sexual arousal to adult women, consistent with their self-reported sexual orientation and sexual history. However, they also showed substantial arousal to pubescent girls, followed by prepubescent girls. In Seto (2018), I suggested the potential for casual or opportunistic CSEM demand—involving depictions of older adolescents—is hinted at in the popularity of pornography genres such as teens, barely legal, high school girls, and fauxcest ("stepdaughter"; see the Escalation From Legal to Illegal Content section in Chapter 2). Peters et al. (2014) discussed how different text, visual, and verbal cues denote youthfulness in legal adult pornography and can hint at the idea that the depictions involve minors. Though a lot of policy and practice attention has focused on chronic CSEM offending, some individuals who commit CSEM offenses may only do so occasionally or for a short time because of curiosity or thrill seeking (see Chapter 2). Third, most minors are sexually attracted to their peers and are, therefore, interested in content depicting their peers. This can include sexting, resharing images (even without consent), and searching for adolescent content online.

There is a wide spectrum of antisocial and criminal behavior online, ranging from daily harassment, trolling, and bullying to international organized crime syndicates using encrypted messaging and cryptocurrencies to conduct their illegal businesses. Online technologies have many obvious and widely recognized benefits in terms of accessing information, entertainment, and interacting with others. However, there are also significant online costs, in part because of design features and the mismatch between our psychologies and this novel modern environment. Indeed, online technologies provide both general and specific affordances that can facilitate sexual offending (see later in this chapter). This facilitation includes scale in the degree of access and affordability of illegal content (e.g., CSEM) and interactions (e.g., sexual solicitations of minors), as well as the broad disinhibition of behavior because of perceived anonymity, perceived lack of consequences, and the absence of direct social feedback (see Cooper, 1998; Suler, 2004).

A central reason the internet is so powerful is its potential reach. A search engine can provide access to all the information currently hosted on the clearnet.[1] That is much more powerful than going to a local library or asking experts (though a problem with the internet is finding old pages and websites, unlike our ability to access paper archives). Similarly, someone who is interested in possessing CSEM can access content globally through the internet, whereas someone who is interested in physical CSEM has to find someone locally who is willing to trade or sell. Another example would be the sexual solicitation of minors; most people meet a limited number of young adolescents in their daily lives, but hundreds of millions of young adolescents are online at any given time if someone is interested in sexually interacting with them.

Types of online sexual offending are enshrined in specific laws, including CSEM offending and online solicitation of minors. Newer laws, such as those in Canada, criminalize the nonconsensual sharing of sexual images of adults (any sharing, whether "consensual" or not, of minors is already illegal under CSEM laws). Only some countries have laws about digital voyeurism, and only some countries have laws about child sex trafficking and child sex tourism. Because laws are so variable, my definitions rely on what is illegal in Canada and the United States, the two nations I know best in terms of their federal legislation.

Online sexual offending is a truly global phenomenon, though it is not evenly distributed due to differences in terms of law enforcement, public policy, and technology itself. For example, technology companies based in the United States, such as Meta, Apple, Google, and Microsoft, are legally obliged to report CSEM on their platforms to the National Center for Missing and Exploited Children (NCMEC). Therefore, this misses CSEM discovered by non-U.S.-based companies, such as those based in China. The reports to NCMEC are truly global—indeed, more reports involve Asian users than American users (Bursztein et al., 2019)—and point to how we must improve our cross-cultural understanding of the etiology of online sexual offending to develop better prevention strategies. We cannot rely on clinical and criminal justice responses alone, though they too are part of a comprehensive response to this problem. I am particularly interested in prevention strategies for individuals at risk of online sexual offending and technology-facilitated deterrence in the forms of specific interventions (e.g., blocking the transmission of known CSEM, detecting previously unknown CSEM and sexual solicitations) and changing both specific and general affordances that facilitate online sexual offending at the ecological level.

---

[1] *Clearnet* refers to the publicly visible part of the internet, which can be indexed by popular search engines. This can be contrasted with the *darknet*, which is invisible to typical search engines and is usually accessed using the Tor browser, which has been optimized for privacy and security at the expense of speed and convenience.

THE PREVALENCE AND IMPACT OF SEXUAL HARM

My primary motivation for this work is to prevent sexual harm. For this reason, research on the impacts of online sexual offending on victims is an important starting point. In the first edition of this book, there was little research, so I briefly described case studies by Burgess et al. (1984) and Svedin et al. (1996) about CSEM victimization that may not have involved any internet technologies. There has been more research since the first edition, including the Canadian Centre for Child Protection (2017) survey of 150 CSEM victims, the Gewirtz-Meydan et al. (2018) survey of 133 CSEM victims, and the WeProtect Global Alliance and ECPAT[2] (2022) interviews with 42 CSEM victims. Across these studies, younger online CSEM victimization is associated with perpetration by relatives or by family friends, most likely due to their access and opportunity with younger children. There is also a rapidly growing literature on the impacts of image-based sexual victimization (see Henry et al., 2020). Across studies (Canadian Centre for Child Protection, 2017; Thorn, 2022), girls are consistently more likely than boys to be victimized in CSEM, solicitation, trafficking, and child sexual abuse tourism. Women are much more likely to be victims of technology-facilitated sexual assault than men. The gender differences for image-based victimization are smaller but still often observed.

Respondents to the Canadian Centre for Child Protection's (2017) survey had to be adults to participate in the survey and victims of contact child sexual abuse that was recorded—this means that someone who was photographed nude or told to pose in a sexually suggestive way or who sent images of themselves, would not have been eligible for this survey. Notable findings from the Canadian Centre for Child Protection sample include the following: A majority (70%) of respondents worried about being recognized by someone because of CSEM and, indeed, 20% (30/150) said someone who saw their CSEM had identified them. Half (56%) of the respondents said the abuse began before the age of 4, and 87% said it began when they were 11 or younger. Almost half (42%) were abused for more than 10 years, which again is consistent with what is known about intrafamilial sexual abuse (and is consistent with other research on the production of CSEM; see Chapter 2, this volume). In terms of perpetrator tactics, two thirds (67%) of the victims said they were threatened with physical harm, over half (55%) were shown adult pornography, and a sizable minority (42%) were shown CSEM, possibly as part of the abuse (e.g., to show the child what they were supposed to do) or as part of a grooming process (e.g., to desensitize victims to what was happening).

Most Canadian Centre for Child Protection (2017) survey respondents said they were recorded in photos (95%), and 72% were recorded in videos. A minority (14%) had their sexual abuse live streamed and thus shared with others. A 24% of respondents were audio recorded, and 13% were involved in

---

[2]ECPAT was formerly known as End Child Prostitution and Trafficking and is an international nongovernmental organization (NGO) focused on eliminating child sexual exploitation, particularly in the forms of sexual trafficking of minors and child sexual abuse tourism. WeProtect is an international alliance of governments, NGOs, and tech companies concerned about online child sexual exploitation and abuse.

written accounts. Both audio and text depictions of children in sexual situations could have met the Canadian legal standard but not the American legal standard for CSEM. (Everyone who had audio recordings also stated that video content was created.) A majority (71%) of respondents were aware that their sexual abuse was being recorded at the time; presumably, others were too young to realize they were being recorded, the camera was hidden, or they did not notice they were being recorded while being sexually abused. A further 17% were not sure. Regarding intentionality and the contrived nature of CSEM content, 91% were told to do something in addition to sexual acts; in the subset who answered an open-ended follow-up question, respondents said they were told to pose in a certain way (44%), smile (38%), or wear a particular costume (38%).

The Canadian Centre for Child Protection (2017) report acknowledged several survey limitations, including its complete reliance on self-report and the possibility that some respondents completed the survey multiple times. The report authors also recognized that there likely was a selection bias in terms of how the survey came to the attention of respondents because some unknown fraction of respondents were already involved with the Canadian Centre for Child Protection or an international working group representing advocates and survivors.

Some of the Canadian Centre for Child Protection (2017) results are unusual. In particular, one in five respondents said they had been identified by someone who saw their CSEM, which means not only were they recognized but they were also aware that they were recognized. This seems odd because it assumes that CSEM has such a wide reach that a victim might encounter someone who saw their content, even though only some CSEM is shared with others. It is also hard to imagine that a CSEM user would acknowledge they recognized someone from that content because they would then be admitting to criminal behavior. This 20% rate may be more understandable if others who recognized the respondent included people already known to them, such as a nonoffending family member who became aware of the CSEM, or if it included situations in which a police investigator was able to identify them as a victim from distributed CSEM.

Another unusual finding from the survey is that almost 50% (74/150) reported they were victims of organized sexual abuse, which involves coordination among multiple perpetrators (Canadian Centre for Child Protection, 2017). Organized child sexual abuse certainly does occur, but not at this rate in child sexual abuse cases. This unusual finding might be explained by an association between the production of CSEM and having multiple perpetrators or by greater survey participation by respondents who had been victimized in an organized way. The high levels of organized child sexual abuse may also help explain the high rates of concerns respondents expressed about being recognized because recognition might include co-perpetrators.

Though I have described two unusual findings, many of the results reported by the Canadian Centre for Child Protection (2017) are consistent with observations in the survivor survey by Gewirtz-Meydan et al. (2018). Nearly half of the 133 survivors in this second survey were worried about being recognized or others assuming they were willing participants. However, they were not asked if they were recognized, unlike in the Canadian Centre for Child Protection

(2017) survey. In the Gewirtz-Meydan et al. (2018) survey, nearly half of the sample thought the effects of CSEM exploitation differed from other kinds of child sexual exploitation or abuse. One third refused to talk about it, and 22% denied there were CSEM images. In terms of characteristics of the CSEM victimization, most (93%) had contact sexual offenses recorded, 83% were age 12 or younger, and the CSEM offending tended to persist. Half (52%) were victimized by a relative, with women reporting family members more than men and men reporting acquaintance perpetrators more than women. Half (48%) were aware that the CSEM was shared with others. Approximately a quarter reported their victimization to child welfare or police authorities, but only 16 cases resulted in charges, with an 88% conviction rate. Again, this survey also had a selection bias because the survivor respondents were recruited through service organizations and support groups, versus a more wide-open survey recruitment that might recruit participants who reported different characteristics or experiences (recognizing that a broader survey might have to recruit large samples to identify a sufficient sample of CSEM survivors).

WeProtect Global Alliance and ECPAT (2022) interviewed 42 women survivors of online sexual exploitation, which could include CSEM but also other forms of offending, such as sexual solicitation by adults. The women were between 18 and 23 years old at the time of the interview and 12 to 17 years old at the time of the offenses. All were connected with ECPAT or a partner agency so, again, there was likely a selection bias for those who saw it as serious, negative, and/or long-lasting. Qualitative findings included the following: Most were not aware of formal reporting mechanisms beforehand, suggesting a need for education and awareness efforts; they mentioned women perpetrators, despite there being almost exclusively men represented in official data and clinical and criminal justice research (see Gender section later in this chapter); and perpetrators were often known to the victim and in positions of power over them (e.g., adult family relative, teacher), countering the public focus on "stranger danger." This last observation is not to suggest that strangers do not pose a risk to children online or to suggest that strangers do not account for a large fraction of online child sexual exploitation. However, much more attention is paid to these solicitations by strangers, even as most of the solicitations are ignored by the targets (Thorn, 2021, 2023). In contrast, sexual solicitations from someone already known to the minor are more likely (I suspect) to result in CSEM self-production, engaging in sexual activities online, or meeting in person.

An important qualitative finding from the WeProtect Global Alliance and ECPAT (2022) study was the importance of a nonjudgmental, supportive, and caring person if the young person was thinking about disclosing their online victimization. Fear, guilt, and/or shame were identified by victims as impediments to disclosure. Unfortunately, a willingness to disclose did not mean the reporting was easy or effective. Though our social, health, and legal systems require disclosures to activate responses for victims, the friction in making these disclosures—including sometimes active resistance and discouragement—helps explain why sexual offenses are so highly underreported, with dire consequences in terms of providing appropriate victim services, identifying perpetrators, and intervening to prevent further or new offending (see Thorn, 2021, 2023). Disclosure is only a necessary first step in the process of intervention.

There is surprisingly little data on the psychological impacts of being sexually solicited online, and these data come from qualitative or small-sample research (e.g., Hamilton-Giachritsis et al., 2020; Joleby et al., 2020; Whittle et al., 2013). The Thorn (2022) research looked at actions taken in response to online solicitations but not the emotional or other consequences beyond being "uncomfortable" (p. 36).

For image-based offending, one survey of 2,956 Australian adult victims by A. Powell et al. (2019) only asked about how upsetting this experience was: 20% said it was not upsetting, 33% said it was somewhat upsetting, and 47% said it was moderately to extremely upsetting. Women were more likely than men to find the experience upsetting; 13% of women, compared with 27% of men, said it was not upsetting, which is important for understanding variation in impacts and resiliency. I am not aware of any quantitative data on the impacts of technology-facilitated sexual assault of adults, child sexual trafficking, or child sexual abuse tourism.

CHANGES IN ONLINE SEXUAL OFFENDING OVER TIME

Online sexual offending has changed in many ways since the first edition of this book. There have been more arrests and prosecutions for online sexual offending, particularly for CSEM offending and solicitation offending (Savage, 2024; United States Sentencing Commission, 2021), and some jurisdictions have introduced legislation criminalizing other online behavior, such as the nonconsensual sharing of sexually explicit images of adults and digital voyeurism (see Chapter 4). This increase reflects a larger pool of potential perpetrators because many more people have access to the internet now than 10 years ago, and there is more public policy and law enforcement attention. It is hard to know what online sexual offending prevalence rates are, however, because of a lack of centralized data collection. National government data are often outdated or unavailable to the public, and many countries do not count or publicly report these numbers. We must instead rely on other data, such as perpetration and victimization surveys and mandatory reports of CSEM content to NCMEC in the United States for tech companies that operate there.

The technologies that are used to commit online sexual offenses have shifted as part of an ongoing arms race between perpetrators and law enforcement. For example, more CSEM offending involves the use of the darknet than before (Steel et al., 2020a), and tech companies have become better at detecting CSEM offending and solicitation offending by developing automated detection systems based on machine learning. In the first edition, I talked about hash matching software that can flag known CSEM images (PhotoDNA; https://www.microsoft.com/en-us/photodna); there are new technologies to detect previously unknown CSEM content and flag suspicious user interactions as potential sexual solicitation (see Chapter 8). The even greater prevalence of smartphone use means more image-based behavior can occur, including self-generation and sharing of CSEM by youths and production of CSEM and thus nonconsensual resharing and sextortion.

Steel et al. (2022) looked at the technical behavior of 78 CSEM perpetrators recruited from public registries in the United States. Most (95%) were men, 88% were White, and 72% identified as heterosexual. The most common technology used the first time CSEM was accessed was peer-to-peer file-sharing software (42%), followed by clearnet browsing (30%); browsing the darknet for CSEM the first time was rare (7%). Approximately half of the sample used a single technology, typically continuing with their entry technology; for example, if they sought CSEM using peer-to-peer file-sharing software the first time, they continued to use it. Twelve percent never stored CSEM, viewing content only, perhaps in the belief this would result in less digital evidence and a lower risk of prosecution. Steel et al. also asked about the use of countermeasures and compared the use of different countermeasures to a reference sample recruited from Qualtrics panels. Perpetrators engaged in several security countermeasures—to avoid detection—more than the general population, including deleting their browsing history, incognito browsing, secure wiping software, intentionally mislabeling storage devices or directories, and using onion browsing (a way of routing encrypted browser activity so that it is difficult to track to a specific internet protocol address or device). A caveat or limitation to consider in this study is whether there was self-report or selection bias in the participant responses. Another important caveat about this study and any study asking about security countermeasures is that all the participants got caught, suggesting they were either careless, unlucky, or used ineffective countermeasures; it is expected that those who use multiple, effective countermeasures consistently would be much less likely to be caught.

It is worth discussing changes in perpetrator characteristics and content parameters in detail because they both speak to our understanding of perpetration and how we can respond. For example, the National Juvenile Online Victimization survey data showed a trend toward younger perpetrators (a higher percentage of perpetrators age 25 or younger) across three waves of data collection from 2000 to 2009 (Wolak et al., 2012). This is consistent with a survey of CSEM users on the darknet that found most users began viewing CSEM as a minor and, for many, the first exposure was accidental (Insoll et al., 2022). A second example of change over time is the shift in interest to younger or more explicit CSEM content. This suggested honing of pedophilic sexual interests is based on what is reported to clearinghouses like NCMEC, not only what is in the collections of detected perpetrators (Salter & Whitten, 2022). Technology evolves, and users evolve with it, both in perpetration and the race to detect and intercede. Finally, there has been a rapid growth in perpetration prevention resources in the past decade, including helplines in different languages, self-help websites, online guided interventions, and in-person interventions (see Chapter 8).

DIVERSITY AND GENERALIZABILITY CONSIDERATIONS

Almost all the research I describe in this book has been conducted with men from a small number of WEIRD (Western, educated, industrialized, rich, and democratic) countries (see the following section, Gender), which means that most of these men are White as well. We cannot assume that this research generalizes to women, boys, girls, nonbinary persons, or Black, Indigenous, or other people of color. There is substantial evidence of gender differences in sexual offending, including online sexual offending, and there is emerging research about the impact of other diversity considerations, including sexual orientation and race or ethnicity.

Gender

Most perpetrators (80%–90%, depending on the source of the data) of sexual offenses against children are men, with a bigger gender difference found in clinical and criminal justice data compared with self-reported victimization surveys (Cortoni et al., 2017). This gender difference is even starker with online CSEM offending; Babchishin et al.'s (2015) meta-analysis shows that almost all (99% or more) CSEM perpetrators are men. This is in line with the large gender difference in the prevalence of pedohebephilia (most people with pedohebephilia are men; see Seto, 2018) and the strong association between CSEM offending and pedohebephilia (Blanchard et al., 2007; Seto et al., 2006). Little was known about women who commit online sexual offenses (data was mostly available only through case reports), until a 2019 American study showed that women in federal custody for CSEM offenses are likely to be co-perpetrating with a man (77%) and may produce or share CSEM for their partner or money, most often with their own child (71%; Bickart et al., 2019). These data suggest that explanations for CSEM offending by women differ from those offered for offending by men (see Chapter 5), with different risk factors and intervention needs (see Chapters 6 and 7).

Gender differences are smaller or less clear for other forms of online sexual offending. Self-report data has suggested that most sexual solicitation cases involve men soliciting girls (in the large majority of cases) or boys. Some case examples and surveys identify women perpetrators, but unless perpetrator identity is established by meeting or investigation, this may be a lie (e.g., when men pretend to be women to trick boys into sending sexually explicit images of themselves that can then be used for sextortion). Though there are fewer data, it appears that most digital exhibitionism and voyeurism is perpetrated by men, as is the technology-facilitated sexual assault of adults, sexual trafficking of minors, and child sexual abuse tourism (see Chapter 4; Karasavva & Forth, 2022; National Center for Missing and Exploited Children, 2017; Seto et al., 2018; Thorn, 2022). The one form of online sexual offending discussed in this book that shows a smaller gender difference in perpetration (or victimization) is image-based abuse involving nonconsensual sharing of images, though men are still more likely to perpetrate than women, and women are more likely to be victims than men (Henry et al., 2020).

There are several plausible explanations for the large gender differences in most forms of online sexual offending. This includes women being much less likely than men to have paraphilias such as pedophilia or hebephilia (particularly relevant for CSEM offending; see Chapter 2; Seto et al., 2021), having lower rates of compulsive sexual behavior (relevant to some CSEM and solicitation offending; see Chapters 2 and 3; Bőthe et al., 2018), and having lower levels of criminality (relevant to explanations for all online sexual offending; see Chapter 5; Cortoni et al., 2016). Reflecting gender differences in risk factors and perhaps a gender difference in the protective factor of social support as well (see Chapters 5 and 6), women are much less likely to sexually reoffend than men, both offline and online (Cortoni et al., 2010). At the same time, there is a gap between official and self-report data, where 2% of sexual crimes reported to police involve female accused, yet 11% of sexual crimes reported in surveys involve female perpetrators (see the meta-analysis by Cortoni et al., 2017). Moreover, 40% of men who reported being sexually victimized in surveys said the perpetrator was female, compared with 4% of women respondents, yet only 2% of sexual offenses reported to police involve female accused. This suggests that reporting, prosecution, or conviction biases are at play, where online or offline offending by an older man against a young teenage girl is denounced, though the same behavior might be downplayed if the offenses are committed by an older woman against a young teenage boy.

The most parsimonious explanation for the gender discrepancy in online sexual offending is that relatively few women are romantically or sexually attracted to children, and if they are, it is even rarer for women to be preferential or exclusive in their attraction to children. Few women are seen in clinical or forensic settings because of concerns about their sexual interest or behavior involving children (see Seto, 2018). In the community sample recruited in Czechia, Bártová et al. (2021) found that men were four times more likely to report any sexual interest in children than women (2.6% compared with 0.4%), where any interest is a low threshold and would not meet clinical criteria that include intensity, recurrence, and persistence of interest. Other studies also found a large gender difference in sexual interest in children (Joyal & Carpentier, 2022; Seto et al., 2021).

Little is known about women who are attracted to children. Stephens and McPhail (2021) reported on 20 cisgender women who admitted having a sexual or emotional attraction to children. The researchers found that these women reported attraction to both prepubescent and pubescent children, a preference for boys (50%) or both boys and girls (25%), and a high level of attraction without concomitant behavior. This is similar to research on men attracted to children, where attraction to both prepubescent and pubescent children is common, and men tend to prefer girls (see Seto, 2018). However, 42% of the women in the Stephens and McPhail (2021) sample reported emotional but not sexual attraction to children, whereas most men attracted to children reported both romantic and sexual attraction (Martijn et al., 2020). The takeaway for me from this study is that there is some similarity in the phenomenology of attraction to children for men and women, but women differ in important ways from men that influence the likelihood they will engage in sexual behavior involving children, including the use of CSEM or online sexual solicitations.

Madill and Zhao (2022) argued that female interest in child sexual content is expressed differently from male interest in this content, and this might help explain the large gender difference in CSEM offending. Whereas male interest leans toward visual, sexually explicit depictions, more female interest is apparent in the phenomenon of boylove stories (*danmei* in mainland China). If Madill and Zhao's supposition is correct, the high male bias in prevalence in published CSEM research and clinical and correctional samples is partially because the law emphasizes visual depictions, and in the United States, that is the only child content that is illegal. Sexually explicit stories about children would meet the legal standard in Canada or the United Kingdom, but it is plausible that fictional CSEM stories are a lower priority and, thus, are less vigorously investigated or prosecuted than images or videos depicting real children. In other words, the large gender difference in CSEM offending I describe in Chapter 2 would not be as large if nonvisual depictions were a focus of policy and practice as well. Madill and Zhao found that 6% of their Sinophone sample ($N = 1922$) and 12.1% of their Anglophone sample ($N = 1,715$) showed interest in stories describing adult–minor sex, with women reporting more interest than men. Most of the sample consisted of women recruited online through various websites and forums.

Sexual Orientation

Madill and Zhao (2022) also reported that nonheterosexual participants were more likely to report interest in stories describing adult–minor sex than heterosexual participants. Multiple surveys have found that nonheterosexual individuals are more likely to be involved in image sharing and resharing and are more likely to be targeted for online sexual solicitations than heterosexual individuals (e.g., Disrupting Harm surveys; Henry et al., 2020; Seto, Roche, Stroebel, et al., 2023).

Race and Ethnicity

The previous edition of this book did not specifically address racial or ethnic differences, noting only that the available evidence from Canada and the United States was that CSEM perpetrators were disproportionately White, whereas criminal justice populations are disproportionately made up of people of color in Canada and the United States (e.g., Department of Justice Canada, 2022; National Conference of State Legislatures, 2022). Some of this difference from other criminal justice populations might be explained by racial or ethnic differences in internet access because White people have more internet access than Black or Latine people living in the United States (Fairlie, 2017; Ryan, 2017) and so have more opportunity to commit online sexual offenses, everything else being equal. But we cannot ignore the role of inequity, given evidence that, like other sentencing, race is correlated with federal CSEM sentencing (Hartley et al., 2021). Specifically, Black or Latine defendants received longer sentences for CSEM offenses even after controlling for age, sex, criminal history, and presumptive sentence length (specified minimums) in the Hartley et al., 2021 analysis of data from the United States Sentencing Commission from 2006 to 2017.

Other Characteristics

Other characteristics protected in discrimination legislation, such as disability status, religion, or veteran status, have not been systematically explored in online sexual offending research. In a new study, Azizian et al. (in press) identified a subset of CSEM perpetrators who were veterans (53 out of the sample of 224 men seen in an outpatient clinic offering services to individuals on federal probation for CSEM offending). In a study that was not specific to online sexual offending, Paden et al. (2021) compared veterans and civilians who had been civilly committed for sexual offenses in California and found that veterans were significantly more likely to be diagnosed with pedophilic disorder (63% vs. 39%) and half as likely to be diagnosed with antisocial personality disorder (24% vs. 48%), suggesting different pathways to sexual offending. Veterans were more likely to victimize boys aged 13 or younger, while civilians were more likely to victimize girls over 13 and women. Veterans were also distinguished by higher rates of childhood sexual abuse and head trauma.

WEIRD Biases in Research

From Henrich et al. (2010), I can raise the concern that we should not assume that what we know about online sexual offending can be generalized to non-WEIRD countries. In my first book (Seto, 2008), I suggested pedophilia is likely a human universal, but most research on pedophilia has been conducted in a relatively small number of WEIRD countries. We are starting to see more research from other geographies, along with research looking at people of color, but most of this book is still based on research from just a few WEIRD countries, particularly Canada, the United States, the United Kingdom, Australia, and western European Union nations such as Switzerland and Germany.

If I am right that pedophilia is universal, we would expect CSEM offending to occur in every country, with pedophilia being a primary but not exclusive motivation, with mostly men involved, and with the most common content depicting prepubescent girls. This hypothesis is indirectly supported by the international observation that the modal CSEM category is prepubescent girls, whether we compare data from the Canadian Centre for Child Protection in Canada, NCMEC in the United States, the Child Exploitation and Online Protection Centre in the United Kingdom, or Interpol. NCMEC provides a global picture because American law mandates that global big tech companies based in the United States must report any CSEM they discover on their services to NCMEC, even for users outside the United States. From 2008 to 2017, a growing and now majority fraction of all reports come from Oceania and

Asia, along with rapid growth (but still a small fraction) from Africa, whereas reports from Europe and the Americas have been declining over the same period, according to a report by Bursztein et al. (2019).

Other relevant cross-cultural evidence comes from comparing CSEM users responding to anonymous online surveys conducted in English, Spanish, Portuguese, and Russian (Insoll et al., 2024). Though anyone can speak any of these languages, they are associated with particular cultures and geographies, especially Portuguese and Russian. Across all these language groups, sexual interest in children was a common reason given for accessing CSEM, with the most popular content reported to be pubescent girls. There were some differences as well, with Portuguese-speaking participants being the least willing to admit sexual interest in children (a majority chose "prefer not to say" when asked) and Russian-speaking participants being more likely to report their CSEM use came after an escalation in their pornography use toward more extreme or illegal content.

We need more data and research from non-WEIRD societies, we need to understand why or how race and ethnicity might play roles in online sexual offending, we need to address how race and ethnicity affect our response to online sexual offending (e.g., age estimation is poorer for children of color than for White children [Rosenbloom, 2013]; this reflects biases in age estimation models, who is providing the ratings, and other methodological considerations), and we need to find how we can implement evidence-based clinical and risk assessment and interventions in countries with fewer resources and with important cross-cultural and geographic differences.

Sheikh and Rogers (2024) conducted a scoping review of technology-facilitated gender- or sex-based abuse (which is broader than online sexual offending) in low- to middle-income countries and pointed out that there were little data from these countries (e.g., Egypt, countries in sub-Saharan Africa, Brazil, Indonesia). Sheikh and Rogers pointed out that cross-cultural differences in norms could be highly relevant to understanding these forms of abuse, including geographic differences. For example, they noted that even communicating or sharing fully clothed photos with someone of another gender who was related could be negatively viewed in some societies, which may influence sexting and other relevant behaviors. In a rare comparison study, Qu et al. (2022) compared 183 Chinese college students and 86 American college students and found that American students reported a higher rate of nonconsensual sexting.

TECHNOLOGICAL AFFORDANCES THAT CAN FACILITATE ONLINE SEXUAL OFFENDING

One of the core features of the internet is that it provides affordances that can amplify behavior, whether prosocial or antisocial (see Quayle, 2021). The potential scope of CSEM offending is much greater when CSEM comprises digital files that can be infinitely copied and accessed from around the world without any person-to-person contact, which can be contrasted with pre-internet CSEM offending involving a finite number of physical objects such as photographs, videocassettes or DVDs, and magazines that had to be accessed through interacting with other people (see Jenkins, 2001). Similarly, someone who wants to sexually solicit children or youths can potentially contact thousands of children and youths on a major social network, with a low likelihood of detection if they use security countermeasures, which can be contrasted with the risk of directly interacting with the much smaller number of children or youths someone might come into contact with in their daily lives, where young people could immediately draw attention to it or notify a parent or other trusted adult. The same affordances can influence other forms of online sexual offending: Someone who is motivated to expose themselves to unsuspecting persons could only target so many people if they were exposing in-person, with the risk of being detected and caught each time they do it. But now they can expose themselves online to many more people, where most incidents are not reported, and those that are reported rarely result in investigation or prosecution.

Potential reach that extends beyond personal social connections and geography is a form of general internet affordance (cf. anonymity, accessibility, and affordability in what is referred to as "the triple A engine"; Cooper, 1998). User anonymity, in particular, can reduce the likelihood of being detected and facing the consequences for criminal behavior and may also disinhibit behavior because people are acting outside the social contexts in which our species evolved, where we were surrounded by people who knew us and knew our families (Suler, 2004). The central importance of privacy and choice to be anonymous were part of the early internet's DNA because of the libertarian views held by key players, but it is not mandatory and, in fact, was not true in the earliest days, when there were not many users, everyone was using government or military or academic credentials, and many users already knew each other.

Individual apps and platforms can also have specific affordances that influence the likelihood of online sexual offending. For example, a messaging app can allow (or not allow) messages to be sent to strangers without user consent first. Apps that allow unapproved messages can facilitate the sending of unwanted sexual solicitations, dick pics, and so forth, and those that do not reduce the likelihood of this behavior. Phan et al. (2021) did a deeper dive into the affordances of dating apps for different forms of criminal behavior, including sexual harassment, sexual assault, and stalking. Dating apps can also be used for fraud and other scams (Federal Trade Commission, 2022). Apps that provide geolocation can facilitate stalking and, thus, both sexual and nonsexual assaults. Apps that allow the exchange of images can facilitate image-based abuse. Dating apps are particularly relevant because the use of dating apps by minors—even though this is specifically prohibited by the terms of service, which specify that users must be adults—is a robust correlate of image-based victimization (Seto, Roche, Stroebel, et al., 2023; discussed further in Chapter 2).

Another affordance is user search within a platform, which can increase reach in terms of finding potential targets. Service providers can bottleneck or even block the ability of adult users to search for minor users, for example, which would reduce online sexual offending by adults against unknown minors. A major caveat in limiting adult–minor interactions is that many children lie about their age to legally join a service because American law requires users to be at least 13,[3] and some adults will pretend to be minors online. Age verification is an important online safety feature that replicates age gating in real life. Minors cannot legally go to bars or clubs where adults congregate to meet potential sexual or dating partners, and adults who seek out work or volunteer opportunities with high access to children undergo some forms of screening, which might not be effective but does signal concern about the safety of children in these youth-serving positions.

Sometimes, affordances are hijacked. For example, Bluetooth and AirDrop are connectivity functions that make life more convenient for sharing photos or other data between friends, yet these same functions can be used to deliver unwanted images to people who have not selected the necessary security settings; this then puts the onus on potential targets to protect themselves, rather than the safety measure being built into the software (Otterman, 2018).

A serious consequence of these increased affordances to sexually offend (see Quayle, 2021) is that people who are not strongly motivated to engage in online sexual offending might still do it given it is "easy": many opportunities, potential rewards, and the perceived risk of minimal negative consequences. I discuss this in more detail in Chapter 5 when discussing the motivation–facilitation model of sexual offending involving children and the various thresholds in motivation or facilitation that might need to be met before someone takes action.

It is also important to note that these affordances may increase the detection of perpetration as well. One of the inadvertent affordances of online technologies is that it can be easier to study the phenomenon by accessing digital data. Digital forensic techniques can be used to track down CSEM users who are sharing content. As I have already mentioned, machine learning algorithms can help identify and delete known CSEM and flag potential new CSEM or sexual solicitations of minors. These algorithms are essential because they are the only scalable way of proactively moderating content to stem the flow of CSEM and online sexual solicitations; there are only so many content moderators, and content moderation comes with significant human costs. There is limited research, but the impacts of having to review previously reported CSEM can have significant negative effects on those who have to review CSEM and suspicious online interactions. Simonovska et al. (2023) published a study on the impacts of investigating online child sexual exploitation or abuse cases on

---

[3] A user who was 10 but said they were 13 to register for an online service might be considered an adult 5 years later, when they are ostensibly age 18 but are, in fact, 15 years old (see Instagram, 2021; Meta, 2022).

police, for example, finding that most police reported distress in the previous 6 to 8 weeks after exposure to CSEM. Similar research is critical for understanding the impact on content moderators (e.g., Spence et al., 2023).

I hope it is clear that technology affordances are an important domain to consider in explanations of online sexual offending because they point to potential points of intervention in online environments. Indeed, I have been saying for years now that structural changes in how apps and platforms work could have much more impact on online sexual offending than interventions aimed at individuals because structural changes are much more scalable—they can influence all users rather than a subset of users who can be recruited and retained in online interventions. Also, some changes are guaranteed to have an effect, at least initially (e.g., age verification would have a dramatic impact on online sexual offending by adults against minors, even if imperfect, until effective workarounds are deployed). Internet service providers can do a lot to increase or decrease affordances that influence online sexual offending, for example, by installing and using hash matching technology that prevents sharing of known CSEM, and using machine learning classifiers to flag potential new CSEM or suspicious interactions between adult and minor users (see Chapter 8). These interventions affect all users, can dramatically reduce the distribution of known CSEM, can proactively intervene if potential new CSEM is uploaded or if suspicious text interactions occur, and can have these effects whether or not the individuals involved are interested in changing their behavior (which assumes we have tools that can change behavior reliably and powerfully).

I realize this is an unusual position for a psychologist to take in a book published by the American Psychological Association, but psychologists rarely have the opportunity to advocate for changes in environments to shift behavior dramatically. This is one of the reasons I have become fascinated by the problem of online sexual offending. Psychologists and psychology have long recognized the potential impact of environmental factors, but we typically have had little influence over the environment because people can choose where they live and work and who they spend their time with. This is less clearly the case with online spaces, which are mostly privately run; apps and platforms can set their terms of service to promote or downplay user trust and safety.

SUMMARY

Online sexual offending is a global problem that transcends borders and cultures. However, most of what we know about online sexual offending relies on research conducted with men in a small number of so-called WEIRD countries. The prevalence of online sexual offending is likely to continue to grow as more people gain reliable internet access, especially if the technological affordances that facilitate online sexual offending are not addressed. These affordances include accessibility, affordability, perceived anonymity, the online disinhibition effect, and the lack of real age gating to prevent problematic interactions between adults and minors (e.g., on dating apps). These affordances reduce the threshold for individuals to act on their motivations (see the motivation–facilitation model in Chapter 5). For example, someone who is interested in sexual content depicting minors can access seemingly unlimited amounts for the cost of a computing device and internet access, unlike someone in the pre-internet era who would have to figure out how to find and pay for physical items such as photographs or magazines. Moreover, this same person may feel emboldened by their perceived anonymity and a sense that "anything goes" on the internet. They can go even further and solicit sexual content from minors they meet online because there is no real age gating that would limit these kinds of interactions.

Child Sexual Exploitation Material

How is child sexual exploitation material (CSEM) defined legally? Across Canada, the United States, the United Kingdom, the European Union, Australia, and New Zealand—where most online sexual offending research has been conducted—the common elements in CSEM laws are visual depictions of a real person under age 18 involving sexually explicit content, which can include depictions of sexual activity or a "lascivious" focus on the genitals. These laws may not specify an online element, but most CSEM offending reported to police nowadays involves digital images or videos. A majority (72%) of the 192 countries included in the review by the International Center for Missing and Exploited Children (2017) have specific CSEM legislation.

CSEM covers sexual depictions of anyone under age 18, but we now know the modal CSEM image reported to multiple repositories—the Canadian Centre for Child Protection in Canada, National Center for Missing and Exploited Children (NCMEC) in the United States, the Child Exploitation and Online Protection Centre in the United Kingdom, Interpol—is of a prepubescent girl (Quayle et al., 2018; Seto et al., 2018). There is likely a selection bias in reported CSEM because images of older adolescents who might be confused for adults will not be reported unless the identity (and thus, age) of the depicted person is known; for example, if the images were detected as part of an investigation into a sexual relationship between a 16-year-old girl and an adult man. If the specific age is not known, police analysts cannot always classify images of older adolescents as CSEM with confidence, making conviction less likely. There may be more CSEM depicting adolescents than CSEM depicting prepubescent or

---

https://doi.org/10.1037/0000428-003
Online Sexual Offending: Theory, Practice, and Policy, Second Edition, by M. C. Seto
Copyright © 2025 by the American Psychological Association. All rights reserved.

pubescent children online because of self-generated content through sexting and the fact that interest in adolescents is much more common than pedophilia or hebephilia (see Seto, 2017b). However, individuals engaging with CSEM depicting adolescents are less likely to be reported, less likely to be prosecuted, and, therefore, less likely to end up in clinical or correctional settings. There is an intersectional consideration too, given differences in the accuracy of age estimation based on the race or ethnicity of the young person (Rosenbloom, 2013). Politically and publicly, the focus of CSEM policies and practices are depictions of young adolescents, pubescent children, prepubescent children, and infants and toddlers.

Other countries do not have specific CSEM legislation but can prosecute CSEM under general obscenity legislation that typically also specifies other illegal sexual content, such as pornography depicting sexual violence toward adults or pornography depicting human–animal sex. CSEM is not specifically defined in some countries with large populations, including China, Indonesia, and Vietnam. There are also countries that do not criminalize CSEM offending or only criminalize some forms of CSEM offending; for example, Russia prohibits the distribution or production of CSEM but not possession of CSEM. Some countries go further; for example, I have mentioned that Canada and the United Kingdom include nonvisual depictions, and in Canada, CSEM can include fictional characters, as in computer-generated images, drawings, and stories. In the United States, however, a Supreme Court ruling in *Ashcroft v. Free Speech Coalition* (2002) restricted the legal definition of CSEM to visual depictions involving real minors.

Once (estimated) age is determined, police and prosecutors must determine if depictions are likely to meet the legal definition of CSEM regarding sexual explicitness or lasciviousness. An image of a nude child in and of itself might not qualify (e.g., a grandchild in the bathtub, artistic nude photography, or images of children for educational, clinical, or research purposes.) This comes up later in Chapter 6 when I discuss risk assessment and the development and validation of the Child Pornography Offender Risk Tool (CPORT), which distinguishes between CSEM and legal child content such as artistic nude photographs, children in swimsuits, or children in underwear.

PREVALENCE

In this book, I focus on the perpetration of online sexual offending, though I sometimes turn to studies of victimization to examine the impact of perpetration, understand differential vulnerability, and inform thinking about intervention. Here, I summarize a systematic review by Ingram et al. (2023), which identified 18 studies, all but one of which asked about CSEM use, with a total sample of 41,398 people. We found a 5% prevalence for CSEM use in general population studies, which could include accidental CSEM exposure and self-generated CSEM content, and this does not take frequency or persistence of use into account. The odds of CSEM use dramatically increased with the proportion of the sample that was male and the proportion of the sample that said they were attracted to children. This general population base rate for CSEM use can be compared with a rate of 76% for CSEM use in samples of people seeking help for their sexual thoughts or behaviors involving children and 26% in samples of people who self-identified as sexually attracted to children (but were not necessarily seeking help). The relatively high rate for help-seeking people likely reflects an immediate impetus for help seeking—for example, feeling distressed about their CSEM use or being concerned about social or legal consequences for CSEM offending, as well as a greater willingness to admit illegal behavior as part of their help seeking. Though the rate for child-attracted persons was five times higher than found in the general population, it was still a minority and lower than found in help-seeking individuals. This may reflect an important distinction between sexual attraction and corresponding behavior (e.g., Seto et al., 2021), explicit anti-offending positions taken by some child-attracted persons, and/or socially desirable responding. Ingram et al. (2023) also found a few studies that reported on the prevalence of other forms of online sexual offending, with two studies of online solicitation and two studies where online technologies were used to facilitate contact sexual offending.

We have prevalence rates for the nonconsensual sharing of others' images from the Thorn (2022) child and youth survey of 394 children between the ages of 9 and 12 and 602 youth between the ages of 13 and 17. Approximately one in 10 of these young people reported they had nonconsensually shared images of others. I am not reporting data on generating and sending sexts between similar-aged minors because this is common flirting and dating behavior for a minority of youth, even though it could meet the legal definitions of CSEM production, distribution, and/or possession. Other studies are available: Patel and Roesch's (2022) meta-analysis of 20 independent samples of adolescents and/or adults (total $N = 32,247$) found that, overall, 12% had shared sexts beyond the intended recipient, 2.7% had threatened to share sexts, and 8.9% had nonconsensually taken an image. Perpetration rates across studies were not moderated by publication year, mean participant age, proportion of female participants, or study setting.

I consider nonconsensual resharing a serious problem because it is done without the consent of the person depicted in the image and because this reshared content can be distributed further online. It is also a problem because it is not rare. In Madigan et al.'s (2018) meta-analysis of nine studies published between 2004 and 2015, the aggregated prevalence rate was 12%. In a survey of 5,000 young adults (across 54 countries) reported in the WeProtect Global Alliance's (2021) Global Threat Assessment, 29% had an image of them as a minor shared without their consent, with only one in five telling an adult or peer about it and only one in five reporting this to the app or platform where it happened. The dramatic difference between Madigan et al.'s (2018) rate and the WeProtect (2021) survey might be due to the emergence of smartphones and mobile apps in the interim, with the iPhone introduced in 2007 and an Android phone introduced in 2008. Mori et al. (2020) found similar rates in a systematic review and meta-analysis of studies that appeared since the review by Madigan et al. (2018), suggesting prevalence rates are plateauing rather than continuing to increase.

I am not aware of direct data collection from children on the prevalence of CSEM victimization, which would be challenging because it would require large samples and parental consent for younger children. Moreover, some children are not aware that images were taken of them or were too young to remember being photographed. This also does not capture nonconsensual resharing unless the depicted child becomes aware of the resharing; some youths may not realize that self-generated images may have been shared without their consent and are now being circulated as CSEM (see Self-Generated CSEM and Sexting section). We do know about known nonconsensual sharing victimization from systematic reviews by Madigan et al. (2018) and Mori et al. (2020). The Patel and Roesch (2022) systematic review I mentioned also looked at victimization rates based on cases where the person knew they had been recorded or their images had been nonconsensually reshared. The pooled victimization prevalence rates were 8.8% for nonconsensual resharing, 7.2% for threat of sext distribution, and 17.6% for having an image taken without permission. Most online sexual victimization surveys have focused on sexting and, to a lesser extent, sexual solicitations.

An exception and a high-quality survey that did not appear in the Patel and Roesch (2022) meta-analysis was reported by Finkelhor et al. (2022). These authors recruited 2,639 survey participants from a representative online market panel (50% female, 54% White) and reported the following victimization rates: 11% image-based sexual abuse, 7.2% nonconsensual sexting, 5.4% online sexual solicitation by someone 5 or more years older (not necessarily an adult), 3.1% nonconsensual resharing, 3.5% sextortion, and 1.7% commercial sexual exploitation (sent sexts or engaged in other sexual behavior for money or other goods). This study is notable because of the use of a representative sample through the IPSOS KnowledgePanel and questions about a broad range of victimization experiences, including sexual solicitations by an older minor and commercial sexual interactions. In other analyses of the same data set, this research team found negative emotional reactions were higher when images were involved but were similar for peers compared with adults and a known perpetrator compared with a stranger. Importantly, most perpetrators (88%) were other minors, not adults, which can be contrasted with the current public policy and education emphasis on adult perpetrators (Finkelhor et al., 2023). Most perpetrators (69%) were known to the victim, and the most common type of known perpetrator was an intimate partner. The results suggest that many minor-to-minor cases involve self-generated CSEM that is coerced, nonconsensually reshared, and/or used for sextortion. In a systematic review of 32 studies, Sutton and Finkelhor (2023) found that 44% of online sexual solicitations received by minors came from other minors, and two thirds (68%) of solicitations came from family members or acquaintances, which also contradicts the public policy and education emphasis on stranger danger. Aligning with this finding, Jeglic and Winters (2023) surveyed 332 adult survivors of childhood sexual abuse and found that only 8% met the perpetrator online, but online communication was common, with 35% texting, 27% having online chats, and 33% having phone calls. Forty percent of the perpetrators were minors themselves, which is consistent with what we know about childhood sexual abuse.

CSEM CONTENT

Multiple sources indicate the large majority of CSEM perpetrators are interested in girls, based on the collections seized by police and self-report (Seto & Eke, 2015; United States Sentencing Commission, 2021). Though preferring boys is uncommon, it is associated with a higher likelihood of sexual recidivism in CSEM perpetrators, probably because preferring boys is a stronger indicator of pedophilia than being attracted to girls (Seto, Stephens, et al., 2017) and/or men still have more unmonitored access to boys than girls (see Chapter 6, this volume). We also know from Seto et al.'s (2018) analysis of identified victim data at NCMEC that the age of the child is related to familiality, where family members are more likely identified as suspects in cases of younger children depicted in CSEM, probably reflecting access and opportunity. Familial suspects are also more likely to have more CSEM content involving penetrative acts (Salter & Wong, 2023).

Does the specific content of CSEM matter? The age of children or youth depicted in CSEM is suggestive of the person's sexual interests. Like other sexual content, we expect people to seek what they are most interested in, so we suspect that someone with mostly images of prepubescent children may have pedophilia and someone with mostly images of sexually maturing teens probably does not (Bártová et al., 2021; Joyal & Carpentier, 2022; Seto et al., 2021). Evidence in support of this intuitive association includes the following: (a) a majority of CSEM perpetrators show greater sexual arousal to child stimuli than adult stimuli when assessed phallometrically (Blanchard et al., 2007; Seto et al., 2006); (b) the proportion of CSEM perpetrators who show evidence of pedophilia is higher than for contact perpetrators (Babchishin et al., 2011, 2015), where contact perpetrators include intrafamilial perpetrators, who are rarely pedophilic (Seto, Babchishin, et al., 2015), as well as opportunistic, antisocial perpetrators who offend against unrelated children; and (c) in community samples, Bártová et al. (2021), Seto et al. (2021), and Joyal and Carpentier (2022) found a significant degree of correspondence between pedophilic sexual interests and behavior directed toward children. Bártová et al. asked specifically about pornography use, though not for pedophilia; they did not specifically ask about CSEM use.

Thorne (2020) found that individuals who reported sexual thoughts about younger children were more likely to report CSEM use than those who reported sexual thoughts about older children. Moreover, individuals who reported that their favorite sexual thoughts were about children rather than another theme were more likely to use CSEM than those who did not report that these were their favorite sexual thoughts. They were also more likely to report being willing to act on these sexual thoughts if the child "consented" to be recorded.

Though CSEM age distributions are relevant for the clinical assessment of sexual interest in children, including diagnosis of pedophilic disorder (Seto, 2022), they are not significantly related to the risk of sexual recidivism (see Chapter 6). This may reflect noise in CSEM age distributions in individual collections as a result of several factors:

- Age estimates are imprecise given variability in puberty onset and physical and sexual development.

- CSEM age descriptions or labels may be inaccurate (e.g., images of adolescent girls described as "preteen" content).

- Ages may reflect what is being accessed and downloaded but not preferences (e.g., someone searching for "child" content could get content ranging from infants and toddlers to underage teens). Once downloaded, the person might not delete nonpreferred content or might keep nonpreferred content because it could be traded for preferred content. Relevant here is research by Fortin and Proulx (2019) showing that CSEM perpetrators home in on what they like over time, with some seeking content depicting younger children and others seeking content depicting adolescents. In contrast, a gender search (searching for "boys" rather than "girls") is a clearer indication of gender preferences.

- CSEM ages are relevant but are not as important as gender preferences.

There is evidence that CSEM gender preferences and contact victim gender preferences are strongly related. First, Owens et al. (2016) found a high correspondence between CSEM gender preferences and contact victim gender in a cross-sectional analysis of the subset of their 251 FBI cases who had committed both kinds of sexual offenses. In a subsequent study of 71 cases with both CSEM and contact sexual offenses, we also found evidence of a strong correspondence between past and current contact victims and CSEM gender preference (Eke & Seto, 2023). There was a perfect predictive association among the 14 men who committed a new contact sexual offense, where every man who preferred CSEM depicting boys and committed a new contact sexual offense victimized a boy and every man who preferred CSEM depicting girls and committed a new contact sexual offense victimized a girl. There was also significant correspondence between CSEM and contact victim age preferences, though this association was not as strong as for gender. This study suggests that, beyond gender preference and risk in CPORT, it is worthwhile to note CSEM content in terms of relative risk to potential child victims. I discuss in further detail in Chapter 6 the evidence that CSEM gender matters in terms of predicting sexual recidivism.

I do not want to imply that there is no victim crossover in terms of either child gender or age. It has sometimes been assumed that someone who has offended against girls might pose a risk of sexual recidivism against girls only, not boys, but this is not always the case. Similarly, for age, we cannot assume that someone who shows a preference for prepubescent children only poses a risk to prepubescent children. In a meta-analysis by Scurich and Gongola (2021) of 47 studies involving 35,572 individuals who had committed contact sexual offenses, 19.1% had both child and adult victims, and 15.2% had both male and female victims. These data show that correspondence for both contact victim age and gender is clear, but crossover does sometimes occur. In other words, correspondence information about CSEM content and contact child victim characteristics is useful, but it does not rule out other gender or age groups in terms of risk management and safety planning. Relevantly, N. Davis et al. (2018) examined 136 CSEM perpetrators in Australia and found that those who showed interest across age groups—toddlers, prepubescent children, pubescent children, and underage teens—showed no gender preference and had higher average severity scores for their collections.

It is important to determine what factors predict victim gender or age crossover for online sexual offending, contact offending, and dual offending (e.g., online as well as contact). According to research showing that those who offend against both boys and girls are, on average, at higher risk to sexually reoffend and more likely to show pedophilic sexual arousal in the lab, we expect those who are more clearly pedophilic or otherwise higher risk are more likely to crossover for gender (see Seto, 2018). It is also the case that being interested in both boys and girls doubles the potential target population. I also predict that hypersexuality and criminality are important for understanding victim age crossover, and thus, individuals high on indicators of hypersexuality and criminality would be more likely to offend against multiple victim age groups. I have previously speculated that some paraphilias are relevant as well. For example, someone with an intense interest in exhibitionism may expose themselves to both children and adults as opportunities arise, and someone with an intense interest in biastophilia may engage in coercive behavior against both children and adults (Seto, 2018).

I mentioned that some longitudinal data suggest that CSEM perpetrators hone their preferences over time. Fortin and Proulx (2019) looked at the time lines of CSEM activity of 40 perpetrators over 6 or more months. They identified four different trajectories over time in the average estimated age and severity of CSEM content (from nude posing to sexual activity to the inclusion of violence or other paraphilic themes). An escalation trajectory was the most common (38%), with increasing severity of content and decreasing age, but some trajectories involved seeking images of older children or seeking less severe images of younger children. Fortin and Proulx did not analyze child gender, however, and so could not examine whether some individuals sought more boy or more girl content over time.

Though CSEM victim age distributions are not significantly related to the likelihood of sexual recidivism (see Chapter 6), they are related to perceptions of culpability and risk to reoffend, as reflected in sentencing guidelines (e.g., United States Sentencing Commission, 2021), questions we get about the CPORT (see Appendix), and vignette studies. In Lam et al. (2010), we found that younger victim age was correlated with higher perceived crime severity, irrespective of victim gender. Taylor-Smith (2021) attempted to replicate this study by recruiting students and online participants for a vignette study that manipulated CSEM victim age (5, 11, 17) and perpetrator age (19, 35, 65) for a total of nine vignettes. Victim age affected perceived crime severity, recommended sentence, and estimated likelihood of recidivism. However, victim age did not affect estimates of the probability of past or future sexual contact with a child. It did interact with perpetrator age in affecting the likelihood the perpetrator was deemed to be pedophilic. In a second study by Taylor-Smith, reported in the same paper, perpetrator age and gender had no effect on perceived offense severity, but male perpetrators were considered to be at higher risk of committing another CSEM offense than female perpetrators. In both studies by Taylor-Smith, perpetrators who were thought to be pedophilic were rated as higher in offense severity. Taylor-Smith found victim age was correlated with the likelihood of recidivism, unlike Lam et al. (2010). This could reflect multiple factors, including jurisdiction and sampling, but another possibility is that students and the general public have become more aware that CSEM victim age might matter.

Even if CSEM content parameters are not related to the risk of reoffending or treatment needs, the courts appear to pay attention to these parameters. Fortin et al. (2019) analyzed sentencing decisions for 101 CSEM cases in Quebec. Quantitatively, the top predictors of sentence length were prior sexual offending history and level of engagement in offending (with production judged as higher than distribution, which in turn was judged as higher engagement than possession only). The numbers of CSEM images or videos were unrelated to sentence length. However, a qualitative analysis found that judges often mentioned the size of the CSEM collection, even though it did not come through as a unique correlate of sentence length in a regression analysis. Judges also talked about time invested in CSEM offending and the nature of the content (e.g., inclusion of violence or bestiality) in their sentencing decisions, citing these parameters as relevant to inferring criminal intent and the perpetrators' sexual motivations. As I discuss in Chapter 6, information about CSEM content parameters, such as the number of images or videos, the ratio of CSEM to adult pornography, and age and gender distributions, is valuable for clinical assessment, diagnosis, and treatment planning.

PERPETRATOR CHARACTERISTICS

In the previous edition, I reviewed the evidence regarding perpetrator characteristics one by one. However, there have now been systematic reviews and later studies published after these reviews that have examined the demographic, psychological, and criminological characteristics of individuals who have committed online sexual offenses (Babchishin et al., 2011, 2015). The Babchishin et al. (2015) review identified 30 samples, totaling 2,284 online perpetrators, 2,320 contact perpetrators, and 1,086 individuals with both online and contact offenses. Babchishin et al. (2011) found that online perpetrators—mostly CSEM perpetrators in the studies they covered—are even more likely to be White men with higher education and higher IQs than contact perpetrators. I suggested in Chapter 1 that the gender discrepancy is related to the greater likelihood of pedohebephilia in CSEM perpetrators, and the racial effect is possibly due to opportunity in the form of internet access. The education and IQ effects are probably due to a selection bias for the use of computer technologies in committing CSEM offenses; this effect should diminish over time as internet technologies become easier to use, including the introduction of voice commands and AI agents.

Babchishin et al. (2015) also examined data on psychologically meaningful risk factors (see Mann et al., 2010; Seto, Augustyn, et al., 2023) that are associated with the persistence of sexual offending in samples of contact and non-contact perpetrators (including those who engaged in exhibitionistic behavior, voyeuristic behavior, and online sexual solicitations involving attempted or completed meetings in person but excluding CSEM offending). There was a pattern of both similarities and differences: CSEM perpetrators scored higher on atypical sexual interests than contact perpetrators, with dual perpetrators (CSEM and contact) being the highest; CSEM and contact perpetrators were similar in their emotional congruence with children and offense-supportive cognitions[1] about children and/or sex (see Chapter 5); CSEM perpetrators scored higher than contact perpetrators on empathy, which may explain why they are less likely to have directly offended against children; and CSEM perpetrators are more socially isolated, lonely, and introverted but generally have better social functioning. In a large sample study reported after the Babchishin et al. (2015) review was published, Henshaw et al. (2018) compared CSEM, contact, and dual perpetrators (a total of 1,205 cases) and replicated the meta-analytic finding that CSEM perpetrators are higher on atypical sexual interests and lower on antisocial behavior than contact perpetrators, whereas dual perpetrators were high on both. Another study (Nicol et al., 2021) compared 99 CSEM and 95 contact perpetrators in Australia and found that CSEM perpetrators were significantly older, were more likely to be employed, had fewer criminal charges, and had fewer supervision violations. Because of the meta-analysis and subsequent replications, I am confident that these CSEM and contact perpetrator differences are robust.

Another important finding to highlight from the Babchishin et al. (2015) review was the relevance of opportunity: Online perpetrators had more online access in the form of having multiple devices, private access, and/or time spent online, whereas contact perpetrators had more direct access to children through co-residence or work. Any sensible explanation of CSEM offending and other online sexual offending needs to consider the relevance of opportunity to commit offenses, just as opportunity plays a role in offline sexual offending.

---

[1] *Emotional congruence* with children refers to an emotional connection with children that is separate from sexual or romantic attraction. This emotional congruence can involve liking children more than adults, preferring the company of children over adults, and feeling more childlike.

These group comparison results are important for developing an empirically supported model of online CSEM offending because they suggest that existing models to explain sexual offending involving children can be adapted to this realm. On average, CSEM perpetrators are more likely to show sexual interest in children, which is a risk factor for sexual offending involving children (see Chapter 5). At the same time, however, they show less criminal and antisocial behavior, where greater criminal and antisocial behavior histories are also a risk factor. There were no differences in the psychologically meaningful risk factors—for offline offending at least—of emotional congruence with children and offense-supportive cognitions about children or sex (see Chapters 5 and 6).

This pattern of observations can be contrasted with a hypothetical pattern where CSEM and contact perpetrators were entirely different from each other across psychologically meaningful risk factors, which suggests that unique factors need to be considered in explaining CSEM offending. The observed pattern can also be contrasted with a hypothetical pattern wherein CSEM and contact perpetrators were similar in all respects, which suggests that the different offending behavior is driven by circumstances and not psychological differences. The mixed pattern of results suggests we can have some confidence that what we know about sexual offending involving children can be relevant, including explanatory models of online sexual offending (Chapter 5), clinical and risk assessment knowledge and measures used with contact perpetrators (Chapter 6), and interventions in the form of treatment or prevention (Chapters 7 and 8). At the same time, there are also unique factors about online sexual offending, such as the impact of technological affordances.

An American Cohort of CSEM Perpetrators

Specific to the American context, the 2021 report by the United States Sentencing Commission on federally sentenced CSEM perpetrators described the characteristics of those who had committed CSEM offenses other than production offenses: Almost all (99%) were men, 80% were White, their mean age was 41, and over half had attended college. This is quite different from other federally sentenced perpetrators in the United States, where there are more women, more people of color, and fewer people who have attended college or university.

Another important detail in the report relevant to the risk of recidivism is that 76% were in the lowest criminal history classification level, with 69% having zero criminal history points, meaning they had no prior criminal history. The United States Sentencing Commission (2021) report also showed an apparent plateau in the number of federally sentenced CSEM perpetrators in the years leading up to the publication of the report. This might not reflect an actual plateau in the total number of cases, however, but a shift toward state rather than federal prosecutions, given heavy mandatory minimum sentences at the federal level and resulting judicial overrides.

New CSEM Users

There is often an assumption that CSEM users repeatedly access CSEM and are persistent perpetrators, as suggested by the high likelihood of pedohebephilia in clinical and forensic studies of CSEM perpetrators. However, these individuals may not represent all CSEM users because persistence increases the likelihood of detection and, thus, appearance in clinical or forensic settings. For example, in Seto and Eke (2015), discussed in much more depth in Chapter 6 of this volume, the men convicted of possessing CSEM in this sample had been collecting CSEM for an average of 3.5 years. We have little information about the onset of CSEM and early CSEM use in nonclinical or nonforensic samples. A 2021 ReDirection survey conducted on darknet forums associated with CSEM use was informative about (mostly) undetected CSEM users (Insoll et al., 2022). The ReDirection team obtained responses from 8,484 CSEM users across two different surveys, one for those who endorsed "No need for help" (39%) and a second for those who chose "Help us to help you" (61%). The survey intentionally did not ask about demographic characteristics to reassure participants they could not be identified, so there was no information about gender, age, or other characteristics. The survey was originally launched in English and Spanish, but they got so much response that they translated it into 10 additional languages.

There were several key findings in the ReDirection survey (Insoll et al., 2022). First, most respondents said they had been searching for and viewing CSEM for less than 6 months, and 43% said they had only begun accessing CSEM in the past month. Second, half (51%) said their first exposure was accidental rather than intentional—for example, they were searching for other sexual content (15%), or they were sent CSEM via social connections (14%). It is of concern that 52% said they felt afraid that viewing CSEM might lead to sexual acts involving a child, 44% said viewing CSEM made them think about direct contact with a child, and 37% said they did seek contact with a child after viewing CSEM. Third, and particularly relevant to the opportunity for early intervention and a shift downward in average perpetrator age with digital natives, the large majority (70%) of respondents said they first saw CSEM before the age of 18, and almost 40% said they saw CSEM for the first time before age 13. This finding may reflect that many participants in these darknet surveys were relatively young and, therefore, more comfortable navigating darknet technologies than older participants who only learned to use the internet as adults, sometimes much older adults.

CSEM CHANGES OVER TIME

In this section, I focus on changes over time in terms of CSEM content and then changes over time in CSEM perpetrator characteristics. Though the psychological underpinnings of interest in CSEM and CSEM offending are likely to be robust over time, technological and situational factors can influence both these trends.

An example of a technological factor is video. It is likely that video CSEM has always been desired content because videos are more powerful sexual stimuli than images, but video has only become more common as CSEM content as a result of much higher download speeds and cheap storage; readers who are older (like me) might remember how long it would take to download a large file when using dial-up internet connections. A relevant situational factor might involve the fact that older perpetrators did not go online and discover CSEM until later in their lives as adults. Younger people, however, have grown up with the internet readily available at home, at school, and via mobile devices in their pockets, so they may begin engaging with CSEM at a younger age than older cohorts of CSEM users (Insoll et al., 2022).

There have been suggestions that CSEM content has depicted younger children and more severe content over time, where severe content depicts more intrusive sexual acts, violence, or other paraphilic themes (such as bestiality). In a longitudinal analysis of data on CSEM reported to the NCMEC, we did not find evidence of younger children being depicted over time but did see a trend toward more severe content (Seto et al., 2018). There is some additional support for this idea from an analysis of digitized pre-internet photographs, with more recent digital images from the Canadian Centre for Child Protection, the Canadian clearinghouse, examined by Salter and Whitten (2022). This study found evidence that children in images have gotten slightly younger and content more serious in terms of explicitness. These effects were small, though; Salter and Whitten found 79% of newer versus 71% of pre-internet images depicted prepubescent girls, versus almost no difference for boys. Similarly, the proportion of images rated as severe was slightly higher for contemporary CSEM (50%) than for pre-internet CSEM (46.7%), corresponding to a weak but significant difference.

Quayle et al. (2018) analyzed data from 687 cases of identified CSEM victims. A large portion involved self-generated content shared via sexting, with self-generated content representing 40% or more of images in the sample since 2010. An important qualification is that the self-generated content was coerced in many cases, so it was not simply willingly generated content that was then maliciously reshared. The number of cases involving girls was similar to that involving boys, though girls were more likely to be photographed by a family member (32.8%) than boys (14.9%).

Perhaps the best data on changes over time in perpetrator characteristics are from three waves of data collection for the National Juvenile Online Victimization (NJOV) project, though these data are quite old, with the latest wave from 2009 (the researchers may have some preliminary Wave 4 data by the time this book is published; Mitchell, personal communication, August 1, 2023). The NJOV data collection was completed through telephone surveys of cases investigated, leading to arrests in over 2,000 police services across the United States. All Internet Crimes Against Children Task Forces in the United States were represented. Half the agencies had officers who had received specialized training before 2000; the rest were a random selection of local, county, and state agencies.

Some perpetrator characteristics did not change across waves: Perpetrators were almost always men, the large majority were White, and the most common CSEM in their possession was of prepubescent girls (Wolak et al., 2011, 2012). However, there were some changes over time as well. The proportion of perpetrators between the ages of 18 and 25 increased over time; the proportion of cases involving video also increased, probably reflecting changes in bandwidth and storage capacities, as I have suggested; and there were increases in CSEM distribution and decreases in concurrent contact offending, which likely reflects changes in how people were identified by police. For CSEM distribution, the NJOV data collection was conducted in the era when peer-to-peer file sharing dominated, which is a passive form of distribution involving no direct interaction with other CSEM users, as opposed to active trading with others on darknet forums where there is some kind of interaction with others (see Steel et al., 2022). For concurrent contact offending, it may have been the case that CSEM offending was more likely to be detected during investigations for child sexual abuse in earlier waves or that cases involving the production of CSEM (child sexual abuse is recorded by the perpetrator) were prioritized by police.

More recent police and policy attention and research have focused on the use of darknet sites for accessing and distributing CSEM. For example, van der Bruggen and Blokland (2022) analyzed a large data set of over 400,000 posts to a darknet CSEM forum between 2010 and 2014. Posts were assigned to topics based on the thread and subforum titles. The largest topic in terms of number of posts and number of members was devoted to CSEM in general. The next most popular topics, in descending order, involved explicit girl CSEM, less explicit girl content, administrative posts, explicit boy CSEM, less explicit boy content, and information security posts. Less explicit content included nonnude images and content depicting underage or potentially underage teens. Though there were a small number of members overall, the so-called VIPs were the most active members, representing 4% of members but 32% of all posts. Administrators (including subforum moderators) were even more disproportionately active, representing 0.1% of members but 15% of all posts. Many users were lurkers only, meaning they never posted. Group trajectory modeling was used to identify different user activity patterns: Two large groups (lurkers and browsers) rarely, if ever, post, and VIPs and administrators become less active over time, but there is also a group that escalates in activity over time.

PERPETRATOR COUNTERMEASURES

Some data suggest changes in perpetrator tactics in terms of their security countermeasures, though surprisingly few detected perpetrators use such measures (e.g., 16% in the United States Sentencing Commission, 2021). Security countermeasures include using the darknet, other security software, encryption, hidden files, and cryptocurrencies. Chopin et al. (2023) analyzed data from 199 Quebec men convicted for CSEM and/or solicitation. Only 22% used encryption (19%) or countermeasures such as proxies, virtual private networks, or the darknet (4%). Chopin et al. extended past research by showing that the use of countermeasures was correlated with older age, less employment, admission of pedohebephilia, CSEM offending, sexual offense history, and offense-supportive cognitions. This implies that more chronic or entrenched CSEM users are more likely to use countermeasures. It is highly likely that, in the long run, those who are caught are less tech-savvy than those who are not caught, so countermeasure use may be quite common among undetected perpetrators.

These data need to be interpreted in terms of how police detected CSEM perpetrators because we have newer results suggesting important perpetrator differences depending on the detection method (Seto & Eke, in press). We attempted to replicate prior research by Nielssen et al. (2011), who compared 52 men detected through undercover policing and 53 men detected by other means. Men detected by undercover policing had more CSEM but less contact offending than those detected through other means. In Seto and Eke, we distinguished between four different detection methods in a sample of 336 men convicted of CSEM offenses (discussed further in Chapter 6): (a) 105 men reported by others, such as a family member or the IT department at work; (b) 64 men detected during another police investigation, most commonly for an allegation of child sexual abuse; (c) 80 men detected through website activity, including purchases; and (d) 87 men detected through undercover policing. Those detected through website activity were the least likely to have a prior criminal history of any kind compared with the other groups. The website activity group was also the most likely to admit to sexual attraction to children, whereas those detected by undercover police operations were the least likely to admit this attraction. Most notably, those who were detected by undercover police work were the least likely to commit a new sexual offense during a fixed 5-year follow-up, including when we focused on CSEM recidivism. The highest risk group included those detected during another police investigation, which makes sense, given that they were typically being investigated for an allegation of contact sexual offending against children. Although undercover policing practices have changed since these data were collected, the results of our analysis raise questions about the cost-effectiveness of some undercover police work and the importance of determining whether CSEM offending has taken place when investigating other crimes, especially sexual offenses involving children.

CSEM PRODUCTION

There are different forms of CSEM production, and there may be meaningful differences between perpetrators of these different forms of CSEM production. The most direct CSEM production is through the recording of contact sexual offending, which might be done for multiple reasons, including as a souvenir and later fantasy material, to blackmail victims into maintaining their silence or cooperation, and as valuable new content to be traded online for status or other incentives. Other direct production still involves being in the same space as a child but without physical contact, such as directing a child to engage in sexual behavior with another child, engage in solo behavior (masturbation, penetration with objects), or pose suggestively. Yet another form of production involves interacting with a child online to induce them to produce content, either self-generated or doing something on camera that is surreptitiously recorded (see Chapter 3).

In some jurisdictions, such as Canada, an individual could be charged with production for creating content depicting fictional children (e.g., computer-generated content, drawings, stories) or for creating new content using deep-fake technologies. In our CPORT research, some individuals were charged with production because they digitally morphed the faces of known children onto the bodies of stranger children depicted in CSEM obtained online, presumably to create content that matched their sexual fantasies about the known children (Seto & Eke, 2015). All other things being equal, I expect those who recorded contact sexual offending to be the highest risk (they are dual perpetrators by definition), followed by those who did not have direct contact with children but interacted with them (those who interacted in person being higher risk in turn than those who interacted online exclusively), and then followed by the lowest-risk group, "fantasy-driven" perpetrators who created CSEM without any direct interactions with the depicted children or without any real children involved at all.

There is clearly a robust association between the production of CSEM and contact sexual offending, given the contributions of direct production (e.g., Krone & Smith, 2017; Krone et al., 2017; McManus et al., 2015). Contact offending is not requisite, however. Bickart et al. (2019) found a high correlation between production and contact offending, and Gewirtz-Meydan et al. (2018) found that most (93%) participants who completed their CSEM victimization survey had experienced child sexual abuse as part of the production. Bickart et al. noted that some production cases involving female perpetrators included direct physical contact offending; in other cases, the female perpetrator recorded images or videos of young children in their care.

The United States Sentencing Commission (2021) examined federally sentenced CSEM production cases. Data were extracted from mandatory documents required by federal courts, including charging documents, plea agreements, reasons for the court decision, disposition orders, and presentence reports. Though the number of such cases represented a tiny fraction of those in federal corrections, the federal system saw a 422% increase from 2005 (98 cases) to 2019 (512 cases) in CSEM production cases. The 2021 report presented descriptive information on the 512 cases sentenced in 2019. The majority (57%) involved a single child; the others had from two to 440 victims. Typically (60%), the production perpetrator was in a position of trust, such as family member, teacher, or coach, and had access to victims in this way. However, 35% involved strangers who were met online, which was more than double the rate (14%) in 2010, suggesting the impact of more and younger children having their own devices and being active on major apps and platforms despite age restrictions and differential treatment of minor users, plus a willingness to engage with strangers, including adult strangers. The United States Sentencing Commission data suggest production by a stranger is more likely to result in federal rather than state prosecution for production, perhaps because production may involve individuals in different states or movement across state lines. There may be other selection effects as well, given that many CSEM perpetrators can be charged under state or federal laws, where the federal penalties are usually more severe because of long mandatory minimum sentences, though that depends on the state (e.g., possession of CSEM can result in a 10-year sentence for each image in Arizona, so someone with 20 images could conceivably be sentenced to 200 years in prison).

Compared with our NCMEC–Thorn research collaboration (Seto et al., 2016) and an analysis of Australian cases by Salter et al. (2021), federally sentenced CSEM production perpetrators in the United States who had in-person access had younger victims, with 84% age 12 or younger and 30% being infants or toddlers (United States Sentencing Commission, 2021). In contrast, almost two thirds (62%) of strangers had teen victims. A third (32%) of production perpetrators distributed CSEM they created, and a quarter (23%) distributed other CSEM. A majority (55%) of federal production perpetrators possessed other CSEM besides the content they produced. A third (36%) were part of an online CSEM community (forums). In terms of offending tactics, 20% used threats, coercion, or violence; 5% gave the victim alcohol or drugs to induce cooperation; 19% lied about their age, gender, or identity; and 15% gave bribes (e.g., money or gifts). Many (81%) of the production cases had committed contact sexual offenses too, which is higher than found in other studies of production offending, such as Gewirtz-Meydan et al. (2018). The implication is that committing contact offenses also increases the likelihood of federal rather than state prosecution. NJOV research found that most CSEM cases were prosecuted at the state level, which typically issues lighter sentences than the federal system and its mandatory minimums.

In the CSEM survivor survey conducted by the Canadian Centre for Child Protection (2017), a majority (58%) of the participants said they were abused by more than one perpetrator; in half of the cases with a single perpetrator, the perpetrators were relatives, either a parent (most commonly a biological father, followed by a sociolegal father) or another relative. Most (82%) of the primary perpetrators in multiple perpetrator cases were parents or extended family members. Family relatives are more likely to be involved in CSEM production involving younger children, likely because relatives have greater access and opportunity to produce CSEM with these children than with others. Salter and Wong (2023) completed a systematic review of 66 studies, including pre-internet studies dating back to 1970, and concluded that family members were more likely to be involved in the production of CSEM involving the youngest children and CSEM depicting more intrusive behavior, including women who produced content of their own children, either alone or with a male co-perpetrator. In their clinical treatment sample of 264 CSEM perpetrators, Middleton et al. (2009) found that 12% of the sample had CSEM depicting related children, while most (88%) had CSEM depicting unrelated children.

A lot of education and awareness campaigning is still built on the assumption of "stranger danger," where the greatest risk to children online is perceived to be strangers who might sexually solicit them. Yet a lot of online offending involves perpetrators who are known to the victim (Bickart et al., 2019; Gewirtz-Meydan et al., 2018; Prat et al., 2014; Sheehan & Sullivan, 2010; Shelton et al., 2016; Wolak, Finkelhor, Mitchell, & Jones, 2011). For example, in Gewirtz-Meydan et al. (2018), more than half of the cases (52%) involved a family member, and another large portion (41%) involved acquaintances, consistent with the NJOV data. In other words, only 7% of the cases in Gewirtz-Meydan et al. involved a stranger. Similarly, in an earlier study by Wolak et al. (2008) looking at law enforcement data, the victim and perpetrator met online in only about one fifth of cases, and less than 5% involved a stranger perpetrator. In the Thorn–NCMEC study, we found that family member involvement was associated with CSEM involving younger identified child victims (Seto et al., 2016).

There was a trend in the NJOV data collection waves toward higher proportions of youth-produced content from 2000 to 2009, from 6% to 27% to 63% (Wolak et al., 2012). Most of this involved adult or other youth solicitations, typically via sextortion or nonconsensual sharing. There were concomitant trends toward more acquaintance than stranger perpetrators and more involvement of teens in online sexual solicitations. This trend appears to have increased with the widespread adoption of smartphones and apps for sharing photos and videos, leading to an explosion of research on sexting and self-generated content (e.g., Seto et al., 2022). Sutton and Finkelhor (2023) reported that the majority of CSEM cases involving self-generated minor content are likely to involve other minors.

Several studies have found meaningful differences between adult- and minor produced CSEM: Adult produced images are more likely to involve a family member (51% vs. 6%) and have victims under age 12 (54% vs. 14%), and these individuals were more likely to have other CSEM downloaded from the internet (49% vs. 22%). In a first-of-its-kind analysis of NCMEC data, conducted with financial support from the Thorn Foundation, we conducted two sets of analyses. The first involved an analysis of historical data on actively traded cases (defined as images involved in more than five reports to NCMEC) identified between 2002 and 2013 (Seto et al., 2018). We found no obvious trend over time in terms of victim gender or age categories. In a second analysis of data involving identified victims, the typical case involved depictions of White (85%) pubescent (61%) girls (76%) in a nonfamilial relationship with White (86%) male (98%) perpetrators. Being actively traded was associated with younger children, both boys and girls, with more sexual activity depicted and a familial relationship, especially a nuclear family member. Familial relationships were significantly associated with female victims, female perpetrators, younger children, and more severe content.

A parsimonious interpretation of all these findings is that the production of CSEM involving younger children is more likely to involve family members because family members have more unmonitored access to these younger children, even compared with day care providers, teachers, and other caregivers. If family members then distribute those images, whether for money, to trade, or to brag, those images then circulate and, therefore, are more likely to be actively traded. The study by Bickart et al. (2019) suggests that women may be more likely to produce CSEM involving related children for money or other incentives, whereas men may be more likely to produce CSEM for trading, souvenirs, or blackmail. In contrast, the production of images of pubescent or postpubescent victims is more likely to involve male nonfamily perpetrators, such as a peer who nonconsensually reshared images that were sent to them, an adult who solicited the young person online, or an adult already engaged in a statutorily prohibited sexual relationship, where the minor agrees to the production of CSEM but cannot legally consent to the recording.

NJOV data suggest that production via online sexual solicitations, whether by relatives or others, represents an increasing proportion of CSEM production, as opposed to recording direct child sexual abuse. For example, de Santisteban and Gámez-Guadix (2018) found that 6% of adolescent students had been solicited online for sexual images (which could qualify as CSEM), and 1% sent images. Solicitations increased with age, with older underage girls getting 1.5 times the number of requests of younger girls. Girls were more likely to refuse than boys, however, so they were similar in terms of engaging in online sexual interactions of some kind, which could include sharing CSEM or similar images or videos. The sexual chats, if sufficiently explicit and clear regarding age, could also violate Canadian and U.K. laws.

Self-Generated CSEM and Sexting

A newer form of production that involves CSEM but that is not always criminalized is self-generated sexual content by minors that is shared with similar-aged peers, such as a dating partner. The creator is technically guilty of production and distribution, and the receiver is technically guilty of possession because CSEM refers to any sexual content of persons under the age of 18. This self-generated content can then result in further distribution via nonconsensual resharing or hacking and is becoming a significant source of new CSEM.

Youth sexting is less common than some parents and media stories seem to think, but some youths clearly do engage in sending or receiving sexual messages, including images or video, putting them at risk of nonconsensual sharing and sextortion (Wolak et al., 2018). In addition, some youths may be pressured or coerced into sending sexts, for example, by a partner who threatens to end the relationship otherwise. Sexting prevalence rates are available from Madigan et al.'s (2018) meta-analysis of 39 studies representing a total of 110,380 participants: Sending sexts was 15%, receiving sexts was 27%, nonconsensual sharing was 12%, and own sext being leaked was 8%. In this meta-analysis, sexts included sexually explicit messages as well as images or videos. Prevalence rates were positively correlated with participant age, such that rates were higher for older participants, but gender was not a significant moderator of sexting behavior overall, though some individual studies did find gender effects. For example, in studies conducted since the meta-analysis, such as Gassó et al. (2022), men were more likely to perpetrate coercive sexting, and women were more likely to be victims.

Mori et al. (2020) reported an update of Madigan et al. (2018), with a new meta-analysis of 28 studies reported since the cutoff date for studies to be included in Madigan et al. The prevalence rates in newer studies were similar to those reported by Madigan et al., with 19% sent, 35% received, and 14% nonconsensually sharing, suggesting the upward trend observed by Madigan et al. from 2009 to 2015 had not continued. Study effect sizes were heterogeneous, but none of the moderators (year of data collection, mean participant age, percentage of the sample that was male) were significant. Now that smartphone ownership is so high in some geographies, these prevalence rates are likely to be stable, depending on who is willing to sext under specific circumstances. I expect sexting rates to increase in other geographies as their rates of mobile ownership increase but with geographic variations for as yet unknown reasons (see Disrupting Harm surveys mentioned previously). Optimistically, this plateau in sexting rates might also be due to education and awareness campaigns and shifting norms about sexting behaviors, particularly nonconsensual resharing. Indeed, influencing norms would be a powerful way to address risky behavior based on the robust associations we found for norms in our analysis of a survey of children, where perceptions of what friends do were correlated with sending and receiving sexts, as well as nonconsensually sharing sexts (Seto, Roche, Stroebel, et al., 2023).

Correlates of nonconsensual sharing perpetration are of particular interest in developing more effective policies and practices, so what else do we know? According to a literature review by K. Walker and Sleath (2017), there is not much research on correlates. Considering the general sexual offending literature, one could hypothesize that perpetrators are more likely to be male, be delinquent, have permissive attitudes about resharing (e.g., believing it is just a prank, no harm done), and be sexually active, including engaging in risky sexual behavior such as unprotected sex or having multiple casual partners. The Thorn Foundation has conducted several surveys of children and youth asking about sexting behavior. We conducted an analysis of the 2021 survey identifying demographic, technology use, and social context factors (Seto, Roche, Stroebel, et al., 2023). The sample comprised 394 children between the ages of 9 and 12 and 602 youths between the ages of 13 and 17. Their average age was 13.5 ($SD = 2.50$) years. Most respondents were female (60%), White (56%), and cisgender, heterosexual (79%). One in 10 participants sent images, one in five received images, one in 10 nonconsensually reshared images, and one in 10 had their images leaked. Analyses revealed that gender, gender or sexual minority status, use of dating apps and particular online platforms, self-sharing and resharing attitudes, and friend norms all significantly and uniquely predicted sending images. Age, resharing attitudes, and friend norms all significantly predicted receiving images. Household income, geographic location, resharing attitudes, and friend norms all significantly predicted nonconsensual resharing. Age and friend norms significantly predicted having one's image leaked. The largest effects were for attitudes about sending sexts, attitudes about resharing, and perceived friend norms. There was specificity of attitudes in that attitudes about sending had the strongest correlation with that behavior, as did resharing. There were also large effects for technology use factors such as the use of dating apps, use of encrypted messaging apps, and use of Snapchat (ephemeral image sharing). Sexting is now part of flirting and dating, and the use of encrypted or ephemeral messaging apps suggests that some young people do attend to privacy and security.

Correlations do not prove causation, however. For example, finding that dating apps are correlated with sexting behaviors does not tell us whether the use of dating apps increases the likelihood of sexting behaviors or whether someone who is sexting or is predisposed to engage in sexting seeks out dating apps. To examine possible causality, we need longitudinal designs or quasi-experiments to determine if the association is predictive (e.g., use of dating apps at Time 1 predicting sexting at Time 2) and whether associations remain significant after controlling for other relevant variables. However, I have some confidence that attitudes and perceived friend norms are meaningfully related to behavior because of longitudinal evidence on the theory of planned behavior, which proposes that attitudes and perceived norms influence intentions, which in turn influence behavior (Ajzen & Fishbein, 1980). This hypothesis is also consistent with other research on young adults. For example, Clancy et al.'s (2019) study of 505 young adult Australian participants also found subjective norms and attitudes predict nonconsensual resharing, consistent with the theory of planned behavior. This result suggests an important opportunity for intervention, where social marketing or other strategies could be used to influence attitudes and norms. Consider the successes in shifting behaviors such as wearing seatbelts, smoking less tobacco, and not drinking and driving (Dinh-Zarr et al., 2001; Shults et al., 2001).

Nonconsensual sharing is a global phenomenon, as demonstrated in the WeProtect Global Alliance's regular Global Threat Assessment reports (WeProtect Global Alliance, 2021). In the 2021 survey, over 5,000 young adults (18- to 20-year-olds) from 54 countries (divided into 12 regions for reporting) were asked about "online sexual harms" by the Economist Impact Unit. These harms included, first, an adult or stranger sending them sexual content (without specifying whether the content was unwanted or unrequested); second, being uncomfortable with sexual content (which could include sex education or frank talk); and third, being asked to keep a sexual interaction of some kind secret (which is vague and could include consensual peer-to-peer interactions). The fourth question was a direct example of CSEM-related behavior, which involved having a sexually explicit image or video shared without permission

(29% prevalence overall). Nonconsensual resharing was more likely for non-heterosexual participants (41% vs. 23%), transgender or nonbinary persons (41% vs. 24%), and racialized participants (40% vs. 24%) but did not differ for gender. In a different study, Clancy et al. (2019) found that youths who responded to their survey were more likely to engage in nonconsensual resharing if they were sexually active or dating online. They also found that receiving a sext meant for someone else was associated with resharing.

There were also geographic differences. For example, English-speaking high-income countries had more than twice the prevalence of nations in Eastern Europe or the Commonwealth of Independent States (WeProtect Global Alliance, 2021). What might explain this? Differences in internet access may play a role, but this finding again points out the need for cross-cultural research to understand variation across cultures and geographies. Possibilities include variations in attitudes and beliefs about consent, image generation and sharing, sexual content more generally, and views about girls and women.

Sending self-generated images to others is potentially risky behavior but is now part of the social and sexual landscape for some young people (see the textbox in Chapter 4). Admonishments not to self-generate nudes or to send them to peers is like abstinence-only sex education: It is not going to work. What we need is education about the risks, harm reduction strategies, and the importance of consent (e.g., nudes should not be sent without consent, and nudes that are received from others should never be shown or shared with anyone else without consent).

Live Streaming

There have been growing concerns about live streaming CSEM, where individuals around the world can pay to watch child exploitation or sexual abuse being committed. Little is known about this phenomenon. Almost half (45%) of the respondents to the ReDirection survey said they had watched live-streamed CSEM (Insoll et al., 2022), yet only 1% of federally sentenced CSEM perpetrators in the United States were involved in live streaming, according to the United States Sentencing Commission (2021) report, so this big discrepancy needs to be explained. One possibility is the difference between self-reported and detected offending, where many CSEM users are accessing live-streamed content, but this is not what they are caught for, and they are unlikely to admit to undetected crimes upon arrest and prosecution. Another possibility is that we are talking about results from different populations; ReDirection survey users were younger than the typical federally sentenced CSEM perpetrator, and live-streaming behavior might reflect an age or cohort effect. A third possibility is that live streaming is more popular outside the United States for unknown reasons.

The Internet Watch Foundation (2018) analyzed 2,082 images or videos that met the legal criteria for CSEM and had been shared during a live stream. Of these images, 96% showed children on their own, typically in their bedroom.

Most (98%) depicted children aged 13 or under, and most (96%) depicted girls. All the images or videos had been redistributed from the original site where they had been posted, and the majority ended up in 16 forums that specialized in posts about live-streamed child sexual abuse.

R. Brown et al. (2020) looked at live-streaming cases in Australia where financial records were used to identify suspects who had made payments to Filipino facilitators and where it was highly likely these payments were for access to live streaming, according to arrests in the Philippines and texts about type of child or activities sought. Transactions were believed to be for live streaming because all the facilitators were arrested for child sexual exploitation or abuse offenses, adult content does not require facilitators to accept payment, and the Australian Federal Police indicated contact offending was typically facilitated through cash, not electronic transactions. R. Brown et al. obtained data from 256 Australia-based persons all under investigation (not necessarily charged or convicted yet) for paying for live streaming of child sexual abuse from the Philippines. In total, the Australian suspects sent 2,714 payments to live streaming facilitators. R. Brown et al. suggested the focus on the Philippines was in part because of the relative costs for Australian suspects. A good reason to focus on the financial aspect of live streaming child sexual abuse is that payment incentivizes child sexual abuse, just as money can incentivize sexual trafficking of children and child sexual abuse tourism (see Chapter 4).

Kleijn and Bogaerts (2021) studied 195 cases involving live streaming suspects and operators who pretended to be facilitators of live streaming. These data were collected by Terres des Hommes as part of a campaign where adults posed as Filipina girls between the ages of 9 and 12 in different chatrooms. In 10 weeks, the operators spoke to 20,172 people in 19 anglophone chatrooms. Kleijn and Bogaerts randomly selected 196 of 1,000 suspects and excluded the sole female suspect for a final sample of 195 suspects. The 195 male live-streaming suspects in Klein and Bogaert's analysis were purportedly between 18 and 61, with one third from Europe and one third from North America (mostly Canada and the United States). Kleijn and Bogaerts used thematic analysis to identify the pathways to offending described by Ward and Hudson (1998). In brief, the pathways model distinguishes between approach and avoidance pathways to sexual offending. Approach pathways are distinguished by the person seeking opportunities to offend, whether directly (active) or indirectly, by behaving impulsively or making choices that facilitate offending (passive). In contrast, avoidance pathways are distinguished by the person trying to avoid offending, either actively (employing strategies to prevent offenses) or passively (resisting urges but lacking the knowledge or skills to implement effective strategies and not making an effort to acquire the knowledge or skills). A mixed pathway shows elements of both approach and avoidance elements. Kleijn and Bogaerts found evidence for both approach and mixed pathways, with only 12 suspects assigned to the avoidance pathway. Half of the Kleijn and Bogaerts sample were in an active approach pathway, where they made explicit sexual requests within the first 10 lines of their chat with the putative girl. Even the additional 40 cases in the mixed pathway group were still approach oriented overall; the main difference from those assigned to the approach pathway is that individuals in the mixed pathway also engaged in some small talk and were not always as direct or manipulative.

Cubitt et al. (2023) further analyzed the data for 209 of the 256 suspects from R. Brown et al. (2020) for a new study. Though many suspects had no prior criminal history, those who did had an average of 3.2 criminal offenses, mostly for relatively minor crimes such as traffic violations, public order offenses, and theft, in that order. In this subsample with a prior criminal history, 11% had a prior sexual offense against an adult, and 4.4% had a prior sexual offense against a child. Cubitt et al. did a cluster analysis and found a cluster of people with more frequent live-streaming transactions, more criminal history, and a greater likelihood of having prior sexual offenses. These characteristics suggest this cluster of people is likely to be at higher risk of further sexual offending, given the risk relevance of criminal history, particularly sexual offending history (see Chapter 6). Another reason to be concerned about live streaming is that it is at the higher extreme of an intensity gradient in CSEM, ascending from drawings or stories to images, then videos, and then to live-streamed content. The psychological step from watching live-streamed child sexual abuse to committing these acts oneself is smaller than the psychological step from using CSEM depicting fictional children, such as drawings or stories.

In the first edition, I pointed out my concerns about commercial child sexual exploitation, including live streaming of child sexual exploitation and abuse, sexual trafficking of children, and child sexual abuse tourism. However, little is known about commercial child sexual exploitation (see Chapter 4). Commercial CSEM production clearly takes place, though it appears to be a tiny fraction of CSEM production. Fredlund et al. (2018) surveyed a representative sample of 3,498 Swedish adolescents and young adults and found that 1.5% reported they had engaged in sexual acts for reimbursement of some kind, including money, alcohol, cigarettes, drugs, or basic needs (e.g., food or a place to stay). Most (57%) met the buyer online, and buyers could be male or female. Most buyers (57%) were adolescents themselves, likely peers or older adolescents. Finkelhor et al. (2022) found that 1.7% of their sample had engaged in commercial sexual exploitation, sending sexts or engaging in other sexual behavior for money or other goods. Karlsson and Josephson (2021) reported that many child and youth participants in their survey about nudes online—almost 13,000 participants responding to posts on Snapchat and Instagram stories in Sweden—reported they had been offered money to sell nudes. Almost half (46%) were aged 10 to 13, and over half were aged 14 to 17. For girls, solicitations were predominantly from adults, either adults only or both adults and minors. For boys, the most common solicitations were from minors, either minors only or minors and adults; however, boys were less likely to know the age of the solicitor than girls were. Most participants (80% among those ages 10 to 13) had been sent unsolicited nudes, and significant minorities (15% again of those ages 10 to 13) had their nudes nonconsensually shared.

Karlsson and Josephson (2021) did not mention if respondents were asked if they sold nudes, though some of the quotes from the open-ended responses indicate that some participants did sell their images (e.g., one participant said they made 500 Swedish kroner, or approximately 50 U.S. dollars, for an image). The same report also discussed the different strategies the young participants used to mitigate their risk if they sold nudes. The simplest was not to do it, but others described ways they attempted to mitigate risk by not showing their face in the image or sending nudes to strangers who would be less able to engage in sextortion or nonconsensually reshare the images than someone who knew the sender's identity.

Virtual CSEM and Child Sex Dolls

Some CSEM perpetrators in Seto and Eke (2005) had anime content depicting CSEM themes (illegal in Canada), and boylove story research has shown there is interest in stories about sexual or romantic interactions with children (Madill & Zhao, 2022). In addition, computer image generation technologies are constantly improving and—accelerated by the emergence of AI technology—could be used to create realistic CSEM content; indeed, multiple stimulus sets have been developed for the assessment of sexual interest in children to address the ethical concerns about using stimuli depicting real children (Gress et al., 2013). Child sex dolls have been deemed to constitute CSEM in Canada (Warnica, 2019), and other jurisdictions have proposed banning child sex dolls.

Deepfakes are different from entirely fictional CSEM because they involve the use of images of real children, as when perpetrators create new CSEM by morphing the faces of known children onto the bodies of unknown children (Seto & Eke, 2015). I suspect that deepfakes will become a growing part of CSEM content as the technology becomes easier to use and more widely available. Eelmaa (2022) cited a Netclean report from 2018 suggesting that one in five police investigators had encountered deepfakes during an investigation. Deepfakes involving children can be prosecuted under obscenity legislation or CSEM legislation in some countries, but there are many challenges, including distinguishing deepfakes from real images, clarifying the legality of deepfakes involving adults, and regulating deepfake technology.

The Internet Watch Foundation (2023) published a report on 11,108 AI-generated images that might have been CSEM, identified in a single darknet forum by Internet Watch Foundation analysts. Of these images, 27% were deemed to meet the legal threshold for CSEM in the United Kingdom (which can include child content that does not look realistic, like Canada, but unlike the United States), and of the images deemed to be illegal, only 14% were clearly unrealistic. The most common age category (54%) included children who appeared to be between the ages of 7 and 10 and, thus, were likely to be prepubescent. The second most common age category (39%) depicted children who appeared to be between the ages of 11 and 13 and, thus, included pubescent children as well. The report authors noted how quickly this technology has advanced, demonstrating how Midjourney, as an example, has greatly improved the realism of AI-generated images of adults in less than 18 months, from Version 1, released in February 2022, to Version 5, released 15 months later in May 2023.

Deepfakes

Technology can advance quickly. As I edit this section approximately 18 months after beginning my first draft, there has been an explosion of policy and public attention to the potential for so-called generative AI technology that can be used to create convincing text, images, or video. Like any new technology, there are many potential benefits and risks of generative AI. A specific risk is the use of generative AI to facilitate online sexual offending (Lapowsky, 2023). For example, text generation using large language models could be used to refine online sexual solicitations in terms of approach or content, and image or video generation can produce realistic-looking CSEM.

I am particularly concerned about the use of deepfake technology to create CSEM using images of real children—for example, by digitally morphing images of their faces with CSEM images obtained online. These images could be used to fuel sexual fantasies about a specific child or youth, which may suggest an elevated risk of direct sexual offending against that child. Even if deepfakes do not increase the risk of direct sexual offending, they could still be used to commit sextortion of both minors and adults, particularly girls and women, which could still cause harm if seen by others, even if those others suspect the images are not real.

There is no research on the impact of deepfake technology, given how new this technology is. However, we do have some relevant data from our follow-up research on adult men convicted of CSEM offending, 91% of them between 2000 and 2006 (Seto & Eke, 2015). A third (32%) possessed anime CSEM content, suggesting an interest in fictional content that did not depict real children. A small minority (6%) had created CSEM through morphing, typically using photo manipulation software to combine the face of a known child with the body of an unknown child depicted in CSEM obtained online. Our hypothesis in Seto and Eke (2015) was that morphing was used to create content about a specific child the perpetrator had sexual fantasies about but was unwilling or unable to create CSEM or engage in direct sexual offending against that child.

A preprint on survey studies reported that attitudes about deepfakes are affected by celebrity status, whether the content was used for self-gratification or shared online, and the respondent's psychopathy score (Fido et al., 2022). Eelmaa (2022) qualitatively analyzed 13,293 Reddit comments to identify themes in the Reddit users' views and attitudes about the sexualization of minors in deepfakes and hentai (hentai is a genre of Japanese animation characterized by overtly sexualized characters and content). The analysis captured five major themes in the discussions about the sexualization of minors: illegality, art, the promotion of pedophilia, increase in offending, and general harmfulness.

Deepfakes illustrate several key themes in this book. First, new technology is quickly co-opted for sexual purposes, and that can include harmful and/or illegal purposes. Second, initial efforts can be clumsy or flawed but then are refined over time. Third, the scope of potential harm keeps broadening. With real photos, CSEM production involves some kind of direct interaction with a child, but with deepfake technology, CSEM that convincingly depicts real children can be created without any interaction at all.

OTHER ILLEGAL PORNOGRAPHY

The overwhelming focus of online sexual content offending research, policy, and practice has been CSEM, for understandable reasons. As lawyers will sometimes say in court, it shocks the conscience to realize that sexual images and videos of children are being produced and shared with others who find this content to be sexually gratifying. Sexual exploitation in CSEM is obvious, given children cannot legally consent to being recorded, and in many cases, CSEM production represents the recording of child sexual abuse. I imagine the focus has largely been on CSEM because it mostly depicts real children.

However, other forms of illegal pornography can also cause harm to others. For example, obscenity laws often prohibit depictions of sexual violence. I think there should be a similar level of policy attention for the possession, distribution, or production of depictions of real sexual violence (e.g., a video recording of the sexual assault of an adult) compared with simulated sexual violence involving actors.[2] I think it is worth paying attention to other illegal pornography because the motivation–facilitation model of sexual offending (see Chapter 5) suggests that individuals seeking out content depicting sexual violence are more likely to be sexually interested in this content and more likely to engage in sexual violence if facilitating factors and opportunity were present. In both cross-sectional and longitudinal data, there is evidence that general adult pornography use is associated with sexual aggression toward adults (e.g., a meta-analysis by Paul Wright et al. (2016) that examined 22 studies from seven countries), but it is still unclear whether consumption of violent pornography has a stronger association with sexual violence perpetration than nonviolent pornography.

Some jurisdictions, such as Canada, have criminalized the nonconsensual recording of images or videos (e.g., "upskirting" images, spycam footage) involving adults, though what is covered can vary greatly. Najdowski (2017)

---

[2]Machine learning tools might be useful for distinguishing simulated sexual violence from sexual violence, just as they might be useful for distinguishing AI-generated CSEM from CSEM depicting real children. Another potential use would be to distinguish deepfakes from real images. Another way technology could be brought to bear on this problem is the use of blockchains to authenticate commercially produced pornography involving consenting adult actors. Pornography sites could reduce the inadvertent distribution of CSEM and content depicting real sexual violence.

reviewed 75 state or federal laws in the United States (some states had multiple applicable laws) regarding nonconsensual recording or sharing of images with others, akin to digital voyeurism or nonconsensual sharing of images (see Chapter 4). A quarter of these statutes specified that the law applied only in private spaces, meaning there was no legal protection for women being surreptitiously recorded in public spaces. Only one in five laws addressed the specific situation when images were taken with consent but then reshared without consent. It is also worth pointing out that, even when laws exist, they may not be applied. For example, the nonconsensual sharing of images is a relatively new criminal offense in Canada that is rarely invoked, even though self-report survey data suggest that many people are affected. Karasavva and Forth (2022) found that over a quarter of their university student sample reported their images had been nonconsensually reshared.

In a representative sample of young Swedish men, Seto, Babchishin, et al. (2015) found that self-reported viewing of depictions of adult–child sex (which would meet the legal definitions of CSEM) was positively correlated with viewing content depicting sexual violence but not with viewing content depicting bestiality. This suggests some overlap in the factors contributing to an interest in viewing content that involves harm or potential harm to other people. Seto and Eke (2015) found that approximately one in 12 CSEM perpetrators in their Canadian sample had content depicting rape that was considered indicative of sexual interest in rape because of the amount, level of organization, and/or evidence the content had been recently viewed. Approximately one in seven CSEM perpetrators were deemed to have indicative content depicting bestiality. Both content depicting sexual violence and sex with animals is illegal in Canada, but all the perpetrators were identified and included in the study because they had been convicted of CSEM offenses, not other illegal pornography offenses.

Another reason to be concerned with illegal pornography besides CSEM is the possibility that it is a step in the escalation of pornography use. Some individuals who commit CSEM offenses claim that they began watching mainstream adult pornography and then progressed to more unusual pornography, such as bondage, discipline, sadism, and masochism or fetish content, and then taboo and illegal content, such as sexual violence or CSEM, as they became habituated at each step (see Perpetrator Explanations section in Chapter 5). Seigfried-Spellar and Rogers (2013) analyzed data from an online survey and found some evidence of what they described as a progression from the early onset of the use of adult pornography to bestiality content to CSEM. They did not ask about other types of atypical pornography use. However, Landripet et al. (2019) did not find evidence of content progression from mainstream to violent pornography in analyzing the pornography use patterns reported by a large sample of Croatian adolescents.

Escalation From Legal to Illegal Content

Another consideration in our understanding of CSEM offending is legal content that some would describe as CSEM-adjacent, including legal pornography that plays with the social taboos about sexual interest in minors, including the barely legal, "schoolgirl," and faux incest genres (so-called fauxcest, e.g., "stepdaughter" pornography). These are popular genres, as demonstrated in analyses of older pornography use data in the book *A Billion Wicked Thoughts* (Ogas & Gaddam, 2011) and more recent Pornhub Insight (https://www.pornhub.com/insights/) analyses about search terms, where "teen" content is usually at the top or highly placed. I have mentioned already that Henek and Bartels (2020) demonstrated that there was an overlap in interests for barely legal pornography and CSEM in a community sample of 87 men. Self-reported interest in adult-as-schoolgirl fantasies was correlated with fantasies about innocence (a partner pretending to be a virgin or inexperienced or a partner acting innocent—a top feature in G. Wilson & Cox, 1983; see also Martijn et al., 2020) and, most important, with self-reported interest in or proclivity to have sex with children.

Escalation in pornography use can be shaped by invisible technology algorithms, where an initial interest in "barely legal" content leads to recommendations of "petite schoolgirls" and other content that pretends to depict minors. From there, it may be a small step to search for real content depicting minors. There is relevant experimental analog evidence from Paul and Linz (2008), who found exposure to "barely legal" pornography primed participants to make more child and sex associations in a lexical decision-making task. A counterargument here is that men have a preparedness to respond to post-pubescent youthfulness (recall the sexual response gradient discussed in Chapter 1), and so we would expect the CSEM content of those who escalate in their sexual content use to differ from those with pedophilia, in that those who escalate are more likely to seek content depicting underage adolescents and less likely to see content depicting prepubescent or pubescent children.

A. Walker et al. (2016) did a Google Trends analysis and found that teen pornography searches increased from 2004 to 2014, whereas searches for "lolita" pornography (where Lolita was a codeword for CSEM) had gone down. State-by-state analytics suggested searches for teen pornography were positively associated with the proportion of minors in the state population, which may reflect minors seeking content depicting minors. Searches for teen pornography were negatively associated with state income and education indicators. A caveat for A. Walker et al. (2016) and other studies of "teen pornography" is that "teen" is just a label, capturing young adolescents (13) to young adults (18 or 19). Peters et al. (2014) analyzed videos to look for text, visual, and other cues in purported teen pornography. A lot of this pornography looked like any other pornography, simply with the teen label added. However, some of the content did include text and other cues to hint at adult–minor sex (e.g., referring to a "teen" as a "good girl" or "little girl" and actors speaking in a childish voice, wearing knee socks or school uniforms, with pigtails and the absence of makeup and actors with slim builds and small breasts).

Turner-Moore and Waterman (2017) conducted a study of sexual fantasies about minors in a sample of 279 men (93 had sexually offended). A large minority of the sample (44%, which also included nonoffending community men) reported child-related fantasies that described oral and penetrative sex with an unknown, attractive adolescent girl (13–15 years old), with school uniforms often mentioned, similar to the legal pornography content that plays with age norms. The next most common fantasy was "mutually" enjoyable sex with a child under age 12. And the third most common fantasy (17%) was sex with a child known to the participant.

Henek and Bartels (2020) obtained responses from a convenience sample of 87 men and found that having schoolgirl fantasies could be a proxy for sexual interest in children, with the important caveat that age was not specified, so legally "child" could refer to anyone under the age of 18. Adult-as-schoolgirl fantasies were predicted by partner-as-innocent fantasies but not sexual dominance or submission.

Another fuzzy boundary in the legal regulation of child content is child content that is not sexually explicit but that, nonetheless, could be sought because of someone's sexual or romantic attraction to children. This could include content depicting child celebrities, child models, and ordinary children in everyday situations. Legal, nonsexual content can nonetheless be sexualized by some individuals, such as depictions of children in swimsuits or underwear or engaging in gymnastics or yoga (see Grannò et al., 2020). This child content does not meet legal criteria for CSEM but nonetheless can be problematic for individuals who are sexually or romantically attracted to children.

It is meaningful that Seto and Eke (2015) found that legal child content is still relevant to the risk of sexual recidivism, with those who prefer legal boy content being at higher risk than those preferring legal girl content; most CSEM perpetrators in our sample had both legal and illegal child content (see Chapter 6 review of the CPORT). What we were not able to determine in Seto and Eke (2005) was whether possession of content depicting fictional children was related to the risk of sexual recidivism. The closest variable we had was possession of any hentai CSEM content, coded simply as yes or no; about a third of our sample had anime CSEM content, and whether the individual possessed hentai CSEM (because content depicting fictional children is still illegal in Canada) was not significantly related to sexual recidivism. We did not code anime gender preferences, but I am curious to know whether the anime depicted boys more than girls would have enhanced the prediction of sexual recidivism.

Bestiality, Violence, and Other Forms of Extreme Pornography

Several studies have examined individuals convicted of other illegal pornography offenses. One Swiss study compared juveniles convicted of CSEM and those convicted of other illegal pornography crimes involving bestiality, violence, or human excrement (Aebi et al., 2014). Aebi et al. found that the 54 juveniles convicted of CSEM had more frequent and extensive involvement with illegal content but had less criminal history than the 42 juveniles convicted of other illegal pornography offenses. There was no significant difference in recidivism rates between the two groups, with low recidivism rates overall. It is probable that the juvenile CSEM perpetrators were more likely to have atypical sexual interests than the juveniles convicted of other illegal pornography crimes, but they were less antisocial than the others (see Chapters 5 and 6).

Another relevant study, also conducted in Switzerland, followed adults convicted of illegal pornography offenses (Goller et al., 2016). Most were in legal trouble for CSEM offenses, but some were in trouble for other illegal pornography crimes. Goller et al. followed 4,612 illegal pornography perpetrators convicted between 1973 and 2008; most (92%) were convicted of illegal pornography offenses only, and the rest were also convicted of contact sexual offenses against children. Most (93%) had been convicted of CSEM offenses, but many were also convicted of possessing content depicting bestiality (54%), excrement (39%), or violence (27%). Not all the cases were available for follow-up, but this study showed again that dual perpetrators (illegal pornography plus contact) were at much higher risk than illegal pornography perpetrators, though the 3-year reconviction rate for contact sexual offending was less than 3% even for the dual perpetration group. The most common type of sexual recidivism involved another illegal pornography offense, again even for dual perpetrators.

McGlynn and Bows (2019) examined data from police records for a total of 571 cases accused of "extreme pornography" offenses between 2015 and 2017 in the United Kingdom, which has laws prohibiting extreme content depicting serious injury, necrophilia, bestiality, or sexual violence. Bestiality content was the most common, representing 87% of the charges, which does not map onto either the prevalence of paraphilic interests (zoophilia is rarer than a paraphilic interest in sexual violence in surveys of paraphilic interests; e.g., Seto et al., 2021) or the prevalence of human–animal content in analyses of pornography repositories. Another finding was the variation in charge rates across cases, from 40% for necrophilic content cases to 79% for cases involving content depicting acts that threaten a person's life; this suggests an impact of police or prosecution discretion on whether to charge someone with an extreme pornography offense. Of those accused, 97% were male, again in line with the extreme gender discrepancy in CSEM offending, suggesting the discrepancy is not specific to CSEM but perhaps a more general male bias toward illegal pornography offending. Also, 67% of this sample was White, which can be compared with census data from 2019 indicating that 78% of the population in the United Kingdom was White, suggesting disproportionate representation of Black, Indigenous, and People of Color (BIPOC) persons (Office for National Statistics, 2021).

CSEM ECOSYSTEMS

This section covers three environments I believe are relevant to CSEM offending and online sexual offending more broadly: (a) technology environments, (b) legal and policy environments, and (c) social environments.

I briefly discuss the relevance of these different but overlapping environments to online sexual offending.

Technology Environments

Technology environments can directly facilitate or mitigate online sexual offending because of intentional or unintentional affordances. In Chapter 1, I talked about the facilitating impact of differential access to the internet, particularly high-speed internet, on opportunities to offend. The ability to anonymously transfer large volumes of data using encryption is an important affordance for internet security and privacy, but it can also facilitate CSEM offending. Steel et al. (2023) described four eras in online CSEM offending in terms of the evolution of technologies and thus affordances, from "open" sharing via email, chat, or bulletin boards to closed websites to peer-to-peer file sharing to the darknet. The general trend has been toward greater anonymity and privacy protection.

The ability for technology users to interact with each other online can foster communication and community building, but it can also mean adult users can interact with minor users and engage in online sexual solicitations. Dating apps and platforms have proliferated as a way for adults to meet potential romantic partners. These same apps and platforms can also be used to sexually solicit minors who sign up or facilitate sexual assaults of adults.

Woodhams et al. (2021) looked at the posts and messages of 53 suspects monitored by police in the United Kingdom because of their activity on darknet forums. These researchers did not look at messages from other users except those of undercover police. All suspects were members of one of four darknet forums dedicated to sexual interest in children or CSEM, each with a different focus (e.g., general sexual interest in children vs. one forum that focused on child torture and sadism). Consistent with their engagement on these forums, most users (97%) admitted sexual interest in children, and only one person said they were only interested in adults. Only 11% reported sexual interest in adults, indicating a high proportion of exclusive pedohebephilia among these suspects. In terms of age preferences, 14% said "pubescent" (this would be considered postpubescent in my chronophilias categorization, referring to older adolescents; see Seto, 2017b), 31% pubescent, 45% prepubescent, and 34% children under age 5. This is an interesting observation because it again highlights the relative popularity of prepubescent CSEM content online, and it also indicates that many suspects had multiple age interests because the percentages add up to more than 100%. Eleven CSEM suspects were eventually identified and charged, eight for CSEM offenses and three for contact sexual offenses. All but one suspect said they were male, and 13% had senior roles in the forum—for example, as a moderator or owner. A quarter (28%) said they had their own children, and 34% reported having regular access to children. In terms of offending, 76% showed evidence they used CSEM, 64% showed evidence they had committed contact offenses, and 43% showed evidence of both forms of sexual offending. A small minority (14%) said they produced CSEM, but they did not specify whether they were recording contact sexual offending or had engaged in online sexual solicitations of children. Consistent with their use of darknet versus clearnet sources for CSEM, suspects took a range of security countermeasures, including anonymous emails and encryption. In terms of their stated reasons for forum involvement, 32% said they were on the forum for CSEM and 23% to associate with like-minded people.

I have mostly focused on affordances that can facilitate online sexual offending, but there are also affordances that can be used to mitigate these behaviors. All forms of online sexual offending would be mitigated if real identity credentials were required, but this would come at the expense of privacy, safety, and the risk of repressive government tactics. I have already discussed how more effective age-gating online would emulate the protection minors have by being barred from adult-only spaces such as bars or nightclubs. Last, online technologies leave digital traces that can aid police in the investigation of crimes, including online sexual offending. I discuss other ways that technology can be used to mitigate online sexual offending in Chapter 8.

Legal and Policy Environments

Though the internet is borderless in some respects, criminal justice and other responses are organized locally, regionally, and nationally. The International Center for Missing and Exploited Children has completed surveys of international law regarding CSEM and online sexual solicitations of minors and developed model laws. Perhaps the most notable conclusion from their regular updates is the change over time; the first edition of their review of CSEM laws was produced in 2006, and the most recent edition in 2018. In that period, the number of countries deemed to have sufficient anti-CSEM legislation went from 27 to 119, and the number of countries with no pertinent legislation went down from 95 to 16 (International Center for Missing and Exploited Children, 2023). That is quite a big change in legal environments in 12 years. However, there has been little movement (from 41 to 38 countries) on criminalization of CSEM possession without intent or actual distribution.

Something I did not examine in the first edition was online sexual solicitation laws, which had not been reviewed yet by the International Center for Missing and Exploited Children. The first edition of their review was posted in 2017 and reported the following: 63 countries (much fewer than for CSEM) have legislation regarding online sexual solicitation, but the majority of countries (133 out of 196) did not. Of these 133 countries without specific legislation, 51 did have legislation criminalizing showing pornography to a minor, which can be part of online sexual solicitations, but 82 had no legislation at all, which means someone could legally and knowingly engage in sexual chats with a minor, getting into trouble only if they sent or received CSEM. There may be a similar trend in online sexual solicitation legislation by 2029, as was seen for CSEM, which would mean many more countries will have specific laws in less than a decade.

Similarly, few countries have criminalized the nonconsensual sharing of intimate images—one country that has is Canada—but more countries may bring in specific legislation as the harmful consequences of this behavior become more widely acknowledged. Few countries prosecute digital exhibitionism, even though it may already violate existing laws regarding indecent exposure, and countries vary in whether and how they prosecute digital voyeurism.

Also relevant to this legal and policy environment issue is a survey of a set of low-middle-income countries conducted by UNICEF (n.d.). It showed variation across these countries in their adoption of legislation and other public policies, distinguished further by whether they are members of the WeProtect Global Alliance or designated an "End Violence Pathfinding country." Being part of the WeProtect Global Alliance or being designated a Pathfinding country implies a national commitment to addressing online child sexual exploitation and abuse and benefiting from this membership or designation by drawing on international resources. An important caveat in examining the UNICEF survey is that many of the partial or complete adoption of policies are about whether there are frameworks, policies, or mechanisms in place. But the devil is in the details: Having a reporting portal is not worth much if there is no mandate to report, reporting is inconsistent, or data quality is poor. Similarly, having a law on the books is a start, but it likely has little impact if it is rarely applied, as with the nonconsensual resharing of images law in Canada. These challenges are acknowledged in the UNICEF report.

Whether laws and other public policies are having the desired impacts is impossible to assess without benchmarking data on the incidence of online sexual offending. There is relatively little benchmarking available, though there is some movement on this with the WeProtect Alliance's annual Global Threat Assessments (the latest is WeProtect Global Alliance, 2023) and other international efforts to ask minors about their experiences online (e.g., Thorn, 2021, 2022, 2023). It is still the case that most of this research is WEIRD (Western, educated, industrialized, rich, and democratic), and we cannot assume that results generalize to other parts of the world. Even if results generalize, not having a more diverse base of knowledge means we are missing out on potentially important sociocultural factors.

A good example of both legal and cultural environments having an impact on online sexual offending is Japan, which stands out internationally in terms of historical and cultural tolerance for content depicting minors in sexualized contexts, including pubescent and even prepubescent children. I have previously discussed the relevance of this in terms of sexualized content depicting children in Japanese anime, manga, and popular culture (see Seto, 2018). Ogaki (2018) discussed the evolution and forms of *jyoshi kousei* (JK; "high school girls") businesses in Japan. These so-called JK businesses involve a range of activities, including selling worn and unwashed underwear or other clothing, going out on dates with adults, or offering other services involving high school girls, such as photo shoots or massages. As part of these JK businesses, illegal activities can occur, including the production of CSEM or payment for sex with a minor. Indeed, the age of consent in Japan only changed from 13 to 16 in 2023, suggesting that adults could legally have had sex with high school girls if no payment was involved (Yamaguchi, 2023).

Cultural Environments

Though I have just discussed Japan as an outlier in some cultural aspects, I am particularly thinking about internet culture in this section rather than cultures based on geography, shared language, or religious affiliations. In particular, core principles associated with the emergence of internet technologies continue to have an impact on online behavior, including online sexual offending. These include antiauthoritarian principles, libertarianism, and beliefs about the relative value of individual privacy and freedom of speech (e.g., Rheingold, 2000). These ideals are not inherent to the internet; like other cultural beliefs and norms, they can shift over time and across spaces. More specific online cultures can also be shaped by and influence individual beliefs and perceived norms wherever individuals who are interested in CSEM, children, or sexual coercion congregate. Kloess and van der Bruggen (2023) conducted a literature review that included studies of online forums for individuals who are sexually attracted to minors. Many of these studies were qualitative, and most relied on analyses of posts, not direct messages between users. These forums create and reflect specific subcultures, including subcultures involved with online sexual offending and subcultures of persons who are sexually attracted to minors, including pre-pubescent or pubescent children. An example of the subcultures is users posting their views about CSEM and whether it is victimless or at least less victimizing or the idea that most men are attracted to underage girls (for example) but will not admit it to themselves, much less others (see Chapters 5 and 6).

SUMMARY

Among all the forms of online sexual offending covered in this book, CSEM offending has continued to receive the most attention in terms of research, policy, and practice. Pedophilia and hebephilia are important paraphilic motivations for this form of online sexual offending when detected, and I am confident that this is one of the findings that will be robust cross-culturally and over time. At the same time, CSEM offending is not homogenous, and it is not always explained by pedophilia or hebephilia. It is possible that a lot of undetected CSEM offending involves content depicting older adolescents, which tends to be a lower priority in law enforcement and is less likely to result in convictions, given ambiguity about the age of the persons depicted unless their identities are known. Many men who prefer adults are nonetheless also sexually interested in older adolescents, and minors themselves are interested in their peers and may produce or engage with content depicting their peers. Technological affordances are a grave concern, given evidence that many CSEM users began as minors and are relatively new to CSEM.

There is growing evidence that CSEM involving prepubescent children is more likely to be produced by family members, whereas CSEM involving pubescent children or postpubescent adolescents is more likely to be self-generated or created as a result of online sexual solicitations. CSEM offending clearly demonstrates the relevance of technological affordances, illustrated partly by the technological arms race between perpetrators and police. In addition to technology, legal and cultural factors also influence how CSEM is operationalized and promulgated.

CASE EXAMPLES

The following are two case examples of individuals adjudicated for CSEM offenses, to illustrate some of the ideas in this chapter. These case examples include details from real clients as well as fictional elements to protect client confidentiality. Subsequent chapters will also return to Adam and Bart.

Adam (Lower Risk CSEM)

Adam was a 46-year-old man living with his long-term partner and his partner's daughter from a previous marriage. He had no prior psychiatric or criminal history. Adam was employed by a major financial services company, and CSEM was discovered on his work computer during a routine IT service (detected by a third party). The CSEM comprised thousands of images and videos depicting prepubescent and pubescent girls, including explicit sexual activity with adults, which raised alarm bells for police and others because his stepdaughter was 11 at the time.

Adam reported escalating use of pornography over the previous 5 years as a result of relationship conflict and reduced sex life. He said that he began using mainstream adult pornography but quickly went down a rabbit hole of more unusual themes, including fauxcest content ("daddy–daughter"). Adam's claim of escalation in his pornography use over time was consistent with forensic digital evidence indicating he frequently used pornography sites, including paid subscriptions. His high level of pornography use was facilitated by the technological affordances of easy access to unconventional, then taboo, and then illegal pornography content, as well as algorithms he subsequently claimed had shown him ads and suggestions for content depicting young-looking adult models (the "barely legal" content) and content that pretended to be CSEM, such as "stepdaughters." Adam readily admitted his guilt and his sexual interest in the CSEM content but denied any sexual interest in his stepdaughter or any other specific children. Adam did not volunteer or work with children and reported minimal contact with children besides his stepdaughter and her friends. He denied having offense-supportive cognitions regarding children or sex. He also denied experiencing romantic attraction to children and emotional congruence with children (see Chapter 5). Both he and his partner said he was a social drinker with no history of drug use. His family of origin remained supportive but was shocked and mystified by the criminal charges. His partner ended the relationship and moved away.

Bart (Higher Risk CSEM)

Bart was a 32-year-old man who lived alone and worked as a freelance graphics and commercial designer. He reported no long-term relationships and few friends. His criminal record showed a prior contact sexual offense when he was 17, committed against a 13-year-old boy he knew from school. He received a term in residential treatment plus probation, which he completed without incident. Bart was arrested as part of an international, undercover police investigation of an active darknet trading ring focusing on sexually explicit depictions of prepubescent and pubescent boys. Bart was identified as a moderator who was active in the ring and posted that he had many opportunities to offend and could create new content. Bart quickly admitted he was sexually and romantically attracted to boys following his arrest and explained that he sought out CSEM because the images already existed, and the content was a substitute for interacting with boys offline. Forensic analysis of his computing and storage devices determined he had a large, organized collection of CSEM that predominantly depicted boys, though there were also some images and videos of boys and girls together or girls alone. Bart also had pornography content depicting other paraphilic themes, including boys in bondage and boys engaged in sexual acts with animals. In addition to CSEM, Brad had a large amount of legal content depicting boys, including stock photos, child models, and child celebrities from TV and movies. He was familiar with games, music, and other cultural interests popular with children and said he was more comfortable with children than with adults because of his social anxiety and introversion.

3

Sexual Solicitation of Minors

I wrote in the 2013 edition of this book that most research on online sexual offending has focused on child sexual exploitation material (CSEM) offending; this is still the case 10 years later. Yet many parents, educators, and policymakers are also concerned about the risk posed by adults using internet technologies to contact children and adolescents for sexual purposes, with recent recognition that this can also include older minors sexually soliciting younger children. I refer to this form of online sexual offending as sexual solicitation offending,[1] where the older person is contacting a minor to solicit some kind of sexual interaction, whether that is sending images that would constitute CSEM, engaging in sexually explicit chat, sending pornographic content (e.g., sending nudes of themselves or other CSEM), or in some cases, proposing to meet in person where contact sexual offending can take place.

Laws that have been created to criminalize this behavior do not refer to sexual solicitation but instead typically use terms such as *luring*, *enticement*, or *grooming*. I think these legal terms can be misleading because the criminal behavior being described does not necessarily involve enticements such as gifts or attention (luring or enticement) and are not necessarily gradual, linear, or subtle (grooming); indeed, some solicitations can be quite aggressive, involving

---

[1] Adults can also engage in unwanted sexual solicitations of other adults, but this is usually not pursued criminally unless the behavior is repeated or the target is frightened by the person who is soliciting them. Online sexual harassment of adults by other adults—particularly harassment of women by men—is, unfortunately, a common and toxic experience (A. Powell & Henry, 2019).

https://doi.org/10.1037/0000428-004
Online Sexual Offending: Theory, Practice, and Policy, Second Edition, by M. C. Seto
Copyright © 2025 by the American Psychological Association. All rights reserved.

direct threats or use of force. Also, solicitations can be abrupt rather than gradual, such as immediately asking someone for nudes in the hope that anyone responds or being aggressive or even hostile in the initial interactions.

PREVALENCE

Most of what we know about the prevalence of online sexual solicitation comes from victimization data, particularly anonymous surveys. Wager et al. (2018) summarized evidence about online child sexual exploitation victimization, including 21 self-reported victimization surveys about online sexual solicitations and unwanted exposure to pornography. These surveys help us understand victimization prevalence rates but often did not ask about the age or relationship to the solicitor, thus blurring potential differences when the soliciting person is also a minor, young adult, or much older adult and when the person is a stranger versus someone already known to the minor. In Table 5 in Wager et al., focusing on online requests that were unwanted and/or involved an adult (intentionally excluding wanted interactions with a peer), about one in four girls (28%) and one in 10 boys (10%) reported receiving this kind of request. The prevalence rates were higher for older respondents and for longer time frames (e.g., lifetime vs. 1 year). The 1-year prevalence rates were 15% to 19% for girls and 5% to 8% for boys.

The following point was not discussed by Wager et al. (2018): These kinds of 1-year rates, relative to lifetime prevalence rates, support my suspicion that online sexual solicitations are not random. If they were, lifetime rates would continue to increase as youths spend more time online and are, therefore, exposed to the risk of sexual solicitation. Instead, it appears that a minority of young people are vulnerable to being repeatedly solicited sexually for reasons such as having a sexually suggestive username or profile photo, being on forums that address sexual topics, or posting about problems such as family dysfunction, loneliness, mental health issues, or substance use, which are seen by others as evidence of vulnerability to sexual solicitation. This observation applies to sexual solicitations by strangers; research discussed later indicates that most sexual solicitations come from older minors or adults who already know the young person, and there may be differences in vulnerabilities for these different groups of perpetrators. Also, most solicitations to meet do not result in a meeting; who agrees to meet with the solicitation perpetrator is also unlikely to be random. In some cases, the other person is already known and older but not much older, and the young person is open to a sexual interaction (e.g., because they see themselves in or developing a romantic relationship with the soliciting person).

Since the Wager et al. (2018) review, the Thorn (2022) grooming report revealed that harassment has become "normal" for many internet users: More than a third (40%) had been asked for a nude online, with no major difference between boys and girls. One in seven minors reported being asked for nudes by strangers online on at least a weekly basis. There was evidence of a gender and age interaction, where boys between the ages of 9 and 12 were more likely to be asked than girls in the same age group (31% vs. 25%), whereas girls between the ages of 13 and 17 were more likely to be asked than boys in the same age group (51% vs. 42%). Almost two thirds of LGBTQ+ youth (64%) had been sexually solicited in this way. Most minors had been asked to move from a public online space to a private online space (e.g., from a public gaming forum to a private messaging app).

Victimization prevalence data provide important insights, but they do not directly tell us about the prevalence of perpetration because an individual perpetrator could sexually approach multiple targets; indeed, one quarter was shown to do so in the analysis of solicitation reports by the National Center for Missing and Exploited Children (NCMEC; 2017). Gledhill's (2016) thesis was the only general population study identified in the Ingram et al. (2023) systematic review that reported on solicitation perpetration prevalence, albeit in a convenience sample of 71 participants recruited from different online sites. In this study, 4% (3/71) acknowledged online sexual solicitation of a minor, with a majority (2/3) acknowledging they solicited a minor in the hope of facilitating contact sexual offending.

A few other studies have looked at sexual solicitation perpetration in mixed or noncommunity samples that are less informative about general prevalence rates. For example, Schulz et al. (2016) surveyed 2,828 respondents regarding sexual solicitations of adolescents and children. However, they oversampled from pedophilia forums ($n = 386/2,828$), where we would expect sexual solicitations of children to be much more likely and, indeed, forum members accounted for 79% of sexual solicitations of children (1% overall in the large sample) and 49% of solicitations of adolescents (4.5% overall). If we do some reverse arithmetic, that means six of 2,442 (0.2% of the general website sample) had sexually solicited a child, and 2.5% had sexually solicited an adolescent; depending on the age of the adolescent and the specific law that applied in their jurisdiction, this would constitute criminal behavior.

Regarding official crime records, Canadian data for police-reported incidents and charges were analyzed by Ibrahim (2023) from 2014 to 2020. In police-reported incidents of luring (online sexual solicitation), the incidence rate increased from 50 per 100,000 population to 131 per 100,000, an increase of more than 2.5 times during this period. However, these rates for police-reported incidents are much lower than the incidence rates suggested by self-report victimization surveys, highlighting again the huge gap between youth experiences and police reporting (Thorn, 2023). Of all online sexual offenses, 77% were for sexual solicitations; CSEM offenses were also reported in about a fifth of these incidents. Consistent with research described elsewhere in this chapter, most of the victims were girls, 73% involving girls between the ages of 12 and 17 and 13% involving girls under age 12. Targeting girls under the age of 14 can suggest pedophilia or hebephilia, whereas the luring of older adolescents does not.

I concluded in the first edition that most online sexual solicitation does not involve pedophilia because data from the National Juvenile Online

Victimization (NJOV) studies found no real solicitation victims under the age of 12 (undercover police officers may pose as younger children) for those who met or attempted to meet in person (see Wolak et al., 2008). Most victims were between the ages of 13 and 15, with a modal age of 14, which can be compared with the mean age of 15 reported by NCMEC (2017) in their analysis of online enticement reports (see Online Solicitation Tactics section). Some of these cases, but not all, may involve hebephilia. This might not fully reflect the range of possible sexual motivations because there are men who would like to solicit younger children if they could reach these children, but younger children are less likely to be online while unsupervised compared with older children and adolescents. This has changed as children get phones at a younger age and have more unsupervised access to online platforms and apps (including knowing how to circumvent parental and other controls). Though American law sets the age threshold for social platforms and apps at 13, many younger children knowingly lie about their age to join. Indeed, the Thorn (2022) research shows that children below the age of 12 are sexually solicited online, including in sexual chats, requests for sexual images, and sending of sexual images. Solicitations of children below the age of 12 do suggest that pedophilia or hebephilia may be relevant motivations. Solicitation of younger children is much more likely to be fantasy driven (see the Fantasy- Versus Contact-Driven Solicitations section) because attempting to meet in person is unrealistic (though possibly still desired by perpetrators).

In the Ibrahim (2023) analysis of Canadian online sexual offending data, among all online sexual victims, 39% were initially strangers, with another 25% being casual acquaintances. Someone closer than an acquaintance was less common, with 8% being friends, 7% being relatives, and 7% being intimate partners. The involvement of intimate partners presumably does not include luring because there is already an existing sexual relationship, but it could include CSEM and nonconsensual sharing of sexual images. Consistent with research on online CSEM sexual offending, most perpetrators (91%) were male, with a mean age of 24 years overall but a much younger mean age for nonconsensual sharing, suggesting this is more of a peer-involved phenomenon. The data reported by Ibrahim are also consistent with my speculation that online offenses are more likely to result in convictions than offline offenses, probably because of the digital evidence available for online offenses, compared with the reliance on victim testimony, witness testimony, and circumstantial evidence in many offline cases.

PERPETRATOR CHARACTERISTICS

It is still the case that there is much less research on solicitation perpetrators than CSEM perpetrators. Much of what we know about perpetrators still relies on the NJOV studies, where the third wave was completed in 2009, an eon ago when it comes to technology (though there is a fourth wave being collected now). Almost all identified solicitation perpetrators in the NJOV studies were male, either older adolescents or adults. Perpetrators were significantly older than their targets, though the age differences decreased over time. Given the ages of the targets they were approaching, NJOV perpetrators were highly unlikely to be pedophilic, though some may have been hebephilic, and more recent perpetrators may have pedophilia or hebephilia because children under the age of 12 are being solicited (Thorn, 2022).

I extracted some key findings regarding solicitation perpetrator characteristics and behavior from the Wolak et al. (2012) bulletin summarizing some of the data from 2000, 2006, and 2009, focusing on pertinent trends over the three NJOV waves (see Table 3.1). Notable trends included an increasing proportion of perpetrators across the three waves that were already known to the minors, from half in 2000 to three quarters in 2009. An increasing proportion of perpetrators were age 25 or younger, so the age difference between perpetrator and target was smaller over time, just as CSEM perpetrator age decreased over the same period. Though rates remained low, victims were more likely to have lied about being an adult, so at least the initial contact by the solicitation perpetrator was ostensibly with an adult (the highest was 22% in 2009). There was a decline in the proportion who possessed CSEM at the time of their arrest, but there was an increase in the production of CSEM, possibly directly linked to online sexual solicitations (e.g., asking for self-generated CSEM or taking screenshots of live-streamed sexual activity; again, see the concomitant decrease in concurrent contact offending for CSEM cases).

Importantly, there were also some solicitation perpetrator characteristics and tactics that did not change over the three NJOV data collection waves, which I suspect have not changed since 2009. The first is that only a minority

TABLE 3.1. NJOV Trends Over Three Data Collection Waves in 2000, 2006, and 2009

Characteristic	2000	2006	2009
Already knew in person	**49%**	**59%**	**72%**
Offender age 25 or less	**11%**	**26%**	**47%**
Possessed CSEM[a]	**52%**	**44%**	**28%**
Produced CSEM[a]	**36%**	**57%**	**59%**
Offender lied about being a minor	5%	20%	15%
Victim lied about being an adult	**9%**	**14%**	**22%**
Offender lied about sexual motives	21%	15%	15%
Offender met victim in person	76%	73%	66%
If met, travelled less than 50 miles	51%	67%	59%
If met, two or more meetings	72%	53%	63%

Note. Bolded figures indicate a notable change over time. Already knowing the person increased by almost 50%, the perpetrator being age 25 or younger increased in proportion by more than four times, and whether the perpetrator possessed child sexual exploitation material (CSEM) decreased by half. NJOV = National Juvenile Online Victimization project.
[a]Those who met solicitation victims online were more likely to possess CSEM and more likely to produce CSEM than those who solicited minors they already knew.

of adult perpetrators lie about being a minor, some youth lie about being an adult, most perpetrators do not lie about their sexual motives, and meeting in person is more likely when real minors interact with someone they already know. Meetings are likely to be local, though there are examples of individuals who traveled long distances, even internationally, to meet in person. This suggests that online solicitations by an adult already known to the minor have some resemblances to statutory sexual offending, as I suggested in the first edition. Statutory sexual offending applies when adults have mutually willing sex with minors below the legal age of consent. These trends would not necessarily apply to perpetrators who are strangers and interact online only, though I suspect they are still mostly not lying about being minors and are still being explicit about their sexual motives.

In contrast to clinical or criminal justice data, a WeProtect Global Alliance and ECPAT report from 2022 found that a fifth of solicitation perpetrators were women, according to 36 women and six men reporting about their juvenile experiences. This is consistent with the gender discrepancy found in the broader sexual offending literature, where 90% or more of individuals convicted of sexual offenses against children are male, yet self-reported victimization surveys suggest that up to 20% of perpetrators are female. Figure 10 in the WeProtect Global Alliance and ECPAT report summarized estimates from a survey of 413 frontline workers in six different countries. This is presumably based on what victims have told them, where they may not know perpetrator gender for certain unless they met in person or obtained other proof. This is intriguing, but we do not know about the actual representation of female perpetrators without confirmation of identities.

ONLINE SOLICITATIONS COMPARED WITH GROOMING

Individuals who sexually offend against children vary in the tactics they use. *Grooming* is a common term used to refer to some of these tactics. Craven et al. (2006) defined it as follows:

> A process by which a person prepares a child, significant adults and the environment for the abuse of this child. Specific goals include gaining access to the child, gaining the child's compliance and maintaining the child's secrecy to avoid disclosure. (p. 297)

Grooming tactics include building trust with a child by rewarding them with affection, positive attention, or gifts; teaching the child their interactions are special and secret; and gradually introducing the idea of sex. Grooming can be manipulative and deceptive, as when seemingly innocuous behavior such as tickling or play wrestling is introduced as an intentional prelude to more direct sexual touching.

Grooming may be more likely by individuals who report romantic attraction to children (Martijn et al., 2020) or an emotional congruence with children where they feel closer to children than adults and prefer the company of children over adults (McPhail et al., 2013; see Chapter 5, this volume). However, as noted already, grooming can be a misnomer for offline sexual solicitations as well because perpetrators can also be directly coercive, including by using their position of power or authority (e.g., a parent, teacher, coach, or religious leader), blackmail, threats, or force. I am not aware of any research that has tested this hypothesis, but I expect that perpetrators who use coercion or violence to gain victim compliance are more antisocial (in terms of personality traits such as callousness) and less likely to report romantic attraction to children.

As with CSEM offending, the venues for sexual solicitation of minors are different, but the underlying criminal behavior and psychology are not new. Ringenberg et al. (2022) conducted a scoping review of both offline and online solicitation research and noted both similarities and differences between offline and online solicitations. For example, they described how both offline and online solicitation perpetrators assess the risk of disclosure and, therefore, the risk of being detected and arrested. Online solicitation perpetrators, however, also have to assess the risk that an unknown minor they contact might be lying about their age or might even be an undercover police officer posing as a minor. This is not a risk for offline solicitation perpetrators who have some in-person interaction with a real minor. This, in turn, reflects a difference in the likelihood that a perpetrator is unknown to the minor; it is much more likely online, whereas offline solicitation usually involves a minor who is somehow known to the adult, whether through family, friends, work, or volunteering. Internet technologies can allow online solicitation perpetrators to contact hundreds, even thousands of strangers quickly.

Most of the minors approached by strangers will ignore or block sexual solicitation requests, but if even one in 1,000 minors is susceptible and responds in some way, this low-cost "spamming" strategy can pay off for soliciting persons. And it might not be in one in 1,000 solicitations: Mitchell et al. (2007) found that one in 65 youths complied with an online request to send a sexual image of themselves, most often to other adolescents, but sometimes to adults. Fewer youths comply with such requests now (Thorn, 2023), though the absolute numbers may be higher given that many more youths are online, and the prevalence of solicitations may have increased since Mitchell et al.'s (2007) study.

Gámez-Guadix et al. (2018) proposed a model of online grooming that involved three main strategies: Deception, bribery, or forming a nonsexual relationship to build trust toward forming a sexual relationship. Gámez-Guadix et al. tested this model in a sample of 2,731 youths between the ages of 12 and 15, 51% of them girls. The following model fits the data, where 196 youths (7%) in the sample had been sexually solicited online in the past year by

> talking about sexual things with an adult on the internet, having sent an adult photos or videos with sexual content of his or herself, having maintained a flirtatious relationship with an adult online, having met in person an adult previously met on the internet, and having met offline to have sexual contact. (Gámez-Guadix et al., 2018, p. 14)

The individual rates for different solicitations were not reported, but I assume that talking and flirtation were the most common, meeting offline for sex was the rarest, and being sent photos or meeting an adult initially encountered online were intermediate in prevalence. One caveat about these results is that the survey asked about experiences with deceit, bribery, or trust building in the past year, but these experiences were not specifically tied to online sexual solicitation. So, this study reports that youths who described experiencing deceit, bribery, or nonsexual trust building were also more likely to report sexual solicitation experiences. The two sets of experiences might not be connected except as co-occurring online events. It is also worth pointing out that Gámez-Guadix et al.'s model does not explicitly include the use of threats, coercion, or force in online sexual solicitations, focusing instead on solicitations that involve grooming.

An important aspect of grooming is that some children are more likely to be targeted, and different tactics are used for different vulnerabilities (see Target Vulnerabilities section later). The risk of online sexual solicitation is not randomly distributed: Children who are socially isolated, live in chaotic families, or have mental health problems are more vulnerable to both offline and online sexual solicitations by older juveniles or adults, just as these children are also more vulnerable to bullying and physical or sexual abuse more generally. In terms of differential tactics, extra attention might be more effective for lonely, socially isolated, or emotionally neglected children, whereas gifts of money, alcohol, or drugs might be more effective for children in impoverished circumstances.

In an early study about tactic choice among contact perpetrators, Conte et al. (1989) interviewed 20 men who had sexually offended against children and found they intentionally targeted vulnerable children. This included targeting children who were needy, unhappy, sad, or previously victimized or, conversely, targeting children who were particularly friendly and trusting. Most of this small clinical sample of men befriended children and groomed them before initiating sexual contact. Budin and Johnson (1989) reported that the perpetrators in their sample targeted their own children or sought "passive, quiet, troubled, lonely children" (p. 79) from single-parent homes. Online perpetrators may similarly look through public posts and profiles to identify minors who may be more vulnerable to sexual solicitations.

M. B. Powell et al. (2021) analyzed 38 chat logs from real sexual solicitation cases obtained from police. All involved men (mean age 31) soliciting single targets; 36 targets were girls between the ages of 13 and 15, and two targets were boys ages 13 or 14. The mean duration of the interactions was 41 days, ranging from one to 17 conversation sessions. M. B. Powell et al. analyzed the transcripts to see what sequences of messages cohered as "moves" made by the perpetrators. They identified the following moves: initiating sexual interaction (35% of all moves); managing target resistance (15%; e.g., by flattering the target or apologizing or checking in later, often co-occurring with an attempted sexual interaction); establishing target attributes such as age, sexual experience, sexual interests, and appearance (12%); attempting to define the online relationship (10%); acknowledging wrongdoing (8%; e.g., mentioning the age difference); asking for or sending images (8%); and discussing meeting in person (7%). The interactions were heterogeneous, dynamic, and haphazard, varying greatly in length, the rapidity of the first sexual request, and the duration between sexual requests.

M. B. Powell et al. (2021) also attempted a cluster analysis with data from 38 solicitation perpetrators and identified three clusters of people. The majority (20 cases) had an impetuous, "hit and run" (M. B. Powell et al.'s label, p. 8) style, with the shortest conversations and initiated sexual requests early, sometimes in their first message (what I called a spamming strategy earlier). Thirteen cases were described as opportunistic and were average in many respects, not differing from the overall sample in terms of tactics or length of conversations—they were less direct and more tangential (e.g., talking about their own sexual fantasies or behavior) and seemed less socially skilled. Five cases were described as devious, with a fixation on the target being young, lots of fantasy content, the most detailed sexual requests, and a greater likelihood of suggesting a meeting in person and demanding secrecy. Devious cases could be aggressive but softened this aggression with flattery, empathy, or apologies. M. B. Powell et al. saw the devious cluster as the most predatory of the three clusters they identified.

ONLINE SOLICITATION TACTICS

There is evidence that offline grooming tactics differ depending on the perpetrator–victim relationship. For example, Kaufman et al. (1998) found that related perpetrators were more likely to commit sexual offenses in the context of routine care (e.g., bathing or dressing a child) or use bribes, whereas unrelated perpetrators were more likely to offer alcohol or drugs. Adolescents were more likely to use threats or force than adults, but the use of threats or force was rare in either group. Lang and Frenzel (1988) also found that related perpetrators were more likely to commit offenses in the context of routine care or play (e.g., tickling games; see also Elliott et al., 1995; Wortley & Smallbone, 2006; Young, 1997). Therefore, it is quite plausible that online grooming tactics differ according to the perpetrator–victim relationship. For example, imagine what grooming might look like when the perpetrator is a much older adult compared with a young adult or another minor, familiar versus a stranger, and if known, related, versus unrelated to the target. I speculate that young adult or minor perpetrators can be more direct than older adults about their sexual interest in the target, especially if they are already known to the target. Suggestions or plans to meet may be more likely from known rather than stranger perpetrators. Related perpetrators may use online technologies to secretly communicate with the target to avoid discovery by the target's parents or other family members because they may already be meeting in person.

In an early study of online solicitation, Malesky (2007) found that perpetrators used grooming tactics such as looking for signs of neediness or hints the child might be receptive to sexual topics. One of his participants reported,

"Neediness is very apparent when a child will do anything to keep talking to you" (p. 27). Some experts have speculated that young people who use suggestive profile pictures or usernames are more likely to draw attention. Some online spaces are higher risk than others, such as a sexuality forum compared with a gaming or sports forum. Some vulnerabilities can become apparent in initial conversations—for example, if the youth posts about mental health problems, being bullied, or being different from the majority in some way. In the Disrupting Harm survey research by the WeProtect Global Alliance (2021), youths who were LGBTQ+, belonged to a racial or ethnic minority, or had a disability were more likely to have an adult or stranger send them sexual content or have their own sexual image or video shared without permission, suggesting these characteristics are part of the calculus when perpetrators are choosing potential targets.

Solicitation perpetrators in the NCMEC (2017) study used the following tactics, in descending order: 34% engaged in chat or role-play; 29% tried to establish rapport with the target; 23% sent nudes of themselves; 20% pretended to be younger than they were; 10% offered nudes of themselves but did not send them; 9% offered an image exchange; and 8% offered money or gifts. Most adolescents ignore these solicitations, but some do respond because of boredom, loneliness, or curiosity; because of other vulnerabilities such as mental health concerns, social isolation, or being bullied; or because they are young or immature (see Thorn, 2022). It is worth noting that many of the tactics used by solicitation perpetrators in the NCMEC (2017) analysis set involved CSEM, either as requests or sent as part of the grooming or part of a proposed exchange. This is likely partly due to the special legal role that NCMEC plays in the United States, where reports of CSEM offending to NCMEC are mandatory. Nonetheless, the NCMEC data also indicate an overlap between CSEM and solicitation offending. Indeed, solicitation is becoming a major source of CSEM via self-generation, either directly or after nonconsensual sharing (Thorn, 2021, 2023).

A large Finnish survey of children from 499 schools in Finland asked about solicitation victimization by a stranger (Save the Children Finland, 2021), and some of the data speak to perpetrators and perpetration tactics. The survey received responses from 1,762 young people ages 11 to 17 recruited through schools or social media. Almost all children (99%) recognized that the following were examples of online solicitation: being asked for nudes, sent sexual messages, and sent self-nudes by perpetrators. Around three quarters understood that being asked to keep the conversation secret and insincere efforts to befriend the child might be evidence of grooming. A majority (60%) thought being asked for contact information was potential evidence of grooming, and half saw praise as such. Most children (73%) thought they could detect grooming if it happened to them.

A study by Joleby et al. (2021) of 50 Swedish court cases—representing 50 perpetrators, with 122 victims ranging in age from 7 to 17 (median age 13)—further shows that solicitation tactics vary, including "sweet talk" (flattery, acting like a friend, professing love) and "coercion" (p. 1; including threats, bribes, and nagging). Those who engaged in sweet talk tactics were younger and targeted older minor victims, meaning there was a smaller age difference (cf. statutory sexual offending) than with those who used coercion tactics. For interested readers, Table 1 in Joleby et al. (2021) is an extensive summary of qualitative and small-sample research on solicitation tactics. In another study, Joleby et al. (2020) compared cases in which the offending all took place online (81 victims) with those that involved offline offenses as well (17 victims). Reflecting the reach of the internet, the online cases were more likely to involve children aged 12 or younger, might have lasted only a day (not repeated), and were more likely to involve strangers.

Several studies show that deception is uncommon in online sexual solicitations because perpetrators often do not hide their identities or pretend they have innocuous motivations (E. Bergen et al., 2014; Broome et al., 2020). However, identity deception was associated with a higher likelihood of receiving images or engaging in cybersex or sexual contact in E. Bergen et al. (2014). Many solicitations are abruptly sexual, in line with a spamming strategy (Kloess et al., 2019). Perhaps the most important takeaway from all these studies is that tactics can be quite varied and adjusted according to the youth and the specific situation (de Santisteban & Gámez-Guadix, 2018). This suggests that solicitation interventions, including prevention campaigns, need to be tailored to different kinds of solicitation tactics.

FANTASY- VERSUS CONTACT-DRIVEN SOLICITATIONS

In a small descriptive study of men convicted of solicitation offenses after engaging with undercover police officers posing as minors, Briggs et al. (2011) proposed a distinction between 21 fantasy-driven and 30 contact-driven sexual solicitations. Fantasy-driven solicitations were focused on the online interactions, comprising sexually explicit messages, requests for CSEM, sending pornography, or live video interactions. Contact-driven solicitations, in contrast, focused on convincing the target to meet in person, where contact sexual offending might take place. Briggs et al. found that the fantasy-driven solicitation cases involved longer and more frequent interactions, whereas the contact-driven solicitations tended to be brief and blunt. A subsequent study by DeHart et al. (2017) analyzing police transcripts and other records from undercover police investigations also found evidence for the fantasy- versus contact-driven distinction, along with a new third group that engaged in both kinds of interactions, across interactions or across targets. Soldino and Seigfried-Spellar (2024) analyzed data from 98 police reports, resulting in data for 120 unique suspects and 234 unique victims. Of the 120 suspects, 36% were deemed to be contact driven because they made specific and detailed plans to meet or committed contact sexual offenses, according to the police reports; the rest were deemed to be online focused, which is similar to what I have called fantasy-driven solicitation. There were no differences between the online-focused and contact-driven perpetrators in terms of age or criminal history. Contact-driven perpetrators differed by being more likely to send nudes, offer an exchange in return for nudes, and have male and older victims, even though most victims were girls. Another notable observation from this study was that about half the perpetrators exclusively provided their real identities, and the other half exclusively provided fake identities, which I suspect is related to whether the perpetrator was a stranger because a stranger would be more motivated and able to give a fake identity. There was no difference between online-focused and contact-driven perpetrators in the use of deception.

An unpublished study also sheds light on the distinction between fantasy- and contact-driven solicitation (Desjardins, 2021). Desjardins analyzed police data for 52 dyads involving 18 perpetrators and 52 victims (51 girls, ages 11 to 17), comprising 829 conversations ($M = 16$ per dyad; $M = 64$ days in duration). The majority of perpetrators (12 of 18) interacted with more than one target, and four perpetrators engaged in both fantasy- and contact-driven solicitations. Of the 52 dyads, there were 22 online-only dyads, 10 where contact was requested, and 22 where offline contact occurred. All cases involved strangers with no prior interactions, and all were one-on-one online interactions. Desjardins did not have information on interactions that took place via audio or video calls. It was not specified in their thesis, but Desjardin presumably had access to all text interactions identified by police across apps or platforms. Desjardin's analysis distinguished between contact requests and actual contacts. Future research on this would be helpful because some contact requests are not seriously intended—as when vaguely talking about meeting is part of the online fantasy—whereas other requests were serious and did not result in meetings only because they were thwarted (e.g., parents grounded youths for unrelated behavior.) Desjardins found significant differences in victim behavior between those dyads where contact was requested compared with those dyads where contact occurred: Consistent with the fantasy- versus contact-driven distinction, the former dyads had significantly more conversations and significantly more sexual content in conversations, the perpetrator was more likely to ask the victim about offline contact, and the victim was significantly more likely to send pictures to the perpetrator and to request the perpetrator's picture.

Broome et al. (2018) conducted a review of 22 solicitation studies—not only of comparisons but also exclusively fantasy-driven or contact-driven solicitation—and found significant overlap between these two putative types; for example, both fantasy- and contact-driven groups engaged in online behavior that can result in sexual gratification, and both engaged in behaviors that could have led to in-person contact. Broome et al. concluded that the distinction between fantasy- and contact-driven solicitation is fuzzy, noting, for example, that 54% of the cases that DeHart et al. (2017) categorized as fantasy-driven mentioned meeting offline but never made specific suggestions about meeting. I have already addressed how simply mentioning meeting in person may not be a serious suggestion and may still reflect fantasy-driven behavior. Broome et al. (2018) argued instead for using a European Online Grooming Project typology that distinguishes between intimacy-seeking, adaptable, and hypersexualized types of online sexual solicitations (Webster et al., 2012). This typology focuses more on patterns of interaction than motivations. In this typology, *intimacy-seeking solicitations* involve prolonged and frequent interactions, with sexual content introduced slowly, leading to the planning of offline meetings. *Adaptable solicitations* can involve both online fantasy and offline contact, where the communication style and pattern of interactions vary depending on the target response. Last, *hypersexual solicitations* introduce sexual content quickly and frequently involve CSEM or extreme adult pornography. Individuals of this type are viewed as more likely to engage in identity deception, not interested in forming a relationship, and less likely to suggest meeting offline. The European Grooming Project typology is also likely to be fuzzy, with cases that are not prototypical or that blend features of multiple types.

Unlike Broome et al. (2018), I think the distinction between fantasy- and contact-driven solicitation still has merit. It is intuitive, parsimonious, and can accommodate variation in online sexual solicitation when considering individuals who engage in both forms of solicitations. The distinction between fantasy- and contact-driven solicitation can be reliably made according to whether serious attempts to meet or actual meetings occur. A different approach to the typology recommended by Broome et al. is to refine the definitions and operationalization of fantasy- and contact-driven solicitation. For example, contact-driven solicitation could be operationalized as not only talking in a vague or indirect way about meeting but also explicitly proposing and then trying to arrange a meeting, making concrete plans such as setting a date, making travel arrangements, and showing up to a meeting in person. It could also acknowledge that contact-driven solicitation can involve online sexual gratification. The critical distinction—and the focus of much policy and law enforcement—is whether the person attempts to or does meet in person. A mixed type of solicitation involves both fantasy- and contact-driven tactics, either within the full scope of interactions with a target or across targets. For example, a mixed solicitation perpetrator might mostly engage in fantasy-driven solicitations but occasionally suggest meeting in person when the person is close geographically (DeHart et al., 2017). Independent of the fantasy- versus contact-driven distinction is the level of interaction, ranging from abrupt to prolonged interactions that resemble classical grooming, thus capturing more of the interaction style elements of the European Grooming Project typology.

Here, I expand on the idea that an online solicitation typology can distinguish between fantasy- and contact-driven solicitations while taking into account differences in patterns of interactions (frequency and duration of interactions), types of sexual interactions (how soon, what kind of interactions, whether offline meeting for sex is discussed), target choice, and outcomes. These additional considerations include the complexities captured in the European Online Grooming Project typology regarding the duration and frequency of online interactions and communication styles. For example, fantasy-driven solicitations can vary from those involving immediate demands for sexual content or sexual interactions online to those that involve frequent and prolonged interactions building up to the introduction of sex. Similarly, contact-driven solicitations can involve a lot of online sexual interaction as well or can focus primarily on attempting to meet in person.

Multiple motivations for sexual solicitation are possible. In cases that resemble statutory sexual offending using online technologies (see the Target Vulnerabilities section), I expect the motivation to be sexually conventional, typically targeting underage minors who are sexually mature looking or approaching sexual maturity and who are likely to be known to the perpetrator. These perpetrators are interested in a sexual and perhaps romantic relationship, so interactions are likely to be frequent and ongoing, with a mix of short and long interactions typical of ordinary dyads. Sex may be introduced gradually, and sexual interactions will probably involve both online and offline sexual behavior. These cases are unlikely to be reported by the minor; instead, they are more likely to be reported by others, as when a parent discovers evidence of message exchanges or when a friend is concerned because the minor is spending so much time with a much older person. For other online sexual solicitations, a high sex drive may be the motivation. In these cases, I expect multiple contacts, many, if not all, with unknown targets, where sexual requests are made quickly, typically involving requests for CSEM, sending pornography, or live sex chat or streaming. Individuals with hypersexual motivations are likely to show other evidence of excessive sexual conduct, including extreme pornography use, high frequency of masturbation, activity on hookup or dating apps, and use of commercial sex services. Finally, some solicitation perpetrators may target pubescent or even prepubescent children, suggesting that hebephilia or pedophilia (respectively) are pertinent motivations.

Interactions depend on whether the child is already known to the perpetrator. If already known, interactions can be prolonged and aimed at relationship building, akin to classical grooming. If not known, interactions can involve grooming as well but can also be brief and intense, as the perpetrator scans for potential vulnerabilities such as loneliness (see Target Vulnerabilities section) or aggressively requests CSEM or other content. Some sexual solicitations may be examples of trolling, pranking, or bullying behavior and do not reflect sexual motivations per se.

COMPARISONS WITH OTHER PERPETRATOR GROUPS

Surprisingly little research has compared solicitation perpetrators with other online or offline perpetrator groups. In Seto et al. (2012), we compared 70 solicitation perpetrators with 38 CSEM perpetrators and 38 (lower risk) contact perpetrators on sociodemographic characteristics and risk measures. Solicitation and CSEM perpetrators were better educated than the contact perpetrators but otherwise did not differ sociodemographically. Solicitation perpetrators were rated by evaluators as having less capacity for relationship stability and were rated lower in sexual preoccupation and atypical sexual interests than CSEM perpetrators, but they were rated higher on sexual preoccupation and again lower in capacity for relationship stability compared with contact perpetrators. There were inconsistent group differences on the risk measures, but I expect contact perpetrators to be at higher risk of sexually reoffending, on average, than either CSEM or solicitation perpetrators if a full range of contact perpetrators were included.

Solicitation perpetrators who attempted or had contact with children could be scored using well-established and widely used risk measures, such as the Static-99R,[2] and they can easily fit into existing treatment and supervision paradigms designed for contact perpetrators. But what about fantasy-driven solicitation perpetrators? Are they more like CSEM perpetrators in that their sexual behavior does not involve direct contact with children? I suspect there is a gradient of risk to directly offend sexually against a child, in the following ascending order: access or possession of CSEM; remote production of CSEM or fantasy-driven solicitation; contact-driven solicitation; and contact sexual offending, which includes individuals who produce CSEM by recording their contact offending behavior. As I discuss further in Chapter 4, these different groups of online perpetrators would then be expected to differ in the likelihood of pedohebephilia, hypersexuality, or antisocial tendencies such as impulsivity and risk taking.

Merdian et al. (2018) suggested a distinction between fantasy-driven and contact-driven CSEM perpetrators, where the former used CSEM for sexual fantasies and as part of collecting behavior, while the latter used CSEM as a substitute for contact offending, to facilitate contact offending (showing targets as part of grooming), or as a record of contact offending they had committed. All things being equal, contact-driven CSEM perpetrators are higher risk than fantasy-driven CSEM perpetrators.

Reavis et al. (2023) compared 113 CSEM and 35 solicitation offenders, further dividing CSEM perpetrators into those with or without other criminal history. In this study, both CSEM and solicitation perpetrators were low overall in terms of psychopathy. Both groups showed some evidence of psychopathology, including elevations in personality disorder traits, assessed using a self-report personality and psychopathology inventory. However, socially desirable responding was high, likely driven by the fact that the data were mostly obtained as part of presentencing assessments where men might have been trying to look better than they were in terms of psychopathic traits or psychopathology.

There is an overlap between CSEM and solicitation perpetration, as already noted, where some solicitation perpetrators seek or share CSEM as part of their offending. In the third NJOV wave, 20% of solicitation cases also had evidence of CSEM offending (Wolak & Finkelhor, 2013), and in our follow-up research on CSEM perpetrators, 10% had engaged in online sexual communications

---

[2]The Static-99R is the most widely used sexual offending risk assessment tool (https://saarna.org). It comprises 10 static risk factors that cannot change as a result of intervention (see Chapter 6). Factors include the perpetrator's age at the time they have the opportunity to reoffend; criminal history, particularly sexual offense history; and victim characteristics such as victim gender and relationship to the victim. Studies have repeatedly demonstrated its predictive validity for noncontact and contact perpetrators in multiple countries.

with a minor (or undercover police officer posing as a minor; Seto & Eke, 2015). Paquette and Fortin (2021) analyzed 137 CSEM or solicitation cases and examined their overlaps with each other and with contact offending. Curiously, the CSEM plus solicitation group was the least likely to endorse offense-supportive beliefs, whereas the dual perpetrators (CSEM and/or solicitation plus contact offending) were the most likely to endorse these beliefs.

A thesis by Schaaf (2022) examined archival data from the United States and Canada to compare CSEM perpetrators distinguished by whether they engage in online solicitation offending as well. A sample of 247 cases was divided into CSEM only (n = 189), CSEM plus online conversations (fantasy driven; n = 27), and CSEM plus attempted meeting (contact driven; n = 31). The results are consistent with my speculations regarding perpetrator characteristics and the motivation–facilitation model described in Chapter 5. CSEM-exclusive perpetrators were more likely to report the use of preteen CSEM, whereas the CSEM plus attempted meeting group was more likely to report the use of teen content; the CSEM plus online conversations group was intermediate in terms of the ages they sought. In addition, the CSEM plus attempted contact group was more antisocial than the others, according to their substance use and delinquency histories, whereas the CSEM only group showed more evidence of sexual preoccupation, including reported escalations in their pornography use over time (see Chapters 5 and 6). The CSEM plus attempted meeting group showed more evidence of using the internet to cope with negative feelings and general internet preoccupation.

The NCMEC enticement report (2017) is the largest analysis of online sexual solicitation cases I am aware of, comprising 5,917 solicitation cases reported to NCMEC. Unlike CSEM, American law does not mandate reporting solicitation cases to NCMEC, so this is not an exhaustive or representative sample of such cases. Some of the cases reported to NCMEC, but not all, may have resulted in law enforcement action or at least confirmation of solicitation. Because they are cases, and solicitation perpetrators may engage with multiple targets, the number of cases does not equal the number of perpetrators. Most (78%) of the targets in these NCMEC cases were girls whose mean age was 15. A quarter (23%) of perpetration suspects appeared to have multiple targets; this is likely an underestimate because it is based only on targets who reported the crime or when the crime was detected by others (e.g., as part of a police investigation), and many solicitation suspects may have had undetected targets. Of the solicitation suspects, 82% were male, and 9% were female, with missing information in the remaining cases. Only 2% were known by targets, so most reports involved strangers, contrary to the research suggesting that most solicitations involve someone known to the target. The simplest explanation for this discrepancy is that solicitations involving strangers are much more likely to be reported to NCMEC. Many of the reports to NCMEC were from internet service providers or parents rather than the youths themselves. Indeed, the Thorn research (2021, 2023) suggests that many youths do not report sexual solicitations, either to the platforms where the solicitations occur or to their parents. In the subset of 118 known perpetrator cases in the NCMEC data set, half involved family members, and a little over half were male; this indicates that female perpetrators were much more likely to be involved in known cases. In terms of solicitation goals, CSEM was the most common (60%), followed by sexual contact (32%). These perpetration goals were more likely to be achieved if older boys were targeted.

Target gender differences appear again and again in the empirical literature on sexual solicitation offending, with girls more likely to be targeted than boys. Solicitation perpetrators act differently when targeting girls than boys. van Gijn-Grosvenor and Lamb (2016) analyzed data from 101 convicted perpetrators who had engaged with adult decoys (Perverted Justice vigilantes), 52 with decoys posing as girls and 49 with decoys posing as boys. Analyzing these transcripts, van Gijn-Grosvenor and Lamb found that those who engaged with decoy boys were older but pretended to be younger, whereas those who engaged with decoy girls were less direct, put more effort into establishing rapport, were less sexually explicit even though they talked more about sexual topics, and used more strategies to conceal their contact with the decoys (e.g., asking if anyone could observe online conversations, asking where their parents were, asking them to keep online interactions a secret). Reflecting this greater investment in grooming, interactions with girls were longer than with boys.

METHODOLOGICAL CONSIDERATIONS

In Broome et al.'s (2018) review, one of the major methodological confounds they noted in this literature—which I also noted in the first edition of this book—is that many of the studies in their review involved decoy victims, whether undercover police officers posing as minors or nonpolice adults posing as decoys for vigilante purposes, such as members of the vigilante group Perverted Justice. In particular, many linguistic analysis studies of online sexual solicitations have relied on vigilante decoy data, where adults posing as minors can differ in important ways from real minors. For example, to "catch" perpetrators, I expect decoys are more compliant or willing to engage in sexual interactions than real minors, but decoys may simultaneously be less likely to initiate sexual interactions in case this would lead to a successful entrapment defense if the case were to go to court. Similarly, decoys are not going to block or report suspects engaging in suspicious behavior, unlike many real youths when they are sexually solicited, because they are waiting to see if the suspect engages in illegal behavior, such as sending adult pornography to a minor, requesting or sending CSEM, or attempting to meet in person with someone who cannot legally consent to sex with an adult. In short, discoveries made about linguistic patterns with decoys or undercover police officers may not generalize to online sexual solicitations involving real minors.

For these reasons, data involving solicitations of real minors—such as the cases analyzed by NCMEC (2017)—are critically important. Wolak et al. (2008) found most solicitation perpetrators were male, and most targets were girls.

Victims were typically between the ages of 13 and 15, with no victims below the age of 12. I summarized the changes over time in Table 3.1. A study by Chiu et al. (2018) is also valuable because they did a linguistic analysis of 36,029 words in 4,353 messages from 107 chat sessions between four fantasy-driven and five contact-driven perpetrators interacting with 12 real youths. Contact-driven perpetrators were more likely to use first-person pronouns, negative emotion words, and positive emotion words, suggesting more self-disclosures. These self-disclosure messages elicited corresponding self-disclosures by youths. More research is needed to compare the linguistic and interaction patterns of cases involving adult decoys (vigilantes or police) with real minors.

TARGET VULNERABILITIES

Youths are not uniformly at risk of online sexual solicitations; otherwise, the 1-year incidence rates reported by Wager et al. (2018) would accumulate to high lifetime prevalence rates. Some youths are clearly more vulnerable to sexual solicitations, and some youths are targeted multiple times by different perpetrators. The focus of this book is on online sexual perpetration, but part of understanding perpetration is also understanding who they target. Early evidence from the NJOV studies suggested that girls are at greater risk than boys, and among boys, those who were nonheterosexual were at greater risk, presumably because most detected solicitation perpetrators are men. The risk of being a target of sexual solicitation increases with age. These results have been replicated by Thorn (2022).

The Save the Children Finland (2021) survey, like many prior survey studies, found that girls were more likely to be solicited; the researchers did not examine age or sexual orientation. Most interactions were short, with the modal response being a few hours (44%), followed by a few days (24%). Only 16% of interactions lasted a month or longer. Meeting in person (6%) or engaging in a live video interaction (9%) was rare; the most common reaction was to block the soliciting person, in line with Thorn (2022). Unlike the Thorn survey results, most respondents told a friend, but consistent with other research, few told a parent (see also Colburn et al., 2023). Among those who did not disclose to anyone, three quarters thought it was not a serious problem. Notably, having a close friend and talking to a parent about online behavior were protective factors for being solicited; however, 8% of the sample said they did not have a close friend they could tell. This points to the vulnerability of the lonely, ostracized, or friendless as potential targets of online sexual solicitations. I return to victim reporting and the roles of family and friends in protecting minors in Chapter 8 on prevention. There has been more attention to policy, tech deterrence, and interventions, but there is much potential for efforts to influence peer and parent attitudes and norms (see Thorn, 2021, 2022, 2023).

Among the 975 children who answered about the other person's age in the Save the Children Finland (2021) survey, 39% said the other person was slightly older, 31% said they were 5+ years older, 19% did not know, and 10% thought the person was the same age. Only 1% thought the other person was younger. Some of the differences in how the participants responded to the online solicitation may be partly attributable to the fact that the plurality of solicitations was from someone "slightly" older, likely still a minor. For example, solicitations from an older minor might be associated with the participant telling a friend but not a parent.

The Save the Children Finland (2021) survey looked at children's explanations for responding to a stranger online: Among the 660 children who answered this question, the most common reason given by participants was that they were bored (55%), followed by curiosity (40%). Other reasons included feeling lonely, not feeling like they could refuse, wanting to please the stranger, being afraid to say no, or being pressured (26% or lower). A third (32% of 1065) were offered an incentive for sexual acts, and 32% were told not to talk about the interaction.

What are the social or psychological vulnerabilities of targeted minors? De Roos (2017) analyzed 169 cases identified using legal databases and found that grooming was associated with living in a single-parent home (47%), having a vulnerable mother because of mental health or other issues (34%), and distress at home (38%). Noll et al.'s (2022) study about online behaviors of girls who had been sexually abused found that sexually abused girls were at higher risk of online victimization. Other research suggests vulnerable youth are vulnerable not only to online sexual offending but also to maltreatment of other kinds, including bullying and ostracism. Gámez-Guadix and Mateos-Pérez (2019) looked at longitudinal data from 1,497 Spanish youth ages 12 to 14, assessed twice 1 year apart. Almost half had been cyberbullied at both points. Sexting at baseline predicted being solicited and cyberbullied 1 year later, and being solicited or cyberbullied at baseline predicted sexting 1 year later, suggesting some common etiology. In their systematic review of 24 studies, Hu et al. (2023) identified eight longitudinal studies of adolescents and found that sexting significantly predicted future sexual behavior, such as intercourse onset. Curiously, the evidence for sexting at baseline predicting sexting 1 year later was mixed, and no studies examined whether sexting at baseline predicted other online sexual behavior 1 year later.

Vulnerability affects not only who is approached online but also who responds to online sexual solicitations. Gámez-Guadix et al. (2018) found that 12.6% of the Spanish youths (ages 12 to 15) in their study had been sexually solicited by an adult in the past year, and 7.9% had engaged in any sexualized interaction. This did not necessarily represent a one-on-one correspondence because the interactions could be initiated by the youths, but it does suggest that many youths who are solicited might then engage in sexualized interactions. In their survey of 1,260 youths between the ages of 12 and 17 (56% female), Calvete et al. (2021) found that youths who were sexually solicited by an adult were more likely to engage in sexualized interactions at the 1-year follow-up.

SUMMARY AND CONCLUSIONS

Unlike CSEM offending, sexual solicitation offending is unlikely to evoke pedophilia because the targets are usually pubescent children (which might be consistent with hebephilia) or postpubescent adolescents. Sexual solicitation offending is heterogeneous, and only some cases resemble grooming in the sense of being gradual, linear, and deceptive or manipulative; many solicitations are abrupt and/or aggressive. There is clear evidence that there are different types of sexual solicitation, and subsequent research has confirmed an initial distinction between fantasy-driven and contact-driven solicitation, where some individuals engage only in online interactions, whereas others attempt to set up meetings where contact sexual offending might take place. An advance since the first edition of this book is evidence that some individuals have mixed intentions, showing both fantasy-driven and contact-driven behavior across sessions or targets. Another important advance since the first edition is the recognition that many sexual solicitations are from someone already known to the target, including other minors.

HYPOTHETICAL CASE EXAMPLE: SEAN (SEXUAL SOLICITATION)

Sean was a 28-year-old man working in construction, characterized by relatively short terms of employment because he frequently quit jobs or was fired because of his "bad attitude," as evidenced by regularly showing up late and occasionally getting into arguments with supervisors. He had several longer term dating relationships as an adolescent or young adult but had never lived with a lover. He was convicted of CSEM and sexual solicitation offenses for sexually communicating and exchanging sexual images with both known (friends of his younger siblings) and unknown adolescent girls between the ages of 13 and 16. Though there were differences across victims, Sean's general pattern was to engage in a seemingly friendly, then flirtatious way with girls across a variety of popular social media apps and platforms. His online sexual solicitations were discovered when a girl's mobile was examined by a parent, and they became concerned about the conversation thread, which included explicit messages about her sexual fantasies and behavior.

Sean was arrested, and his mobile and laptop computer were seized by police. Forensic analysis revealed evidence of multiple sexual conversations with girls that varied in duration and content. Some conversations were prolonged, including discussions of social interests, private life, dating history, and sexual history. Most of these conversations were with girls Sean already knew offline. Other conversations were short and immediately explicit, asking for nudes or sexual chat; these conversations were entirely with girls he did not know. Sean suggested meeting in person for sex with several of the girls he knew offline, and there was evidence they did sometimes meet in social situations, but none of the girls reported ever meeting with him for sex, and there was no evidence to suggest he had sex with them. Forensic analysis and interviews with identified girls found evidence that nudes were exchanged and that Sean had engaged in live-stream interactions with minors involving nudity and concurrent masturbation. Sean had both a juvenile and adult criminal history involving misdemeanors such as shoplifting, petty theft, being intoxicated in a public place, and possession of small amounts of marijuana and marijuana paraphernalia, with criminal charges for these offenses on five different occasions. He had no criminal record or allegations of prior sexual or violent offenses.

Sean was deemed to be a mixed type of solicitation perpetrator because he engaged in online-only interactions with some minors, but he also suggested meeting with minors he did know. There was no evidence that he had sex with any of the girls he came into contact with, though sexual contact offending could not be conclusively ruled out because some minors were never identified in the police investigation. When asked about the juvenile and adult history of nonsexual offending, Sean admitted that he had engaged in impulsive and antisocial behavior from a young age, including behavior problems at school, underage alcohol use, drug use, and shoplifting.

4

Other Online Sexual Offending

Most of the attention to online sexual offending has focused on child sexual exploitation material (CSEM) offending, followed by online solicitation of children and youth. But there are other forms of online sexual offending as well, including digital exhibitionism (sending unsolicited sexual self-images, such as "dick pics"), digital voyeurism (surreptitiously observing someone doing something private, such as changing or showering), and other image-based sexual abuse, such as sharing someone's sexual images without consent. Websites are devoted to illegal content like this, such as "upskirting" images and videos, as well as legal simulations of digital voyeurism (where the depicted individuals are actors pretending to be surreptitiously recorded). Both digital exhibitionism and voyeurism have been described as forms of image-based sexual abuse. I discuss these and other forms of image-based abuse in the next section.

DIGITAL EXHIBITIONISM

Digital exhibitionism includes sending unsolicited genital images (dick pics when sent by people with penises) or exposing oneself in a live video chat. Most research on digital exhibitionism has focused on prevalence rates, perpetrator and target characteristics, and self-reported motivations. Online exhibitionism is so prevalent that it has become tolerated as an unavoidable nuisance—particularly for women—simply for being online. The limited evidence on

https://doi.org/10.1037/0000428-005
Online Sexual Offending: Theory, Practice, and Policy, Second Edition, by M. C. Seto
Copyright © 2025 by the American Psychological Association. All rights reserved.

digital exhibitionism suggests motivations for sending unsolicited dick pics can be varied, including pranking, trolling, aggression, and even the (misguided) hope for reciprocity (see Oswald et al., 2020; discussed in more detail later). For some men, the motivation is paraphilic; they are sexually aroused by the idea of exposing themselves to an unsuspecting person. I suspect that paraphilic motivation is more likely if the person engaged in the behavior repeatedly, fantasized about engaging in the behavior, and masturbated to these fantasies or when recalling engaging in this behavior.

March and Wagstaff (2017) surveyed 240 people (72% women, the majority of whom were heterosexual) who had sent unsolicited genital images. Answers to questions about sending images (number of people sent to, enjoyment of sending images, whether they thought the target enjoyed receiving images) were explained by gender (men reported more recipients, enjoyment, and estimated target enjoyment than women), self-rated attractiveness (people who rated their attractiveness higher had higher scores), and so-called dark personality traits (individuals higher in Machiavellianism, psychopathy, or sadism had higher scores on sending images).

Oswald et al. (2020) did an online survey of 1,087 heterosexual men, 523 of whom had sent an unsolicited dick pic. They found that the most common motivation for sending an unsolicited dick pic was transactional, motivated by the hope of receiving an explicit image in response. Other common motivations were flirting and the hope it would "turn on" the recipient. Power and control style motives (e.g., forcing someone to see their penis without consent, making someone angry, feeling powerful) were rare. Indeed, the most hoped-for reaction (82%) was sexual excitement of the target person. Sending unsolicited dick pics was associated with higher narcissism and greater ambivalent or hostile sexism, which is consistent with the motivation–facilitation model, suggesting that antisocial personality traits, attitudes, and beliefs facilitate acting on motivations to engage in problematic sexual behavior (Seto, 2019; see Chapter 5, this volume). These quantitative results are also consistent with the qualitative analysis from focus groups by Mandau (2020) with 29 young adults (20 women and nine men). Women found unsolicited dick pics to be intrusive and assumed the motivation was a misguided attempt to be flirtatious. Men thought that sending dick pics was a way of showing off, getting nudes in return, or potentially hooking up.

The responses in Oswald et al. (2020) can be compared with those of 238 men seen at a clinic for in-person exhibitionistic behavior decades earlier (Freund et al., 1988). Most men in the clinical sample reported a wish for sexual contact with the target person: 62% wished to touch the target person, and 52% hoped to have intercourse with the target person. This can be compared with the third of Oswald et al.'s (2020) respondents, who hoped that the target person would want to have sex with them after being exposed to their unsolicited dick pic. Another 14% of the clinical cases seen by Freund et al. (1988) hoped for admiration, and 11% hoped for any kind of reaction from the target person. Only a few hoped for fear, anger, or disgust as a response to their exhibitionistic behavior. Two thirds of the men had exposed themselves to strangers, but some had exposed themselves to someone they knew. Two thirds exposed themselves to a different person every time they engaged in this behavior.

A quarter (27%) of the men who had sent unsolicited dick pics in Oswald et al. (2020) indicated that sending dick pics turned them on, consistent with a paraphilic motivation; by implication, almost three quarters of men who sent unsolicited dick pics were not motivated by exhibitionism per se. I speculate that the likelihood of exhibitionism being the primary motivation will be related to how dick pics are sent (entirely out of the blue or after sustained flirting and conversation), who they are sent to (a single person met on a dating app vs. multiple strangers on general forums), whether the person fantasizes or masturbates to fantasies about exposing themselves, and any co-occurrence of in-person exhibitionistic behavior.

In an analysis of self-reported digital exhibitionism perpetration and victimization in a sample of 810 men and women, Karasavva et al. (2023) looked at expectations versus experiences with regard to "cyberflashing," mostly in the context of sending unrequested nude or sexual images in online interactions with people they had not met in person before. Almost half (42%) of the sample had sent unrequested images (46% women, 30% men), and 68% (71% women, 60% men) had received unrequested images. The observation that more women than men engaged in cyberflashing behavior in Karasavva et al. may be surprising, given my observations that online sexual offending is highly gendered overall. A potential explanation is that the questions about sending unrequested images did not address frequency or context. I expect men engage in repeated cyberflashing more than women, women are more likely to cyberflash within dating apps or platforms, and men are more likely to cyberflash in other contexts.

There were other gender effects as well: Women were more likely to report expecting a flirty or positive reaction than men, and conversely, men were more likely to expect a negative reaction (Karasavva et al., 2023). Yet women were more likely to report a negative reaction when they received unrequested images, whereas men were more likely to report a positive reaction. Sending unrequested images was associated with expecting a flirty or positive reaction and not expecting a negative reaction, suggesting behavior is partly related to a mismatch of expectations and likely reactions between sender and receiver. This study suggests that many cyberflashing events are not intended to be aversive because a majority (77%) expected a flirty or positive reaction, as likely or unlikely as that might be. Karasavva et al. suggested naivety helped explain this large gap between expectations and reality. Also, a Pew survey reported by Anderson et al. (2020) found young women were twice as likely to be sent unsolicited explicit images (57% vs. 28%) than young men and were twice as likely to report threats of physical violence accompanying these images (19% vs. 9%). These experiences were more prevalent for young women and men than for older women and men.

DIGITAL VOYEURISM

The prevalence of digital voyeurism is unknown, but offline voyeuristic behavior is common according to several self-report surveys, so I would expect high levels of online voyeurism perpetration and victimization as well (Bártová et al., 2021; Joyal & Carpentier, 2022; Långström & Seto, 2006; Seto et al., 2021). Unlike most CSEM offending, sexual solicitation offending, and digital exhibitionism, many digital voyeurism targets are unaware they have been victimized—for example, because they were observed using hidden cameras.[1] As a result, digital voyeurism is difficult to study because we only know about cases where the voyeuristic behavior was detected by the targets and targets were willing to report this.

Lewis and Anitha (2023) conducted a systematic review of scholarship on upskirting, where 16 of the 26 sources they found in the review took a legal perspective. Lewis and Anitha considered how upskirting was framed in these sources and how perpetrators and targets were understood. For example, they analyzed how upskirting was framed as a behavior for sexual gratification (the majority of sources), a privacy issue, or an example of gendered power or violence (these explanations are not mutually exclusive). Lewis and Anitha made an interesting point about *homosociality*, the status achievement among other misogynistic men for engaging in this behavior. In her thesis, C. Thompson (2019) referred to upskirting as "everyday misogyny" (p. 3). In this perspective, digital exhibitionism and voyeurism can be understood as part of a spectrum of gender-based sexual harassment.

Karasavva (2020) surveyed 816 participants (72% women) about their experiences with image-based sexual abuse victimization and perpetration, which includes behavior other than digital voyeurism. Karasavva found a 14% lifetime prevalence for image-based perpetration and 28% lifetime victimization. Perpetration and victimization were correlated with each other, with 10% of men and 8% of women endorsing both. Men were more likely to perpetrate than women, and women were more likely to be victims. The most common perpetrator–victim relationship was with a partner or ex-partner, followed by a friend; strangers were rare. About 9% of victims said they did not know who the perpetrator was, whereas 17% of perpetrators said they did not know who the victim was, suggesting they were resharing images of strangers that others had already shared. Overall perpetration was 11% (15% men and 9% women). The most common form of sharing was of topless photos, followed by nudes and recordings of sexual activity. More clearly voyeuristic forms (upskirt or "down blouse" images) were rare (less than 2%). Image-based perpetration was positively and significantly correlated with self-reported proclivity and with three of four so-called dark personality traits, referring to narcissism, psychopathy, and sadism; perpetration was not significantly related to attitudes

---

[1]There is enough anxiety about hidden cameras that there are special apps and advice on how to protect oneself (Hendrickson, 2024).

about the behavior or Machiavellianism. Almost half (46%) of the sample were unaware that image-based sexual abuse was illegal in Canada, and whether someone knew it was illegal was unrelated to perpetration. This suggests that criminalization and law enforcement will not be sufficient to address this problem.

Liu (2022) conducted a unique study because they looked at male–male digital voyeurism and did so in a non-Western context by studying a Chinese forum with a voyeurism channel. Liu concluded that this channel was mostly used by mainland Chinese individuals because most posts used Mandarin slang terms that are common in mainland China among men who have sex with men. Liu defined voyeurism as taking and sharing images of someone who was unaware or did not give consent, which I think conflates digital voyeurism (unsuspecting targets) and nonconsensual resharing (being aware the image was taken but not consenting to further sharing, discussed in the next section). Most posts (63%) that described how the image was obtained indicated the poster had taken the photo, most commonly in a public bathroom. Most images (77%) were of strangers, but 11% were of a roommate or classmate or someone known to the sender; pictures of relatives were rare (1%). A sixth (17%) of the posts included a text description suggesting other nonconsensual behavior—for example, sexual contact with someone while they were asleep or intoxicated. Liu focused their analysis of these forum posts using neutralization theory from criminology and found evidence of victim blaming, minimization of harm, and objectification (collecting images for fun; see offense-supportive cognitions in Chapters 5 and 6).

OTHER IMAGE-BASED OFFENDING

Henry et al.'s (2020) book describes the cumulative results of their surveys regarding imaged-based offending victimization and perpetration, with data from 6,109 respondents in Australia, New Zealand, and the United Kingdom, ages 16 to 64. The data did not come from a probability sample, but the sample was age and gender stratified. The surveys asked about a range of imaged-based offending, and over a third (38%) had experienced one or more forms: 33% had a nude or sexual image taken of them without consent, 21% had their image shared without consent, 19% were threatened with image resharing, and 14% experienced all three forms of offending. Of those who were victimized, the majority (61%) were victimized by a prior or current partner, and image-based abuse was associated with other forms of abuse, suggesting an important link between image-based abuse and intimate partner violence (see also Dardis & Richards, 2022, and Henry et al., 2020). At the same time, 20% of the sample were victimized by acquaintances, with strangers, family members, and coworkers all under 10%. Victimization rates were similar across gender and ethnicity but were much higher for LGBTQ+ respondents and younger respondents.

One in six participants (18%) had perpetrated at least one form of image-based abuse, with 16% saying they had taken a nude or sexual image of someone without consent, 11% had reshared an image without consent, and 9% had threatened to reshare an image without consent; 8% of the sample had engaged in all three behaviors (Henry et al., 2020). Unlike victimization, gender was correlated with perpetration, with men being twice as likely as women to engage in one of these forms of image-based abuse. Perpetration was also more likely for LGBTQ+ respondents, younger participants, and non-White participants. In a regression analysis, perpetration was positively and uniquely correlated with being male, nonheterosexual, and having a disability. Perpetration was also significantly associated with endorsing victim-blaming attitudes and with the participants' experience of self-generating sexual images and image-based victimization (suggesting quid pro quo and/or mutual perpetration or victimization). The associations were stronger for self-generating images and victimization experience than attitudes or demographic characteristics. In terms of reported motivations for engaging in this behavior, some participants said they thought it was funny or sexy, and some thought it would impress their friends; however, others clearly knew it could harm the people in the images and intentionally did it for control or revenge. Many perpetrators reported multiple motivations for their behavior.

Sparks et al. (2023) surveyed 541 young adults (61% female) and found that image-based victimization and perpetration overlapped for nonconsensual resharing and cyberflashing but not for coerced sexting. The strength of these associations is illustrated by the fact that victims of nonconsensual resharing had almost three times the odds of perpetrating this behavior, and victims of cyberflashing had almost four times the odds of perpetration. Consistent with the motivation–facilitation model (Seto, 2019; discussed in more depth in Chapter 5), those who had both victimization and perpetration experiences scored higher in self-reported interest in exhibitionism, sexual compulsivity, offense-supportive attitudes, and antisocial personality traits such as Machiavellianism and impulsivity than those with only victimization experiences or neither experience. Those with both victimization and perpetration experiences did not differ from those who had perpetration experiences only on any of these factors.

Henry et al. (2020) pointed out that image-based abuse beyond digital voyeurism or exhibitionism also has nondigital, offline equivalents, and social norms have changed over time. They begin their book by describing how *Hustler* magazine introduced its Beaver Hunt section in 1980, where readers could submit sexually explicit photographs. Though these photographs were ostensibly consensually taken and shared with the magazine, it subsequently became clear that some photographs were not shared with consent, and some were intentionally submitted for revenge purposes by ex-partners, in a literally analog version of what now takes place digitally.

Perpetration motivations were varied in the Henry et al. (2020) study and were not necessarily paraphilic. We have limited data about nonsexual motivations: The study by Oswald et al. (2020), cited in the previous section regarding digital exhibitionism, identified pranks, trolling, and aggression as nonsexual motivations. Similarly, 49 victims of nonconsensual resharing or threats in a study by Pacheco et al. (2019) identified nonsexual motivations, such as pranking (19%), extortion (money, 17%), aggression (revenge, humiliation, intimidation, 26% cumulatively), or control (12%), rather than sexual motivations (sexual thrill or pleasure, 3%). Dodge (2021) reviewed Canadian legal cases and found examples of nonconsensual sharing that were motivated by intimidation and control (e.g., to force agreement on divorce terms), showing off (e.g., teen boys resharing images to brag to their friends), and jealousy or competition (e.g., teen girls who reshared images of a girl that a boyfriend or love interest was involved with).

Maas et al. (2021) conducted a study of so-called "slutpages," online sites for the nonconsensual sharing of nudes and other sexual images. In a survey of 1,867 students (mean age 20, 64% cisgender women), slutpage use was associated with younger age, being a man, and fraternity or sorority or team sport involvement. Slutpage use was correlated with drinking alcohol and using pornography more frequently.

Ringrose et al. (2021) examined image-based harassment and abuse in a survey of 336 youth between the ages of 13 and 18 and focus groups involving 144 youth ages 12 to 18. Ringrose et al. defined harassment as the sending of unsolicited nudes (typically dick pics) and unwanted sexual solicitation, and they defined abuse as nonconsensual resharing of images. Although age was often unknown, most perpetrators were minors when age was known. Like other studies I have mentioned, these events were gendered because girls received unsolicited images and were sexually solicited more often than boys. This study suggests there is a big gap when laws and public policies focus on perpetration by adults because minors face sexual harassment or abuse from peers or older minors.

Gámez-Guadix et al. (2018) looked at the temporal stability over 1 year of image-based victimization and perpetration in a sample of 1,820 Spanish adolescents (mean age 13.4 years, 51% female). They found perpetration rates of 4.9% for nonconsensual sharing and 0.7% for sextortion perpetration. Nonconsensual sharing showed stability over 1 year, whereas engaging in sextortion (with a much lower base rate) did not. Both forms of victimization were significantly, though modestly, stable over time. These data suggest that perpetration and victimization are not necessarily chronic.

Pedersen et al. (2023) looked at correlates of contact sexual abuse and image-based sexual abuse in a large sample of almost 10,000 Swedish youths. Contact sexual abuse was defined as being forced into having intercourse or other sexual activities, and image-based sexual abuse was defined as nonconsensual sharing of nudes, including "revenge porn" or upskirting. The 1-year incidence rates were 4.3% for contact sexual abuse, 2.9% for image-based abuse, and 1.7% for both. Again, girls were more likely to be victims of contact sexual abuse, and this was associated with being bullied or cyberbullied, substance use, earlier sexual onset, and commercial sexual exploitation history; those with both contact and image-based abuse were even higher on these vulnerability factors.

SEXTORTION

In this section, I look more closely at sextortion data from the National Center for Missing and Exploited Children (NCMEC; 2017), based on 1,428 sextortion cases reported to their Cybertipline between 2013 and 2016. Of these reports, 78% involved girls, and the mean age of targets was 15, ranging from 8 to 17. This wide age range suggests the targets ranged from prepubescent children to sexually mature looking adolescents who might have been mistaken for adults, and this, in turn, suggests different motivations for offending and different offending dynamics. I suspect that sextortion cases involving young children involve pedophilia or hebephilia, demands for more CSEM, and threats that releasing the images would mean the child gets in trouble as well, with their parents or with authorities. In contrast, sextortion involving teens is unlikely to involve pedophilia or hebephilia but is likely to involve demands for more images or sexual interactions online or offline and threats that releasing the images would destroy the teen's reputation. Sextortion involving children is likely to involve strangers met online, while sextortion involving teens may be more likely to involve someone known to them, particularly a former or current sexual partner.

Most of the sextortion cases (56%) described in NCMEC (2017) involved a single app or platform, typically an app or platform used for messaging, video chat, or social media. Tactics used by perpetrators varied, ranging from grooming as described in Chapter 3 and "consensual" sharing by the young person to cases involving deception, threats, or hacking. In most (78%) of the cases, the goal of sextortion was to obtain more sexual content, with girls reporting this goal more than boys. In 7% of cases, the goal was to obtain money or goods from the target, and this was reported more by boys than girls. In 5% of cases, the demand was for sexual contact. The time duration was known in only a third of cases (39%) in the NCMEC data set, and in this subset where duration was known, 80% involved sextortion on the same day, though in some cases, the attempted blackmail happened months or even years later. A report from the International Center for Missing and Exploited Children (2018) on sextortion pointed out that some sextortion cases involve bluffing, where perpetrators claimed to possess sexual content that they did not have, in the hope the target had created and shared content and so could not be sure if it was reshared without their consent.

Wolak et al. (2018) surveyed 1,385 young adult sextortion victims, 91% of whom were female. Again, most (60%) knew the perpetrator, usually a partner or ex-partner. This survey also found that the motive in most cases was to obtain more sexual content. Two thirds felt pressured, and one third were physically threatened. Three quarters of the targets in the survey did send images after being sextorted. Only half of the respondents ever disclosed what happened to them, and few reported it to the police, pointing out the limitations of relying on reports to parents, police, or technology companies to intervene in sextortion.

O'Malley and Holt (2022) qualitatively analyzed data from 160 sextortion cases they found by searching court documents and news. These data are, therefore, highly unlikely to be representative because newsworthiness and sensationalism influence what is reported in media stories. Nonetheless, I think this study is worth describing here because it highlights that sextortion can also involve adults. A slight majority (53%) of the cases in this analysis involved minors, with a mean age of 14, and strangers who pressured the target to produce CSEM or meet for sex. The fact that a stranger was involved may increase the likelihood the case made it into the news because "stranger danger" appears to be driving online safety policies and laws. Another 12% of cases involved a partner. These partner-perpetrated cases were different from the other cases because a majority (58%) of these demands were nonsexual (e.g., to enter or leave a relationship, end a friendship, or quit a job). In these partner-perpetrated cases, sextortion again seemed to be part of a broader pattern of coercive control. Another 21% of cases looked like cybercrime, mostly targeting females, where strangers obtained images through hacking, scamming, or theft and then used their possession of these images to blackmail the targets, sometimes for money or other goods.

TECHNOLOGY-FACILITATED SEXUAL ASSAULT OF ADULTS

Dating apps and platforms are commonly used now. For example, a Pew survey found that 53% of adults under age 30 had used a dating app or website; the rates were lower as age increased (Anderson et al., 2020). Henry et al. (2020) surveyed 5,798 Australian women and found that one in 10 reported an unwanted sexual experience with someone they first met online. They also cited National Crime Agency data from the United Kingdom suggesting a six-fold increase in the number of sexual assaults during a first date with someone met online, though the absolute number of cases was relatively small (33 in 2009 and 184 in 2014). In a small study by Rowse et al. (2020) involving sexual assault investigations that included a forensic examination, 11 of 76 cases (14%) involved a woman (all under age 30) who met a man on a dating app. Most alleged sexual assaults took place in the perpetrator's residence, and intoxication was a factor in most cases.

A. Powell and Henry (2019) reported that one in 10 respondents reported a sexual assault facilitated by a dating app. A majority (62%) of the sample reported experiencing any form of technology-facilitated sexual abuse, most commonly online sexual harassment, then partner-controlling behavior, followed by unwanted sexual requests. The prevalence of technology-facilitated sexual abuse was negatively correlated with age, likely reflecting a greater use of dating apps in younger respondents. There were both gender similarities and differences in the results, with a small gender difference for receiving unwanted sexual texts or images, but perpetrators were twice as likely to be male than female. Women reported being more upset by these experiences than men, likely based on the potential threat and risk of further victimization that women anticipated. Consistent with other studies I have reviewed, nonheterosexual respondents reported more unwanted experiences than heterosexual participants. Finally, contributing to the underrepresentation of technology-facilitated sexual violence against adults in the clinical and criminal justice sectors, victimization was highly underreported. Most victims (54% overall) ignored the behavior, and most of the rest told the perpetrator to stop (e.g., 43% of female respondents, 33% of male respondents). Few complained to the app or platform (15% overall) or reported their experience to police (7% overall).

Pooley and Boxall (2020) suggested the use of dating apps, in particular, increases the risk for sexually or nonsexually violent victimization due to their affordances, including a wider reach of potential targets, the disinhibiting effects of anonymity, and specific features, such as GPS tracking (see also Phan et al., 2021). This observation aligns with what we found in Seto, Roche, Stroebel, et al. (2023), where children or youth who used dating apps were more likely to have their sexual images shared without consent, presumably because dating apps facilitate generating and sharing these kinds of images.

Moreover, Teunissen et al. (2022) found that 12% of almost 10,000 Australian survey respondents who had used a dating app or website in the past 5 years reported that they had been asked by someone on that app or website about sexually exploiting a child in their care, such as their own child. This included requests for sexual information, requests for sexual images or videos, and requests for live streaming. Men were more likely to receive such requests than women. This study connects the use of dating apps and platforms to the risk of CSEM production, as well as technology-facilitated sexual assault (and harassment) of adults.

Echevarria et al. (2023) surveyed 277 people who used dating apps about their experience with technology-facilitated sexual violence and again found that women were at greater risk of victimization than men, and nonheterosexual participants were at greater risk than heterosexual participants. Most participants experienced some form of technology-facilitated sexual violence while using dating apps, with 87% reporting sexual harassment, 42% reporting receiving unwanted images, and 45% reporting coercive experiences. Victimization was correlated with scores on measures of depression and anxiety, loneliness, low self-esteem, and external locus of control, but these data were cross-sectional, so it is not possible to determine if these psychological factors are antecedents, consequences, or correlates of technology-facilitated sexual violence experiences.

In their scoping review of the literature regarding sexual violence and the use of dating apps, Filice et al. (2022) identified 55 relevant studies, many reporting on the prevalence of sexual abuse, perceptions, and mitigation strategies. Half (53%, 29) of these studies were qualitative, and another 20 were surveys. Three quarters of the reviewed studies were conducted in the United States, Canada, or Australia. Many involved small convenience samples, a major exception being the Australian studies of image-based abuse reported in Henry et al. (2020). Importantly, dating app abuse was correlated with intimate partner violence victimization, including emotional abuse, physical abuse, coercive control, and forced social isolation.

In another scoping review, this time by Gewirtz-Meydan et al. (2024), 12 studies were identified. Prevalence of sexual harassment (e.g., unwanted sexually explicit messages or images) was reported in five studies; sexual harassment on dating apps was common, ranging from 57% to 88% of respondents. Women and sexual and gender minorities were at greater risk of sexual harassment. Experiencing sexual harassment was associated with higher levels of anxiety, depression, traumatic stress, loneliness, adverse childhood experiences, and low self-esteem.

Does some of what we know about offline perpetration of harassment, sexual coercion, and sexual assault generalize to technology-facilitated sexual violence? M. P. Thompson and Morrison (2013) found that online harassment and coercive behavior were predicted by the same kind of risk factors identified in Malamuth et al.'s (1995) confluence model of sexual aggression by men against women, including rape-supportive beliefs, peer approval of coerced sex (norms), number of sexual partners, and exposure to pornography (impersonal sexuality). M. P. Thompson and Morrison (2013) surveyed 571 respondents and found that 5% tried to get someone online to talk about sex when they did not want to, 2% asked someone for sexual information when they did not want to tell, 3% asked someone to do something sexual they did not want to, 16% nonconsensually reshared sexual messages or photos, and 21% engaged in any of these forms of technology-facilitated sexual coercion.

We do not know from these data how much overlap there is between online and offline behavior. For example, it may be the case that individuals who were sexually coercive with dates they previously met in bars or other public or private spaces are now sexually coercive with dates they meet via apps because so many more people use dating apps now. Alternatively, the affordances of online technologies, such as anonymity and search, may have increased the number of people who are engaging in sexually coercive behavior, and there may be overlapping but distinct populations of individuals who are coercive online versus offline.

In a rare study outside the heteronormative context, Dietzel (2021) conducted a qualitative thesis study of 25 males who have sex with males. Participants ranged in age from 18 to 62, most were White, and 24 of 25 identified as men; one participant identified as gender fluid. Most (23 of 25) of the participants used Grindr, but many used other dating or hookup apps, spending from 1 to 23 hours a week on these apps. The mean duration of use of dating or hookup apps was over 4 years. Participants reported both sending and receiving unsolicited sexual messages or dick pics, as well as several examples of sexual coercion mediated by dating or hookup apps. Participants pointed out how assumptions were made about sexual interest or consent based on profile information—for example, assuming that someone interested in a hookup would be open to receiving unsolicited dick pics. There was also a racialized component, where non-White men were treated differently than White men online. This is an important study because men who have sex with men are more likely to use dating and hookup apps than heterosexual men (Anzani et al., 2018), and therefore, they may be at greater risk of technology-facilitated sexual violence.

As I am writing this section, attention has been drawn to the technological facilitation of stalking and sexual harassment. In particular, Eva Galperin of the Electronic Frontier Foundation has raised concerns about *stalkerware*, specific apps that can be used to track someone without their knowledge or consent (see Parker, 2021). There have also been multiple news reports about how AirTags or similar devices can be used to track someone's whereabouts surreptitiously. Stalkerware or tracking devices can be used by former or current partners as part of a pattern of coercive control within an abusive relationship, and they can also be used by strangers engaging in stalking behaviors. There has been media attention, some attempted tech fixes (e.g., AirTags will notify people if there is an "unknown accessory," but that only works for iPhone users), and some legal and policy discussion, but no systematic social science research I am aware of.

SEXUAL TRAFFICKING

I turn next to the use of internet technologies to facilitate sexual trafficking, starting with minors, then adults, though almost no research has been done on the use of online technologies for the sexual trafficking of adults. Sexual trafficking of minors is just one form of commercial sexual exploitation of minors, but any commercial sexual activity involving a minor is considered to be sexual trafficking in American law and policy because someone under the age of 18 cannot legally consent to sex work. At the same time, many sex workers start before the age of 18 as part of "survival sex"—for example, as teen runaways to pay for basic needs, drugs, or other expenses. In their systematic review of 23 sexual trafficking of minor studies, Baird and Connolly (2023) found that online recruitment was the most common tactic used by traffickers, cited in seven studies. Typically, an older male presented himself as someone interested in a romantic relationship or friendship with a minor he contacted via messaging, games, or social network apps or platforms. A common pattern was the "boyfriend pimp," where an older male would establish a relationship with a minor target that would progress to sexual exploitation through pressure or force. Another common pathway that could involve online recruitment was befriending by other girls, again where friendship progressed to trafficking. Family members were more likely to be involved for younger children. Dalley (2010) and O'Brien and Li (2020) suggested minors who posted sexually explicit images or were already selling sexual services online were more likely to be targeted, though O'Brien and Li made this suggestion based on input from professional service providers, not data from traffickers or trafficking victims themselves. In contrast, Gezinski and Gonzalez-Pons (2022) concluded from their review that there were few examples of individuals who were recruited online into sexual trafficking, with more evidence of the use of online platforms for advertising sexual services. They also concluded that the prevalence of sexual trafficking was unknown.

Reid et al. (2015) compared 15 family-facilitated cases with 43 nonrelative trafficking cases from social services data for 92 girls, with trafficker information available for 62 girls. Among these 62 girls, 29% were trafficked by a stranger, 36% by a partner, 31% by a relative, 3% by a drug dealer, and 2% by an employer. Girls involved in family-facilitated cases were, on average, 3 years younger than other girls (mean 11.5 years old vs. 14.7 years old). Victims of family-facilitated cases were also more likely to witness domestic violence and experience other child maltreatment (child sexual abuse, child physical abuse, child neglect, and polyvictimization) and were less likely to have ever run away than those trafficked by nonrelatives. These results fit with what we know from the broader literature on sexual trafficking with minors. From their review of 15 studies published in English from January 2010 to September 2017, Franchino-Olsen (2021) concluded child maltreatment, caregiver strain, running away or being thrown away, substance use, peer influences, witnessing family violence or criminality, poverty, difficulty in school, conflict with parents, poor mental health, involvement with child protection services, juvenile delinquency, and prior sexual victimization were risk factors for being sexually trafficked as a minor. A caveat of this review is that a mix of studies was included, including studies of professional perceptions (which are not always accurate) and child sexual abuse victims in general rather than trafficked children specifically. Some studies did focus on this target group. The role of online technologies was not systematically explored in any of these studies. An implication of Franchino-Olsen's review is that the major risk factors are not unique to sexual trafficking because all the specific risk factors mentioned are also relevant for other concerning mental health and social outcomes. Consistent with the idea that a rising tide can lift all boats, these studies suggest that general, mainstream interventions to address early childhood and family well-being can have many benefits, including reduced risk of (online) sexual trafficking victimization.

We also need to address the use of internet technologies to facilitate the sexual trafficking of adults, as when adults are deceived or coerced into sex work (recognizing that some adults may also knowingly and willingly engage in sex work.) We know little scientifically about this form of technology-facilitated sexual offending (see Gezinski & Gonzalez-Pons, 2022). Sarkar (2015) suggested that adults typically are recruited in their home countries under false pretenses, such as sham online employment or marriage agencies. Once they are recruited, victims are sexually trafficked by traffickers using online apps or platforms to advertise for sexual services. To shed light on this phenomenon, Sarkar surveyed 97 female trafficking victims, 64 traffickers, and 85 clients in India, Nepal, Thailand, Hungary, and the United Kingdom, using semistructured, open-ended questions. Victims were primarily identified through nongovernmental organizations or brothels, traffickers were primarily identified through police or other authorities, and how clients were recruited was not specified. Highlighting only a few observations, victims reported using social networks to advertise their sexual services, closely monitored by traffickers. Traffickers rarely worked alone; instead, they worked with a business partner or a larger group. Clients indicated that they searched online for sexual services and commonly were interested in purchasing sexual services because they were tourists or traveling businesspeople.

The Polaris Project (2016) reported on the cantina-based trafficking of both minors and women from Central and South America. Minors were trafficked by definition, according to American policy, and at least some of the women were trafficked because they were not told they would be required to do sex work (e.g., they were falsely told they would be doing domestic or factory work). Data were from hotline calls representing 201 cases reported between December 2007 and March 2016. These cases involved an estimated 1,300 potential victims (potential because we do not know about individual consent, and some potential victims might have been suspected, but their identities were not known). Most of these potential victims were adults,[2] but an estimated 42% of trafficking victims were below the age of 18 at the time of the reporting, with 29% between the ages of 15 to 17 and 13% being 12 or 13. There were few victims below the age of 12. Given that the large majority (87%) of potential victims were age 15 or older, it is reasonable to infer that many buyers do not have pedohebephilia and are instead interested in buying sex with postpubescent adolescents or adults, even if they were aware or suspected that the person was being sexually trafficked. In many ways, these data reinforce the importance of opportunity and access (cf. motivation–facilitation model, see Chapter 5) and facilitation of sexual offending through alcohol use because these illegal activities took place in bars and clubs.

Cockbain and K. Olver's (2019) chapter described U.K. data from 2009 to 2014 for confirmed trafficking victims. For sexual exploitation, there were 298 cases involving minors and 808 cases involving adults; for both minors and adults, most victims were female. Whereas child victims were most commonly trafficked for sex (45%), followed by labor (34%), then domestic servitude (11%), adults were most commonly trafficked for labor (47%), followed by sex (39%), then domestic servitude (13%). In the same chapter, Cockbain and K. Olver analyzed data from cases involving the trafficking of British minors for sexual exploitation, with only a minority for money (other incentives included alcohol, drugs, and clout). Across six investigations, 55 men were convicted of offenses against 43 core victims; these men were described as unremarkable in terms of background and criminal history.

As this brief section makes clear, there is relatively little social science research on sexual trafficking involving minors, and most of this work has focused on victims of trafficking rather than the perpetrators.

---

[2]These were the ages of the victims at the time of the Polaris Project (2016) study; some of these adults may have been minors when they were first sexually trafficked.

CHILD SEXUAL ABUSE TOURISM

Sexual trafficking of minors is related to child sexual abuse tourism, which is another form of commercial sexual exploitation of children. Both domestic and international trafficking can involve children and youth who are then commercially exploited for the sake of both domestic and international tourists who travel to gain access to sex with young people who are under the legal age of consent in their home jurisdictions. For example, buyers from wealthier countries like the United States, Canada, the United Kingdom, or the European Union might travel to poorer countries in Southeast or South Asia, Central or South America, and Africa. Child abuse tourism is more likely to involve prepubescent or pubescent children than the broader phenomenon of sexual trafficking of minors.

In 2003, the U.S. government passed the PROTECT Act, which made it illegal for U.S. residents to travel to foreign countries to have sex with persons below the legal age of consent. Other countries have similar laws; for example, Canada has criminalized child sexual abuse tourism since 1997. There are few systematic data about this phenomenon yet many broad announcements or conclusions. For example, the 2016 ECPAT regional report on Cambodia explained that it has become a well-known destination country because it is inexpensive for travelers from middle- to high-income countries, detection is less likely, and there has been more law enforcement and nongovernmental agency attention to the problem in better known destination countries such as Thailand (ECPAT, 2016a). The International Justice Mission has done the soundest studies, in my opinion, given the methods they used and the data obtained. For example, in contrast to a government estimate that 30% of sex workers in Cambodia are minors, the International Justice Mission (2013) found 8% of sex workers in the cities of Phnom Penh, Siem Reap, and Sihanoukville were minors, and most (seven out of eight minors) were 16- and 17-year-olds; this means less than 1% of all sex workers in the International Justice Mission study were age 15 or younger. A follow-up study by the International Justice Mission in 2015 found an even lower rate, with less than 3% of sex workers being minors and few aged 15 or younger. Qualitatively, this change was attributed to more attention to child sexual abuse tourism in Cambodia. Similar results were reported in International Justice Mission (2014) research conducted in the Philippines, where a survey of 90 commercial sex establishments in metropolitan Manila found that 8% of sex workers were minors; a 2014 follow-up study of a broader area found a prevalence rate of 5%.

J. D. Davis et al. (2017) interviewed 51 male sex workers in the Chiang Mai region of Thailand. Approximately one in five began working before age 18. Just over half the buyers (51%) were judged to be foreign, pointing out that domestic trafficking of minors is also a major concern. The involvement of foreign buyers varied by area; the market area had the highest proportion of foreign buyers (estimated 82%) because it is highly traveled by tourists. Some buyers were women, but they were much younger than men who bought sex (estimated ages of 20 to 30 years old, compared with 30 to 70 years old for men, where the mean age of sex worker respondents was 22, ranging from 15 to 35). Most sex workers came to the Chiang Mai region for employment, including from nearby Myanmar.

A German market panel survey of 8,718 men found 36 men (0.4%) admitted to traveling for sex with children (Koops et al., 2017). Koops et al. compared these 36 men with another 96 men (1.1%) who admitted sexual offending against a child but without travel. There was no significant group difference in age, education level, or being in a committed relationship for 2 or more years. There was also no group difference in reporting pedophilic sexual interests or hypersexuality, but the child sex tourism group was more likely to offend against boys (which is associated with pedophilia, see Seto, 2018), twice as likely to use CSEM (78% vs. 34%), and much more likely to pay for sex with children (78% vs. 5%). The child sex tourism group also rated their risk of sexually offending as higher and were more likely to have prior violent or sexual offenses. All these findings suggest the child sex tourism group is a higher risk group than individuals who do not travel to commit sexual crimes against children.

SUMMARY

Forms of online sexual offending other than CSEM offending and sexual solicitation of minors have received much less research attention. This is not because they are rare, however. Digital exhibitionism is common enough that it appears to have become a tolerated aspect of a hostile online environment for women, and prevalence research suggests that nonconsensual resharing of images is not rare among minors or adults. We do not know how common technology-facilitated sexual assaults are, but they are likely to be common, given how much sexual violence occurs in dating contexts and given that the majority of younger adults use dating apps and platforms to meet. The prevalence of commercial sexual exploitation of children through either trafficking or tourism is unknown, but it has nonetheless been the focus of international policies to prevent wealthier people from traveling to low- and middle-income countries to exploit children sexually. Overall, there has been less attention to online sexual offending targeting adults, with policymakers and practitioners focusing on offending involving minors.

There is also overlap across forms of online sexual offending. Nonconsensually resharing images of minors also constitutes CSEM offending, images obtained through digital voyeurism can also be nonconsensually reshared, and individuals who engage in the commercial sexual exploitation of children in person, through trafficking and/or tourism, may also engage in live streaming (CSEM offending) or sexual solicitations of minors online.

A general trend is that men are more likely to perpetrate these forms of online sexual offending, and girls, women, and persons who are sexual or gender minorities are at greater risk of being targeted. Motivations for the forms of online sexual offending covered in this chapter vary, with paraphilic motivations likely for digital voyeurism and commercial sexual exploitation of children through trafficking or tourism and nonparaphilic sexual motivations more likely for digital exhibitionism and technology-facilitated sexual assault of adults. At the same time, there is evidence of nonsexual motivations as well, particularly for digital exhibitionism that is sporadic and the nonconsensual resharing of sexual images.

CASE EXAMPLES

The following hypothetical case examples were created from combining details from real cases with fictional elements to protect client confidentiality. The case examples are intended to illustrate points made in this chapter about different forms of online sexual offending and will be revisited in subsequent chapters.

Elvis (Digital Exhibitionism)

Elvis was a 25-year-old single male student reported to both police and tech companies for sending unsolicited close-ups of his genitals on dating apps and other social media. Most of this behavior was ignored by the recipients or reported only to the platform, but he sent images to a 16-year-old girl, and the parents discovered this and pursued the matter with the police. Elvis was identified as a suspect because he was careless about his security and privacy settings, and thus, the image sent to the 16-year-old girl was traced to him. He had two minor charges as an adolescent (once for shoplifting and a second time for a fight at school) but no criminal involvement as an adult. He denied any sexual motivation for his behavior, instead claiming he sent images to strangers out of curiosity and boredom. However, at another point in the assessment, Elvis also said he hoped that the recipients would be interested in receiving his photos and reciprocate by sending their nudes to him.

Vince (Digital Voyeurism)

Vince was a gym employee in his early 40s who was identified and charged after a police investigation discovered that he had set up a hidden spy camera in the women's changing room at the gym. He had no prior criminal history as a juvenile or adult. He initially denied it but eventually admitted during a clinical interview that he was sexually aroused by the idea of observing, without their knowledge, women undressing. He admitted saving the videos—hundreds were found by police stored on his seized computer equipment—and masturbating while rewatching them. Vince denied any interest in minors and stated that he was most attracted to young adult women. His longest romantic relationship lasted 4 years, and he lived with his partner for 3 of those 4 years. However, he had videos of women of many different ages, including teen minors and older women. As a result, Vince was also charged with CSEM offenses because the ages of the teen minors could be determined by examining gym membership records.

Jack (Nonconsensual Sharing and Sextortion)

Jack was a 21-year-old male college student investigated and charged with nonconsensual sharing of images after his 20-year-old victim, a fellow student and ex-partner, went to the police and disclosed that he had shared these images to a "revenge porn" website after the dissolution of their year-long relationship. The victim believed that Jack was the culprit because he was the only person she had ever shared nudes with, and forensic analysis determined that the photos had been uploaded from Jack's mobile. The victim also alleged that Jack had threatened to post the photos when she began talking about breaking up and that this threat caused her to delay ending the relationship. The victim also reported a pattern of coercive control, including becoming more socially isolated from her friends and having to turn on a phone location feature so that Jack knew where she was at all times.

Adrian (Technology-Facilitated Sexual Assault)

Adrian was a 31-year-old single man charged with six counts of sexual assault and three counts of administering a noxious substance with intent after a group of women came forward and reported their experiences during dates they had with Adrian after matching on a dating app. The women had discovered each other in a private Facebook group about dangerous men active on dating apps. There was digital evidence, and, in one case, physical evidence corroborating the women's reports, and Adrian quickly admitted that he used dating apps to meet women whom he would then try to get drunk or secretly administer a sedative to have sex with them. He admitted he wanted to have sex with the women but denied any paraphilic interest in sex with an unconscious woman (which would be evidence of somnophilia) or engaging in sexual aggression. He had no prior juvenile or adult criminal history and denied any unreported sexual assaults. However, he did admit to an extensive history of excessive alcohol and illegal substance use, and he claimed that he was sometimes intoxicated or high when he met women for dates. Adrian said he used substances to cope with chronic feelings of anxiety, low self-esteem, and depression. He minimized his culpability for the offenses by repeatedly pointing out that he was often intoxicated or high.

Smith (Commercial Sexual Exploitation of Children: Child Trafficking and Child Abuse Tourism)

Smith was a 59-year-old man who traveled frequently internationally and was arrested during his most recent trip by local police after other tourists observed him sexually touching a child in a public place. An investigation revealed photographs and videos of Jones engaging in sexual acts with a variety of boys between 11 and 14 years of age (most were pubescent in appearance). Local investigators were able to determine that the children had been trafficked from neighboring, even poorer countries and forced into sex work. Smith was referred to the police in his home country because his home country had legislation specifically criminalizing transnational sexual offending involving children. A search warrant revealed evidence that he had regularly communicated via darknet forums with individuals about how to travel to Country X so he could purchase sexual access to boys. In addition to engaging in child sexual abuse tourism, Smith was also directly involved in the sexual trafficking of children because he had specific preferences regarding appearances and paid for a boy to be brought from a nearby region to the town he was staying in to sexually abuse the child. Smith was charged and convicted of CSEM offenses as well because digital evidence indicated he had purchased access to live streaming child sexual abuse in the same country and had photographed many of the boys he committed contact sexual offenses against. Smith readily admitted to being sexually attracted to pubescent and then prepubescent boys and reported viewing CSEM (including live streaming) for years. Smith had no prior criminal record and denied that he had committed undetected sexual offenses in his home country. He reported no psychiatric history or concerns.

The Etiology of Online Sexual Offending and the Motivation–Facilitation Model

In this chapter, I examine key questions: What are the causes of online sexual offending? Do they differ from the factors involved in offline perpetration? What can a better understanding of the etiology of online sexual offending tell us about prognosis (risk assessment, Chapter 6), needs assessment (Chapter 6), treatment (Chapter 7), and prevention (Chapter 8)? In the previous chapters, I covered relevant information about perpetrator psychology and behavior across forms of online sexual offending. It is clear that there can be heterogeneity of motivations even when the behavior is similar (e.g., sending "dick pics" can be an expression of paraphilic motivation but can also be used to bully or harass someone), as well as heterogeneity of behaviors even when the motivations are similar (e.g., sexual interest in children can be expressed through child sexual exploitation material [CSEM] use, online solicitations of younger children, or commercial sexual exploitation of children). Because most of the literature on online sexual offending has focused on CSEM offending, a great deal of this chapter focuses on this form of offending as well, particularly in my discussion of the motivation–facilitation model (Seto, 2019). However, the motivation–facilitation model could apply to other forms of online sexual offending as well, including offending against adults.

---

https://doi.org/10.1037/0000428-006
Online Sexual Offending: Theory, Practice, and Policy, Second Edition, by M. C. Seto
Copyright © 2025 by the American Psychological Association. All rights reserved.

PERPETRATOR EXPLANATIONS

It is easy to dismiss self-reported perpetrator explanations because of self-interest, such as to minimize culpability or deny something as stigmatizing as being sexually attracted to prepubescent or pubescent children. Nonetheless, a valuable starting point in understanding etiology is to ask perpetrators directly about their offending. In an early study of self-reported explanations for CSEM offending, we found (to my surprise) that a plurality of 84 CSEM perpetrators acknowledged they were sexually interested in children and CSEM, though many initially claimed the access was accidental or due to curiosity (Seto et al., 2010). Other reported motivations included more general sexual self-regulation problems, such as having a pornography use problem or having indiscriminate sexual interests in a variety of taboo or paraphilic themes (see Chapter 2). Similar results have been obtained in other small-sample studies. Merdian et al. (2013) found that a third of 39 CSEM perpetrators in their sample admitted sexual interest in children. Others claimed nonparaphilic sexual motivations; 23% said there was an escalation in their pornography use over time, from typical mainstream adult pornography to more taboo content to CSEM (recall the case example of Adam). The most common explanation (38%) given by Merdian et al. was the use of CSEM to cope with unpleasant feelings such as loneliness, depression, or anger, which could include both paraphilic and nonparaphilic sexual motivations.

Surjadi et al. (2010) looked at the self-reported motivations of 43 CSEM perpetrators and found that the most common reason given for using CSEM was avoidant behavior (e.g., using CSEM to cope with unpleasant feelings) followed by sexual motivations (pedophilia or another sexual motivation). Curiously, a third claimed they never masturbated to CSEM, belying a sexual motivation for engaging with this content. Consistent with the idea of escalation of use over time, 27% of the perpetrators in Surjadi et al. admitted they masturbated the first time they viewed CSEM, whereas 40% claimed they did not begin masturbating to this content until later, most commonly 2 months after their first viewing of CSEM.

In another small study by Steely et al. (2018) of 25 CSEM perpetrators in the southern United States, almost a third (8/25, 32%) said they escalated from adult to CSEM content, either because they were drawn by the taboo nature of the child content, or they realized they were sexually attracted to minors. Another eight respondents (32%) admitted they searched directly for CSEM, either because they were attracted to children or out of curiosity. Like Seto et al. (2010), seven (28%) said it was accidental access, but overall, almost half (48%) admitted they were motivated by a sexual interest in children. The respondents went further and explained that part of their attraction was to innocence and inexperience, echoing the attractive features identified by G. Wilson and Cox (1983) and Martijn et al. (2020).

I find it remarkable that these studies—differing in samples, methods, and geographies—have consistently shown that the top three motivations for CSEM offending reported by perpetrators are (a) sexual interest in children and thus

CSEM; (b) escalation of pornography use over time from mainstream to taboo to illegal child content; and (c) sexualized coping, where the use of CSEM was a way to cope with unpleasant feelings such as loneliness, boredom, depression, or anxiety. The escalation and coping explanations are less stigmatized than admitting pedohebephilia, which may explain why some perpetrators provide these explanations instead of acknowledging their sexual interest in children.

It is unclear to me why someone would escalate to CSEM depicting younger children or why they would use CSEM instead of continuing to use adult pornography (even if taboo or illegal) to cope with unpleasant feelings; both the escalation and coping explanations still lead to social and legal culpability. Indeed, in a vignette study by Kliethermes (2021), whether someone was motivated by sexual arousal to the content, compulsive pornography use, or risk taking was unrelated to respondent ratings of offense severity, recommended sentence, and estimated risk of sexually reoffending. Kliethermes did find that perpetrator age mattered, such that a 65-year-old was viewed as more culpable than a 15-year-old, possibly because participant judgments are more forgiving for juveniles or because there is a much smaller age difference for a teen perpetrator and the young people depicted in the content. A caveat to note about this study is that the vignettes were rated by a convenience sample in which a high proportion of people said they knew sexual offense victims or perpetrators of CSEM, and thus, their views might not reflect those of the general public.

Consistent with the escalation of pornography use explanation, Seigfried-Spellar and Rogers (2013) found evidence in a survey of 630 respondents regarding ages of onset of pornography use that mainstream adult pornography use preceded the use of zoophilic pornography ($n = 54$), which in turn preceded the use of CSEM ($n = 33$). A study by Fortin and Proulx (2019) suggests some individuals escalate their CSEM use over time, as described in Chapter 2. My interpretation of the Fortin and Proulx study is that many individuals home into the content that best matches their sexual interests, most commonly more explicit content depicting younger children. However, other profiles identified by Fortin and Proulx went in other directions, including those who preferred less explicit content depicting young children or preferred content depicting adolescents. Changes in CSEM use over time are salient when we consider again the results of the ReDirection survey I described in Chapter 2, in which a majority of CSEM users said they were juveniles the first time they saw CSEM, and it was often accidental access (Insoll et al., 2022). Prevention and early intervention for early CSEM access could have important impacts downstream, as I discuss further in Chapter 8.

A newer study covered different ground in the explanations given by perpetrators by examining the sentencing remarks for 29 single-perpetrator cases out of 140 initial cases, excluding cases who had prior CSEM or contact sexual offenses or concurrent CSEM and contact offenses or who were appealing their conviction (Christensen & Tsagaris, 2020). From professional evaluations or submissions from the defense, explanations given by perpetrators for their CSEM use included denial or minimization of intent (e.g., CSEM use was evidence of collecting behavior rather than being sexually motivated), poor mental health, partner conflict, pornography addiction, and substance use, presumably submitted as potentially mitigating factors that might lead to a less severe sentence. Nonetheless, seven of the 29 (24%) suspects explicitly acknowledged having a sexual attraction to children, even though they might also frame this as an addiction to CSEM.

Another relevant study by Rimer and Holt (2023) qualitatively analyzed statements given by 103 CSEM users who participated in a group treatment program (in the United Kingdom) or were interviewed while in prison (in the United States) at different times, from pretrial to serving time in prison. Rimer and Holt described similarities in themes across setting and timeline, with three main themes: (a) pornography use progression; (b) addiction, such as a perceived lack of control, ignoring negative consequences, and symptoms of withdrawal; and (c) more rarely, statements about responsibility and control and the recognition that calling CSEM use an addiction might be face saving because it is more palatable than admitting sexual interest in children.

MOTIVATION–FACILITATION MODEL

I believe a large proportion—but not all—of online sexual offending can be understood through the motivation–facilitation model (see Figure 5.1), which organizes what we know about motivations for sexual offending and the factors that facilitate acting on those motivations. The original version of this model was developed to explain contact sexual offending against children (Seto, 2008), but I then expanded it to include online sexual offending (Seto, 2013) and other forms of sexual offending (Seto, 2019).

In this chapter, I describe motivations and facilitation factors suggested in previous chapters that can also inform case formulation. I then discuss decisions about assessment and treatment in the following chapters. In brief, the motivation–facilitation model focuses on three sets of factors. *Motivation factors* are primarily sexual and explain why someone would want to engage in illegal online sexual behavior. For accessing CSEM and commercial sexual exploitation of prepubescent or pubescent children, the primary motivation is pedohebephilia (see Chapters 2 and 4). For sexual solicitation, paraphilic interests are less prominent but can still be relevant when the individual is targeting prepubescent or pubescent children, which seems more common in research conducted in the past decade. Common, though socially sanctioned, sexual interests in postpubescent adolescents help explain most sexual solicitations by men of older adolescents, some digital exhibitionism toward older adolescents, and sexual trafficking or tourism involving older adolescents who are under the legal age of consent in the person's home jurisdiction. Pedophilic or hebephilic sexual interests are more likely to be relevant for sexual solicitations of younger children. Exhibitionism is a relevant paraphilic motivation for some digital exhibitionism (recall that Oswald et al., 2020, found that a quarter of their sample reported

FIGURE 5.1. Motivation–Facilitation Model

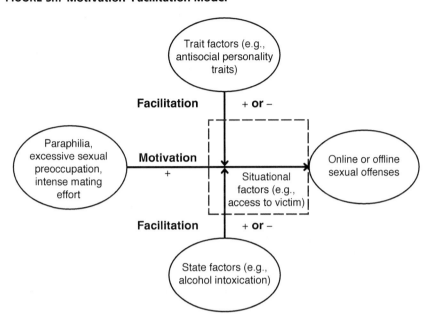

Note. Adapted from "The Motivation–Facilitation Model of Sexual Offending," by M. C. Seto, 2017a, *Sexual Abuse* [advance online publication, p. 3]. Copyright 2017 by Sage. Adapted with permission.

being turned on by the idea of sending an unsolicited sexual image), and I suspect that voyeurism is a paraphilic motivation for most digital voyeurism. Sexual motivations are less obviously connected to image-based abuse involving the nonconsensual sharing of images, in contrast to image-based abuse involving sextortion (e.g., for more sexual content or sexual interactions).

Having one or more of these sexual motivations is usually not sufficient, however. Whether someone acts on their motivations to sexually offend depends on the presence of a second set of factors involving trait or state facilitation. *Trait facilitation factors* include persistent factors such as antisocial personality traits (especially impulsivity, risk taking, and callousness), offense-supportive attitudes and beliefs, and social norms that tolerate the illegal behavior. In applying the motivation–facilitation model to CSEM offending, someone who is sexually attracted to prepubescent or pubescent children is more likely to seek out CSEM if they are more impulsive (and thus do not reflect on the potential legal and social consequences of their actions), more tolerant of the risk they might get caught, and/or indifferent to the effects of the CSEM use on the children who are depicted. Similarly, someone who believes that the children in the images are not harmed by the images being viewed is more likely to seek CSEM, just as someone who believes that minors who have sexually suggestive usernames, profile photos, or posts are inviting sexual attention from adults is more likely to sexually solicit these minors. The third example reflecting the role of perceived social norms is someone who believes that sending unrequested dick pics is common on dating and hookup apps and, therefore, "not a big deal"; this individual is more likely to engage in this form of online transgression. *State facilitation factors* are more dynamic than trait facilitation factors, by definition, and they also influence acting on motivations to offend. Examples of state facilitation factors include mood (seeking out CSEM to cope with stress or depressed affect) and substance use (acting more recklessly when intoxicated).

Finally, the third set of factors in the motivation–facilitation model involves *situational factors* that affect access and opportunity to offend. For online offending, this includes access to the internet and online opportunities to engage in illegal behavior, such as finding CSEM or sexually soliciting children (see the Technological Affordances That Can Facilitate Online Sexual Offending section in Chapter 1). Other situational factors that affect access and opportunity include parental supervision of children's online activities and, for solicitations focused on potential sexual contact, opportunities to meet in person. In a small qualitative study of participants in an online intervention, McMahan et al. (2023) suggested that pandemic restrictions—resulting in more time online and more social isolation—affected urges to find CSEM. Using call and website visit data from Stop It Now! USA and Stop It Now! UK & Ireland, Seto, Roche, Coleman, et al. (2023) found some evidence of an increase in help seeking by people concerned about their sexual thoughts or behaviors involving children during the first pandemic lockdown of Spring 2020 when many people shifted to remote work or school. This meant minors and adults had more opportunities to interact online; adults who were at risk of CSEM or online sexual solicitation were also feeling bored, lonely, or stressed; and adults who normally could regulate their sexual thoughts about children in their residence spent more time with those children.

The motivation–facilitation model bears a great debt to the dual control model of sexual arousal (Janssen & Bancroft, 2007) and the self-control theory of crime (Gottfredson & Hirschi, 1990). The dual control model of sexual arousal suggests that the cumulative and interacting effects of excitation and inhibition processes affect the experience and expression of sexual arousal. Sexual excitation increases responsiveness to sexual stimuli and may include the effects of sex drive, motivations for sex, and available outlets. Sexual inhibition decreases responsiveness to sexual stimuli and may include the effects of anxiety, guilt, and fear of negative consequences. These ideas are reflected in the motivation–facilitation model because paraphilic motivations and hypersexuality can contribute to sexual excitation, whereas reflectivity, risk avoidance, empathy, and prosocial attitudes and beliefs about sex and children can contribute to sexual inhibition.

The self-control theory of crime (Gottfredson & Hirschi, 1990) was developed as a general theory of crime based on the factors that affect self-control. Both sexual motivations and facilitation factors are expected to influence self-control when it comes to sexual criminal behavior. However, this general theory of crime does not specifically address atypical sexual motivations such as pedohebephilia. Another precursor to the motivation–facilitation model is an implicit model in the meta-analytic findings of Hanson and Bussière (1998) and Hanson and Morton-Bourgon (2005), where the two primary risk dimensions across many sexual recidivism studies reflect atypical sexuality (motivation factors) and antisociality (facilitation factors).

The motivation–facilitation model was originally formulated to explain the persistence of sexual offending against children, given meta-analytic evidence that indicators of sexual interest in children (self-report, sexual arousal to children in the lab, having multiple child victims, having boy victims, having unrelated victims) are robust predictors of sexual recidivism (Hanson & Bussière, 1998; Hanson & Morton-Bourgon, 2005). The same meta-analyses have also shown that indicators of facilitation factors (antisocial personality, offense-supportive cognitions, substance use) are robust predictors of sexual recidivism. Variables reflecting motivation (sexual interest in children) or indirectly reflecting antisocial tendencies (criminal history) predict sexual recidivism among CSEM offenders (see Chapter 6).

The results of Klein et al.'s (2015) analysis of a large German market panel sample of men are consistent with the motivation–facilitation model, being relevant to the onset of sexual offending. In their analysis of responses from 8,718 men, self-reported CSEM offending was correlated with sexual fantasies about children and high sex drive; self-reported contact sexual offending against children was predicted by sexual fantasies about children and prior criminal history. Similarly, the results reported by Bailey et al. (2016) are mostly consistent with the motivation–facilitation model. Bailey et al. surveyed an anonymous sample of 1,102 men who self-identified as sexually attracted to children. Although the group was homogeneous for sexual attraction to children, there was still variation in the strength of their attraction, and questions tapping this variation (e.g., preferential vs. nonpreferential attraction to children) were correlated with self-reported sexual offending: Participants who reported more attraction to children than to adults were more likely to report having criminal charges for sexual offenses. In addition, participants who were attracted to boys rather than girls (and, therefore, were more likely to have pedohebephilia) were more likely to have criminal charges. There was also support for situational factors in the survey data because men who had repeatedly worked in jobs with children (and thus were more intensely attracted to children and/or who had more opportunities) were more likely to have sexually offended. However, offense-supportive attitudes about child–adult sex were uncorrelated with sexual offending, as was the frequency of sexual fantasies about children.

Two other factors I have not yet discussed—having fallen in love with children and childhood sexual abuse history—were also correlated with sexual offending in the Bailey et al. (2016) survey. Though childhood sexual abuse history appears to be associated with the onset of sexual offending because individuals who have sexually offended are much more likely to have experienced childhood sexual abuse than individuals who have committed other kinds of offenses, childhood sexual abuse history does not predict sexual recidivism among individuals who have been convicted of sexual offenses

(Hanson & Bussière, 1998; Hanson & Morton-Bourgon, 2005; Jespersen et al., 2009; Seto & Lalumière, 2010). Thorne (2020), however, found no significant correlation between childhood sexual abuse history and the use of CSEM in a convenience sample of 119 individuals reporting sexual thoughts about children.

APPLYING THE MOTIVATION–FACILITATION MODEL

In the following sections, I discuss how the motivation–facilitation model can be applied to different forms of online sexual offending to guide case formulation, which can then guide assessment and treatment decisions. The clearest utility of the model is for CSEM offending, and I have already given examples of how it can be applied. However, the motivation–facilitation model is also useful for other forms of online sexual offending that are clearly sexually motivated.

CSEM Offending

Paquette and Cortoni (2021) found that pedohebephilic sexual interests (motivation), sexualized coping (facilitation), and offense-supportive cognitions (facilitation) distinguished both CSEM and dual perpetrators from a comparison group of men who had committed nonsexual offenses exclusively. However, sexual preoccupation (another highlighted motivation) and perceived anonymity (situational facilitation factor) did not distinguish men who had committed online sexual offenses from those who had committed nonsexual offenses. Gewirtz-Meydan et al. (2018) examined motivations for producing CSEM offending. Perpetrators did not give explanations in almost half (48%) of the cases, but among the remaining cases, the reasons were personal use (16%), use of CSEM to blackmail the victim (16%), and to sell or trade with others (16%). Some also reported other reasons than those already listed (23%); the explanations did not add up to 100% because respondents could report multiple explanations (e.g., personal use and blackmail). Not everyone recognizes or reports sexual motivations for CSEM use—whether acknowledging pedohebephilia, reporting escalation in pornography use, or reporting sexualized coping. Morgan's (2015) thesis completed a thematic analysis of 12 CSEM users in New Zealand who were in treatment or had participated in treatment. They cited factors such as stress, boredom, social isolation, and progression from adult content as onset factors and collecting behavior, coping with negative emotions, and addiction as maintenance factors. Only a tiny sliver of CSEM perpetrators responded (78/2508 eligible, so 3%, and likely a strong selection bias) to an online survey conducted by Steel et al. (2023), but they too claimed nonsexual motivations or sexual motivations other than pedohebephilia.

What is likely to distinguish paraphilic motivations, nonparaphilic sexual motivations, and nonsexual motivations for online sexual offending? We can ask people, but they might lie, claiming it was curiosity or thrill seeking or some other nonsexual motivation first and then (reluctantly) acknowledging a more general sexual regulation problem before admitting to pedohebephilia

(Seto et al., 2010). How and when to identify pedohebephilia is beyond this book, but ideally, it includes self-report, observations, and an objective assessment of sexual arousal patterns (see Seto, 2018).

For CSEM offending, I think the relevant questions for clinical assessment (see the next chapter) include the frequency and persistence of CSEM use, the type of CSEM in terms of ages and gender that were accessed, the variety of CSEM used, the ratio of CSEM to adult content, and self-reported behavior and mood during the use of CSEM. In research that I cover in more detail in the next chapter, indicators correlated with admitted sexual interest in children included duration of CSEM activities and use of text or videos in addition to images (Seto & Eke, 2017). In terms of CSEM to adult content ratio, I suggest that someone with a small fraction of total content involving CSEM could more plausibly claim they had escalated their pornography use over time, whereas someone with a tiny fraction of adult compared with CSEM content would have a weak claim. Similarly, evidence of having a variety of content depicting many other atypical or taboo pornography themes could be consistent with a sexual compulsivity explanation, as would other sexual behaviors such as hiring sex workers, engaging in many casual sexual relationships, and engaging in other, noncriminal paraphilic behavior.

I also expect those who are motivated by paraphilic or hypersexual motivations to be more likely to continue engaging in online sexual offending despite any distress or impairment they experience as a result. In contrast, someone who engages in online sexual offending opportunistically would be expected to desist if they become distressed or impaired. This speculation—if correct—has implications for interventions. Technological deterrence through reducing affordances or adding friction could dramatically reduce online sexual offending, but it would probably be less successful for those who are motivated by paraphilic motivations because these individuals are more likely to be entrenched in the behavior in terms of frequency and/or duration than those with non-paraphilic motivations. This minority requires more intense intervention, consistent with the risk-need-responsivity framework that I discuss in more detail in Chapters 6 and 7.

Solicitation Offending

In the first edition, I proposed that solicitation perpetrators were unlikely to be pedophilic, given their targets were predominantly adolescents below the legal age of consent. However, this does not mean they do not fit within the motivation–facilitation model because some could be motivated by hebephilia or even ephebophilia (a sexual preference for postpubescent adolescents who are not yet sexually mature rather than sexually mature adults; see Seto, 2017b). Studies in the past 5 years have shown that children below the age of 12 are also sexually solicited (e.g., Thorn, 2022), suggesting pedophilia is becoming more relevant. Other solicitation perpetrators are motivated by hypersexuality—resulting in approaches to underage teens—or typical sexual interests in sexually maturing adolescents that are not inhibited by social norms. Regardless of what kind of motivations they have, many online solicitation perpetrators resemble statutory sexual offending perpetrators in that they target younger people who might be more susceptible to their approaches, whereas women their age would be unimpressed.

Sexualized coping may also be relevant for some solicitation offending: E. Bergen et al. (2015) compared 640 adults who had sexually interacted with other adults online with a group of 77 adults who admitted they had sexually interacted with a child or adolescent online. The latter group had significantly more sexual arousal and shame before their online interactions than the adult–adult group. Engaging in the sexual interactions reduced negative affect, but this was offset by a surge in shame after the interaction.

Image-Based Offending

I suspect some digital exhibitionism and a higher proportion of digital voyeurism are motivated by paraphilic sexual interests, consistent with the motivation–facilitation model (see Oswald et al., 2020). Some digital exhibitionism appears to be motivated by misguided sexual interests, given that some survey participants said they hoped the exposure might lead to a positive, sexual response (Karasavva & Forth, 2022; see Chapter 4, this volume). It is also clear that some digital exhibitionism and a large proportion of other image-based offending is not sexually motivated and, instead, is an expression of bullying, trolling, seeking revenge, or other nonsexual explanations (Oswald et al., 2020). Sextortion is different from other image-based sexual abuse because it is mostly sexually motivated, either to get more CSEM or coerce sexual interactions, including online interactions in the case of sexual solicitation cases.

Karasavva and Forth (2022) found that image-based sexual abuse was correlated with narcissism, psychopathy, and sadism, where sadism might be a (sexual) motivation for the behavior while narcissism and psychopathy can facilitate acting on motivations. Fido et al. (2023) found that a self-reported proclivity for digital voyeurism in an online vignette study was associated with past voyeuristic behavior (which may indicate a paraphilic interest in voyeurism) along with higher psychopathy scores, reflecting facilitation. Proclivity was also associated with target attractiveness, being male, and being older. In another study, Sparks et al. (2023) found that cyberflashing (sending unrequested images) was correlated with self-reported interest in exhibitionism and with sexual compulsivity (a sexual motivation), as well as offense-supportive attitudes and antisocial personality traits such as impulsivity (facilitation).

Technology-Facilitated Sexual Assault of Adults

We do not have enough evidence to determine if technology-facilitated sexual assault of adults fits with the motivation–facilitation model. The behavior seems to be sexually motivated, but we do not know if facilitation factors such as antisocial personality traits, offense-supportive cognitions, and lifestyle instability play a role. Research specifically testing this model—and other models, such as the confluence model to explain sexual aggression by men against women—is needed. In the previous chapter, I pointed out that M. P. Thompson and Morrison (2013) found that online harassment and coercive behavior were predicted by the same kind of risk factors identified in Malamuth et al.'s (1995) confluence model, including rape-supportive beliefs, peer approval of coerced sex (norms), number of sexual partners, and exposure to pornography (impersonal sexuality).

In some ways, technology-facilitated sexual assault of adults is the clearest example of how the distinction between online and offline offending will further blur. If more and more people meet and communicate via dating apps, social networks, or other online platforms (e.g., multiplayer gaming), technology will be increasingly involved in sexual assaults of adults. There is an important distinction, however, between more opportunistic involvement of technology (e.g., someone who sexually assaults a date they met via an app while they both were intoxicated) and more intentional use of technology, as when a serial perpetrator intentionally uses dating and hookup apps to identify potential targets, pretending to be someone trustworthy and genuinely interested in meeting and dating new people.

Sexual Trafficking and Child Sexual Abuse Tourism

Both sexual trafficking of children and child sexual abuse tourism fit well within the motivation–facilitation model, where the sexual motivation may be pedophilia or hebephilia for younger children and hypersexuality for older adolescents. Technology-facilitated involvement with sexually trafficked women, where the person knows or is suspicious that the woman has been trafficked, could fit as well because the person was sexually motivated and willing to act on this motivation despite the moral and legal prohibitions.

LIMITATIONS OF THE MOTIVATION–FACILITATION MODEL

The motivation–facilitation model was initially developed to explain the onset and persistence of contact sexual offending against children (Seto, 2008) and then extended to explain CSEM offending (Seto, 2013). As a result, the motivation–facilitation model emphasizes sexual motivations and de-emphasizes nonsexual motivations for online sexual offending, such as curiosity or thrill seeking for CSEM offending, anger or revenge for some image-based sexual abuse (hence the popularization of the term "revenge porn"), and hostility or trolling for some digital exhibitionism. For sexual solicitations of children, romantic attraction to children or emotional congruence with children might also be motivations; although these constructs are correlated with pedohebephilia, neither construct is essentially sexual in nature.

Another limitation of the motivation–facilitation model—and the online and offline sexual offending literature—is the absence of protective factors in the model. I did not consider protective factors when developing the motivation–facilitation model because the research literature was scant, abstract, and confusing. Indeed, there is debate about how to define and conceptualize protective factors, with some authors suggesting that this can include the absence of a risk factor and others suggesting protective factors are not simply the absence of risk and, instead, are factors that help buffer the person from the effects of other risk factors. For example, not having antisocial friends would be the absence of a risk factor (antisocial peer influences), whereas having prosocial friends is not simply the absence of antisocial friends because someone could have many antisocial and prosocial friends. Instead, the prosocial friends can buffer the person from the criminogenic effects of their antisocial friends.

The only protective factor I believe there is sufficient empirical support for is positive social support—from family, friends, and others—which can buffer the person against the urge to act on their sexual motivations, even in the presence of facilitation factors such as antisocial personality, offense-supportive cognitions, and antisocial norms (Seto, Roche, Stroebel, et al., 2023). Positive social supports can provide healthier ways to cope with negative feelings, detect and intervene early if they see risky behavior or other warning signs, and counter offense-supportive cognitions and norms. A meta-analysis of studies involving adolescents or college students identified parent monitoring and family functioning as candidate protective factors for sexual violence perpetration in these younger individuals (O'Connor et al., 2024). The motivation–facilitation model can be updated to include protective factors when this literature is more developed.

The third limitation of the motivation–facilitation model is that the research synthesized to build the model is primarily based on data from men who have committed sexual offenses, with some relevant evidence from boys as well. This evidence has accumulated in a small number of WEIRD (Western, educated, industrialized, rich, and democratic) countries (see Chapter 1). We do not know yet if the motivation–facilitation model is relevant for women, girls, men, or boys who have sexually offended in nonWEIRD societies. A promising, though small, study by Erkan et al. (2023) reported that prior contact sexual offending was correlated with evidence of pedophilic disorder, exclusivity of interest in children, high levels of sexual activity, and emotional congruence with children (see the Emotional Congruence With Children section in Chapter 5) in an anonymous online sample of 42 women who self-identified as being attracted to children.

CSEM PATHWAYS

Merdian et al. (2018) applied the pathways model of sexual offending (see the Live Streaming section in Chapter 2 for a brief overview of the pathways model) to CSEM offending, suggesting there was evidence of both approach and avoidance pathways in CSEM offending. Synthesizing this pathways model and the motivation–facilitation model, Merdian et al. (2020) developed a case formulation model from interviews with 20 CSEM perpetrators, identifying seven germane themes: developmental context, individual risk and protective propensities, personal circumstances, permission-giving thoughts, internet environment and behavior, evaluation of consequences for the individual, and desistance (see Figure 5.2). Developmental context included lack of connection to others, including estrangement from family or social isolation, and unmet sexual needs, including sexual victimization. Individual propensities included dysfunctional coping, negative emotional states, and sexual interest in children. Internet environment and behavior referred to the affordances discussed in Chapter 2. Permission-giving thoughts included ideas that viewing CSEM was harmless, or the children depicted in the content were not real. Consequences of offending could be positively or negatively reinforcing (e.g., sexually arousing and gratifying, relieving negative mood state). Desistance included social connection and confidential help.

FIGURE 5.2. Case Formulation Model

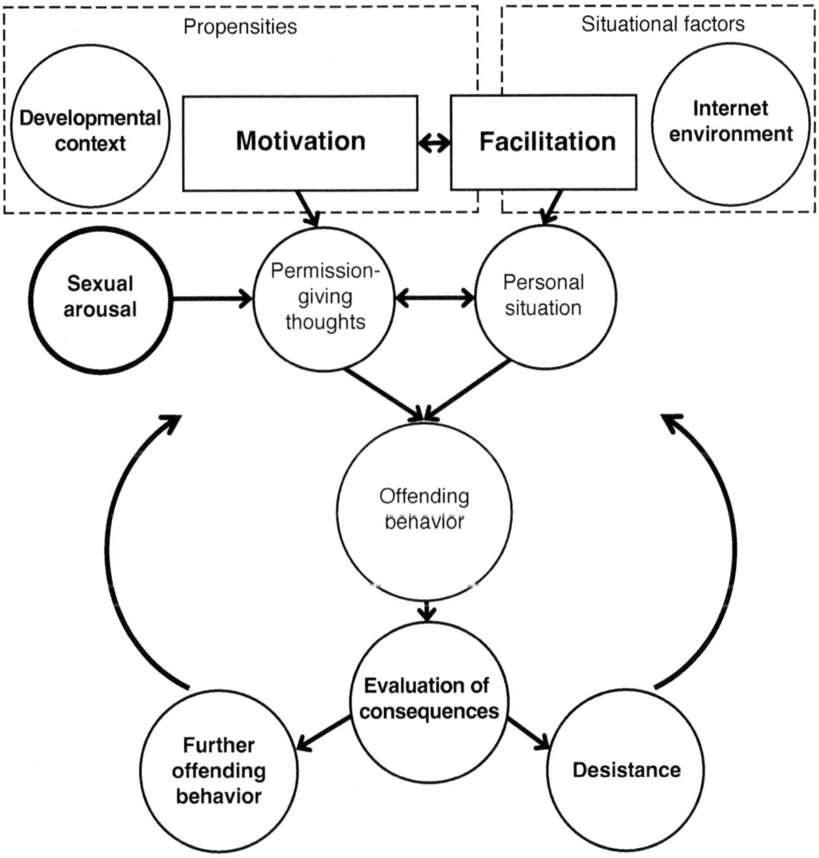

Note. This model builds on the motivation–facilitation model described by Seto (2019). Adapted from "Development of a Case Formulation Model for Individuals Who Have Viewed, Distributed, and/or Shared Child Sexual Exploitation Material," by H. L. Merdian, D. E. Perkins, E. Dustagheer, and E. Glorney, 2020, *International Journal of Offender Therapy and Comparative Criminology, 64*(10–11), p. 1066 (https://doi.org/10.1177/0306624X17748067). Copyright 2020 by Sage. Adapted with permission.

Merdian et al.'s (2020) case formulation model provides a clinically useful way of organizing the concepts discussed in the previous chapter and the clinical and risk assessment foci described in the next chapter. The case formulation model included some modifications of the motivation–facilitation model. For example, offense-supportive cognitions (offense-permissive thoughts) are viewed as an offshoot of motivation, whereas I see it as a form of facilitation; someone who holds these attitudes and beliefs can justify acting on their sexual motivations but is not motivated by these cognitions per se. Current sexual arousal is seen as contributing to the motivational pathway, via cognitions, and this offending pattern can be reinforced by rewards of offending behavior. A new component in Merdian et al.'s model that is not in the motivation–facilitation model is the evaluation of consequences after sexually offending, where positive appraisals lead to more offending and negative appraisals lead to less offending. This modification is fully within accepted behavioral principles of reinforcement and social learning.

Sexual Motivations

The motivation–facilitation model for online sexual offending prioritizes sexual motivations, though nonsexual motivations also exist. Sexual motivations, in turn, can be paraphilic or nonparaphilic. An obvious example of paraphilic motivation is someone with pedophilia or hebephilia engaging in online sexual offending as an expression of their sexual interest in prepubescent or pubescent children. Nonparaphilic sexual motivations include hypersexuality, as when someone who is excessively sexually preoccupied engages in escalating pornography use, culminating in illegal pornography use, or typical sexual interests expressed despite social norms and legality (as when someone solicits an adolescent they find sexually attractive and disregards the fact they are a minor). I have already discussed these different motivations in previous chapters, but I go into further detail here about each type of motivation.

Pedophilia and Hebephilia

Pedophilia and hebephilia (or pedohebephilia) are central to understanding a large fraction of online sexual offending involving prepubescent or pubescent children. In line with the motivation–facilitation model, pedohebephilia is the most prevalent motivation for CSEM offending (Blanchard et al., 2007; Seto et al., 2006, 2010); helps explain the solicitation of prepubescent or pubescent children; explains some image-based offending, such as sextortion to get more CSEM involving younger children or to coerce sexual conversations or other interactions; and the commercial sexual exploitation targeting prepubescent or pubescent children. Pedohebephilia cannot explain all online sexual offending involving minors, however, particularly behavior directed toward older adolescents who are postpubescent in appearance. Involvement with CSEM depicting postpubescent minors may help explain why one quarter of the sample in Seto et al. (2006) did not show an absolute preference for children over adults because the focus of the phallometric testing was sexual arousal to prepubescent or pubescent children. (Another contributing factor would be attempts at faking, as well as nonsexual motivations such as thrill seeking or curiosity.) Age is not a great proxy for sexual maturity, but adolescents between the ages of 15 and 17 would typically be postpubescent in appearance. Some men are interested in finding sexual content or having online sexual interactions with these adolescents, and their offending behavior is not explained by pedohebephilia. Online offending involving adults, such as the use of online technologies to facilitate sexual assault, digital exhibitionism or voyeurism targeting adults, or image-based abuse involving adults, does not invoke pedohebephilia either.

Readers are referred to Seto (2018) to learn more about pedohebephilia, but the key details are that pedohebephilia is much more common in men than women, with my best guess being a 1% prevalence rate in the male population. Also, pedohebephilia can be thought of as a sexual orientation for age that is similar to sexual orientation for gender in the sense that there are neurodevelopmental precursors; the typical age of onset is in adolescence, after puberty; and it appears to be stable over the lifespan (Seto, 2012, 2017b). Importantly, when we discuss interventions in Chapters 7 (treatment) and 8 (prevention), there is only weak evidence that we can change pedohebephilia so that individuals are no longer sexually attracted to prepubescent or pubescent children. Instead, the focus of interventions has been to reduce the strength of the motivation through self-regulation (e.g., coping strategies when experiencing sexual urges), reduce the influence of facilitation factors and thus the likelihood of acting on sexual motivations (e.g., addressing offense-supportive cognitions), and increase protective factors that can buffer the person against the effects of these risk factors (positive social support). Some interventions also address situational factors through personal risk-management plans and professional monitoring (e.g., treatment check-ins, probation, or parole supervision with conditions about access to the internet or being with children without a responsible adult present).

An important finding from several community surveys is that only some people who report sexual interest in children have acted on that interest. Bártová et al. (2021) found significant and positive correlations between sexual interest in children and both CSEM use and other sexual behavior, with stronger correlations for other behavior. In contrast, the association between bondage, discipline, sadism, and masochism interests with pornography use and with other sexual behavior was similar. This result is counterintuitive to me because pornography use is less risky than contact sexual offending because it does not involve another person and is less likely to be detected or reported. We also found that there was a positive association between pedohebephilic interests and behavior in an online community sample (we did not distinguish between CSEM use and child contacts), but it was smaller for pedohebephilia than for other paraphilias such as sadism or masochism (Seto et al., 2021). Joyal and Carpentier (2022) reported that 0.6% of their sample reported a sexual interest in children and, of these individuals, two thirds had acted on this interest. Other paraphilias are relevant to online sexual offending as well. As discussed in Chapter 2, some paraphilic interests motivate seeking out illegal pornography content such as bestiality (zoophilia) or sexual violence (biastophilia or sexual sadism). Some acts of digital exhibitionism and voyeurism are motivated by the corresponding paraphilias. There is a significant and positive—though nowhere close to perfect—correspondence between a variety of paraphilic interests and their corresponding behaviors (Bártová et al., 2021; Joyal & Carpentier, 2022; Seto et al., 2021). An important caveat in interpreting these studies is they were all nonrepresentative samples recruited for surveys about a broad range of paraphilic interests and behavior.

Hypersexuality

Pedohebephilia is not the only sexual motivation for CSEM offending (Seto et al., 2010). Hypersexuality may be a valid explanation when someone honestly reports spending a lot of time viewing mainstream adult pornography, becoming habituated to this content, and then seeking increasingly taboo and then illegal content such as CSEM (corroborated by forensic digital evidence when available). Escalation of pornography use toward CSEM is consistently identified as one of the top three explanations by perpetrators (Merdian et al., 2013; Schaaf, 2022; Seto et al., 2010; Surjadi et al., 2010). I noted earlier that Seigfried-Spellar and Rogers (2013) found evidence that the use of pornography depicting bestiality or sexual violence preceded the use of CSEM, whereas Landripet et al. (2019) did not find evidence for escalation from mainstream to violent pornography use. Escalation of pornography use is plausible in some cases, though we do not have much more data than this, and we have sparse objective evidence about changes in pornography viewing over time, as could come from a forensic analysis of digital files and activities over time.

There is an obvious potential for self-report bias, where it is more palatable to claim that hypersexuality motivated the use of CSEM (or other online sexual offending) rather than pedohebephilia, given the huge stigma associated with being sexually attracted to children. I am more skeptical of a claim of hypersexuality as a motivation for CSEM offending involving content depicting prepubescent and pubescent children than for content depicting postpubescent adolescents. Why would someone look for younger child content[1] if they had no predisposition or existing sexual interest in this content, given that most men are not sexually interested in prepubescent or pubescent children and prefer sexually mature–looking persons (Seto, 2017b)? Hypersexuality is a more believable explanation if the person is in trouble for CSEM depicting underage but mature-looking adolescents because this is consistent with the sexual response gradient observed in men.

---

[1] I thank Lyne Piché (personal communication, October 19, 2023) for reminding me that pornography choices are not simply a result of active searching. Algorithms suggest videos and ads based on viewing behavior and history, so these algorithms can amplify choices. For example, someone searching for "college student" pornography might be served suggestions and ads for "cheerleader" or "babysitter" content and then content depicting petite, young-looking women with small or no breasts. Individuals who are high in impulsivity or hypersexuality may be more likely to click these suggestions and thus migrate over time toward faux CSEM or actual CSEM. This suggests that changes in these algorithms could deter engagement with CSEM.

In essence, my argument by analogy is this: Is there any evidence that hypersexual straight men engage in regular use of gay pornography, even though they report no sexual interest in men? Some heterosexual men may occasionally view gay pornography out of curiosity or a desire for novelty or might see gay pornography accidentally while searching for other content, but how many would return to this content repeatedly and accumulate large collections? Extending the analogy, many men may occasionally view unconventional or taboo pornography depicting fauxcest or faux CSEM ("high school girls"), but would they continue viewing this content if they realized it was, in fact, true depictions of incest or CSEM? Would they choose this content despite the plethora of novel adult pornography that is available online? At the same time, we know that behavior does not always reflect sexual interest, and thus, some pornography use may not reflect what the person is truly interested in (Bártová et al., 2021; Joyal & Carpentier, 2022; Seto et al., 2021).

Hypersexuality can be a plausible explanation for some sexual solicitations targeting underage adolescents. For example, someone who feels a compulsion to engage in a wide range of sexual interactions online might not be inhibited by the knowledge that the target is a minor or might even find it more exciting because it is taboo or illegal (but not stigmatized to the same extent as sexual interactions with a prepubescent or pubescent child). Similarly, someone who intentionally seeks sex with underage minors through sexual trafficking or sexual abuse tourism involving postpubescent adolescents is possibly motivated by hypersexuality and unlikely to be motivated by pedohebephilia.

Last, hypersexuality is not mutually exclusive of paraphilic interests. Someone could show signs of both—for example, by compulsively pursuing sexual outlets involving children despite negative social and other consequences or gradually moving from boundary-pushing content (e.g., barely legal "schoolgirl" pornography) to actual CSEM depicting adolescents and then CSEM depicting younger adolescents and then children.

Intense Mating Effort

Sociosexuality (referred to as "intense mating effort" in Seto, 2019, p. 3) describes individual differences in willingness to engage in casual sex (Simpson & Gangestad, 1991). Individuals with unrestricted sociosexuality are more likely to have casual sexual partners, seek novel partners, and have multiple partners and are less likely to seek or stay in committed sexual relationships. Sociosexuality is a relevant motivation for online sexual offending because individuals with less restricted sociosexuality would be expected to be more active on dating and hookup apps and platforms and more likely to interact with older adolescents or adults online in the hope it may lead to casual sex. Sociosexuality is not significantly correlated with sex drive, so it is distinct from hypersexuality. Lalumière and Quinsey (1996) found that men who were less restricted in sociosexuality were more likely to engage in sexually coercive behavior, so sociosexuality may be important in technology-facilitated sexual assaults.

Facilitation

The motivation–facilitation model suggests that facilitation factors are key in understanding if and when someone will act on their motivations for online sexual offending (Seto, 2019). Individuals who are high in both motivation and facilitation factors are at the greatest risk of offending. There is a calculus across motivation and facilitation in that someone who is highly motivated may require relatively lower levels of facilitation to act, whereas someone who is less motivated may only act when facilitation factors are strong. Both motivation and facilitation factors can be dynamic, changing due to time, situation, and other influences.

Antisociality

I use *antisociality* as a broad umbrella term for multiple, correlated facilitation factors. Antisociality factors include antisocial personality traits such as impulsivity, callousness, and risk taking; offense-supportive cognitions such as the belief that children can benefit from sexual interactions with adults; and lifestyle instability in terms of occupation (education and employment), housing, and social networks (family and friends). Individuals who are impulsive, callous, or high in risk taking are more likely to act on sexual urges than individuals who are reflective, empathic, or low in risk tolerance. Individuals who endorse offense-supportive attitudes and beliefs are more likely to act because they see their behavior as less egregious or culpable. Finally, individuals with high life instability have less to lose for sexual offending than someone with a steady job, strong family and friend relationships, and a positive reputation in their communities. These factors are correlated because individuals high in antisocial personality traits are more likely to espouse (or admit) offense-supportive attitudes and beliefs and are more likely to have unstable relationships, employment, and community involvement. Many of these factors are discussed in more depth in the next chapter.

On average, online CSEM perpetrators are lower on measures of antisocial personality traits and offense-supportive cognitions than contact perpetrators (Babchishin et al., 2011, 2015). This might be a level of antisociality sufficient to facilitate committing CSEM offenses but not high enough to facilitate contact offenses, including online solicitation offenses that result in in-person meeting, technology-facilitated sexual assault of adults, or commercial sexual exploitation of minors through trafficking or tourism.

Something that was not explicitly incorporated in the original motivation–facilitation model is the idea that the level of facilitation required to act on motivations depends on the level of inhibition, and the level of inhibition depends on the severity of the behavior. In this revision of the model, the level of facilitation required for accessing CSEM is expected to be lower than for distributing or producing CSEM, lower for nonproduction CSEM offending than fantasy-driven sexual solicitation that involves some direct interaction with a minor, and lower for fantasy-driven sexual solicitation than for technology-facilitated contact offending. This logic can apply to other online sexual offending;

for example, fantasy-driven solicitation, where there is no attempt to meet in person, should require less facilitation for offending behavior than showing up to meet a solicitation target.

Situational Facilitation

Babchishin et al. (2023) discussed how situational risk factors may play a relatively more important role in CSEM offending than contact offending because the steps from interest to behavior are shorter for CSEM offending. For example, someone who is sexually interested in children can act on that interest by returning to websites (once they are discovered) to access more CSEM. The risk of being detected for this criminal behavior is statistically low, given the number of CSEM users at any given time and the limits on law enforcement and tech company resources. This means less facilitation is required to act on the sexual interest in children. In contrast, contact offending means seeking opportunities to commit an offense. Even if the victim is already known or shares a residence, it still requires efforts to avoid detection by others, prevent disclosure by the victim, and engage in the criminal behavior. Offenses can be impulsive, and situational factors still matter—for example, waiting until no responsible adults are present—but sustained facilitation is probably required for contact offending.[2]

Problematic Internet Use

Problematic internet use does not motivate online sexual offending. Indeed, Marx et al. (2021) found that CSEM users were online less and reported less compulsive internet use than comparison groups of people concerned about their online pornography use or their online gaming. Problematic internet use is not a facilitation factor either unless it is an expression of facilitation factors such as thrill seeking or risk taking. Instead, problematic internet use could be viewed as an opportunity factor because someone who is online a lot necessarily has more chances to commit online sexual offenses than someone who is rarely online. Indeed, one of the hallmark needs of CSEM perpetrators in the clinical literature is internet self-regulation deficits in addition to sexual self-regulation deficits (e.g., Piché & Schweighofer, 2023; see Chapter 7, this volume).

Some perpetrators claim problematic pornography use, typically defined as excessive or compulsive use of pornography that can also include extreme or even illegal content. Soldino et al. (2021) examined data from 100 Spanish men who had sexually offended. A third was excluded for socially desirable responding, which unfortunately reduced the statistical power to detect significant effects in this study and may have excluded higher risk individuals, given that risk to reoffend is positively correlated with socially desirable responding in general offending research (Mills & Kroner, 2005). In the remaining sample,

---

[2] I thank Kelly Babchishin for pointing out this argument and elaborating on it in her review of an earlier draft of this manuscript.

those who had committed online sexual offenses scored higher on an online sexual addiction questionnaire than those who had exclusively committed contact sexual offenses. Thorne (2020) analyzed self-report data from an online sample of 119 individuals who reported having sexual thoughts about children 10% or more of the time they had sexual thoughts. Use of CSEM was uncorrelated with age of first pornography use, but it was significantly correlated with younger age at first masturbation and having sexual experiences with peers as a child.

The fact that some CSEM perpetrators attribute their offending to problematic pornography use or a broader problem of sexual addiction or compulsivity does not mean it is true. Research by Grubbs et al. (2019) and others has found that many individuals who self-report concerns about problematic pornography use do not differ in their frequency of pornography use or other use parameters from those who do not report concerns. Instead, the problematic pornography use group differs in terms of having moral or religious qualms about pornography use and relationship problems connected to their use of pornography.

METHODOLOGICAL ISSUES

In this section, I discuss several important methodological issues to consider in reviewing and interpreting the research evidence described in this book. Some of them are fundamental to this literature and have already been mentioned. For example, most of what we know about online sexual offending comes from detected offending, particularly in clinical and forensic studies of perpetrators, and we do not know whether the results generalize to undetected offending. It is likely that perpetrators who are savvier about encryption and other security countermeasures are less likely to be detected by police or other authorities and, thus, less likely to be in clinical or forensic samples. This may explain the perhaps surprisingly low rates of countermeasures identified in many studies, including the National Juvenile Online Victimization research (Steel et al., 2020a; Wolak et al., 2012). Detected perpetrators may differ in other important ways from undetected perpetrators as well. For example, detected perpetrators might be more impulsive, reckless, or careless and, therefore, differ on these risk- and intervention-relevant traits from those who remain undetected. We might also expect that the likelihood of detection is correlated with the frequency or persistence of online sexual offending, where those who engage in high levels of illegal behavior are more likely to be detected than sporadic perpetrators. For all we know, detected perpetrators may represent the tip of the iceberg in terms of numbers, seriousness of their behavior, and potential impacts on victims. Anonymous surveys of undetected perpetrators and victimization reports are therefore critical in attempting to fill in the gaps.

Besides security precautions and the frequency and persistence of online sexual offending, there may also be other selection biases that affect our understanding of perpetrator characteristics. For example, anonymous surveys that recruit via online forums people who are sexually attracted to children seem to recruit a higher proportion of individuals who report being attracted to boys compared with clinical or forensic samples. This implies that those who are attracted to boys are more likely to belong to forums or volunteer for research; conversely, it may be the case that those who are attracted to boys are less likely to end up in clinical and forensic settings—for example, if boys are less likely to disclose their victimization to the police. Given the importance of child gender preferences for the assessment of pedophilia and the risk of sexual recidivism, this affects our interpretation of research conducted using online forums. For example, in research on pedophilia and sexual offending against children (Seto, 2018), those who prefer boys are more likely to be pedophilic (Seto & Lalumière, 2001; Seto, Stephens, et al., 2017) and more likely to sexually reoffend (Hanson & Bussière, 1998; Hanson & Morton-Bourgon, 2005). This implies research using online forums may overestimate risk and stigma in samples of all child-attracted persons.

I have already discussed how CSEM perpetrator samples skew toward those with an interest in prepubescent or pubescent children because age estimation is less reliable with older adolescents, and thus, someone without any identified CSEM victims might not be prosecuted because it could not be determined with sufficient confidence whether the images are of a sexually mature looking minor or an immature looking young adult. Online solicitation cases skew toward those involving undercover police officers because those involving real minors are unlikely to be reported to police—unless detected by parents or other responsible adults—especially if it is a statutory sexual offending situation, where the young person sees themself as being in a relationship with the older person (see Thorn, 2022). Telling parents is embarrassing and might result in negative consequences (from the point of view of the young person), such as more rules or loss of access to devices or apps, and there is cynicism about the impact of reporting to tech companies (and the youths may view it as too severe a consequence if the solicitor is known). Sexual solicitations could involve younger children if younger children were online and unsupervised by parents or teachers.

I raised in Chapter 3 the caveat that many analyses of online grooming tactics—including linguistic analyses—are based on transcripts of cases involving undercover police officers or vigilantes, which may differ in meaningful ways from interactions involving real minors. In particular, undercover operators can pretend to be young children (under age 12) who are active online and interacting with strangers, and so more cases involve individuals interested in young children. In contrast, Wolak et al.'s (2008) summary of research on solicitation cases involving real minors rather than undercover officers suggests that most solicitation targets are between the ages of 12 and 15, with a modal age of 13; solicitation targets below the age of 12 are rare. Also, undercover police are likely to be less cautious if they are pretending to be another perpetrator (e.g., interested in trading CSEM); though they may show some caution to be realistic, they are also attempting to maintain engagement. However, undercover police are reluctant to send CSEM images, unlike real children who might initiate conversations or who can be persuaded or coerced into sending self-generated CSEM. Consistent with this speculation, Schneevogt et al. (2018) compared logs of all 622 archived Perverted Justice interactions with interactions involving real children and found there were linguistic differences, where perpetrators interacting with adult decoys are unlikely to use overt persuasion or extortion. Finally, child sexual abuse tourism is likely to skew toward wealthier individuals who can afford to travel internationally to commit contact sexual offenses against children.

For online target research, targets who respond to surveys or report their experiences to police or technology companies may be more distressed or concerned about what happened, which may mean more serious cases are selected for study or that the impacts of online sexual offending are overestimated because those who were not bothered by what happened are underrepresented in the research. This is suggested by the Thorn (2022) research described in previous chapters, where most minor targets do not report their experiences to parents, police, or tech companies, instead opting to block perpetrator accounts.

It is important to acknowledge that the motivation–facilitation model and other models of online sexual offending are derived from clinical and criminal justice research, which might capture those who offend more persistently or compulsively. We might expect a higher proportion of paraphilias and hypersexuality in these samples. In contrast, we might see more transient motivations in community samples, with larger representations of curiosity, risk taking, or other motivations. Indeed, we can compare the results of the clinical and forensic studies reviewed in this book with the large darknet survey sample from Insoll et al. (2022). In this survey, where self-report bias might be less pronounced because respondents were anonymous and would not face negative consequences for admitting atypical motivations, 70% said they first saw CSEM before age 18, and almost 40% said this was before age 13. Yet more than half of these respondents said their first CSEM exposure was accidental, meaning they did not search for CSEM. From this survey, we might hypothesize that there is a higher prevalence of atypical sexual motivations in clinical and criminal justice settings and a lower prevalence in the general community. This, again, emphasizes the value of tech deterrence and other more scalable solutions in reducing the overall volume of offending behavior, paired with more intense interventions for those who are at greater risk of high frequency or persistence (see Chapters 7 and 8).

IS CSEM OFFENDING A GATEWAY OFFENSE?

My first online sexual offending study (Seto & Eke, 2005) began when I was asked about a surge of clinical referrals for CSEM offending, including questions about perpetrator characteristics, their risk of sexually offending, and their intervention needs. In particular, I was asked if CSEM use might be a gateway to contact sexual offending—for example, by inciting more sexual thoughts and feelings about children that might be acted on if there were opportunities.

The assumption that CSEM use increases the risk of contact sexual offending can be understood as part of a larger debate about the effects of adult pornography or violent pornography on the risk of committing sexual violence. Multiple systematic reviews have concluded that there are negative effects of mainstream pornography use on antisocial behavior, but much of this seems to involve individuals who already have a predisposition to antisocial behavior, such as nonsexual aggression and sexual aggression, suggesting an interaction rather than a main effect of pornography (Allen et al., 1995; Wright et al., 2016). In other words, violent pornography is not likely to increase the risk of sexual violence overall, just as most people can consume violent television, movies, or video games without significant harm. (Though it is important to point out that even small effects can have important impacts at the population level; see Carey et al., 2023.)

CSEM might be a step on the way to solicitation or contact sexual offending against children for some CSEM users, and there clearly is overlap in these different forms of offending, as discussed in Chapters 2 and 3. In particular, the Seto et al. (2011) meta-analysis found that one in eight detected CSEM perpetrators have a criminal record for contact sexual offending, and about half admit or are known to have committed contact sexual offenses in studies that included self-report information—for example through polygraph interviews or treatment disclosures. I have also discussed how dual perpetrators are the most likely to be pedohebephilic and are at higher risk of sexual recidivism than CSEM exclusive perpetrators (Seto & Eke, 2015). At the same time, most CSEM perpetrators do not go on to commit contact sexual offenses (Helmus et al., 2024; Seto et al., 2011). In Chapter 3, I pointed out how a minority of solicitation cases involve CSEM, either requests for self-generated CSEM, using CSEM for sextortion, sending CSEM as part of grooming, or producing CSEM as a souvenir of online or offline interactions.

A study conducted by Eke et al. (2019) looking at the temporal ordering of sexual offenses for men who had committed at least two distinct sexual offenses in their criminal history is relevant here. We looked at the first two recorded sexual offenses of 85 men from the combined sample and distinguished between those who committed CSEM offenses only (CSEM then CSEM; 40/85 = 47%), those who showed de-escalation (contact then CSEM, 35/85 = 42%), and those who showed escalation (CSEM then contact, which was a small minority of perpetrators, 10/85 = 12%). We then looked at whether they had a new sexual offense after these two sexual offenses in their histories. Both the stable and de-escalation groups were relatively low in sexual recidivism, and both groups were more likely to commit a new CSEM offense than a new contact offense if they did reoffend. In contrast, the escalation group had a higher sexual recidivism rate than the other two groups, and the escalation group was relatively more likely to commit a new contact sexual offense, about equal to their likelihood of a new CSEM offense (Babchishin et al., 2022).

SUMMARY

In this chapter, I argued that the motivation–facilitation model provides a useful theoretical and clinical framework for considering the factors that help explain online sexual offending, which is helpful for case formulation and then guiding assessment and treatment decisions. Many incidents of online sexual offending appear to be sexually motivated, either as a result of paraphilias, excessive sexual preoccupation, or intense mating effort. Whether someone acts on these sexual motivations depends on the level of trait and state facilitation factors that exist and opportunities to offend. Trait facilitation factors include antisocial personality traits and offense-supportive cognitions. State facilitation factors include intoxication and emotional stress.

Given that the motivation–facilitation model is based on what we know about the factors associated with both the onset and persistence of sexual offending more generally, I am confident that the motivation–facilitation model is relevant to online sexual offending as well. A caveat, however, is that this may only be true for detected perpetrators because the research underlying the motivation–facilitation model was based on detected perpetrators. It is unclear how well this model applies to the many individuals who have not been detected yet. Also, some forms of online sexual offending do not fit well within the motivation–facilitation model. In particular, online sexual offending that is singular or sporadic and not sexually motivated may not fit as well. This includes someone who sends unsolicited dick pics to a specific individual to bully or troll them, someone who shares images of someone to humiliate and hurt them, and someone who engages in sextortion for financial gain only.

In extending the motivation–facilitation model from Seto (2019), there is a balancing of motivation and facilitation factors in that someone with strong motivations to sexually offend online will require less facilitation than someone with weaker motivations. Similarly, someone who is high in facilitation factors may require less motivation to act than someone who is relatively low. Finally, the motivation–facilitation model suggests higher thresholds for both motivation and facilitation factors for online sexual offending to occur, depending on the relative seriousness of the online sexual offending, both across and within forms. For example, across forms, I would expect stronger motivations and/or stronger facilitation factors in someone who engages in contact sexual offending against adults or children than someone who engages in online interactions only, as in accessing CSEM or other illegal pornography or engaging in fantasy-driven solicitation exclusively. Within forms, I would expect someone who produces CSEM by recording a child or by sexually soliciting a child to be higher on motivation and/or facilitation than someone who views CSEM, and

I would expect someone who engages in contact-driven solicitation to similarly be higher on motivation and/or facilitation than someone who exclusively engages in fantasy-driven solicitation.

CASE EXAMPLE FORMULATIONS

In the following sections, I return to hypothetical case examples introduced in previous chapters to suggest clinical conceptualizations of these cases in light of the motivation–facilitation model and factors discussed in this chapter. These conceptualizations anchor my suggestions in the next chapters regarding assessment and intervention for these cases.

Adam (Lower Risk CSEM)

Adam invoked problematic pornography use and excessive sexual preoccupation as explanations for his CSEM offending, where he consistently claimed pornography was used excessively to cope with his negative emotions and then escalated over time. Despite his denial, the evaluator suspected pedophilia, given the persistence of his use and focus on prepubescent and pubescent children instead of a broader range of taboo and illegal content such as BDSM, bestiality, and other paraphilic themes. Adam was not diagnosed with pedophilic disorder, however. Adam was low on antisociality factors overall, with little evidence of antisocial behavior in his history beyond the two minor charges as a juvenile and his low scores on measures of antisocial personality traits. His low level of antisociality helped explain why he had not committed any direct sexual offenses (contact or noncontact). The clinical interview revealed that his use of pornography increased when he was using alcohol or drugs (state facilitation). The other major factor identified in the evaluation was problematic internet use, given how much time Adam spent online compared with his peers, which increased his situational risk in terms of the opportunity to access illegal content.

Bart (Higher Risk CSEM)

There was consistent and robust evidence that Bart met the diagnostic criteria for pedophilic disorder. Like Adam, Bart was also relatively low on antisociality, suggesting little facilitation was required for Bart to act on his sexual interest in children by contact offending as a juvenile and then persistent CSEM offending as a juvenile and continuing into adulthood. Bart denied any additional contact child victims, no victims came forward when his CSEM offending was announced in local news, and there were no police or court documents suggesting further adjudications as a juvenile or adult. Bart explained that he did not commit any further contact sexual offenses because he limited his contact with children, given the consequences of his juvenile adjudication, despite his romantic attraction to children and emotional congruence with children. Bart's CSEM offending was clearly facilitated by his active involvement in darknet forums, which allowed him to trade CSEM with a large number of other CSEM users. His role as a moderator also gave him social status in this online community, which Bart acknowledged was meaningful to him because he felt like a "nobody" in his life offline. Bart expressed a range of offense-supportive cognitions in his clinical interviews, including his view that CSEM was a safe substitute for contact offending, that the harm done to victims was not compounded by his viewing CSEM, and that some children agreed to be recorded and seemed happy in the images and videos.

Sean (Sexual Solicitation)

Sean acknowledged that he had a long-standing interest in adolescents around the legal age of consent, suggesting he may have ephebophilia, a sexual attraction to postpubescent adolescents who were not yet sexually mature (see Seto, 2017b, for chronophilias). However, this interest was not exclusive because he also reported an interest in adults and had been in several adult relationships. He reported using adult pornography on occasion. In addition to this sexual motivation for his online solicitations of both known and unknown adolescents, Sean was high in facilitation factors, particularly antisocial personality traits such as impulsivity, recklessness, and irresponsibility. As noted, he had an extensive nonsexual offending history, and he admitted to impulsive and antisocial behavior from a young age, including his unstable employment record.

Elvis (Digital Exhibitionism)

Elvis was suspected of having a paraphilic interest in exhibitionism, but there was no evidence that he had ever exposed himself to an unsuspecting person offline, and he denied any sexual motivation for his behavior except indirectly, in that he hoped someone would respond and send him nudes. The evaluator decided it was inconclusive if Elvis met the diagnostic criteria for exhibitionistic disorder. There was evidence that his online sexual offending was facilitated by technological affordances (the ease of connecting with strangers online and the ease with which unsolicited images could be sent from seemingly anonymous user accounts) and by Elvis's emotional immaturity.

Vince (Digital Voyeurism)

Vince's admission that he was sexually aroused by the idea of observing unsuspecting women undress, that he masturbated when he watched the videos he secretly recorded, and that he had been doing this for more than 6 months was taken as sufficient evidence that Vince met the diagnostic criteria for voyeuristic disorder (American Psychiatric Association, 2022). Later, in treatment, Vince admitted that he had begun engaging in voyeuristic behavior as an adolescent when he would trespass at night and try to watch adolescent girls or women through their windows. Vince also admitted during treatment that he regularly viewed voyeuristic content online, especially content posted on forums claiming to be content of real unsuspecting targets (as opposed to pornography that depicted voyeurism themes but clearly involved paid adult actors). Acting on this paraphilic motivation was facilitated by Vince's poor sexual and general self-regulation deficits; he knew he was putting himself in social and legal jeopardy but nonetheless felt compelled to install a spy camera to act on his sexual fantasies and obtain sexual gratification as a result.

Jack (Nonconsensual Sharing and Sextortion)

Jack denied ever receiving images in his prior relationships with two girls he dated in high school. Both girls were in the same grade as him at the time. He initially denied using controlling behavior with his ex-partner, but he eventually acknowledged that he was jealous and worried that she would cheat on him or leave him for someone else. He described being devastated when the victim left and said he impulsively uploaded the images of her because he was feeling angry and wanted to hurt her. He expressed regret for doing this but simultaneously minimized the harm because the website took down the images he posted after legal action was taken. He did not answer when asked about the impact of his actions on his ex-partner and when he was asked about the possibility that other forum users had already downloaded (and possibly shared) the images that Jack posted.

Jack stated that his apparently nonsexual motivation to share images of his ex-partner was to hurt her as an act of revenge. The evaluation identified major facilitation factors, including Jack's hostile and adversarial views of women, both in general and specific to his ex-partner; impulsivity; and jealous and controlling behavior toward his ex-partner as well as previous dating partners.

Adrian (Technology-Facilitated Sexual Assault)

The clinical evaluation did not reveal any evidence that Adrian had a paraphilic motivation for the sexual assaults he committed in that he denied it, and objective testing of his sexual arousal patterns did not indicate any interest in sexual coercion (biastophilia) or causing victims harm (coercive sexual sadism). He also denied having somnophilia, a paraphilia where someone is sexually aroused by the idea of having sex with an unconscious person. Instead, Jack's series of sexual assaults were seen as an expression of his high mating effort (sociosexuality), where he was highly motivated to seek casual sex with novel partners and was willing to provide alcohol or drugs to gain the compliance of the victims. Adrian repeatedly minimized his culpability by pointing out he was often drunk or high at the time.

Smith (Commercial Sexual Exploitation of Children)

Smith was confidently deemed to meet the diagnostic criteria for pedophilic disorder and hebephilic disorder, given his history of CSEM offending and contact sexual offending against children. In addition to pedophilia and hebephilia, Smith reported experiencing a romantic attraction to children and emotional congruence with children. He minimized his culpability for his offenses by explaining how he had romantic feelings for the children he sexually exploited and that he made sure they were treated well. He also made a point of saying that he was never violent and that the children participated willingly. Smith's sexual motivations to engage in CSEM and contact offending were facilitated by many offense-supportive cognitions, including his belief that the children participated willingly, that they knowingly benefited from his actions by earning enough money to support their families, and that the countries he went to knowingly tolerated trafficking and tourism for these economic benefits.

6

Risk and Other Clinical Assessment of Online Sexual Offending Perpetrators

In this chapter, I review assessment approaches and domains to focus on during the clinical and risk assessment of individuals who have committed online sexual offenses. Again reflecting the research evidence, most of the chapter focuses on the clinical and risk assessment of individuals who have committed child sexual exploitation material (CSEM) offenses. However, I do discuss the assessment of other forms of online sexual offending using existing sexual offending risk-assessment tools.

I organize the content of this chapter according to the factors reviewed in the previous chapter on etiology and using the risk–need–responsivity framework described by Bonta and Andrews (2024) with regard to effective correctional rehabilitation. The risk–need–responsivity framework has been repeatedly shown to be important in designing and delivering effective interventions to reduce future offending. In brief, the *risk principle* states that interventions are more effective when titrated to the risk of reoffending, where low-intensity interventions are not sufficient for relatively high-risk individuals and high-intensity interventions are unnecessary for those who are at relatively low risk and may even be harmful. The *need principle* states that interventions are more effective when they focus on factors associated with reductions in future offending. Treatment of depression or anxiety symptoms may improve client well-being, for example, but will not directly reduce future offending because neither depression nor anxiety is a risk factor for future offending (though they may be indirectly related to the risk of offending, when, for example, the individual uses illegal sexual behavior to cope with these unpleasant feelings).

---

https://doi.org/10.1037/0000428-007
Online Sexual Offending: Theory, Practice, and Policy, Second Edition, by M. C. Seto
Copyright © 2025 by the American Psychological Association. All rights reserved.

Finally, the *responsivity principle* states that interventions are more effective when they are structured, cognitive behavioral in orientation, concrete, and tailored to the individual. Someone with reading difficulties, for example, is less likely to benefit from an intervention that relies on a great deal of written material and exercises than an intervention that involves more visual aids and in vivo interactions. Following this risk–need–responsivity framework, I first discuss what we know about risk assessment because it can inform intervention decisions, both in terms of intensity of intervention (risk principle) and what interventions focus on (need principle). I then discuss clinical assessment domains that go into more depth about what interventions need to address (need principle) and how interventions are delivered (responsivity principle).

RISK ASSESSMENT

Because risk assessment is a big topic covered in much detail in the sexual offending literature, I provide only a high-level overview of fundamental risk assessment concepts here. This overview will set the foundation for summarizing what we know about factors associated with sexual recidivism among those who have committed online sexual offenses and then describing the development and independent validation of the Child Pornography Offender Risk Tool, an offense-specific risk tool for men who have committed CSEM offenses (Seto & Eke, 2015). Fundamental risk concepts include the distinction between actuarial and structured assessment approaches, the distinction between static and dynamic risk factors, the concept of protective factors, and how risk information is relevant to the risk–need–responsivity framework. Readers interested in a deeper dive should check out Otto and Douglas (2011), Harris et al. (2015) for violence risk assessment, and Hanson (2022) for prediction analyses and statistics.

Risk Assessment Approaches

Broadly speaking, online or offline sexual offending risk assessments are unstructured, structured, or actuarial. *Unstructured* risk assessment involves assessing the person and using an idiosyncratic model—based on the evaluator's training, experience, and biases—to estimate the likelihood of someone reoffending. It is unstructured because the personal model is not consistent across evaluators because each evaluator develops their own model, may not be consistent from case to case, and might not even be explicitly acknowledged by the evaluator. Unstructured risk assessment was universal before the development and validation of risk assessment tools using a structured or actuarial approach. This form of unstructured judgment is inaccurate (Monahan, 1981) for multiple human reasons, including cognitive biases that affect subjective judgments, such as the primacy effect, recency effect, and saliency (Gigerenzer & Gaissmaier, 2011; Kahneman & Tversky, 1977). Even if evaluators pay attention to relevant risk information, such as criminal history, they may also pay attention to irrelevant information, such as expressions of remorse or guilt, or they may suboptimally weigh information, such as considering criminal history to be less relevant for sexual recidivism than someone's age.

Structured professional judgment tools are an improvement over unstructured judgments because they restrict the information that is considered in the risk assessment so that all evaluators are considering the same set of information. Information can be static (historical or unchanging) or dynamic (naturally changing over time or due to an intervention). This information is typically combined subjectively to arrive at an opinion about risk. Constraint is important partly because now the person has to explain what they considered and how it is relevant instead of facing the black box of their mind. However, structured measures do not produce probabilistic estimates, still allow evaluators to combine information idiosyncratically, and do not explicitly consider the optimal weighting of risk-related information.

Actuarial measures such as the Static-99R (Hanson & Thornton, 1999)—the most commonly used tool in the sexual offending field (Kelley et al., 2020)—are usually composed of static (unchangeable) risk factors that can be combined empirically to provide probabilistic statements about the likelihood of sexual recidivism. Static factors can include historical factors, such as criminal history, and factors that do not change or cannot be changed through intentional intervention, such as current age or criminal history. These tools are actuarial in the same sense that insurance is actuarial, where large data sets are analyzed to identify the important, unique correlates of an outcome of interest. For example, car insurance is actuarial: Insurers determine the appropriate premium to charge customers given the estimated probability that customers will make a claim (for a collision, theft, or other insured loss) in a specified period, based on empirically established risk factors such as driver age, gender, typical mileage, make and model of car driven, and any previous claims. Similarly, an oncologist can actuarially estimate the probability of someone surviving cancer over a specified time by relying on factors such as patient age, gender, type of cancer, and cancer stage. The relevance and weight of each factor can be determined from analyses of large data sets, allowing insurers to determine the unique associations of each risk factor for claims, estimate weights, and derive precise probabilistic estimates.

In the sexual offending field, we now have cumulatively large data sets that help us identify the most important risk factors for sexual recidivism (Hanson & Bussière, 1998; Hanson & Morton-Bourgon, 2005; Whitaker et al., 2008). The meta-analysis by Hanson and Morton-Bourgon (2009) suggested that actuarial and structured risk assessments are both moderately accurate. Hanson and Morton-Bourgon (2009) concluded that actuarial measures produce higher predictive accuracies than structured measures in sexual offending risk assessment, whereas Singh et al. (2011) found that actuarial and structured measures were similar when both violent and general recidivism was included. However, structured assessment tools tend to be more popular with evaluators more generally (e.g., nonsexual violence risk assessment) because they allow more user autonomy (Otto & Douglas, 2011). Viljoen et al. (2021) pointed out that direct comparisons of actuarial, structured, and unstructured assessments—with the same samples in the same settings—are needed (e.g., Wertz et al., 2023).

The field is clearly aligned with actuarial and structured approaches, which I cover in this section. Many such tools exist, and some are widely used to assess risk for future violence, including sexual violence (Kelley et al., 2020; Singh et al., 2011). However, the research base is much more limited for online sexual offending. Later in this chapter, I discuss the assessment tools that have been evaluated.

Static Versus Dynamic Factors

More is known about static than dynamic risk factors (Harris et al., 2015). As I have already noted, static factors either cannot change (e.g., criminal history) or cannot change as a result of intervention (e.g., age). Static factors have the advantage over dynamic factors for longer term prediction, such as the risk of sexual recidivism over 5 or 10 years, but static factors cannot directly inform intervention decisions. Dynamic factors—factors that fluctuate naturally or can change as a result of intervention—have an advantage over static factors in the short term, and they can more directly inform intervention decisions because they can comprise treatment targets that can be periodically reassessed. We also need to pay attention to situational factors, especially in treatment or supervision situations, which can be more stable over time (e.g., having internet access) or less so (e.g., a responsible adult nearby).

An important note about dynamic risk factors is that to be truly dynamic, it is not sufficient to show that one's score on a putatively dynamic risk factor, such as offense-supportive cognitions, can predict sexual recidivism. Because this factor is measured at a single point, the score is not dynamic; instead, it represents someone's cognitions at a single point, which becomes a static factor in the future. To be dynamic, it is necessary to reassess the factor periodically and show that changes in scores over time on a putative dynamic risk factor can predict sexual recidivism. It is also helpful to know if information about dynamic risk factors can add to the prediction of sexual recidivism using static risk factors. Some clinicians and researchers have argued that dynamic risk factors can be understood as time-dependent expressions of an underlying, more static risk factor (Harris et al., 2015). For example, someone's endorsement of offense-supportive cognitions about sex with children may be a time-dependent expression of a more enduring factor such as callousness. Someone's use of substances may be a time-dependent expression of a more enduring predisposition toward risk-taking. Fortuitously, van den Berg et al.'s (2018) meta-analysis found that dynamic risk factor scores can predict recidivism even after taking into account the prediction provided by static risk assessments, and changes in scores (in six studies) were related to recidivism. The effect sizes were modest, but still clinically meaningful.

Static and dynamic information can be simultaneously assessed using the same risk assessment tool or two different tools that fit the purpose. For example, the STABLE-2007 (Hanson et al., 2007) is a dynamic risk tool that provides incremental validity over the Static-99R, an actuarial and static risk assessment tool, and the results can be quantitatively combined according to the scoring guides (Brankley et al., 2021). The STABLE-2007 is typically scored every 6 months or after a major life event, and its predictive validity decreases with time since the last assessment (S. C. Lee et al., 2024). Another popular sexual offending risk assessment tool, the Violence Risk Scale–Sexual Offense Version (M. E. Olver, 2003) includes both static and dynamic risk items. Importantly, studies are showing that changes in dynamic item scores are associated with sexual recidivism, even after controlling for baseline risk (Eher et al., 2020; M. E. Olver et al., 2020). Empirically supported dynamic risk factors for contact sexual offending are summarized in Table 6.1, taken from Seto, Augustyn, et al. (2023). These risk factors are a valuable starting point for thinking about dynamic risk factors for online sexual offending. As we will see, there is a substantial overlap in the evidence so far.

Protective Factors

Since the first edition of this book, the field has started to pay more attention to protective factors (see Cording & Beggs Christofferson, 2017; de Vries Robbé et al., 2015; Nolan et al., 2023). Definitions are debated, but I argue that protective factors buffer someone against the effects of risk factors; they are not simply the absence of a risk factor. For example, having antisocial peers is a well-known dynamic risk factor, where individuals with many antisocial peers are more likely to reoffend than those with few such peers (Bonta & Andrews, 2024). The corresponding protective factor is having prosocial peers, which is protective because someone could have both antisocial and prosocial friends at the same time, where the prosocial friends can buffer the person against the criminogenic effects of the antisocial friends. The protective factor is not the absence of antisocial peers because someone could have no antisocial peers by having no friends at all. Indeed, the absence of friends can be a dynamic risk factor when experiencing loneliness, social isolation, and lack of social support. Several candidate protective factors have been suggested in sexual offending research, particularly in studies of the Structured Assessment of Protective Factors against Sexual Offending (SAPROF-SO; de Vogel et al., 2011), a sexual offending risk tool that includes protective factors as well as risk factors (Willis et al., 2021). Lifespan research on high-risk delinquent boys suggests that protective factors for general offending include a long-term, committed relationship and stable employment (Laub & Sampson, 2009).

In our review of dynamic risk and protective factors for sexual offending (generally, not specifically online), we identified positive social support as an empirically supported protective factor that can change over time. In a qualitative study, Farmer et al. (2012) concluded that social support distinguished individuals who were judged to be low risk from those who were judged to be at high risk of sexually reoffending. Farrington (2015) conducted a systematic review of outcome studies and concluded that positive social support from volunteers and professionals had a beneficial impact on sexual recidivism. Lasher and

TABLE 6.1. Dynamic Risk Factors for Contact Sexual Offending

Risk domain	Risk factor	Indicator(s)
Atypical sexuality	Sexual preoccupation	Thinking about sex and/or masturbating more than what is normative for age and gender; pursuit of casual, impersonal sex and disinterest in long-term or committed relationships; paying for sex
	Paraphilic sexual interests	Self-report, behavior, or phallometric results indicating sexual interest in prepubescent or pubescent children, coercive sex, or other offense-related paraphilias such as exhibitionism or voyeurism
Self-regulation problems	Impulsivity	A pattern of unplanned behavior seen across various contexts (e.g., financial, social, vocational, leisure)—for example, living from paycheck to paycheck, incurring gambling debts, leaving jobs without having another to go to, driving recklessly
	Lifestyle instability	Unstable employment, residence, or use of leisure time not due to circumstances outside one's control (e.g., poor job market)
	Emotional-regulation deficits	Intensity of negative emotional response is disproportionate to stressor or trigger; maladaptive coping strategies in response to emotions (e.g., substance use, interpersonal aggression, excessive sexual activity)
	Problem-solving deficits	Sets unrealistic goals; is unable to identify potential obstacles or problems, generate and evaluate reasonable solutions, or carry out a plan of action
Antisocial cognitions	Offense-supportive attitudes and beliefs	Data from self-report measures and/or inferences from statements about sexual offending suggestive of attitudes that support engagement in crime generally (e.g., grievance thinking), sexual offending in general (e.g., sexual entitlement), sexual offending against children (e.g., children enjoy sex), or sexual offending against adults (e.g., women wish to be raped if they dress provocatively)
	Hostile masculinity	Data from self-report measures and/or inferences from statements about women suggestive of adversarial gender beliefs (believing there is a battle of the sexes between men and women), hostility toward women (anger and suspicion targeted at women), and gender-role stereotyping
	Noncompliance with supervision and interventions	Poor attitudes about treatment or other interventions, demonstrated by not attending supervision or treatment meetings, not complying with any conditions, not willing to participate genuinely in intervention (e.g., withholding information, lying)
Relationship problems	Incapacity for adult intimacy	Absence of long-term relationships, dysfunctional intimate relationships (e.g., infidelity, conflict, abuse)
	Emotional congruence with children	Preference for the company of children and/or children's activities, identifies with children more than adults, sees children as friends or romantic partners
	Negative social influences	Peers engage in criminal behavior, are supportive of individual's offending, and/or interfere with the development of a prosocial lifestyle

Note. Data from Seto, Augustyn, et al. (2023).

McGrath (2017) concluded that social stability was an important protective factor, where social stability included positive social influences and stable employment, stable housing, problem-solving skills, and emotional regulation skills. A. Walker et al. (2020) found that stable family support was linked to lower rates of sexual recidivism, even after statistically controlling for major risk factors.

ACCUMULATING RISK KNOWLEDGE

In this section, I provide an overview of research on risk factors for sexual recidivism among online sexual offending cases to identify building blocks on the way to the development of online sexual offending risk tools. All this research has been conducted with CSEM perpetrators, which can suggest risk factor candidates for other forms of online offending that require empirical validation. The first building block is to know what the sexual recidivism base rates are.

Sexual Recidivism Rates

In the Seto et al. (2011) meta-analysis, we identified nine samples of mostly CSEM perpetrators with an average follow-up time of 3.4 years (total $N = 2,630$). Across studies, approximately 5% committed a new sexual offense of some kind, with most of these individuals being more likely to commit a new CSEM offense (3.4%) rather than a new contact sexual offense (2.1%). Several studies reported no sexual recidivism during their follow-up periods, which may be related to crime reporting rates, criminal justice processing, length of follow-up, or quality of their recidivism data sources. These rates are less than half of the aggregated sexual recidivism rates found in studies of contact perpetrators, with an aggregate rate of 13% after 4 or 5 years of opportunity (Hanson & Bussière, 1998; Hanson & Morton-Bourgon, 2005). There have been multiple follow-up studies since the Seto et al. (2011) meta-analysis, generally finding that sexual recidivism rates among CSEM perpetrators are lower than for contact perpetrators. Goller et al. (2016) reported a large national cohort sample, bigger than all the other samples combined, with 4,249 individuals convicted of illegal pornography offenses (mostly CSEM offenses) and 363 dual perpetrators. Their sexual recidivism rates after 3 years were low, at 0.2% and 2.6%, respectively, but there was clearly a difference between dual and illegal pornography perpetrators. Notably, there are no recidivism studies from Global South countries; all the studies in Seto et al.'s (2011) review and those published since that review have been conducted in Global North countries such as Canada, the United States, the United Kingdom, and nations in the European Union.

Only one juvenile recidivism study has been published so far (Aebi et al., 2014), with a small sample of only 54 youths who committed CSEM offenses compared with a larger group of youths who had committed other illegal pornography offenses (bestiality, sexual violence, or excrement). The sexual recidivism rates were low in this study, with 1.9% of the youths who committed CSEM offenses committing any kind of new sexual offense and 2.4% of the youths who committed other illegal pornography offenses. Their combined rate of 2.1% was not notably different from the 2.4% of youths in Aebi et al. who committed direct offenses against children or peers.

An unpublished systematic review by Helmus (2023) updated the meta-analysis by Seto et al. (2011) by integrating these additional studies. Importantly, there was a difference when distinguishing CSEM perpetrators by contact offending history; dual perpetrators were at the highest risk, with a 10% sexual recidivism rate, and were more likely to commit contact offenses than CSEM offenses, whereas those with any other kind of criminal history were more likely to commit CSEM offenses than contact offenses. The key conclusions from this updated meta-analysis by Helmus (2023) are (a) CSEM perpetrators are lower risk, on average, than contact perpetrators, according to the aggregated recidivism rates reported in the Hanson and Bussière (1998) and Hanson and Morton-Bourgon (2005) meta-analyses, because they had an average sexual recidivism rate that was less than half of that found for offline perpetrators in a similar time frame; (b) dual perpetrators were the highest risk group, followed by CSEM-exclusive perpetrators and those with other kinds of criminal history; and (c) CSEM and contact sexual recidivism rates were similar for CSEM-exclusive perpetrators, CSEM recidivism was higher for those with other criminal history, and contact recidivism was higher for dual perpetrators.

This recidivism research has multiple implications for policy and practice. First, the focus on CSEM offending can be justified for many reasons, but the idea they are a high-risk group that is likely to go on and directly offend sexually against children is not supported by the sexual recidivism results. Second, the risk principle suggests that only a fraction of CSEM perpetrators require intensive intervention, and many individuals require low-intensity or no treatment (see Chapter 7). Third, we should prioritize dual perpetrators in our intervention strategies because they have also committed contact offenses, and (as we will see later in this chapter) they are at higher risk of sexually reoffending. We should also prioritize CSEM production offending because that usually involves some kind of direct interaction with a child, whether recording abuse or convincing a child to self-generate images. Last, we should pay more attention to other online offending groups; a study from Australia (Dowling et al., 2021) suggests solicitation perpetrators are at higher risk to sexually reoffend than contact perpetrators, though this is only the first recidivism study for solicitation offending.

The contact sexual recidivism rates reported in the studies reviewed by Helmus (2023) might not have taken pseudo-recidivism into account, which would mean that true contact recidivism rates are lower than reported. I use the term *pseudo-recidivism* to refer to new charges or convictions that result from historical sexual offenses coming to light when someone has been detected for CSEM offending. For example, someone charged with possessing CSEM might be mentioned in a local news story, which may cause a previously undetected contact victim to come forward and report their experience to the police. It is not possible to determine if new charges or convictions represent historical offenses from criminal records alone; inspection of police and court documents is typically necessary. The study we reported in Eke et al. (2011) stands out because we were able to access police reports, not only national criminal records, to determine the nature of the offending behavior and, thus, count pseudo-recidivism. Historical sexual offenses should be addressed for the sake of victims and justice, but the risk principle is driven by the risk of future behavior, not future adjudication for prior behavior (though adjudications are how we usually measure recidivism). We found that over a third of new contact sexual charges or convictions in Eke et al. were, in fact, for historical offenses. Of the 34 men in Eke et al. who were charged for contact sexual offenses during the follow-up period, 13 (38%) were charged for historical sexual offenses that came to light after their index CSEM offending. At the same time, our high-quality information was also able to detect recidivism that might not have been counted if relying solely on criminal records (e.g., new nonsexual charges that, in fact, were laid for sexually motivated behavior).

Initial Empirically Established Risk Factors

The first empirically established risk factor was criminal history, and this is no surprise given that criminal history has always been relevant across different offending groups, jurisdictions, and time, as well as across demographic characteristics such as gender, age, and mental disorder status (Bonta & Andrews, 2024). Because of this robust evidence, in Seto and Eke (2005), the first-ever peer-reviewed recidivism study following men convicted of a CSEM offense, we looked at whether someone having any criminal history was relevant. We found that whether someone had any criminal history was associated with all outcomes, including conditional release failure, general recidivism, and, specifically, sexual recidivism. Criminal history has continued to be relevant in other follow-up research of CSEM perpetrators (Cohen, 2023; Eke et al., 2011; Howard & Wakeling, 2021; Wakeling et al., 2011).

In Eke et al. (2011), we followed the sample reported in Seto and Eke (2005), expanding the sample to 541 men convicted of CSEM offenses, followed for an average of 4 years. A third committed any kind of new offense during the follow-up period, 7% committed a new CSEM offense, and 4% committed a new contact sexual offense. A further 2% were charged with historical contact sexual offenses that came to light following their CSEM conviction (so again, about one third of contact sexual recidivism was pseudo-recidivism). We found that younger age and, again, criminal history, particularly sexual offending history, predicted sexual recidivism. This study suggested three risk candidates to consider in a structured or actuarial risk assessment of CSEM perpetrators: perpetrator age, any criminal history, and sexual offending history. I also expect these factors to be risk relevant in other online sexual offending groups, such as solicitation offending and image-based offending, because the first two factors are essentially universal across types of crime, and sexual offending history is consistently an important risk factor in the larger sexual offending literature (Hanson & Bussière, 1998; Hanson & Morton-Bourgon, 2005).

As noted, Goller et al. (2016) found that dual perpetrators were more than 10 times as likely to sexually reoffend than illegal pornography perpetrators (2.6% vs. 0.2%). Dual perpetrators—those with both CSEM offending and contact sexual offending—are the most likely to be pedohebephilic. Sexual interest in children is also a robust risk factor for sexual recidivism among individuals who have committed contact or noncontact offenses against children, which suggests that sexual interest in children is a strong risk candidate for online sexual offending against children as well (Hanson & Bussière, 1998; Hanson & Morton-Bourgon, 2005).

Indeed, the sexual offending literature emphasizes the importance of atypical sexual interests, whether pedohebephilia for CSEM, hebephilia or ephebophilia (postpubescent adolescents) for solicitation, exhibitionism for some digital exhibitionistic behavior, voyeurism for some digital voyeuristic behavior, biastophilia (coercive sex) or sexual sadism (suffering, humiliation) for some technology-facilitated sexual assaults of adults, and again, hebephilia or ephebophilia for sexual trafficking and child sexual abuse tourism.

Candidates for an Offense-Specific Tool

This background accumulation of information about risk-relevant details informed our choice of candidate factors in developing the Child Pornography Offender Risk Tool (discussed in more detail later in this chapter). We expected atypical sexual interests to be relevant, so we tried to capture this in multiple ways: admissions of sexual interest in children, CSEM-to-adult pornography ratio, age and gender distributions of the minors depicted in CSEM, whether the content was organized (which might suggest the level of engagement), whether the person had stories or audio in addition to images or videos, and whether they created CSEM by morphing images (e.g., placing the face of a known child on the body of an unknown child in images obtained online). In addition to atypical sexual interests in children, we also coded whether the individual had pornography content that suggested other paraphilic sexual interests, such as biastophilia, zoophilia, sadism, or masochism.

We were also interested in other child content, not only CSEM, given Howitt's (1995) qualitative study finding that men who were sexually attracted to children created their own sexual content using legal images from magazines or other sources, partly because CSEM was harder to find in this early internet era and perhaps partly because of the fear of consequences. This is still the case; there are forum posts about creating content or using content that does not violate the law, such as anime or text CSEM in the United States. This can also include child content that is sexualized by users, such as YouTube videos of children engaging in yoga or gymnastics (Grannò et al., 2020). Users bookmark or like this content on YouTube and other apps or platforms to draw attention to child content for other users. In addition, McCarthy (2010) found that dual perpetrators were more likely to be exclusively interested in children, and they were also more likely to be accessing legal images of children, such as child modeling sites. Intuitively, having other child content that does not meet the legal definition of CSEM can still be evidence of sexual interest in children, just as adults who are interested in other adults may seek nonexplicit images of adults they find attractive, including adult models, adult celebrities, and the like. Having other child content may also indicate romantic attraction to children or emotional congruence with children.

Community Data

There is much less evidence regarding candidate risk factors for sexual recidivism in the general community outside of clinical or forensic settings. A reanalysis of the Swedish data reported by Seto et al. (2010) found that ever viewing depictions of adult–child sex was significantly associated with viewing violent pornography, suggesting commonalities in viewing illegal or atypical content (though the association of viewing adult–child sex with viewing depictions of sex with animals was positive but not statistically significant). Another significant correlate was social norms, represented by having friends who had viewed adult–child sex, friends' attitudes about adult–child sex, and being willing to join if a friend was having sexual contact with a child (all these correlations were significant and moderate in magnitude; Seto, Babchishin, et al., 2015). Self-reported interest in sex with a child was also correlated with viewing adult–child sex depictions, which is consistent with the clinical and forensic literature.

It is reasonable to assume that other risk and protective factors identified in clinical and forensic research are also relevant for community samples. Another possibility is that there are additional factors in the community that are not typically covered in the clinical and forensic literature. For example, the motivation–facilitation model, routine activities theory, and many other criminological theories predict that time spent online and where time is spent online are relevant situational factors because opportunity is a key consideration for any offending. Yet clinical and forensic research has focused on psychologically meaningful factors consistent with a clinical or forensic interest in individualized risk assessment, treatment planning, and service delivery.

RISK PRIORITIZATION TOOLS

In this section, I discuss risk assessment tools that have been adapted or developed for assessing individuals who have sexually offended (see also the scoping review by S. J. Brown (2024) which includes expert recommendations in addition to empirical evidence). Again, most of the data has been with CSEM perpetrators, and we do not know if these measures might be valid for other types of perpetrators.

Risk Matrix 2000

The first risk assessment validation study for online sexual offending that I am aware of was published by Wakeling et al. (2011), who examined a sexual offending specific risk assessment tool, the Risk Matrix 2000 (RM2000/S; Thornton et al., 2003), and a general risk tool, the Offender Group Reconviction Scale 3 (OGSR3; Howard et al., 2009), in a sample of 994 online (mostly CSEM) perpetrators after a 2-year follow-up, with a sexual reconviction rate of 3.1%; three quarters of new sexual offenses were internet-related. Both the RM2000/S and OGSR3 significantly predicted sexual recidivism, with predictive accuracies comparable to previous research using the RM2000/S. The OGRS3 worked even though it is a general recidivism risk tool, and online perpetrators scored lower than offline perpetrators on the OGRS3. Interestingly, a similar finding was reported by Cohen (2023), who compared the predictive accuracy of a general recidivism risk tool used in federal probation in the United States with the Child Pornography Offender Risk Tool (see later), a CSEM-specific risk assessment tool. Both the general and specific risk assessment tools were significantly and similarly predictive. In the Wakeling et al. (2011) study, the RM2000/S and OGSR3 combined to provide better prediction of violent (including contact sexual) recidivism, suggesting the mixture of general and sexual offending specific risk factors did better for this task. However, the predictive performance of the RM2000/S was driven by 26 people in the Very High Risk category, where there was no apparent difference in sexual recidivism across the other three risk categories. I infer from the RM2000/S items that individuals could not be put in the Very High Risk category without having committed contact offenses as well and, thus, being dual perpetrators.

Kent Internet Risk Assessment Tool–Version 2

The Kent Internet Risk Assessment Tool–Version 2 (KIRAT-2; Long et al., 2016) was developed as a prioritization tool for police by focusing on discriminative rather than predictive validity, where higher scores on the KIRAT-2 are associated with a higher likelihood of dual perpetration among suspects, given that law enforcement prioritizes identifying victims and intervening in ongoing contact offending. From a sample of 374 police files for men convicted of CSEM offenses between 2001 and 2013 (60% from Kent Police), Long et al. distinguished 170 cases who had an allegation or conviction of contact sexual offending from those with no known contact sexual offenses. The researchers coded 166 variables with good interrater reliability and generated a model that they validated in a 70:30 sample split. They identified 17 variables that fed into nine items in a four-step decision tree, where the first step determines the risk of dual perpetration from low to very high (four levels), and other steps modified this risk level: (a) previous allegations and convictions for sexual offenses; (b) access to children; (c) solicitation behavior; and (d) other criminal behavior, including intimate partner violence and substance abuse. The area under curve

(AUC)[1] was .89 in the generation sample and .91 in the entire sample; results were not reported for the validation sample on its own, but it must have been higher than in the general sample, given the entire sample value. The KIRAT-2 had higher sensitivity than specificity, where sensitivity reflects the number of dual perpetrators correctly identified as such according to their higher scores on the measure, and specificity reflects the number of non-dual perpetrators correctly identified according to their lower scores on the measure. This makes sense for a prioritization tool like the KIRAT-2, where 98% of dual perpetrators were allocated to higher risk levels, and 62% of CSEM perpetrators were allocated to lower risk levels. Though useful for distinguishing CSEM suspects who are likely to be dual perpetrators from others, I am unaware of any research examining the predictive validity of the KIRAT-2 or of any independent replication of these discriminative results.

OASys Sexual Reoffending Predictor–Internet Version

The United Kingdom's Ministry of Justice developed a brief prioritization tool, the OASys Sexual Reoffending Predictor–Internet Version (OSP/I; Howard & Wakeling, 2021), for CSEM perpetrators that is based solely on history of sanctions for sexual offenses, ultimately demonstrating that individuals with prior CSEM sanctions are at greater risk of further CSEM offending. Howard and Wakeling found that this internet offending modification of the OASys Sexual Reoffending Predictor measure used in U.K. corrections could significantly predict CSEM recidivism, with an AUC of .74, based on four descending levels of risk: multiple CSEM sanctions, single CSEM sanction, multiple contact sexual offense sanctions, and any other sexual offending sanctions. The AUC obtained suggests there is good predictive accuracy for a tool that simply ranks people according to the number and type of sexual offense sanctions they have. In the same report, Howard and Wakeling compared the RM2000/S and OSP/I in a large sample of 2,728 individuals convicted of sexual offenses, two thirds against children and 9% involving CSEM offending. The OSP/I was significantly related to new CSEM convictions (the base rate was 3.3%) in a mean 4.5-year follow-up for the entire sample, where most of the sample was low risk because they had no prior CSEM sanctions. The OSP/I did not significantly predict new contact sexual offenses (AUC = .49) but did significantly predict new CSEM convictions (AUC = .74) for the entire sample. The report did not specify how the OSP/I performed with the CSEM perpetrators only, but it likely still worked, given that the CSEM recidivism rates were 3.4%, 8.8%, and 32.4% in the medium, high, and very high-risk categories (so, excluding the low-risk category, which means no CSEM or contact sexual

---

[1] The area under the curve (AUC) is a useful statistic for expressing the predictive accuracy of a risk assessment tool (Hanson, 2022). The AUC can be described as the probability that a randomly chosen recidivism case has a higher score on the tool than a randomly chosen nonrecidivism case. Thus, an AUC of 50 represents chance prediction, and an AUC of 1.0 represents perfect prediction.

offense sanctions). Few people were assigned to the very high-risk category; if this risk group is combined with the high-risk group so that the OSP/I ranks those with zero sanctions, one sanction, or two or more sanctions, the risk of sexual recidivism is clearly driven by those with two or more sanctions. For the OSP/I, 47 cases were in the very high-risk level, where a third (32%) committed another CSEM offense, compared with 9%, 3%, and 1%, respectively, for the other three levels. Howard and Wakeling's study found that the OSP/C,[2] a general sexual offending risk assessment tool, did not work for CSEM prediction, and the RM2000/S had an AUC of .62, which was significant but not as good as the AUC for the OSP/I.

Static-99R

All the tools mentioned previously have been developed or evaluated for the risk assessment of CSEM perpetrators. Dual (CSEM and contact) perpetrators can be assessed using the Static-99R (Hanson & Thornton, 1999) and other tools developed for those who have directly offended against a victim, though the utility becomes less clear the longer it has been since the contact offenses were committed. Sexual solicitation perpetrators can be assessed using the Static-99R if there was some kind of direct interaction with a minor or undercover police officer posing as a minor (https://saarna.org/). The Static-99R or other well-known risk tools should still work for other forms of contact sexual offending facilitated by internet technologies, including sexual assaults of adults, child sexual trafficking, or child sexual abuse tourism. My logic is that these types of online sexual offenses also involve attempted or actual contact with victims. However, we do not yet have follow-up studies demonstrating that existing risk tools work for other online sexual offending groups, including digital exhibitionism and voyeurism and image-based abuse, given that these forms of behavior involve heterogeneous motivations and individuals who would not previously have been subject to clinical or forensic interventions.

DYNAMIC RISK ASSESSMENT TOOLS

Static factors are useful for long-term prediction, and dynamic risk factors can be useful for short-term prediction and guiding intervention. Babchishin et al. (2023) examined the predictive validities of the STABLE-2007 and ACUTE-2007 (Hanson et al., 2007) in a large sample, with 1,042 men who committed contact offenses as a comparison, 228 men who committed CSEM offenses exclusively, and 80 men who committed both contact and CSEM offenses. I have already

---

[2] The OSP/C is based on the total number of sanctions, number of sanctions for contact sexual offenses against an adult, number of sanctions for contact sexual offenses against a child, number of sanctions for noncontact sexual offenses, and number of sanctions for CSEM offenses, as well as the date of the most recent sexual offense sanction and whether any sexual offenses involved a stranger.

mentioned the STABLE-2007, and I discuss the items and domains later in this chapter in the Criminogenic Needs Assessment section. The ACUTE-2007 is another dynamic risk assessment tool that can be completed more frequently than the STABLE-2007, such as at every supervision meeting or monthly case conference. The ACUTE-2007 comprises seven items, rated on a four-point scale from "no problem" to "intervene now": (a) access to victims, (b) emotional collapse, (c) change in social supports, (d) hostility, (e) rejection of supervision, (f) sexual preoccupations, and (g) substance abuse. Access to victims is a situational risk factor, and the remaining items can be viewed as current expressions of more stable risk factors (emotional collapse, hostility, rejection of supervision, sexual preoccupation, and substance abuse) or a loss of a supported protective factor (social supports).

Babchishin et al. (2023) found that both dynamic risk tools could predict sexual recidivism among those who had committed CSEM offenses, including any sexual recidivism, and then specifically CSEM and contact sexual recidivism. This was also true for CSEM-exclusive cases, so the results were not driven by dual cases where their contact offense(s) would have made them already eligible for both dynamic risk tools. Dual cases had higher recidivism rates than CSEM-exclusive cases, mostly due to a difference in contact recidivism: The any sexual recidivism rates were 8.8% versus 3.9% (5.2% overall); contact recidivism was 3.8% versus 0.4% (1.3% overall), and CSEM recidivism was similar for the two groups, at 3.8% versus 3.5% (3.6% overall).

CHILD PORNOGRAPHY OFFENDER RISK TOOL

Demand for a valid risk prioritization tool for CSEM perpetration led to our development of the Child Pornography Offender Risk Tool (CPORT, pronounced "seaport"), which began in the early 2010s with a grant from the Ontario Mental Health Foundation and negotiations for access to closed investigation files from 10 participating police services (Seto & Eke, 2015). Our original goal was to develop a risk prioritization tool for police investigators, which is why we relied on data from closed police files for men convicted of CSEM offenses rather than clinical files, where clinical files would have been richer in terms of clinical assessment, diagnosis, and other information. The police case files were rich in terms of police contacts and criminal record information, as well as interviews with suspects soon after the investigation began, either through transcripts or audio or video recordings, whereas individuals seen in clinical settings may have had weeks, months, or even longer to reconsider their explanations and other statements. We also had criminal records, police occurrence reports that are created whenever a police officer has contact with someone, and perhaps most uniquely, direct access to the CSEM content seized by police, as well as some digital information about other pornography, other legal child content, and online communications with minors.

We initially thought the user pool for the CPORT would be law enforcement, but we soon recognized there was also widespread clinical demand.

This is demonstrated by the uptake of the CPORT since its publication by Seto and Eke (2015). The CPORT is now used by probation officers and clinicians in Canada, several state departments of correction in the United States, the Scottish Risk Management Authority, and corrections in New Zealand. To summarize the initial CPORT development research, we had detailed information for 301 men convicted of CSEM offenses; almost all had possession convictions, and some also had distribution and production offenses. In this sample, 266 men were at risk in the community for at least 5 years, therefore, excluding those who were still in correctional custody, at risk for less than 5 years, or who were deported or died before 5 years at risk in the community. We collected data in the following domains: demographics, criminal history, any police contacts with the suspect, self-reported information during the interviews, forensic analysis of CSEM and other child or sexually explicit content, and any reports or other information obtained during the investigation (e.g., witness statements). Our coding was informed by theory, empirical research on risk factors for offline offending, and early research on risk factors for CSEM offending (e.g., Seto & Eke, 2005; see Chapters 2 and 5, this volume).

Building on the earlier research identifying risk-relevant factors, including younger age, criminal history, and prior contact sexual offending, Seto and Eke (2015) tried to code information that tapped the two major risk dimensions identified by Hanson and Bussière (1998) and Hanson and Morton-Bourgon (2005). These same dimensions are represented in the motivation–facilitation model, where motivations include sexual interest in children, other paraphilic sexual interests, and sexual preoccupation, and facilitation factors include evidence of antisociality, such as criminal history, delinquency, and substance abuse (see Seto, 2019); all are significant correlates of sexual recidivism in conventional samples of sexually offending men (Hanson & Bussière, 1998; Hanson & Morton-Bourgon, 2005). Given that there was already evidence of the predictive validity of some variables from our preceding studies, using an overlapping sample of men who had been placed on the Ontario Sex Offender Registry, we expected that sexual recidivism would be associated with younger age, prior criminal history, and prior contact sexual offending (Eke et al., 2011; Seto & Eke, 2005). We further hypothesized that evidence of sexual interest in children, such as admission of this interest (Hanson & Morton-Bourgon, 2005), a preference for CSEM content depicting younger children, a preference for CSEM depicting boys, and evidence of greater involvement with CSEM, such as larger CSEM collections, longer duration of CSEM use, or engagement in the form of organizing would be associated with a higher risk of sexual recidivism. Our logic for including CSEM content parameters follows our assumption that people would seek out content that matched their sexual preferences, just as straight people are expected to primarily seek heterosexual pornography, or individuals interested in bondage, discipline, sadism, and masochism seek out this kind of sexual content (Bártová et al., 2021).

The explanation for boy content is less direct and is based on research showing that an interest in boys is associated with greater sexual arousal to children and a greater likelihood of pedohebephilia (Seto & Lalumière, 2001; Seto, Stephens, et al., 2017). In addition, having boy victims is associated with a greater likelihood of sexual recidivism in men who have committed contact sexual offenses against children (Hanson & Bussière, 1998; Hanson & Morton-Bourgon, 2005).

Seto and Eke (2015) also wondered if possession of other child content mattered because that can also be evidence of sexual or romantic attraction in children (e.g., McCarthy, 2010, and accessing child modeling sites.) We further looked at CSEM-specific behavior based on investigator suggestions from their extensive experience with these cases, such as whether CSEM content was organized, whether there was anime as well as images of real children, and whether they participated in online pedohebephilia forums.

Some of the hypotheses were supported. The following candidate risk factors did not uniquely and significantly predict sexual recidivism: amount of CSEM, proportion of CSEM to adult pornography, age distributions in CSEM content, presence of other paraphilic content, and substance abuse (Seto & Eke, 2015). In the end, seven items were useful in predicting any sexual recidivism in our development sample (see Appendix for scoring guidance). Any sexual recidivism included new contact offending, new noncontact offending, and new CSEM offending and was found in 11% of cases, with 3% involving new contact offenses and 9% involving new CSEM offenses. The following items were scored dichotomously to keep coding simple and maximize interrater reliability: perpetrator age 35 or younger; any prior criminal history on record; any failure on conditional release; any contact sexual offending, prior or concurrent; evidence of sexual interest in prepubescent or pubescent children; more boy than girl CSEM; more boy than girl other child content. Each item is scored as yes or no, so total scores could range from 0 to 7; all scores were represented in the development sample, but the sample mean score was just below 2. The CPORT showed moderate predictive accuracy for any sexual recidivism (AUC = .74) and performed slightly better if there was no missing information.

I am aware of some confusion about one particular result from Seto and Eke (2015): When the sample of 266 men was divided by criminal history, CPORT was not significantly predictive for the CSEM-exclusive group with no other criminal record. This is an important issue because the CSEM-exclusive group is common in clinical practice, and other risk assessment tools are suitable for those who have committed other kinds of sexual offenses. The effect size for this CSEM-exclusive group was similar to the effect sizes for other groups, despite focusing on a subgroup with a lower CPORT score by definition because they could not have any contact sexual offending history and likely had no prior criminal history unless it was a prior charge or conviction for CSEM offending. This was clarified in a subsequent study by Eke et al. (2019), which found that the CPORT was a significant predictor of sexual recidivism in a small validation sample and a significant predictor for CSEM perpetrators without any contact sexual offending when the development and validation sample were combined. Subsequently, the CPORT can significantly and specifically predict CSEM recidivism (like the OSP/I), and researchers have examined how the CPORT compares with other risk assessment tools such as the Static-99R and RM2000/S (Helmus, Eke, Farmus, & Seto, 2024; discussed later in this chapter).

CORRELATES OF ADMISSION OF SEXUAL INTEREST IN CHILDREN SCALE

We developed the Correlates of Admission of Sexual Interest in Children Scale (CASIC; Seto & Eke, 2017; see Appendix, this volume) because we were concerned that the item regarding admission of sexual interest in children or CSEM would be vulnerable to faking as the CPORT items became better known. We, therefore, reanalyzed the data set used to develop the CPORT to identify behavioral correlates of admission of sexual interest. The following variables were significantly and uniquely related to this CPORT admission item: (a) never married or common-law; (b) possessed one or more CSEM videos; (c) possessed CSEM texts, including stories or journals about sexual interactions with children; (d) evidence that CSEM offending spanned 2 or more years; (e) volunteered in a position with high levels of access to children; and (f) engaged in online sexual communications with a minor or undercover police officer posing as a minor.

Several independent studies[3] have examined the predictive validity of the CPORT or modifications of the CPORT, where modifications typically mean dropping items because they could not be coded from archival data or were not present in the data sources. Table 6.2 summarizes seven independent validation studies that were conducted across different countries. Many of these validation studies used modified versions of the CPORT because they could not score all seven items. Most commonly, these researchers did not have information about CSEM or other child content; they sometimes also did not know about admissions of sexual interest in children. Though not ideal for research validation purposes, this reflects field utility because most clinicians may not have objective information about CSEM or other child content, and some police services may not record all the relevant information (e.g., not recording child content that does not meet the legal definition of CSEM.) Most of these studies were theses or dissertations (Bell, 2020; Black, 2018; Gunnarsdóttir, 2019; Pilon, 2016). The Pilon (2016) sample likely overlapped with ours, given that the data were also collected in Ontario, but the extent of this overlap is unknown. Two samples were larger than our combined sample—Black (2018) and Bell (2020)—and both of these studies found that the first four items of the CPORT significantly predicted sexual recidivism, including specifically CSEM recidivism. Soldino et al. (2021) did not find that the CPORT was a significant predictor of sexual recidivism in Spain, but curiously,

---

[3]Several of these studies were published in *Sexual Abuse*, the journal for which I served as editor-in-chief between 2015 and 2023. This is not unusual because *Sexual Abuse* had the highest impact factor among journals focusing on sexual offending perpetration during this period. To avoid any perceived conflict of interest as a codeveloper of the CPORT, I strictly followed the recommendations of the action editors assigned to the submission without any override (favorable or unfavorable) by me. The journal did not receive and therefore did not reject any manuscripts reporting unsuccessful replication of Seto and Eke (2015), and Soldino et al. (2021) was recommended for publication by the action editor despite reporting a nonsignificant effect for the CPORT.

TABLE 6.2. Summary of Independent CPORT Validity Studies, in Chronological Order

Study	Sample (location)	Base rates	Finding
Pilon (2016)	279 (Canada)	3% any sexual recidivism after M = 3 years	Missing items 6, 7 AUC (any sexual) = .56
Black (2018)	552 (New Zealand)	8% contact recidivism, 13% CSEM recidivism after M = 7 years	Missing items 5–7 **AUC (any sexual) = .77** **AUC (CSEM) = .77** **AUC (contact) = .74**
Gunnarsdóttir (2019)	106 (Iceland)	16% any sexual recidivism, 10% CSEM after 5 years	Missing item 5 **AUC (any sexual) = .77**
Bell (2020)	1,256 (Australia)	12% any sexual recidivism and 10% CSEM recidivism after 5 years	Missing items 5–7 **AUC (any sexual) = .67** **AUC (CSEM) = .67**
Soldino et al. (2021)	304 (Spain)	2% sexual recidivism (mostly CSEM) after 5 years	CPORT AUC (CSEM) = .57 **CASIC AUC (CSEM) = .70**
Savoie et al. (2022)	141 (Scotland)	9.9% any sexual recidivism, 7.8% CSEM recidivism after 5 years	**AUC (any sexual) = .78** **AUC (CSEM) = .74**
Cohen (2023)	5,768 (United States)	4.5% sexual rearrest after 5 years	Items 5–7 Self Report **AUC (any sexual) = .62**

Note. Bolded AUC values are statistically significant. AUC = area under curve; CASIC = Correlates of Admission of Sexual Interest in Children Scale; CPORT = Child Pornography Offender Risk Tool; CSEM = child sexual exploitation material.

the companion measure to assess sexual interest in children (CASIC) significantly predicted CSEM offending.

Bell (2020) reported the largest validation so far, with 1,256 CSEM perpetrators (23% dual) at risk for at least 2 years and 882 CSEM perpetrators at risk for a fixed 5-year follow-up (19% dual). Information was only available for the first four CPORT items, like Black (2018). Bell (2020) found significant predictive accuracy for any sexual recidivism and CSEM recidivism specifically, with 12% any sexual recidivism after 5 years and 10% CSEM recidivism. Most new sexual offenses were for CSEM offenses, with similar rates to those reported by Seto and Eke (2015). The first four CPORT items were significantly predictive in the CSEM-exclusive group. This study suggests that predictive accuracy is affected by not having information about sexual interest in children or preference for boys. Nonetheless, this is reassuring because four validation studies—Pilon (2016), Black (2018), Gunnarsdóttir (2019), and Bell (2020)—have found the remaining CPORT items have predictive validity without the two content items and, in some cases, the sexual interest in children item too.

Savoie et al. (2022) used data from 141 men in Scotland convicted of CSEM offenses and followed for at least 5 years. The CPORT was scored as intended, unlike previous validation studies that modified or dropped items. Savoie et al. used the CASIC if no information was available about admissions of sexual interest in children, and they also examined predictive accuracy if the CASIC was used instead of the sexual interest in children item, whether or not there was missing information on this item. The CPORT worked well, with an AUC of .81 for any recidivism (24.8%), AUC of .78 for sexual recidivism specifically (9.9%), and AUC of .74 for CSEM recidivism (7.8%, which is about 79% of all sexual reoffending). Effect sizes were similar for CSEM groups, distinguishing dual from others, but the group sizes were quite small.

Despite this growing evidence, Scurich and Krauss (2023) criticized the use of the CPORT by American evaluators, pointing out the limited validation so far, the lack of a validation study using an American sample, and the limitations or caveats we have noted about the independent validation studies that have been conducted (e.g., missing items, some inconsistency in results). These are valid criticisms, though Scurich and Krauss did not explain what they would recommend instead, given the number of CSEM perpetrators who require risk assessment for criminal justice and clinical decision making. I hope they are not suggesting a return to unstructured clinical judgment and all the problems that can bring or the use of unvalidated risk assessment tools.

Relevant to one of the criticisms made by Scurich and Krauss (2023), Cohen (2023) published results of a follow-up study of 5,768 individuals under federal probation supervision for CSEM offenses; 89% were White, and their mean age was 46. Over 90% were convicted of possession or distribution offenses, and about 1% were convicted of production. Three quarters were in the low-risk category on the Post Conviction Risk Assessment (Johnson et al., 2011), the standard general risk assessment tool used by federal probation officers. The sexual rearrest rate was 4.5% after 5 years of opportunity. The CPORT was scored from administrative data and an automated tool for extracting information from unstructured text. The scoring of the CPORT differed from the development sample by relying on admissions of gender preferences without access to the underlying collections and by relying on admission of sexual interest without the CASIC. CPORT was significantly predictive of sexual recidivism, albeit with a weaker effect than reported by other validation studies (AUC = .62); this value was similar to the AUC found for the Post Conviction Risk Assessment (AUC = .61), which is coincidentally what Wakeling et al. (2011) found as well when comparing the RM2000/S and OGRS3, which are sexual offense and general recidivism risk tools, respectively. Adding additional risk items to the CPORT produced an AUC of .65, which is marginally higher. The results of Cohen (2023) and Wakeling et al. (2011) suggest there could be value in using both CSEM-specific and general risk assessment items in evaluating CSEM perpetrators.

Given the similar AUCs found for the OSP/I (Howard & Wakeling, 2021) compared with the CPORT, why would anyone want to use the CPORT instead of a four-level categorization based on sanction history? The OSP/I researchers used everyone with a sexual offending sanction in their sample because contact and noncontact perpetrators might commit new CSEM offenses. However, from the perspective of assessing the risk of the 593 cases already known to have committed CSEM offenses, these cases were sorted into two groups only, single versus multiple CSEM offenses, with the latter having more than three times the recidivism rate of the former group after 5 years (9% vs. 32%). Most of the predictive accuracy of the OSP/I then is driven by the stark difference in CSEM recidivism rates between those with no prior CSEM sanctions (though they may have committed other sexual offenses, including contact sexual offenses against children or sexual offenses against adults) and those with multiple CSEM sanctions. Sanction history is useful for the criminal justice system because it is easily obtained from administrative records, and the OSP/I can efficiently inform decisions about security level, treatment eligibility, and supervision conditions. The CPORT can still provide additional value because there are more than two risk levels for those with CSEM offenses and because the scoring provides additional information for case formulation, such as whether someone is at more risk because of atypical sexuality (the last three items, in particular) or antisociality (the first three items). The CPORT can also predict CSEM recidivism, in addition to any sexual recidivism. Helmus, Eke, and Seto (2024) reviewed the evidence on risk assessment tools for men convicted of CSEM offenses.

Helmus, Eke, Farmus, and Seto (2024) found that the CPORT risk assessment tool had higher predictive accuracy than the RM2000/S in a Canadian sample. We reported that the CPORT was higher than the RM2000/S in predictive accuracy in a sample of 365 men convicted of CSEM offenses, followed for an average of 8 years. The cases were from the sample reported by Eke et al. (2019) but not the full sample because some did not have enough information to score the RM2000/S retrospectively. The sexual recidivism rate in Helmus, Eke, Farmus, and Seto (2024) was 16%, two thirds of which (11%) was for new CSEM offenses. In a fixed 5-year follow-up analysis, the AUC was .73 for the CPORT versus .66 for the RM2000/S, and .74 versus .67 for CSEM specifically. The latter comparison was not statistically significant, but the effect sizes were similar to those for any sexual recidivism. In general, the CPORT produced higher AUCs than the RM2000/S, though the comparison was statistically significant only for any sexual recidivism in the full sample and among CSEM perpetrators who did not have contact sexual offenses.

Angela Eke, my CPORT codeveloper, presented results at the national conference of the Association for the Treatment and Prevention of Sexual Abuse in 2022 of a study using our combined sample ($N = 348$ with complete data for this analysis) comparing the predictive accuracy of the CPORT with the Static-99R, distinguishing further between 108 cases who were eligible for the Static-99R because of prior or concurrent sexual offending (including solicitation offending involving an attempted or actual meeting) and 240 cases who were not eligible. The Static-99R had significant predictive accuracy for predicting any sexual recidivism (AUC = .63), and this was similar to the AUC of .67 for the CPORT, but the Static-99R did not do as well for predicting CSEM recidivism, with an AUC of .62 compared with .73 for the CPORT. The Static-99R and CPORT scores were significantly and positively correlated ($r = .69$). The CPORT scores were more strongly correlated with Static-99R's sexual criminality factor ($r = .57$, which includes sexual offense history and sexual victim characteristics) than the general criminality factor ($r = .29$) comprising prior sentencing dates and nonsexual violence history.

The CPORT can be scored "by the book" as an actuarial risk assessment tool using information available in police case files, or it can be scored as a structured professional judgment tool, using all available information, including subsequent clinical evaluations. I have described the CPORT and CASIC items in the Appendix. It is hard to ignore, for example, if the person has no criminal record for contact sexual offending but admits such offenses during an evaluation or if they did not answer questions about their sexual interest in children when interrogated by police but admit it during clinical assessment. We are currently working on the third version of the CPORT scoring guide that discusses how to consider additional information, such as admissions or assessments of sexual interest in children in clinical settings. Scoring by the book allows evaluators to refer to the probabilistic estimates of sexual recidivism, though cautiously, given the relatively small cumulative sample (compared with, for example, the norms available for the Static-99R, which are based on thousands of cases, including "routine" and "high-risk/high-need" samples; https://saarna.org). In the current scoring guide, we were cautious about reporting probabilities of recidivism, given the small samples so far. There is a current effort by Helmus, Eke, Farmus, and Seto (2024) to combine data to see whether scores perform robustly, whether accuracy is there for an omnibus sample, and what probabilities look like for larger sample norms.

THE SCREENING SCALE FOR PEDOPHILIC INTERESTS (SSPI AND SSPI-2)

The revised Screening Scale for Pedophilic Interests (SSPI-2, pronounced "Spy 2"; Seto, Sandler, & Freeman, 2017; Seto, Stephens, et al., 2017) is a revision of the Screening Scale for Pedophilic Interests (SSPI; Seto & Lalumière, 2001), which was created as a proxy measure for phallometrically assessed sexual arousal to children, relative to adults, in men who have committed contact sexual offenses against children. Relative sexual arousal to children is an important risk factor and treatment target for men who have sexually offended against children (Hanson & Bussière, 1998; Hanson & Morton-Bourgon, 2005). Relative sexual arousal to children is more useful than an absolute index of sexual arousal to children because relative arousal takes individual differences into account. To illustrate using circumferential data, someone who produces a 10 mm change in penile circumference to child stimuli and a 20 mm change to adult stimuli has the same relative sexual arousal (50%) as someone who produces a 20 mm change to penile circumference to child stimuli and a 40 mm change to adult stimuli. The person with greater penile changes overall would look like they are showing greater arousal to children if one focused on absolute values. Phallometric labs to assess genital sexual arousal are not always available because of cost, technical expertise required, or geography (e.g., phallometric testing is not permitted in Germany). Some eligible individuals will refuse testing even if it is available, and some individuals who agree to testing will not produce interpretable responses due to older age, medical conditions, or other reasons. Finally, phallometric testing is widely perceived as an intrusive procedure, and some commentators have raised ethical concerns about the use of child stimuli and putting potentially vulnerable people through the testing procedures (Bourget & Bradford, 2018).

Though there are many correlates of sexual arousal to children, including adult sexual partner history, romantic attraction to children, and emotional congruence with children, Seto and Lalumière (2001) chose to focus on behavioral correlates that are not reliant on self-report and that are usually easily obtainable in clinical assessments and criminal justice files in creating the SSPI. The SSPI had only four items, scored for contact or noncontact (e.g., exhibitionistic behavior) with sexual victims under age 14: having boy victims, having multiple child victims, having at least one child victim under the age of 12, and having extrafamilial child victims (Seto & Lalumière, 2001). The SSPI has since been used in multiple studies as a clinical or research proxy measure for sexual arousal to children. The SSPI-2 took the same four items, now coded for victims aged 15 or younger to match a change in Canadian law regarding the age of consent, removed the double weight for having a boy victim, and added a fifth item: CSEM offending based on self-report or criminal records. SSPI-2 scores are significantly, positively, and moderately correlated with relative sexual arousal to children (Seto, Stephens, et al., 2017) and significantly associated with sexual recidivism in two studies (Faitakis et al., 2023; Seto, Sandler, & Freeman, 2017). In the Seto, Sandler, and Freeman (2017) study, following a large sample of men released from the New York state prison system, the SSPI-2 was more strongly associated with sexual rearrest in 5 years than the SSPI, indicating the addition of the CSEM item increased predictive validity in a sample of men who had directly offended against children.

The SSPI-2 is not intended for CSEM perpetrators without any contact or noncontact offenses against children because it was developed and then validated on samples of men who had committed at least one direct offense against a child aged 15 or younger. But the SSPI-2 is still relevant for this book because it points out how both CSEM and contact offending against children are indicators of sexual interest in children (see Seto et al., 2006) and how dual offending (CSEM and contact) is associated with a higher risk of sexual recidivism. The SSPI-2 is also applicable to men who meet minors below the age of consent for sexual purposes after sexually soliciting them online and men who engage in the sexual trafficking of children or child sexual abuse tourism so that it could be a useful clinical assessment tool for some online perpetrators.

In additional research on the SSPI-2 described in a Portuguese master's thesis, Gouveia (2024) calculated the SSPI-2 for 85 men convicted of sexually offending against children. A fifth (22%) had a score of 4 or 5, which is associated with showing greater sexual arousal to children than to adults and, thus, a sexual preference for children. The SSPI-2 was positively associated with the Sexual Violence Risk–20 ($r = .37$; Boer et al., 1997), a structured risk assessment tool, and uncorrelated with scores on a measure of psychopathy.

CRIMINOGENIC NEEDS ASSESSMENT

The need principle in the risk–need–responsivity framework is important for determining intervention targets to reduce the risk of reoffending (Bonta & Andrews, 2024). By definition, these needs must be potentially dynamic, meaning they can change over time—and importantly, they need to be reassessed periodically. My understanding of dynamic risk factors is informed by Mann et al.'s (2010) review of psychologically meaningful risk factors, where factors were considered to be supported if at least three studies showed at least a modest effect size. The following dynamic factors (and the number of supportive studies) were identified as supported by Mann and colleagues: sexual preoccupation (six studies), any atypical sexual interests (16 studies), multiple paraphilic interests (four studies), offense-supportive cognitions (nine studies), emotional congruence with children (three studies), conflicts in intimate relationships (four studies), general self-regulation problems (15 studies), impulsivity or recklessness (six studies), employment instability (15 studies), poor cognitive problem solving (four studies), noncompliance with supervision (three studies), hostility (11 studies), and negative social influences (seven studies). We updated the Mann et al. review and concluded that hostility toward women as part of a broader pattern of hostile masculinity and emotional regulation deficits also supported dynamic risk factors (Seto, Augustyn, et al., 2023). We also identified positive social support as an empirically supported dynamic protective factor.

Most of the following subsections correspond to the dynamic risk domains described in the STABLE-2007, a reliable and validated dynamic risk tool for men who have sexually offended (Hanson et al., 2007; an exception is problematic internet use). The risk domains and items in the STABLE-2007 are useful heuristics for assessing intervention needs, especially with evidence that the STABLE-2007 predicted any sexual recidivism and CSEM recidivism specifically in a sample of men who had committed CSEM offenses (Babchishin et al., 2023). Interestingly, the distribution of STABLE-2007 scores in the CSEM sample was similar to those observed in dual perpetrators. In the STABLE-2007, each of the 13 items is rated by evaluators, with the total risk score associated with different risk categories. The items are significant social influences, capacity for relationship stability, emotional identification with children, hostility toward women, general social rejection/loneliness, lack of concern for others, impulsive acts, poor problem-solving skills, negative emotionality, sex drive/preoccupation, sex as coping, deviant sexual preference, and cooperation with supervision. We can think of these STABLE-2007 items falling into the following domains:

- sexual self-regulation problems (paraphilic sexual interests such as pedohebephilia, sexual preoccupation, the use of sex to cope with negative feelings)
- emotional congruence with children (described here as emotional identification with children)
- relationships (the capacity for relationship stability, hostility toward women, social rejection or loneliness)
- offense-permissive cognitions (hostility toward women)
- delinquent peers (significant social influences)
- antisocial tendencies (lack of concern for others, impulsivity, poor problem-solving skills, negative emotionality, poor cooperation with supervision)

An advantage of the STABLE-2007 is that it can be combined with Static-99R while taking the time being offense free in the community into account (because research has shown that risk to reoffend drops dramatically the longer someone remains in the community offense free; Hanson et al., 2018). Since the first edition of this book, research has provided evidence of true dynamicity for some factors; one of the criticisms previously raised was that any putatively dynamic risk information assessed at only one point is essentially a static risk factor. True dynamicity needs to show change over time and show that change over time predicts sexual recidivism over and above static information (Eher et al., 2012; M. E. Olver et al., 2020). We do not yet know if STABLE-2007 scores can be empirically integrated with CPORT scores or how to interpret differing risk assessment predictions (e.g., lower risk on the CPORT or STABLE-2007, with higher risk on the other measure).

Given that static risk assessments tend to be more accurate over the longer term and dynamic risk assessments must be repeated periodically, I suggest the following: Relatively low scores on the CPORT suggest the person is unlikely to reoffend sexually, particularly with reference to the overall sexual recidivism rates observed in follow-up studies. However, even low-risk individuals may benefit from additional support and monitoring when dynamic risk factors are high. Conversely, someone with a higher score on the CPORT still warrants higher intensity intervention even when their STABLE-2007 scores might suggest few current concerns. Evidence for the relevance of the same dynamic risk factors for CSEM offending—particularly paraphilic sexual interests and sexual preoccupation (Kuhle et al., 2017) and offense-supportive cognitions (Paquette & Cortoni, 2021)—have led me to recommend using the STABLE-2007 as a structured risk assessment tool. This is further supported by Babchishin et al. (2022), who showed for the first time that STABLE-2007 and ACUTE-2007 scores can predict sexual recidivism among CSEM perpetrators.

What about other forms of online sexual offending? Seto et al. (2012) found few significant differences on some putative dynamic risk factors when comparing CSEM and solicitation offenders. No research is available, but my best guess is that the STABLE-2007 would also work for these groups, especially for those involving direct interactions with victims (sexual solicitation, sexual assault of adults, sexual trafficking, and child sexual abuse tourism). Persons who committed sexual offenses involving contact or attempted contact with a victim can also be assessed using the Static-99R. It is less obvious to me if these dynamic risk assessment tools (or static risk assessment tools) will work for digital exhibitionism, digital voyeurism, and other image-based offending, given that these offenses can involve heterogeneous motivations (see Chapter 4) and may not fit with the motivation–facilitation model because they are not necessarily sexually motivated. However, levels of facilitation should still be relevant across different forms of online sexual offending, so static or dynamic measures of antisociality could be predictive (e.g., criminal history, antisocial personality traits, offense-supportive cognitions).

ASSESSING DYNAMIC RISK FACTORS FOR ONLINE SEXUAL OFFENDING

I discussed the relevance of paraphilic sexual interests and hypersexuality as explanations of online sexual offending in Chapter 5, focusing mostly on CSEM offending because this form of offending is still the main focus of clinical and research attention. Here, I describe how to assess these and other dynamic risk factors for treatment planning, supervision conditions, and prevention efforts.

Paraphilias

The easiest way to assess pedohebephilia is through self-report. Questionnaires can be easier for disclosures than interviews, but interviews allow the evaluator to ask follow-up questions for clarification and determine whether someone's expressed interests might meet the criteria for ascertaining a paraphilia or diagnosing a paraphilic disorder using the *Diagnostic and Statistical Manual of Mental Disorders* (5th ed., text rev.; *DSM-5-TR*; American Psychiatric Association, 2022). People might lie, though, especially if facing big social or legal consequences. That is why clinical forensic sexology has developed alternative methods.

The gold standard for the assessment of atypical sexual interests in men is the phallometric assessment of sexual arousal to different sexual stimuli. We are particularly interested in relative sexual arousal to children compared with adults; recall that Seto et al. (2006) found that almost three quarters of CSEM perpetrators show a preference for children over adults when assessed phallometrically, and this is significantly greater than men who commit direct offenses against children or comparison groups of men who have sexually offended against adults exclusively or who have not sexually offended (replicated by Blanchard et al., 2007). Phallometric testing is often not available, however, which is why we developed the SSPI and then SSPI-2 for men who have committed contact or noncontact sexual offenses against children. In addition, measures based on relative viewing time for images depicting children versus adults have been developed, including viewing time measures using stimuli that do not depict real people. Multiple studies have shown that viewing time measures can discriminate men who have sexually offended against children from other men, and one study found that viewing time plus self-report could predict sexual recidivism (Gray et al., 2015).

We do not have a SSPI-2-like tool for men who have committed online sexual offenses exclusively, though it is possible the CASIC could be used in a similar way for CSEM perpetrators. Ontario probation data shows CASIC scores are significantly and positively associated with self-reported sexual interest in children, clinical diagnosis, or the combination (any indication of sexual interest in children; Hermann et al., 2024). Similarly, California clinic data from Azizian et al. (in press) showed significant, positive associations between CASIC scores and self-reported sexual interest in children. I would like to know if CASIC scores correlate with phallometric data or viewing time. I expect moderate and positive correlations, consistent with evidence that different methods for assessing pedohebephilia—including self-report, clinician evaluation, and behavioral information—typically correlate moderately with each other (e.g., McPhail et al., 2021). It is also worth mentioning the generally mediocre diagnostic reliability for paraphilic disorders, which is acceptable for pedophilia and worse for other paraphilias, especially those without specified criteria, such as hebephilia (Graham, 2019; Seto et al., 2016).

CSEM content parameters are relevant to the assessment of pedohebephilia. Intuitively, individuals who preferentially seek content depicting younger children are more likely to have pedohebephilia than those who seek content depicting underage teens. Less obviously, a preference for boys should also be relevant, given evidence that individuals who offend against boys are more likely to have pedohebephilia. For example, in our SSPI and SSPI-2 research, we found that having boy victims is associated with greater sexual arousal to children than adults when assessed phallometrically (Seto & Lalumière, 2001; Seto, Stephens, et al., 2017). In turn, having boy victims is associated with a higher risk of sexual recidivism in the general sexual offending literature (Hanson & Bussière, 1998; Hanson & Morton-Bourgon, 2005).

If pedohebephilia has been identified, it is also important to know if the person has a preferential or nonpreferential sexual attraction to children (see McPhail et al., 2018). More preferential interest in children is associated with a higher risk of sexually offending and also a more difficult prognosis, especially if the interest in children is exclusive because the person has few legal outlets for their sexual interests (they could fantasize about legal child content; see McCarthy, 2010). It is also more difficult to fit into society because individuals with an exclusive interest in children are much less likely to have an adult relationship, which can be suspicious to others (Schippers et al., 2023). In contrast, someone with a nonpreferential interest in children can still have mutually satisfying relationships with adults (even if that is restricted to young-looking adults), can use adult pornography (again, perhaps skewing toward content depicting young-looking adults), and has an easier time fitting into society because they can engage in adult relationships.

Hypersexuality

Another aspect of sexual self-regulation that is important to assess is hypersexuality, typically manifested as excessive sexual preoccupation accompanied by significant distress or impairment.[4] Excessive sexual preoccupation can be assessed by asking about sex drive, frequency of masturbation and other sexual behavior, compulsive pornography use, and a self-reported lack of perceived control over sexual behavior. Self-report measures of hypersexuality have been psychometrically validated (M. E. Olver et al., 2022). Ideally, these self-reports are augmented with collateral information, such as digital evidence regarding pornography use, evidence the person purchased commercial sex services, or interviews with past and current sexual partners. Excessive sexual preoccupation might be relevant in up to one quarter of CSEM offending, where sexual interest in children explains the majority of CSEM offending, but some people credibly claim that their CSEM use was a result of high levels of pornography use and habituation to mainstream content (Seto et al., 2006, 2010).

Hypersexuality can co-occur with pedohebephilia because they are not mutually exclusive conditions. So, someone may seek CSEM because of their sexual interest in children and feel they have less ability to regulate this behavior because of their hypersexuality. I speculate that excessive sexual preoccupation is also likely to be relevant for online sexual solicitation and other online offending, including the technology-facilitated sexual assault of adults. Excessive sexual preoccupation is conceptually and empirically related to the construct of impersonal sex in the confluence model, developed by Malamuth and colleagues (2021), to explain sexual aggression by men against women.

Emotional Congruence With Children

Emotional congruence with children (sometimes referred to as emotional identification with children) can be defined as an exaggerated or atypical emotional affiliation with children (R. J. Wilson, 1999). Phenomenologically, it has been described to me as feeling like one has more in common with children than adults, feeling more comfortable with children than adults, and preferring the company of children over adults. In some cases, the person sees themselves as childlike. Emotional congruence with children is positively correlated with but still conceptually distinct from sexual and romantic attraction to children (Hermann et al., 2017; McPhail et al., 2014). We have discussed sexual attraction

---

[4]Though proposed, a hypersexuality disorder is not in the latest version of the American Psychiatric Association's (2022) diagnostic manual, but it is represented in the World Health Organization's (2019) system, the *International Statistical Classification of Diseases and Related Health Problems* (11th ed.), as compulsive sexual behavior disorder.

to children throughout this book. Romantic attraction is common in men who are sexually attracted to children, and it is correlated with having sexual contact with children (Bailey et al., 2016; Martijn et al., 2020).

Different nonexclusive explanations for emotional congruence with children have been proposed. The blockage hypothesis suggests that some individuals feel a greater affinity for children because they are lonely and socially isolated and do not have meaningful adult relationships. The sexuality hypothesis suggests this emotional affinity with children is driven by romantic and sexual attraction to children and, thus, is not a distinct phenomenon. The immaturity hypothesis suggests that affinity for children is motivated by a sense that children, rather than adults, are the person's emotional and cognitive peers. However, none of these hypotheses are strongly supported, so it remains unclear how emotional congruence with children develops (Fraser et al., 2023; Hermann et al., 2017; McPhail et al., 2014). Emotional congruence with children is important to understand because it is associated with higher rates of sexual recidivism among men who sexually offend against unrelated children but not among intrafamilial perpetrators (McPhail et al., 2013). On average, extrafamilial perpetrators score higher on emotional congruence with children than intrafamilial perpetrators.

I expect emotional congruence with children is relevant to online sexual offending, given its significant correlations with sexual and romantic attraction to children. Emotional congruence with children may explain why some CSEM perpetrators seek less explicit content depicting young children (Fortin & Proulx, 2019) and why some solicitation perpetrators spend time in child-oriented online spaces, such as multiplayer gaming platforms, and engage in online interactions with children that are not sexual. A cynical view would be that these individuals are in these spaces and engaging with children as part of their online solicitation tactics, but the literature on emotional congruence with children suggests that this behavior may also reflect a genuine fulfillment of social and emotional needs rather than sexual interests. I predict that individuals who are high in emotional congruence with children will seek more nonsexual interactions with children, which may increase opportunities to offend but as a by-product rather than a goal. Emotional congruence with children might also interfere with the development or maintenance of healthy adult relationships because time spent with children or focused on child-salient culture (e.g., music, games) is time that is not spent with adults and in more adult-salient spaces.

Paquette and McPhail (2020) developed the Cognitive and Emotional Congruence With Children scale to assess emotional congruence with children for both online and contact offending perpetrators. Their sample was a total of 167 men who had sexually offended, including 45 online only, 45 contact only, and 73 dual perpetrators. The scale has 12 items representing three factors: A childlike sense of self, friendship and positive relationships with children, and romantic attraction to children. Scores on this scale were correlated, as expected, with measures of sexual interest in children, sexualized coping, and offense-supportive cognitions about children and sex. Scores on this new measure of emotional congruence with children were also positively correlated with interest in other paraphilic themes, such as voyeurism, consistent with previous research suggesting interest in CSEM is correlated with interest in other atypical content (Seto & Eke, 2015; Seto, Hermann, et al., 2015). Online perpetrators scored similarly to contact perpetrators, consistent with the Babchishin et al. (2011, 2015) meta-analyses using older measures of emotional congruence with children. Unlike the meta-analysis results from McPhail et al. (2013), intrafamilial perpetrators scored higher on the Cognitive and Emotional Congruence With Children scale than extrafamilial perpetrators.

Offense-Supportive Cognitions

Offense-supportive cognitions are sometimes referred to as cognitive distortions. I do not use this term because calling them distortions implies the thoughts are distortions of the truth (i.e., factually wrong.) Some of the relevant attitudes and beliefs are not factually wrong; stating that children sometimes initiate sexual contact with adults is an accurate statement because it does happen in a small number of cases.[5] To be clear, this does not justify responding sexually to a child or using the fact the child initiated sexual contact to minimize the culpability of the adult.

Offense-supportive cognitions are central to neutralization and other criminological theories to explain both sexual and nonsexual crimes (Bonta & Andrews, 2024). People are more likely to engage in criminal behavior if they have attitudes and beliefs that suggest what they are doing is less harmful or less "their fault." As a general example, individuals who do not believe that laws are important or that their behavior does not harm others (e.g., loss due to theft is "covered by insurance") are more likely to commit crimes. These theories, in turn, can be understood as specific manifestations of more general theories of human behavior, such as the theory of reasoned action, where attitudes and perceived norms influence intentions, which, in turn, influence behavior (Ajzen & Fishbein, 1980). Much research supports the importance of offense-supportive cognitions in crimes, using general attitude and belief measures to distinguish those who have offended from those who have not and predict who is more likely to reoffend (Bonta & Andrews, 2024).

There are child and sex-specific cognitions that are associated with a higher risk of sexual offending. These cognitions fall into different categories, including minimization of harm or wrongfulness (e.g., children are not harmed by sexual contact with an adult or by being photographed for CSEM), child agency (e.g., children can initiate and consent to sex or online sexual interactions), and blaming others (e.g., any harm experienced by child targets is due to

---

[5] Anton Schweighofer (personal communication, October 2, 2023) pointed out that a side benefit of referring to offense-supportive cognitions rather than cognitive distortions is that there is no need to argue about whether a belief is accurate. Instead, the focus can be on whether thinking this way will reduce or increase the risk of offending in the future.

society's reactions rather than the experience). Helmus et al. (2013) found in their meta-analysis of 46 studies (total $N = 13{,}782$) that measures of offense-supportive cognitions had a small but consistent relationship with sexual recidivism. Prediction was better with individuals who have offended against children than those who have offended against adults. This suggests these kinds of cognitions might be stronger predictors for child-focused online sexual offending, compared with online sexual offending targeting adults, such as sexual assaults facilitated using dating apps or platforms.

A caution in interpreting Helmus et al.'s (2013) results is that the prediction was similar for pre- and posttreatment scores, raising the question of whether changing these cognitions reduces the risk of reoffending sexually. For that, we need to look at change scores, and there is some evidence that changes assessed using another tool, the Violence Risk Scale–Sexual Offense Version (VRS-SO), can predict sexual recidivism (M. E. Olver et al., 2018, 2021). In addition, a moderator analysis suggested a stronger prediction for clinician-rated cognitions over self-report, again pointing to the vulnerability of relying entirely on self-report when socially desirable responding is likely. The association between cognitions and sexual offending may also depend on the type of cognition, with important conceptual and empirical differences between attitudes, beliefs, values, and justifications (see Nunes et al., 2015).

Offense-supportive cognitions are facilitation factors in the motivation–facilitation model (Seto, 2019). Acting on the motivation of a sexual interest in children by accessing CSEM, for example, might be facilitated by believing that children are not further harmed if someone views their images. Offense-supportive cognitions can be quite specific, where individuals espouse some offense-supportive cognitions but not others. For example, someone who commits CSEM offending may not believe that children can consent to sexual contact with adults but simultaneously believe that children are not further harmed if someone views their images. Other offense-supportive cognitions in the online sexual offending realm include beliefs that children can consent to (online) sexual interactions with adults or that children who share sexual images of themselves with others have brought any nonconsensual sharing or sextortion on themselves.

There are similarities in the offense-supportive cognitions associated with online compared with contact offending. Indeed, Babchishin et al. (2011) found no significant differences in offense-supportive cognitions comparing online and contact perpetrators. At the same time, a systematic review by Steel et al. (2020b) identified 20 studies and concluded that measures developed for contact offending do not work well for online perpetrators. Rimer (2019) suggested in their thematic analysis of statements that CSEM users hold different constructions of children online compared with offline (see also Kettleborough & Merdian, 2017; Paquette & Cortoni, 2020; Rimer, 2019). I compare examples of common offense-supportive cognitions in online and offline perpetrators drawn from these studies in Table 6.3.

Offense-supportive cognitions about children or sex are not explicitly included in the STABLE-2007 (which does include hostility toward women).

TABLE 6.3. Comparison of Offense-Supportive Cognition Themes in Online and Offline Contexts

Theme	Online	Offline
Dehumanization	Children in CSEM are "not real."	Children are the "property" of their parents and have fewer rights than adults.
Minimize harm	Children are not further harmed by viewing CSEM depicting them.	Children are not harmed by nonviolent sexual interactions with adults; they are more harmed by society's reaction.
Children can consent	Children can consent to online sexual interactions (e.g., chat) with adults.	Children can consent to sexual contacts with adults.
Victim blaming	Children who share nudes bring any resharing or extortion on themselves.	Children who act "flirtatious" or initiate physical contact bring any sexual contact on themselves.

Note. CSEM = child sexual exploitation material. Adapted from "Empirically-Based Dynamic Risk and Protective Factors for Sexual Offending," by M. C. Seto, C. Augustyn, K. M. Roche, and G. Hilkes, 2023, *Clinical Psychology Review, 106*, 102355, p. 2 (https://doi.org/10.1016/j.cpr.2023.102355). Copyright 2023 by Elsevier. Adapted with permission.

They are considered in the VRS-SO and described as "cognitive distortions." Specialized measures for online sexual offending might do better than existing cognition measures. Paquette and Cortoni (2020) did a thematic analysis of statements by online perpetrators and developed the Cognitions of Internet Sexual Offending (C-ISO). The C-ISO was used to compare online, contact, and nonsexual perpetrators. In a regression analysis, cognitions—along with sexual interest in children and sexual coping but not sexual preoccupation—distinguished online and contact offending perpetrators. In a subsequent study with 137 men convicted of CSEM and/or online sexual solicitation offenses, offense-supportive cognitions were correlated with some risk-related factors (Paquette & Fortin, 2021). The sample was too small to compare CSEM with solicitation cases, especially given the amount of crossover offending, where I expect some differences only because the target age ranges are different.

Steel et al. (2023) surveyed 78 CSEM perpetrators on public registries regarding their self-perceptions and cognitions and found evidence of offense-supportive cognitions. Jahnke (2018a) experimentally manipulated the gender and maturity of child targets in a vignette study for 183 English-speaking child-attracted persons. Jahnke found that two thirds of the participants had permissive moral attitudes regarding adult–child sex. Neither gender nor maturity affected ratings of moral acceptability of the described sexual acts. Permissiveness was positively associated with more liberal attitudes generally and with pedophilia; two thirds of the sample reported a preference for children, meaning higher ratings for prepubescent compared with pubescent children or adults. Pedophilic participants believed boys were more likely to engage willingly in adult–child sex. There was no significant association between attitudes and known sexual offending (13%), with the caveat that only known offending was reported (same as in Bailey et al., 2016).

Loneliness and Social Isolation

Loneliness and social isolation can be important unaddressed needs for online perpetrators. Time spent online is time that is unavailable for in-person connections, and negative feelings that result from loneliness or social isolation can motivate sexualized coping, such as viewing pornography or masturbating to paraphilic sexual fantasies. Some individuals may seek out interactions with minors as a response to the absence of adult interactions and relationships in their lives. An early Swiss study of 33 online CSEM perpetrators found they spent an average of almost 20 hours a week online (Frei et al., 2005). Webb et al. (2007) scored the STABLE-2000, a widely used dynamic risk assessment measure for contact perpetrators (the precursor to the STABLE-2007), for a sample of CSEM perpetrators, and found that interpersonal deficits were one of the most common needs identified on this clinician-completed dynamic risk measure. L. E. Marshall et al. (2012) found that CSEM perpetrators were higher in loneliness and social anxiety than contact perpetrators. In addition, loneliness was higher in individuals who sexually solicited children online than those who engaged in online sexual interactions with adults in an online survey (Schulz et al., 2016).

The potential relevance of loneliness and social isolation as risk factors came to the fore during the first wave of the COVID-19 pandemic in the spring of 2020, when many people were more socially isolated due to government-imposed restrictions, including remote work and school, limits on social gatherings, and the shutdown of nonessential services and facilities. A qualitative study (McMahan et al., 2023) of 18 individuals participating in an online intervention for CSEM users (see Chapter 8) found that many of these respondents highlighted the negative impacts of this period on their temptations to use CSEM or engage in other illegal sexual behavior.

Nardett et al. (2021) looked at 6 months of call data for Stop It Now! UK & Ireland, a perpetration prevention service offering helpline and self-help web resources, from April to September 2020, during the first 6 months of the COVID-19 pandemic. A small fraction (111/2650, 4%) of these calls specifically mentioned the pandemic in their conversations. However, these 111 callers made 582 calls, accounting for 11% of all calls. The majority (79%) were seeking help for themselves, with about a third already involved with the criminal justice system. Among these 111 callers, 19 said their concerning behavior around children had increased during this time, 16 said they had lost work or income and were stressed as a result, 15 specifically mentioned social isolation as a concern, 12 said they had less professional support because of the pandemic, nine reported a decrease in protective factors such as social support, and three reported more adult pornography use, which was related to their past CSEM use.

Antisocial Peers

Our grandmothers were right: It matters who you hang out with. Antisocial peers are an important dynamic risk factor across different forms of criminal offending (Bonta & Andrews, 2024). The presence of antisocial peers can be assessed through interviews and questionnaires, collateral informant reports about friendships, and any forensic evidence regarding online community activities. Valid psychometric measures exist, such as the Measures of Criminal Attitudes and Associates, which measures general offense-supportive cognitions and involvement with antisocial peers (Mills et al., 2002).

For individuals who are at risk of online sexual offending, their participation in online forums and interactions with others might be particularly salient because these forums provide opportunities for interacting with peers who are already offending (e.g., trading CSEM) and/or who espouse offense-supportive cognitions that might increase the likelihood of offending. Though online forums can also be a source of positive social support (Roche et al., 2022), they could also serve as places that reinforce offense-supportive cognitions and norms and thereby increase risk. Antisocial peers can share offending tradecraft, such as how to obtain CSEM, sexually solicit children, or hide suspicious or illegal activities online in terms of security precautions.

Positive Social Support

Roche et al. (2022) surveyed 353 self-identified child-attracted persons, 95% of whom were active forum visitors; the rest had visited forums in the past. The top reason (82%) given by participants for joining the forum was to not feel alone. Active users had been on forums for an average of 6 years; 60% visited a forum daily. We recognized there was selection bias in who chose to respond to our survey about social support and found that many forum users reported positive effects from being in forums in terms of emotional support (82%) or advice (informational support, 65%); tangible support was rare (12%). Surprisingly, many participants (74%) said someone offline knew about their attraction to children because, I assumed, many users were on forums because they did not or could not discuss their feelings with relatives, friends, or partners.

Positive social support through forums is encouraging because positive social ties were the only supported protective factor we identified in a review of the sexual offending literature (Seto, Augustyn, et al., 2023). Positive social ties can buffer someone against the effects of negative social ties. For example, having family, friends, coworkers, and others who represent positive relationships in someone's life could buffer them from offense-permissive cognitions and antisocial norms they might be exposed to in online forums. Someone could have both antisocial and prosocial influences in their lives. The simplest way to assess social connections is through self-report and collateral interviews when available (e.g., talking to someone's family member or spouse about the people in their lives).

Wilpert and Janssen (2020) reported a curious and contrary finding in their study of 330 people who contacted Stop It Now! Netherlands. Of these 330 people, 169 had offended (73% CSEM offending), and 161 reported no prior offenses. Those who had offended were more likely to have a partner and children, which seems to contradict the effect of positive social support, though it is true that questions about the quality of the relationship with the partner were not assessed. Having their own children may have been a risk factor because it increased contact with potential victims, such as their children's friends (or their children themselves).

Antisociality

Antisocial traits facilitate acting on motivations for online sexual offending, according to the motivation–facilitation model (Seto, 2017a, 2018). There are multiple lines of evidence supporting the relevance of personality traits such as impulsivity, callousness, and risk taking to sexual offending in general (Hanson & Bussière, 1998; Hanson & Morton-Bourgon, 2005). Impulsivity is evidence of poor self-regulation, which is a listed factor on the STABLE-2007, and poor self-regulation can show up in other ways too, such as being more likely to put oneself in risky situations, using alcohol or drugs that can further disinhibit behavior, or going back to online forums that espouse offense-permissive attitudes and beliefs and norms.

Antisocial traits can be assessed through self-report (interviews or questionnaires), clinical observations, and reviews of collateral information, where traits can be inferred from school records, juvenile delinquency, and input from family members or others who know the person well. Ideally, antisociality factors are assessed as directly as possible—for example, through clinical interviews and questionnaires to assess personality traits and cognitions and where self-report can be corroborated by collateral information from a partner, relative, or other people who know the person well. It is sometimes not possible to directly assess or obtain collateral information. Instead, we have to infer antisociality from documented antisocial and criminal behavior, including evidence of childhood conduct problems, juvenile delinquency, and adult criminal records. This can include police, health, or social service information about fighting, stealing, substance use, and other relevant behavior.

There is evidence that antisocial traits play a role in online sexual offending. Reijnen et al. (2009) compared the personality inventory profiles of 22 CSEM perpetrators with both sexual and nonsexual perpetrators. There were no significant differences between the perpetration groups on their personality profiles, and most germane, the CSEM perpetrators showed a clinical elevation on a scale assessing antisocial tendencies. Seiser et al. (2023) found almost a third (32%) of 53 CSEM perpetrators in their clinical sample were diagnosed with antisocial personality disorder, though other studies find a much lower prevalence. Overall, CSEM perpetrators tend to score relatively low on measures of antisocial traits compared with contact perpetrators, but those who are higher on antisocial traits are at greater risk of sexually reoffending (Klein et al., 2015; Seto & Eke, 2015).

Problematic Internet Use

Problematic internet use is not a dynamic risk factor in the broader sexual offending literature and is not represented in the STABLE-2007. However, problematic internet use stands out as a relevant factor to consider when evaluating someone who has committed an online sexual offense. An early Swiss study found that CSEM perpetrators were spending an average of 20 hours online per week, which included not only time accessing CSEM but also time spent online in other forums and activities (Frei et al., 2005). This may not seem like a lot of time, given how many hours internet users spend online every day, but we should remember that the Frei et al. study was conducted before the introduction of smartphones, and thus, those 20 hours were spent on desktop or laptop computers, with many users relying on dial-up rather than broadband access. Intuitively and empirically, time spent online means more opportunities to engage in online sexual offending behavior. Indeed, Babchishin et al.'s (2011, 2015) systematic reviews found that online perpetrators spend more time online than contact perpetrators. Time spent online also means less time invested in in-person activities and connections.

Perhaps the most germane study was reported by A. F. Lee et al. (2012), comparing 113 CSEM perpetrators with 176 contact perpetrators and 60 dual perpetrators. Both the CSEM and dual perpetrators had higher internet preoccupation scores (e.g., "Did people in your life complain about the amount of time you spent on the internet?" "How often did you lose sleep because of late-night log-ons?") than the contact perpetrators. (Simultaneously, the dual and contact perpetrators were distinguished from the CSEM perpetrators by having higher scores on antisocial behavior, including delinquency and criminal behavior.)

OTHER CLINICAL ASSESSMENT TOPICS

In addition to carrying out a risk assessment to identify intervention intensity and what interventions should target, evaluators often have to address other clinical assessment questions, particularly those that are relevant to considering responsivity and other case management decisions. Choices must be made when conducting a comprehensive clinical evaluation because it is impossible to assess everything that might be relevant. What are the priority topics when assessing someone who has committed online sexual offenses, above and beyond basic personal history, criminal history, prior mental health service involvement, and the dynamic risk and protective domains discussed earlier in this chapter?

I am particularly concerned with information that will help with case conceptualization and service planning. Given the risk principle, it is important to consider risk; hence, risk assessment was covered first in this chapter. I have also already addressed common criminogenic needs (dynamic risk domains) to address the needs principle. These domains are also covered in the pathways analysis by Merdian et al. (2021) and the treatment manual by Piché and Schweighofer (2023).

For the responsivity principle, we are interested in both general and specific responsivity, where general responsivity suggests that interventions that are cognitive behavioral, structured, concrete, and skills focused are better than those that are not. Here, the focus is on specific responsivity related to individual differences. The gist is that—like psychotherapy more generally—interventions tailored to the individual are more likely to be effective. Responsivity factors to consider include age, gender, sexual orientation, ethnicity, reading level, intelligence, willingness, comfort, and capacity to be in a group if that is what is offered.

In my opinion, the most important responsivity factor of all is motivation for change. Individuals who are motivated to change will be more active participants in interventions and, therefore, will be more likely to show positive changes that could lead to better outcomes (Harkins & Beech, 2007; McMurran & Ward, 2010; Romano & Peters, 2015). Ideally, individuals are intrinsically motivated to change, but many may have extrinsic motivations—for example, when individuals are pressured by partners, family members, or close friends to participate or when they are mandated to participate because of their involvement with the criminal justice system.

Psychopathology

Online offending occurs in the contexts of a person's sexual and social development, concurrent functioning, and risk and protective factors. This includes an understanding of their mental health, including evidence of psychiatric conditions and psychopathology. An assessment of general psychopathology is often relevant for health and criminal justice systems as well; for example, a diagnosis may be required to access mental health services (or to access health care insurance coverage in the United States), and a diagnosis may be relevant for some legal proceedings, such as the civil commitment of individuals who have sexually offended under so-called sexually violent predator laws (e.g., Perillo et al., 2021). Diagnoses or serious psychopathology might be considered mitigating or aggravating factors in sentencing and other legal decisions. Even without a diagnosis, serious psychopathology can indirectly affect the person's risk of offending (as when they engage in sexualized coping for depression) and directly affect their ability to participate in services.

Paraphilic disorder diagnoses are top of mind, given the role that paraphilic sexual interests play in online sexual offending. In addition, if the evaluator is using the World Health Organization's *International Statistical Classification of Diseases and Related Health Problems* (11th ed.; 2019) instead of the American Psychiatric Association's (2022) *DSM-5-TR*, it is important to assess for compulsive sexual behavior disorder, which is not in *DSM-5-TR*. Though many paraphilic disorders may be relevant, the most salient are pedophilic disorder, exhibitionistic or voyeuristic disorder, and paraphilic disorder not otherwise specified (hebephilic disorder or sexual coercive disorder) in the assessment of online sexual offending perpetrators.

At a minimum, I would want to know the person's sexual history, including both conventional and unconventional sexual behavior, self-reported sexual fantasies, and for pedophilia, relevant correlates such as emotional congruence with children, attitudes and beliefs about children and sex, and work or volunteer contact with children (see Seto, 2018, for more about the assessment of pedophilia and diagnosis of pedophilic disorder; see also Seto et al., 2016, regarding the reliability of the diagnosis of pedophilic disorder). If available, I would obtain objective measures of sexual interest, such as relative viewing time, phallometric responding, or performance on indirect measures, such as choice reaction time, given the fragilities of relying on self-report and behavioral records.

I recognize that most of these measures have been developed for assessing sexual interest in children, though there is also good phallometric research on sexual interest in coercion and violence (Harris et al., 2012; Lalumière & Quinsey, 1994; Seto et al., 2012). I expect individuals who feel emotional congruence for children or have more permissive attitudes and beliefs about children and sex will be more likely to have a sexual attraction to children. Evaluators can also specifically ask about romantic attraction to children, both as a correlate of sexual attraction and sexual offending history (Bailey et al., 2016; Martijn et al., 2020).

I have argued that CSEM use is relevant to the diagnosis of pedophilic disorder in terms of impairment, but sexual content use is excluded under *DSM-5-TR* language for determining that someone has a pedophilic disorder because the use of CSEM does not meet the threshold for determining impairment, in contrast to direct interactions with a child such as sexual solicitations or contact offending, which are considered relevant (Seto, 2022). The use of sexual content does count toward determining that someone is sexually attracted to prepubescent children, so it is still relevant to ascertain whether someone has pedophilia.

We also want to assess for sexual disorder comorbidity. Someone can have multiple paraphilias, for example, and thus potentially have greater service needs or pose a greater concern in terms of sexually reoffending. For example, I would predict that someone who has both compulsive sexual behavior disorder and pedophilic disorder will be more likely to be a high-frequency CSEM user and more likely to have engaged in sexual solicitations of children or to have committed contact sexual offenses against children.

A diagnostic examination is also helpful for ruling out alternative explanations for online sexual offending. For example, traumatic brain injuries, dementia, and other organic brain conditions can result in what has been described as pseudopedophilic behavior, where someone might use CSEM or attempt sexual contact with children without any prior history or evidence of sexual interest in children (Ciani et al., 2019). Though some scholars, such as Ciani et al., have described this phenomenon as "acquired pedophilia" (p. 1), it may also reflect the disinhibition of an existing interest that was successfully suppressed or a more general disinhibition of sexual behavior that includes CSEM use or other child-focused behavior.

It may be worthwhile to specifically assess for the presence of autism spectrum conditions, given clinical observations and speculation that autism may play a role in some CSEM offending (Alley & Dubin, 2018; Alley et al.,

2019). Possible explanations that have been offered include the idea that some persons with autism spectrum conditions have more difficulty recognizing that CSEM images depict real people, feel more affinity for children than adults, struggle to develop and maintain adult relationships, or have an obsessive fixation on sexual content. However, whether this potential association is statistically and clinically significant has not yet been demonstrated.

Several studies have examined general psychopathology in online perpetrators (e.g., Reavis et al., 2023; Thibodeau et al., 2023). I focus here on the largest study, by Henshaw et al. (2018), which compared 456 CSEM perpetrators with 256 dual perpetrators and 493 contact perpetrators. Of the CSEM and dual perpetrators, few had ever been admitted to a mental health facility (10%), and psychiatric diagnoses were rare; the most common psychiatric diagnosis was for a trauma disorder (10%), followed by mood disorder (8%). Diagnosis is a strict criterion for psychopathology, however, and many individuals could have serious mood or other mental health problems without reaching the criteria or, if they do meet the criteria, without being formally diagnosed. Timing may be relevant, for example, when someone is assessed presentencing versus postsentencing; someone being assessed presentence may be more motivated to respond in a socially desirable way, either by denying psychopathology they believe may be seen as aggravating (e.g., paraphilic disorder) or by falsely reporting psychopathology they believe may be seen as mitigating for sentencing (e.g., reporting depression or trauma).

Thibodeau et al. (2023) found high levels of comorbidity in their clinical sample of 62 CSEM perpetrators, with 47% showing evidence of depression, 61% anxiety, and 27% learning disabilities. Many reported childhood maltreatment histories, with 31% reporting childhood sexual abuse and 36% reporting childhood physical abuse. In Reavis et al. (2023), we compared 51 CSEM-exclusive perpetrators with 61 perpetrators who committed CSEM and another offense and 34 solicitation perpetrators. There were few clinical elevations and no differences in psychopathology between the two CSEM groups or the CSEM and solicitation perpetrators.

One challenge for understanding the relevance of psychopathology is that it is often not possible to determine temporality because psychopathology could precede, co-occur, and/or follow sexual offending. Psychopathology could precede or co-occur with online sexual offending as a potential precursor or correlate, as in sexualized coping, and it could follow sexual offending as a result of the legal and social consequences the person faces when detected. Serious psychopathology may be associated with self-harm (see Suicide and Self-Harm Risk). I would argue that identifying and treating serious psychopathology is part of offering humane treatment, even if psychopathology is unrelated to the risk of recidivism. Serious psychopathology can also greatly affect someone's capacity or motivation to participate in services. It is important, however, to be clear about what treatment is for and why to avoid any confusion that treating psychopathology reduces the risk of sexual recidivism.

Suicide and Self-Harm Risk

Suicide risk assessment should be part of a comprehensive clinical evaluation of online perpetrators, especially if it comes early during a police investigation, given the evidence that there is a dramatically elevated risk of self-harm or suicide attempts after arrest. In a review by Key et al. (2021) of 18 studies, with 11 of these studies meeting study quality criteria, there was evidence of a dramatically higher risk of self-harm or suicide among sexual perpetrators, though few studies specifically included CSEM perpetrators. Steel et al. (2023) studied suicidal ideation among 78 CSEM perpetrators recruited from public sexual offending registries in two states. Over 2,500 individuals were eligible in their initial recruitment, but they obtained a low response rate and had to drop cases due to noncompletion or failing attention checks. Three quarters (73%) of the Steel et al. sample reported suicidal ideation and 19% reported a suicide attempt, which is similar to rates found among child-attracted persons (e.g., 23% attempted suicide in Levenson & Grady, 2019) or prison inmates more generally (20%–30%; e.g., Fazel et al., 2017). Thibodeau et al. (2023) found that 19% of the 62 CSEM perpetrators in their clinical sample reported suicidal ideation or attempts. These rates, in turn, are notably higher than in the general population (4.8% for adults in 2021, according to data from the National Institute of Mental Health, 2024).

The impact of becoming a suspect in a police investigation is important because this is a critical time. Being investigated or arrested likely involves the revelation of the allegations to others in the suspects' lives, the perceived threat of prison or other consequences, and the realization that their lives will never be the same, even if they are not convicted, due to negative publicity and notoriety among the people who know them. How investigators treat the suspect is likely to have a major impact. Indeed, investigators were rated poorly in terms of their compassion, fairness, or understanding by the respondents to Steel et al. (2023). The top two concerns reported by participants were their family finding out about the allegations and the fear of prison. In the ReDirection darknet survey I discussed in detail in Chapter 2, half of the CSEM users who responded to the survey said they had thought about self-harm or suicide, and 8% said they had attempted suicide (Insoll et al., 2022). In an analysis of a subset of 121 Finnish respondents, suicidal ideation was predicted by feeling one could not stop or control CSEM use, difficulties coping emotionally after using CSEM, difficulties with daily living activities, and social withdrawal (Nuotte & Sivonen, 2023). The impact of being detected is probably even greater for those who have no prior criminal record, are in a committed relationship, are stably employed, and are well-liked in their communities.[6]

---

[6] I thank Anton Schweighofer (personal communication, October 2, 2023) for this suggestion.

Denial or Minimization of Responsibility

Some individuals who have sexually offended deny or minimize their offending, either by denying they committed a sexual offense entirely or minimizing their responsibility in some way, which might include admitting some but not all of the actions they took, claiming their behavior was due to intoxication, blaming the victim, or suggesting there was less harm than claimed. There is some overlap between denial or minimization of responsibility and offense-supportive cognitions, discussed in the Offense-Supportive Cognitions section earlier this chapter, particularly for minimization that relies on offense-supportive cognitions (e.g., children who initiate sexual interactions are not harmed by it, so the crime was not as bad as it could have been). Denial or minimization of responsibility can be a challenge for treatment because the individual may argue that treatment is not relevant to them, or they can dwell on their stated innocence (in the case of complete denial) rather than engage with treatment. At the same time, denial of the offense is not a predictor of sexual recidivism (Hanson & Bussière, 1998; Hanson & Morton-Bourgon, 2005), and individuals who deny sexually offending can still meaningfully participate in interventions. Moreover, Nunes et al. (2007) found denial was related to sexual recidivism but only for lower risk perpetrators, which is germane here because many online perpetrators are likely to be at lower risk of reoffending than contact perpetrators. Second, denial may be particularly relevant for thinking about responsivity because someone who denies they have offended may be more likely to refuse or drop out of treatment or be disruptive if compelled to attend (see Levenson, 2011; Levenson & Macgowan, 2004).

However, full denial of offending is uncommon in CSEM and online solicitation offending. Several studies have shown that online perpetrators often admit to their offenses, presumably because they realize there is digital evidence in the form of CSEM, saved messages and posts, and other incriminating data. The person might deny intent or culpability, however, such as claiming the digital evidence was due to a virus, hacking, or another user of their computing devices. This was not uncommon in the initial statements made to police in our study of police interrogations (Seto et al., 2010), but these initial claims quickly shifted to admissions of sexual interest in children or other sexual motivations (e.g., pornography addiction, sexual compulsivity) when suspects were pressed by police investigators. As noted in Chapter 2, a significant minority of CSEM users readily admit they are sexually interested in children and/or CSEM, and others admit to sexual motivations outside of pedohebephilia (e.g., Seto et al., 2010).

A study by Bergeron et al. (2023) looked at videotaped interviews with 130 online perpetrators, with 80% charged with online solicitation, 63% with CSEM possession, and 54% with CSEM distribution. All were male adults, and most (75%) had no prior criminal history. Half fully confessed to their online crimes. Regarding change over time, 65% were consistent, either sticking with confession-confession (41%) or denial-denial (24%), but 35% went from denial to confession; nobody went from confession to denial. Most (61%) expressed guilt, and 76% talked about the potential consequences of their charges.

Bourke and colleagues (2015) examined the use of a polygraph at varying points after first contact with the police in a sample of 127 CSEM suspects—the day of the search warrant, within the first 5 days, or 3 or 4 days after the search warrant was executed—and found no difference in disclosure rates. Most suspects admitted their offenses during these times. Grubin et al. (2014) examined the polygraph interviews of 31 men convicted of CSEM offenses and deemed to be low risk by police. A third (11/31) disclosed undetected offending or suspicious behavior, including five who disclosed undetected sexual contact with children, three who disclosed online sexual solicitations, and two who engaged in undetected trading of CSEM with others. Suspicious behavior included filming children on the street, communicating with other CSEM perpetrators, and traveling that might have been for child sexual abuse tourism.

SUMMARY

Clinical and risk assessment of online sexual perpetrators should include an in-depth interview covering the details of their offenses; their explanations for these offenses if not denied; and developmental, sexual, and criminal histories. These interviews should be supplemented with the use of validated self-report measures (e.g., of personality traits and offense-supportive cognitions) and a review of available file information; collateral interviews, if available; and ideally, some kind of objective assessment of sexual interests, whether that involves phallometric testing, viewing time tasks, or other methods that are being developed (e.g., implicit association tasks). A primary focus is to identify risk and protective factors regarding sexual recidivism, but information obtained in these assessments will also be useful for diagnosis, case formulation, and intervention planning.

I recommend the use of validated risk assessment tools when available and appropriate. This includes the CPORT and CASIC for CSEM perpetrators and the Static-99R for online solicitation perpetrators, digital exhibitionism and voyeurism perpetrators, and those who engage in the technology-facilitated sexual assaults of adults, sexual trafficking of minors, and child sexual abuse tourism. Both the CPORT and Static-99R could be used for dual perpetrators (CSEM and contact) because the two risk assessment tools include overlapping but nonredundant information, and the CPORT can help predict CSEM recidivism specifically. As noted earlier in this chapter, the CPORT appears to have an advantage over the Static-99R and RM2000/S for CSEM recidivism (Eke, 2022; Helmus, Eke, Farmus, & Seto, 2024). Also, the CPORT is suitable for individuals who have committed CSEM offenses exclusively because it is a significant predictor of sexual recidivism in this subgroup of CSEM perpetrators (though the predictive accuracy is not as good as for dual perpetrators).

Individuals who commit contact sexual offenses are eligible for assessment using the Static-99R or other well-established sexual offending risk assessment tools. This includes individuals who attempt to meet or do meet minors (or undercover officers posing as minors) in sexual solicitation cases, individuals who engage in the commercial sexual exploitation of children through sexual trafficking or child sexual abuse tourism, and individuals who use technology to facilitate the sexual assaults of adults.

It is unclear if any existing risk assessment tools are suitable for individuals who engage in digital exhibitionism or voyeurism. The Static-99R (and other tools) can be used for individuals who commit noncontact offenses involving exhibitionism or voyeurism, but historically, these offenses have involved interaction with a person (in-person exhibitionism) or the risk of interaction with a person when surreptitiously watching them. Whether the risk factors and risk predictions are valid for individuals who engage in this behavior online only has not yet been examined. Similarly, it is unclear if existing risk tools are suitable for fantasy-driven sexual solicitation. We do not yet have research regarding the risk factors and risk of sexual recidivism among individuals who engage in image-based sexual abuse involving nonconsensual sharing or sextortion.

Because two studies have shown that general recidivism risk measures are valid for CSEM perpetrators and have comparable predictive accuracies (Cohen, 2023; Wakeling et al., 2011), they might be useful across types of online sexual offending. Even if they do not specifically predict sexual recidivism, they are likely to be valid for predicting the risk of general recidivism, which is also useful information for clinicians and other decision makers.

Only one study has demonstrated the predictive accuracy of the STABLE-2007 for CSEM perpetrators (Babchishin et al., 2023). However, I expect this dynamic risk assessment tool to be useful for all online sexual offending cases, given that the domains covered in the STABLE-2007 are implicated in explanations for these different forms of online sexual offending, and scores on the STABLE-2007 can help identify treatment and supervision targets.

Risk assessment also includes the risk of harm to self, given evidence that individuals identified for online sexual offending are at acutely greater risk of self-injury or suicide following their detection. Clinical assessments are needed to address potential responsivity factors such as reading level, intelligence, psychopathology, and denial or minimization of offending.

CASE EXAMPLES

I again return to the hypothetical case examples introduced in earlier chapters. Here, I discuss the results of hypothetical clinical and risk assessments conducted with these individuals, drawing on the research and recommendations in this chapter.

Adam (Lower Risk CSEM)

In the clinical assessment, Adam reported being devastated by his arrest for CSEM offenses and the subsequent impacts on his family. He described symptoms of severe depression after his arrest and admitted that he had persistent thoughts about suicide in the weeks following his arrest but denied any intent, plans, or attempts to harm himself. Adam also recognized that he had experienced depression and stress before his arrest, which he attributed to his marital difficulties. In the risk assessment, Adam received a score of zero on the CPORT and, thus, was judged to be at relatively low risk for any sexual recidivism, including CSEM recidivism. The dynamic risk assessment identified sexual interest in children and the use of sex as a means of coping with dysphoria (particularly his online pornography use) as criminogenic needs.

Bart (Higher Risk CSEM)

In the clinical assessment, Bart reported feeling significant depression and anxiety following his arrest but denied any thoughts of self-harm or suicide. In the risk assessment, Bart received a score of 6 out of 7 on the CPORT and, thus, would be at relatively high risk for any sexual recidivism, including CSEM recidivism. The dynamic risk assessment identified a sexual interest in children, association with antisocial peers on darknet forums, relationship difficulties, social isolation, and emotional congruence with children as criminogenic needs.

Sean (Sexual Solicitation)

A clinical assessment identified no concerns about mental health or self-harm. Sean was assessed for risk of sexual recidivism using the Static-99R because the scoring rules indicate that someone who engaged in sexual interactions with a real, identifiable minor is eligible. Sean engaged in sexual communications with real minors and, in some cases, participated in the production of CSEM through exchanging nudes and live streaming. Sean's score on the Static-99 was 6, placing him in the highest risk category (Well Above Average Risk). Given the number of minor victims, the production of CSEM, and his estimated risk of sexual recidivism, Sean was sentenced to prison and a long probation period on release. The dynamic risk assessment identified sex as coping, sex drive, hostility toward women, and impulsivity as criminogenic needs. The combination of his static and dynamic risk assessment scores suggested Sean is at a well above average risk to sexually reoffend.

Elvis (Digital Exhibitionism)

The clinical assessment did not identify any concerns regarding psychopathology or potential self-harm. Elvis was eligible for risk assessment using the Static-99R because this tool can be used for individuals who engage in exhibitionistic or voyeuristic offenses that involve direct interaction with a victim, even without any sexual contact. However, a caveat is that the Static-99R development and validation research had few, if any, individuals who had used digital technologies to commit these noncontact sexual offenses. Exposing oneself to a stranger in a public place, in person, may be quite different from someone who sends unsolicited images to strangers online. Elvis received a score of 5 on the Static-99R, putting him in the Above Average Risk category. The dynamic risk assessment indicated atypical sexual interests, sex as coping, and social isolation as criminogenic needs, and the combination of static and dynamic risk assessment scores suggested he was indeed in the Above Average Risk category.

Vince (Digital Voyeurism)

Vince was assessed for risk using the CPORT (he created CSEM by recording minors) and the Static-99R for his noncontact sexual offenses. His score on the CPORT was 0, suggesting he was at relatively low risk of committing a new sexual offense, such as a new CSEM offense, compared with other CSEM perpetrators. In contrast, his score on the Static-99R was 2, putting him in the Average Risk category, this time compared with other individuals who had committed contact or noncontact offenses directly against identifiable victims. The evaluator interpreted these seemingly discrepant results as evidence that Vince was unlikely to commit a new CSEM offense or contact sexual offense against a prepubescent or pubescent child (the most common sexual recidivism in the CPORT research) but was average in the risk of committing a new sexual offense involving voyeuristic behavior against adults or older minors who might be mistaken as adults. Dynamic risk assessment identified atypical sexual interests, high sex drive, sex as coping, social isolation, and relationship difficulties as criminogenic needs. The combination of his static and dynamic risk assessment scores suggested he was at average risk to sexually reoffend.

Jack (Nonconsensual Sharing)

The clinical assessment did not identify any significant concerns. Jack was not eligible for the Static-99R, given the nature of his online sexual offense. A dynamic risk assessment was conducted to identify potential intervention needs, and hostility toward women, lack of concern for others, and negative emotionality were identified.

Adrian (Technology-Facilitated Sexual Assault)

The clinical assessment identified elevations on multiple antisocial personality traits, including impulsivity, recklessness, and callousness. Adrian's history included evidence of early behavior problems, including aggression at home and school, persistent lying, stealing, and noncompliance with rules. No psychopathology or concern about self-harm was noted. Adrian's score on the Static-99R was 4, indicating he was in the Above Average Risk category for sexual recidivism. The dynamic risk assessment highlighted concerns about his capacity for relationship stability, hostility toward women, lack of concern for others, and poor problem solving. The combined static and dynamic risk assessment indicated he was in the Above Average Risk category.

Smith (Sexual Trafficking of Minors and Child Sexual Abuse Tourism)

Because of his contact sexual offending, Smith was assessed using the Static-99R and received a score of 4, putting him in the Above Average Risk category. He was also assessed using the CPORT because of the CSEM offending and again received a score of 4. The evaluator concluded that these concordant results suggested Smith was at above-average risk of committing a new sexual offense, either in the form of CSEM offenses or contact sexual offenses against children. The dynamic risk assessment identified sexual interest in children, sex drive, emotional congruence with children, and relationship difficulties as criminogenic needs. The combined static and dynamic risk assessment indicated he was above average in risk of sexually reoffending.

7

Treatment of Online Sexual Offending Perpetrators

As I also wrote in the first edition, there has been more research and, thus, progress in etiology, characteristics, and clinical and risk assessment than in intervention. Challenges for advancing our scientific knowledge about intervention include the institutional and practical challenges of setting up rigorous evaluations, including randomized controlled trials; institutional and public demand for treatment, even if it is not required; clinical demand for services outrunning the knowledge base; and the specific difficulty of detecting significant effects with relatively low base rates of sexual recidivism, require many years of follow-up, and only capture detected offenses. Nonetheless, there have been some encouraging developments in treatment (this chapter) and prevention (Chapter 8) of online sexual offending. There is enough of an empirical foundation in terms of explanations of online sexual offending and assessment to drive interventions, including adapting existing evidence-based interventions and designing new interventions that adhere to sound principles, particularly the risk–need–responsivity framework described in Chapter 6. We have assessment tools such as the Child Pornography Offender Risk Tool (CPORT) that can provide accurate long-term (static or historical) risk assessment for making decisions about intervention in line with the risk principle, and there is justification for using the STABLE-2007 as a dynamic risk assessment tool to identify intervention targets in line with the need principle. Other clinical assessment information is relevant for decisions according to the responsivity principle, including assessments of acute suicide risk, denial, and psychopathology.

---

https://doi.org/10.1037/0000428-008
Online Sexual Offending: Theory, Practice, and Policy, Second Edition, by M. C. Seto
Copyright © 2025 by the American Psychological Association. All rights reserved.

Following the risk principle, higher intensity interventions should be reserved for those who are at higher risk for sexual recidivism. These interventions might include intensive treatment, custody, and/or prolonged community supervision. Moderate risk estimates warrant less intensive treatment and supervision, and those who are at the lowest risk may require minimal or no intervention after pursuing justice for victims in terms of prosecution and sentencing. Henshaw et al. (2020) suggested that most perpetrators who use child sexual exploitation material (CSEM) exclusively would not require treatment, given baseline sexual recidivism rates. At the same time, Seto et al. (2011) found that many CSEM perpetrators had committed undetected contact sexual offenses, and treatment may help reduce the likelihood of future (undetected) sexual offending. The evaluation of an accredited sexual offending treatment program in the United Kingdom found evidence of an iatrogenic effect for CSEM perpetrators, possibly because the treatment was more intense than their average risk to reoffend would warrant (Mews et al., 2017).

When possible, clinics could offer different intensity treatment streams. I recommend different treatment streams for online versus contact or noncontact perpetrators because they are, on average, at different levels of risk for sexual recidivism, they differ in some likely treatment targets (e.g., internet self-regulation for online perpetrators), and different streams would prevent sharing of tradecraft, such that online perpetrators might learn how to commit contact offenses and contact perpetrators how to commit offenses online.

Following the need principle, I can suggest interventions for specific dynamic risk factors that, ideally, are empirically related to outcomes or are at least theoretically and clinically plausible and, thus, become suitable treatment targets, including sexual self-regulation, emotional congruence with children, offense-permissive cognitions, social ties, and general self-regulation. I have recommended the use of the STABLE-2007 as a structured professional judgment guide to identify major treatment and supervision targets. Additional measures may be helpful because the STABLE-2007 does not directly assess offense-supportive cognitions regarding children and sex and does not specifically address problematic internet use, though this could be considered as part of someone's general self-regulation difficulties. This opinion is supported by Babchishin et al. (2023), though we still need evidence that change in STABLE-2007 dynamic risk factors is associated with less sexual recidivism. Another assessment option that combines both static and dynamic risk factors is the Violence Risk Scale–Sexual Offense Version, though the predictive value of this tool has not yet been tested for online perpetrators (Eher et al., 2020; M. E. Olver et al., 2020).

These criminogenic needs can be addressed using evidence-based strategies: Sexual self-regulation deficits can be addressed through mindfulness training, healthy coping skills, and the development of self-management strategies after a thorough behavioral analysis of the antecedents of prior sexual offenses in terms of mood states, thoughts, and situations. Knowing that certain situations or states are associated with having sexual urges can help the person develop strategies to avoid these situations or states and more effectively cope when urges to offend are experienced. For example, behavioral analysis might reveal that someone's sexual urges are stronger when they are depressed or anxious, and treatment can target healthier mood regulation skills, as well as techniques for voluntary control over sexual arousal. There is some evidence this helps because Gannon et al.'s (2019) meta-analysis revealed that programs providing behavioral conditioning to increase voluntary control over sexual arousal had better outcomes than programs that did not.

Cognitive behavior therapies (CBT) are useful for reducing offense-supportive cognitions, building up social ties to positive peers, and reducing reliance on children for emotional or other needs. Emotional congruence with children and positive social ties can be addressed through interventions to increase positive social contact with adults. This could also indirectly influence offense-permissive cognitions. Finally, problem-solving training and other CBT-based interventions can improve general and internet self-regulation skills. For the responsivity principle, interventions benefit from being concrete, skills-based, and practical (general responsivity). Specific responsivity considerations include developmental disabilities, learning disabilities, and perhaps autism spectrum traits, given a yet untested hypothesis about autism playing a role in CSEM offending (Alley & Dubin, 2018; Alley et al., 2019). Even if it does not, individuals with autism may respond differently in group treatment, especially when discussing socialization. Also, Korchia et al. (2022) found a higher prevalence of attention-deficit/hyperactivity disorder (ADHD) in clients with hypersexuality or paraphilic disorders, suggesting that ADHD could affect online perpetrators who have problems with hypersexuality or paraphilic disorders in their ability to participate in treatment and services.

Generally, sexual offending treatment programs that adhered to the risk, need, and responsivity principles produced better outcomes than those that did not (Hanson et al., 2009). Nobody has yet examined the importance of the risk–need–responsivity framework for online sexual offending treatment, however, and there have been almost no evaluations to date. I review the limited evaluation evidence later in this chapter.

TREATMENT MODELS

Table 7.1 summarizes the intensity of better known interventions for online sexual offending—most focusing on CSEM offending, except for Engage Plus, designed for online sexual solicitation offending—and treatment modules or topics. First, it is clear that there is variation in the intensity of treatment in terms of the number of sessions or total hours, ranging from relatively brief programs delivered in 10 sessions to intensive treatment comprising weekly sessions for a year or longer. Second, there are many commonalities across programs. All involve some attention to criminogenic and other needs that were reviewed in the previous chapter, including an understanding of offending pathways or processes, emotional self-regulation, sexual self-regulation, internet self-regulation, and social and relationship skills. However, the order in which

TABLE 7.1. Overview of Different Treatment Programs for Online Sexual Offending

i-SOTP	iHorizon	Inform Plus & Engage Plus	Prevent It	Dunkelfeld	CEM-COPE	Piche & Schweighofer
20–30 sessions	23 group plus three individual sessions	25 hours 10 sessions	Self-guided pace up to 8 weeks	135 hours or more	10 sessions	12–24 sessions
Values	Motivation to change	Intro to group	Welcome and behavioral analysis	Offense analysis	Introduction	Motivation to change
Functional analysis	Treatment goals	Offense analysis	Life balance	Sexual self-regulation	Legal context and internet use	CSEM pathways
Victim awareness	Supporting success	Role of fantasies	Psychoeducation about sexuality	Solutions planning	Emotional self-regulation	Fantasy management
Emotional and social skills	Sexuality	Fantasy and self-regulation	Motivation to change	Social and relationship skills	Sexual self-regulation	Emotions and sex
Collecting, compulsivity, online behavior	Positive relationships	Victim empathy	Self-regulation skills		Problem solving	Thoughts and offending
New life plan	Internet use	Legal issues	Identifying life goals		Interpersonal relationships	Sexuality management
	Moving on	Relationship and social skills	Risk-management skills		Offense formulation	Relationships
		Making change	Maintaining change		Looking forward	Other roadblocks
		Relapse prevention				Internet health
						Safety planning and accountability

Note. The focus of most of these online sexual offending treatment programs is child sexual exploitation material (CSEM) offending, though Engage Plus was adapted from Inform Plus to provide an option for sexual solicitation offending. Technology-facilitated sexual assault of adults or commercial sexual exploitation of children would be addressed in programs for contact sexual offending. It is unclear how individuals who engage in image-based sexual abuse are dealt with in treatment if they are referred for treatment. The table entries represent different content modules, either based on the developer's labels or my summation of the content. There is a high level of overlap in terms of content across treatment programs, reflecting a common treatment literature, but the order of modules can be quite different.

these domains are addressed varies, and the order in which content is introduced may have an impact. There are also some differences across programs; for example, only two programs (Inform Plus and Coping With Child Exploitation Material Use [CEM-COPE]) explicitly address an understanding of the laws regarding CSEM use or other online offending behavior, and only two programs (Internet Sex Offender Treatment Programme [i-SOTP; Middleton et al., 2009] and Inform Plus) explicitly address victim empathy. This does not mean that legal issues and victim empathy are not addressed in the other programs, but they are not built into the core content of modules.

Internet Sex Offender Treatment Programme (i-SOTP)

In the following sections, I describe and then review the limited evidence available for existing online sexual offending treatment programs. I begin with the Internet Sex Offender Treatment Programme (i-SOTP; Middleton et al., 2009), previously offered in the United Kingdom as part of national correctional programming (updated and now offered as iHorizon [Elliot & Hambly, 2023]; see the next section). The i-SOTP program was developed to address the gap in services for online perpetrators; a third of new referrals to probation services (at that time, in the 2000s) were for internet-related offenses. There was concern about combining online and contact perpetrators in treatment and uncertainty about the applicability of existing treatment programs. Recognizing as well that internet perpetrators seemed to be at lower risk than contact perpetrators, which has since been demonstrated empirically (Seto et al., 2011), there was interest in a lower intensity program to match the risk principle. Middleton et al. (2009) developed the i-SOTP drawing from existing models—relapse prevention, the Good Lives Model, 12-step addiction groups, and self-help information—to address dynamic risk factors assessed by the STABLE-2007 tool: general self-regulation (impulse control, delay of gratification), sexual self-regulation (control over sexual preoccupation and atypical sexual interests), offense-supportive attitudes and beliefs (e.g., that children in images are not harmed); and interpersonal deficits (poor social skills, loneliness). Without getting into details about the prior treatment models, such as relapse prevention, they are mostly cognitive behavioral in orientation and designed to provide knowledge and skills to help the person shift cognitions and better manage their behavior in risky situations.

Middleton et al. (2009) evaluated i-SOTP using a methodologically weak pre–post design, which again cannot rule out change due to time, regression to the mean, or selection bias. There were significant pre–post changes on 10 of 12 measures examined in Middleton et al.'s evaluation of 264 online CSEM perpetrators who were on probation and completed the program. Some measures assessed criminogenic needs such as impulsivity (self-regulation deficits), offense-supportive cognitions, emotional congruence with children, and empathy. However, other measures assessed factors that have not been shown to be directly related to the risk of sexual recidivism, including self-esteem, under- or overassertiveness, personal distress, and locus of control. An additional measure of loneliness could be viewed as a measure of the absence of the protective factor of positive social support. Curiously, there were no measures of paraphilic sexual interests or excessive sexual preoccupation, though pedohebephilia was likely for many participants because the mean age of children depicted in CSEM possessed by treatment participants was 8, ranging from 1 to 15 years old. There was no comparison group, and it was unclear how program attrition was handled, so these changes cannot be attributed to the intervention. Moreover, the group overall was at low risk for sexual recidivism: RM2000/S scores were available for 161 of the 264 treatment participants, and of these, 51% were assigned to the low-risk category, 39% were in the medium-risk category, 9% high risk, and 1% very high risk. The sample was generally low risk on the OASys, a measure of risk for general recidivism used by probation services. The inclusion of low-risk perpetrators in treatment is not consistent with the risk principle, and any treatment directed at reducing noncriminogenic needs, such as subjective distress, would not be consistent with the need principle.

iHorizon

Many aspects of i-SOTP were incorporated into iHorizon (Elliot & Hambly, 2023),[1] the currently accredited online sexual offending program in the United Kingdom that parallels Horizon, the main accredited program for individuals who have sexually offended and are in correctional custody or supervision. Individuals who engage in CSEM-exclusive offending are referred to iHorizon, whereas those who also committed contact offenses or who had direct interactions with children, such as through online sexual solicitations, are referred to Horizon. The iHorizon program is intended for men 18 and older with an IQ of 80 or above. Target foci include self-regulation, internet use, sexual interests in children, sexual preoccupation, and interpersonal functioning. Elliott and Hamby conducted a pre–post analysis of 122 iHorizon participants between November 2018 and January 2020, with complete data for 92 participants. The mean age of this sample was 38 years old, ranging from 20 to 75. Most were White (95%) and admitted their guilt (92%). The iHorizon participants were all treated in the community. The pre–post comparison found significant and large changes on a clinician-rated assessment tool capturing different risk domains, such as sexual self-regulation and interpersonal deficits. There were trivial differences in changes across domains, suggesting there was no treatment specificity; this may be due to a nonspecific effect of the intervention, such that feeling hopeful for change may be a rising tide that will lift all boats or a nonintervention-related process, such as the simple passage of time. Though encouraging, a pre–post comparison does not tell us if iHorizon had a specific impact. Observed changes could be due to the simple passage of time,

---

[1] As a reminder, I disclosed in the Introduction that I was part of the advisory panel that accredited the iHorizon and Horizon programs.

regression to the mean, or a selection bias because only those with both pre- and posttreatment scores were included (those who refuse, drop out of, or are kicked out of treatment do not have posttreatment data). In general, offending program participants who drop out of treatment or are kicked out of treatment due to noncompliance or other disruptive behavior tend to be at higher risk and need than those who can complete treatment, irrespective of specific treatment effects (M. E. Olver & Wong, 2011).

Inform Plus

Gillespie et al. (2018) reported a pre–post evaluation of Inform Plus (https://www.lucyfaithfull.org.uk/help-to-stop-offending-online.htm), a brief psychoeducational intervention for CSEM perpetrators offered in the United Kingdom. From data on 92 men, all under investigation but not yet convicted of CSEM offenses, significant pre–post changes were shown after a 12-week follow-up, which is encouraging but inconclusive. Dervley et al. (2017) conducted a qualitative study of 13 Inform Plus program leavers and eight associates of these participants. These participants reported improvements in self-efficacy and motivation not to offend, which was corroborated by their associates; this was a highly self-selected sample, however. Inform Plus makes sense as an intervention option because it is relatively low intensity and, therefore, suitable for lower risk CSEM perpetrators. I would want to add or refer to a higher intensity program for higher risk perpetrators, where risk is assessed using evidence-based measures such as the CPORT or modified RM2000/S.

Engage Plus

Engage Plus (https://www.lucyfaithfull.org.uk/help-to-stop-offending-online.htm) is an adaptation of Inform Plus and is almost identical in its structure and content. Engage Plus is the only online intervention designed for individuals engaging in online sexual solicitations, whether fantasy or contact driven. Engage Plus was initially introduced as one-on-one counseling but has recently been offered in small groups. No evaluation data have been reported.

Dunkelfeld Prevention Project

Results from the Dunkelfeld Prevention Project are relevant because most of their help-seeking participants had used CSEM, and some admitted to contact sexual offending too. Neutze et al. (2011) reported that, in 137 Dunkelfeld cases who reported lifetime offending behavior, excluding the previous 6 months, 31% reported using CSEM, 33% reported direct offending (including noncontact offending, such as exhibitionism), and 36% reported both. Of the 155 cases with recent offending data over the previous 6 months, 41% reported using CSEM, 33% reported direct offending, and 26% had been inactive in the previous 6 months. The Dunkelfeld Prevention Project is a self-referred program for individuals concerned about their sexual thoughts, feelings, or behaviors involving children and who met diagnostic criteria for pedophilic disorder or hebephilic disorder. Individuals who undergo an extensive assessment and are eligible are offered individual and group therapy, with the potential option of sex drive–reducing medications, to address their needs. Because of Germany's narrow mandatory reporting obligations, individuals can confess to using CSEM or direct offending against children without being reported to authorities unless they indicate a risk of homicide.

Beier et al.'s (2015) outcome study suggested evidence of improvement based on a comparison of 53 treated and 22 wait-list controls. However, this conclusion is challenged by a reanalysis by Mokros and Banse (2019), who pointed out that Beier et al. (2015) only looked at pre–post change in the treated and wait-list groups separately, whereas Mokros and Banse (2019) found that the degree of change in scores was not significantly different between the two groups. Moreover, the number of cases Beier et al. (2015) examined in the evaluation was much smaller than the actual number of people who have gone through treatment and an even tinier fraction of those who were assessed; it is concerning that there are so few outcome data at this point. The Dunkelfeld intervention is considered a higher intensity intervention because it involves 135 hours or more of service, compared with the 25 hours involved in the Inform Plus program.

Wild et al. (2020) reported data on a German outpatient treatment program intended for individuals with a self-reported sexual attraction to children or adolescents, whether or not they would identify as pedophilic or meet clinical criteria and whether or not they were detected by the criminal justice system. Limited outcome data were available, with pre–post self-report data for 25 participants and then follow-up self-reports for nine participants. Of the pre–post sample, 18 of 25 had committed CSEM offenses (1/3 of these were dual), and most (22/25) had been detected. Most (22/25) did not meet the diagnostic criteria for pedophilia in the *International Statistical Classification of Diseases and Related Health Problems* (10th ed.; World Health Organization, 1994). There were significant pre–post reductions on the measures, but again, we do not know if this can be attributed to treatment without any comparison or control group. Self-reported offending behavior was obtained from 19 of 25 participants, but it was messy, involving two different measures with only partial completion at different times. I assume there was a nonrandom bias in who completed the self-reported offending measures; those who offend might be less likely to report it, though there is not the same mandatory reporting obligation in Germany as in Canada or the United States.

Coping With Child Exploitation Material Use (CEM-COPE)

I also mention an expert-informed CEM-COPE treatment model by Henshaw et al. (2020) here because I was one of the experts who were consulted by the CEM-COPE team. The CEM-COPE model is explicitly informed by the motivation–facilitation model and an understanding of typical similarities and differences between online and contact perpetrators (Babchishin et al., 2011, 2015). In particular, the program recognized that online perpetrators are more likely to show evidence of atypical sexuality yet will typically score lower on measures of antisociality when compared with individuals who have committed direct offenses against children or adults. The CEM-COPE program is intended to be delivered in 10 2-hour group sessions for CSEM-exclusive perpetrators.

Piché and Schweighofer's (2023) Treatment Model

I also briefly describe the treatment model developed by Piché and Schweighofer (2023; disclosure: I reviewed the book proposal and provided an endorsement for the published version). In a workbook, Piché and Schweighofer described the program they developed and deliver in a community in British Columbia, Canada. Core elements include goal setting, motivational engagement, CBT principles, fantasy management, emotion self-regulation, sexuality, relationships, internet health, safety planning, and accountability. Chapters cover common evidence-based needs, including the motivation to desist and live a better life, general and sexual self-regulation deficits, internet-use management, lifestyle management, and so on. I am pleased they took my advice—if it was my advice they were responding to—to begin with sustained attention to motivational engagement because most existing interventions rely on the assumption that the person is motivated to seek help and will genuinely engage, and motivational engagement content is only briefly addressed. But we know people show up for treatment with different levels of intrinsic and extrinsic motivation. This can range from genuine (they want to change) to ambivalent (they want to see what is involved) to reluctant help seeking (pressured by a spouse or relative or to comply with a court order).

EVIDENCE-BASED INTERVENTION RECOMMENDATIONS

Given the absence of methodologically strong evidence for effective interventions other than the pilot study evaluation of Prevent It by Lätth et al. (2022), how do we proceed? In this section, I provide evidence-based recommendations for adult interventions drawing on what we know about clinical and risk-related needs (see Chapter 6), perpetrator characteristics, motivations and likely facilitation factors, and robust findings from the general sexual offending intervention literature, which might but is not guaranteed to generalize to online sexual offending.

Risk-Need-Responsivity Framework

I have already argued at the beginning of this chapter that any effective intervention for online sexual offending should be consistent with the risk–need–responsivity framework so that interventions are titrated to the level of risk, address dynamic risk factors, and are responsive to the individual (Bonta & Andrews, 2024). Given what we know about the average risk of sexually reoffending, as summarized in Chapter 6, I expect any treatment for online perpetrators to be less intense than similar treatment for contact perpetrators in terms of total hours and parameters, such as frequency and duration of sessions. In some cases, that can include diversion, no treatment at all, or a low-intensity psychoeducational intervention such as Inform Plus if treatment is ordered by the court or is a condition of probation or parole. A plausible explanation for the results reported by Mews et al. (2017) in their evaluation of the nationally accredited sexual offending treatment program in the United Kingdom is that CSEM perpetrators received too much (or mismatched) treatment because those who participated in treatment were more likely to sexually reoffend than those in the comparison group (4.4% vs. 2.9%). The program involved 180 hours of direct service compared with the approximately 135 hours for 1 year of the Dunkelfeld intervention and 25 hours for Inform Plus.

I covered the most likely treatment needs in Chapter 6 in the Criminogenic Needs Assessment section. Though much less is known about specific responsivity factors, general responsivity usually means interventions are cognitive behavioral rather than insight oriented, concrete, and skills based. Any reading or homework needs to be at an accessible reading level. Piché (personal communication, October 20, 2023) has suggested that groups for neurodiverse clients should be smaller, calmer, and slower than typical groups to avoid overwhelming participants.

Other lessons for online sexual offending treatment can be gleaned from Gannon et al.'s (2019) meta-analysis of sexual offending treatment program outcomes, Hanson et al.'s (2009) meta-analysis showing that greater adherence to risk–need–responsivity principles is related to positive impact, and multiple meta-analyses identifying what works in general correctional interventions (see Bonta & Andrews, 2024). Gannon et al. (2019) found that programs delivered in custody or in the community had similar effects (unlike a review by Schmucker & Lösel, 2015); programs led by a psychologist had better outcomes, possibly reflecting program fidelity or evidence-based practices, given the assessment, evaluation, and research training required for psychologists; and programs that included behavioral treatment to address atypical sexual arousal patterns had better outcomes than those that did not include this behavioral treatment.

Motivation to Change

A major responsivity factor that must be addressed by any effective intervention is motivation to change. There is ample evidence that voluntary and mandated treatment clients may differ in outcomes, including treatment completion and recidivism (e.g., Parhar et al., 2008). Even among those who appear to volunteer for treatment freely, there may be differences between those who are intrinsically (they want to change) and extrinsically (they volunteered for treatment because they are being pressured by a partner or their family) motivated. Those who are intrinsically motivated may be more actively involved, more willing to face therapeutic challenges, and more willing to practice and use skills during and after treatment. Thus, assessing and enhancing motivation to change—for example, by using motivational interviewing techniques—is an important task in treatment (e.g., McMurran, 2004, 2009).

Motivation to change is central to treatment or prevention efforts and is an explicit component of many programs listed in Table 7.1. Motivation to change is one of the impetuses for the Good Lives Model, which argues that focusing solely on deficits and absence of offending is less engaging than also considering strengths and how to live a good life without offending (Ward, 2002). In other words, given that offending fulfilled some need in the person—whether it was sexual gratification or temporary reprieve from distress or revenge—how can that need be fulfilled in a more prosocial way? This can be operationalized in treatment as conversations about what the person hopes to accomplish in treatment, their concerns, and what they want in the future.

In their systematic review of 13 studies, Sturgess et al. (2016) concluded that the following factors affected whether perpetrators completed treatment: self-efficacy to change; perceptions of treatment, staff, and peers; emotional regulation; and perceived choice and control. Motivational engagement techniques can address many of these factors by increasing self-efficacy; improving perceptions of treatment, staff, and peers; and feeling more choice and control in treatment. Emotional dysregulation can be addressed as part of treatment as well. Another way to build motivation to change is to enhance the therapeutic alliance. Kozar and Day (2012) have summarized the evidence for building a therapeutic alliance, including warmth, empathy, and unconditional positive regard. Indeed, these nonspecific elements can explain a large proportion of variance in treatment outcomes, and they help explain why there are often small or no differences in outcomes between different treatment models and programs (see Marcus et al., 2014; Wampold et al., 1997).

The Critical Role of Sexual Self-Regulation

I hope it is clear from reading this book that treatment for online sexual offending must address sexual self-regulation, a critical dynamic risk domain in the general sexual offending literature and a common need for online perpetrators in the forms of paraphilic sexual interests or hypersexuality. This could include CBT content and techniques from the general sexual offending literature to teach sexual self-regulation skills. As mentioned, Gannon et al. (2019) found that outcomes were better in sexual offending treatment programs that included behavioral conditioning of sexual arousal as part of treatment, compared with those that did not (or where it was not known if the program included behavioral conditioning). This finding could reflect a positive effect of behavioral conditioning on voluntary control over sexual arousal (see the case example by Campbell-Fuller & Craig, 2009) as part of someone's sexual self-regulation repertoire. It could also be a proxy for programs that pay special attention to atypical sexual arousal because many programs do not and, instead, focus on nonsexual topics and skills, such as impulse control, social skills, or mood regulation, even though the behavior that brought the person to attention was sexual.

Social Functioning

Another prominent dynamic risk factor is social functioning in terms of social isolation, loneliness, or avoidance of offline relationships and interactions. This, in turn, is likely related to stigma regarding attraction to children for those with pedohebephilia, fear of discovery, social skills deficits, social anxiety, or a lack of interest in adult relationships. As discussed in Chapters 2 (CSEM), 3 (solicitation), and 5 (etiology), social functioning is a common need. It is related to problematic internet use because there can be bidirectional effects: Being online more means less time and maybe less motivation to engage with people offline; however, being isolated, lonely, and/or socially anxious makes being online easier. Being online means potentially more opportunities to offend and, in some fora, being exposed to more offense-permissive influences.

For some online perpetrators, specific internet self-regulation deficits—not just general or sexual self-regulation deficits—are unique treatment targets that distinguish this group from other sexual offending groups. Relevant to this suggestion is the finding from Babchishin et al.'s (2015) meta-analysis that found online perpetrators had more access to the internet, reflecting greater opportunity (in contrast to offline perpetrators, who had more contact with children), and evidence suggesting online perpetrators are more likely to be involved in online pedohebephilia forums (Frei et al., 2005). Though online forums can be an important source of positive social support (Roche et al., 2022), some of these forums can facilitate the exchange of CSEM, feed offense-supportive cognitions and norms, and share tradecraft (e.g., how to sexually solicit children online). Surjadi et al. (2010) identified a nonsexual motivation in a small sample of Dutch perpetrators, suggesting they were online engaging with CSEM to distract themselves, connect with others, or enjoy the satisfaction of collecting. This treatment component must recognize that internet use addressed needs that could be met in other ways (cf. good lives model; Ward, 2002). For example, one reason given by many CSEM-offending men for being online so much is that they were socially isolated and lonely, and they found a community online. How could this positive social connection be met in safer ways, where they are not exposed to offense-supportive cognitions, tradecraft, opportunity, or other exposures that may influence their risk of online sexual offending? How else could the person get that social support and build relationships offline?

Women and Juveniles

I am not aware of any formal treatment models or programs for women who commit online sexual offenses. What about treatment for juveniles? Beier et al. (2016) described an adaptation of the Dunkelfeld program for juvenile candidates ranging between 12 and 18 years of age. In the first year of operation, referrals were received for 49 juveniles, most referred by a parent or guardian or professionals; however, eight juveniles (16%) were self-referred. All but one of the referrals were for male juveniles. Of the 49 referred, 31 were invited to participate in the intake assessment, and 27 showed up. Some additional cases who met program criteria but were seen at the clinic before the media campaign for the juvenile version of Dunkelfeld were added to the study, bringing the total to 33 cases. Their mean age was 15. Of these 33 cases, 27 were seen as having a sexual preference for prepubescent or pubescent children. Two thirds preferred girls, 18% preferred boys, and 15% preferred both boys and girls. No evaluation data were reported. In the offline juvenile sexual offending literature, there is evidence that multisystemic therapy, a cognitive-behavioral approach directly involving parents and families, can significantly reduce sexual offending (Letourneau et al., 2013). Reviews of the juvenile sexual offending literature point out that general self-regulation deficits and social skill deficits are more prominent needs, whereas paraphilic sexual motivations are less prominent but relevant for some juveniles who have sexually offended (Seto & Lalumière, 2010; Seto et al., 2003; van Wijk et al., 2006).

WHO DELIVERS INTERVENTIONS, WHERE, AND HOW?

The previous sections covered specific content and skills that can be addressed in treatment for individuals who have sexually offended, based on an assessment of their risk to sexually offend, criminogenic needs, and responsivity considerations, such as motivation to change. However, there are also nonspecific elements of treatment that can influence treatment participation, engagement, and outcome. In this section, I discuss therapist characteristics (who), treatment in custody versus the community (where), and whether treatment should be provided individually or through hybrid or virtual care (how).

Who?

Both the general and offending treatment literature are clear that therapists who are warm, empathic, fair but firm in terms of establishing expectations and rules, and constructive are associated with better outcomes than therapists who do not have these qualities (W. L. Marshall et al., 2003). Qualifications or years of experience are often less important than specific training and adherence to an empirically supported treatment model (Stein & Lambert, 1984). Treatment fidelity is often overlooked, but it is arguably one of the most important levers for improving treatment outcomes because therapists and programs that maintain high fidelity to evidence-based treatment models produce better outcomes than those that do not (Gearing et al., 2011; Moncher & Prinz, 1991). Gannon et al. (2019) found that programs that had a registered psychologist and active supervision involved were associated with better outcomes, possibly because the psychologist or supervisor brought more attention to program fidelity and ongoing evaluation and validated clinical and risk assessment to drive intervention. Similarly, probation officers trained to follow the risk–need–responsivity framework and use repeated evaluations to drive their supervision decisions were associated with better recidivism outcomes than probation officers before this training (Bonta et al., 2021).

Where?

Schmucker and Lösel (2015) found, in studies conducted up to 2010, that sexual offending treatment had a significant and positive effect in community but not prison programs. In contrast, Gannon et al. (2019) found significant effects for both community and prison programs, presumably because newer outcome studies included prison programs, custody did not distinguish between prison and hospital settings, and/or newer outcome studies had significant positive effects. The choice of treatment in custody or the community should depend on risk level and sentencing rather than whether treatment is more effective in that setting. An advantage of treatment in the community over custody is that there are more in vivo opportunities to practice skills and get feedback in treatment. For example, someone working on building social skills and positive social support could work on these goals between sessions, which is more difficult to do in the controlled environment of prison and the reality that fellow inmates could be antisocial influences.

How?

Another responsivity parameter to consider is whether to offer treatment in an individual versus group format. Groups are typically preferred because they are more cost-efficient, and individuals can benefit from positive group dynamics when there is effective facilitation of group sessions. For example, group members can share their experiences, complement each other's strengths and weaknesses, and offer advice with the credibility of being a peer with similar or relevant experiences. In Gannon et al.'s (2019) meta-analysis, programs that provided group therapy fared better than individual therapy.

Individual therapy is still needed as an option when people cannot participate in group therapy (e.g., because of debilitating social anxiety) or need extra support outside of group therapy sessions. Lampalzer et al. (2021) did a post hoc analysis of program measures for child-attracted persons referred to individual or group therapy. No significant differences were found between these two groups, except those referred for individual therapy were more impulsive; other program measures assessed psychopathy, empathy, dynamic risk factors assessed by the STABLE-2007, and readiness to change.

In addition to the individual versus group therapy decision, another decision is whether to provide treatment in person or virtually. The COVID-19 pandemic accelerated the uptake of virtual care via video conferencing or even telephone sessions. Virtual care can be as good as in-person therapy (Fernandez et al., 2021), and even if it was not, it could still be worth it as an adjunct option for people who cannot come to treatment because of distance, physical mobility or disability, family care or other responsibilities, and cost.

DIVERSION

van Wijk and van Esseveldt (2021) compared 88 adult CSEM perpetrators who received a diversion option of treatment and probation supervision—because they had no prior sexual offenses, limited CSEM offending, and did not have high access to children through work or volunteering—with 106 CSEM perpetrators who were not offered diversion and received typical sentences. The diversion group had zero contact sexual recidivism and 17% noncontact recidivism (15/88), which presumably included mostly new CSEM offenses; the contact sexual recidivism rate was 7%, and the noncontact sexual recidivism rate was 5% for the comparison group. This shows that selection for no prior sexual offense history, limited CSEM, and less access to children can result in lower contact recidivism rates. However, the perpetrators who were diverted were more—rather than less—likely to commit another CSEM offense (19% vs. 9%, so approximately double) in an average of 57 months of follow-up, despite having less criminal history (which is a robust risk factor for sexual recidivism among CSEM perpetrators, as described in Chapter 6).

Diversion cases who did reoffend typically did so after treatment and supervision were completed (van Wijk & van Esseveldt, 2021). Therefore, this could result from treatment and supervision "working" and recidivism taking place after these conditions were removed. It could also be evidence of a negative effect, where low-risk perpetrators did not require treatment, and some may have participated in treatment with higher risk perpetrators, risking an iatrogenic effect. A third possibility is that the diversion group differed in other risk factors besides criminal history—for example, being more likely to be pedohebephilic or hypersexual. Also, the authors excluded 11 diversion perpetrators who turned out to have a sexual offense history, presumably because they were not supposed to be eligible for the diversion option. Their recidivism rates might be more like the comparison group that received conventional sentencing, reducing the group difference if they were included in an intent-to-treat analysis. Given the number of CSEM perpetrators identified, many for possession-only offenses and with no other criminal history, diversion may be a viable option for reducing the strain on criminal justice systems if any identified victims are willing and within a restorative justice framework.

Dodge and Spencer (2018) conducted qualitative interviews with 70 police officers who worked in Canadian sex crime units, as well as two focus groups. They found that informal police diversion (police discretion) exists for youth perpetrators of nonconsensual resharing of sexual images because the police respondents thought that existing CSEM and nonconsensual sharing laws were too harsh, stigmatizing, or inappropriate for the case. Some officers also pointed out that this behavior was common among youth, and thus, responding with criminal sanctions would overburden the youth justice system. Finally, some officers reported that victims did not want to criminalize their peers, instead calling the police to have the resharing or related behavior (e.g., bullying) stopped. Police did think criminalization was appropriate in some circumstances, as when someone engaged in sextortion. Dodge and Spencer suggested some of these police decisions could be influenced by patriarchal attitudes or beliefs (e.g., "Boys will be boys") or victim blaming (e.g., "The victim was dumb to send images").

OTHER COMMON TREATMENT QUESTIONS

Should online sexual offending perpetrators be in separate treatment streams, or is it okay to mix them with those who have committed offline offenses? If resources allow, I recommend separate online and offline offending streams, separating those who have only committed online offenses (CSEM) from those who have attempted or committed contact sexual offenses, which can include dual perpetrators (CSEM plus contact), technology-facilitated sexual assaults of adults, child sexual trafficking, and child sexual abuse tourism. Solicitation perpetrators could fit in either an online or offline stream. One option I have recommended is assigning fantasy-driven solicitation perpetrators to the online offending stream because their behavior involved online interactions only and assigning contact-driven solicitation perpetrators to the conventional offending stream. My logic is that attempting to meet, meeting, or having contact with a child is a more serious crime than exclusively online behavior. Also, solicitation offenders are, on average, more antisocial and less sexually atypical than CSEM perpetrators (Seto et al., 2012). Online perpetrators might be transferred if direct offending is discovered—for example, following new allegations or as a result of treatment disclosure.

Separate streams can be more consistent with the risk–need–responsivity framework because the average risk of sexual recidivism is different in the online and offline streams; online-exclusive perpetrators can have some distinct needs (e.g., internet self-regulation deficits), and there may be some responsivity differences as well (e.g., online CSEM perpetrators have higher education and IQ, on average, and so can handle a higher level of reading and content; Babchishin et al., 2011, 2015). If separate streams are not possible, mixing may be acceptable if it is risk based, to avoid potentially iatrogenic effects for combining lower risk online perpetrators with higher risk contact perpetrators, such as learning contact offending tradecraft or being exposed to more entrenched offense-supportive cognitions about sexual offending against children. In addition, mixing types of offending means contact perpetrators might learn about online sexual offending tradecraft. This recommendation to allow risk-based mixing of different types of perpetrators is based on limited evidence that mixing men who have offended against children with men who have offended against adults does not result in worse group dynamics (Harkins & Beech, 2007). Harkins and Beech also found no difference in recidivism, but the sample sizes were so small that this may not be meaningful. Mixing groups, however, would also mean that higher risk contact perpetrators might be exposed to CSEM and online sexual solicitation tradecraft.

We do not know what, if any, treatment is warranted for image-based perpetrators, including those who nonconsensually share sexual images or engage in digital exhibitionism or voyeurism. Their risk of reoffending and their treatment needs are unknown. My educated guess is that many image-based perpetrators would benefit more from education, diversion, restorative justice, and broader prevention efforts (see the next chapter) to shift their attitudes and norms about this behavior than from specialized treatment to reduce their likelihood of committing image-based abuse again. The nature of any intervention may depend on the motivations and pathways to image-based offending. For example, individuals who engage in image-based abuse as part of a broader pattern of intimate partner control (ex-partners or current partners) may benefit from interventions that address intimate partner violence and control. A second example is that individuals who engage in digital exhibitionism or voyeurism because of paraphilic motivations may benefit from interventions addressing sexual self-regulation, as opposed to those who engage in these behaviors because they thought it was funny or it was an act of trolling or bullying.

SUMMARY

In this chapter, I reviewed existing treatment models and examples of programs informed by these models. There is a high degree of overlap in terms of treatment targets, content, and structure, given these treatment models and programs draw from a common literature, including the risk–need–responsivity framework, the motivation–facilitation model, static and dynamic risk assessment, and responsivity considerations, such as motivation for change. Interventions that follow the risk, need, and responsivity principles are more likely to be effective. Following the risk principle means titrating intervention according to the risk of sexually reoffending, from minimal or no intervention (and perhaps diversion) for those who are at the lowest risk and intensive treatment and/or long-term incapacitation for those at the highest risk. Following the need principle means addressing the dynamic risk factors identified in a comprehensive assessment, particularly those pertaining to the motivation or facilitation of online sexual offending. Treatment might, therefore, address sexual and general self-regulation, relationship skills, peer associations, and offense-supportive cognitions. There is much less research available regarding protective factors, but positive social support has the most empirical support, suggesting a focus on building and maintaining positive relationships with family members, friends, and positive influences in the community through education, employment, volunteering, and involvement with institutions such as charities or churches. In addition to these specific treatment elements, treatment providers should consider nonspecific elements such as therapist characteristics, where treatment is provided, and how treatment is provided.

Reflecting the overall literature, most of the focus has been on treatment for CSEM and solicitation offending, with no evaluative data for treatment of other forms of online sexual offending. Given evidence that sexual offending treatment can be effective, online sexual offending programs that adhere to the risk, need, and responsivity principles and use evidence-based strategies for addressing dynamic risk factors have the best chance of success.

CASE EXAMPLES

In the following sections, I return to the hypothetical case examples and discuss how the results of the case formulation, clinical assessment, and risk assessment information described in previous chapters inform recommendations for intervention. Interventions ideally would adhere to the risk–need–responsivity framework, but they may not because of special considerations, such as mandatory treatment for all individuals convicted of particular offenses or a local lack of relevant resources. Whether an individual follows through with recommendations is also never guaranteed.

Adam (Lower Risk CSEM)

Given his low long-term risk for sexual recidivism, Adam was recommended for a brief psychoeducation intervention as part of his sentence and subsequent probation, but he did not participate in any intensive or long-term treatment. The psychoeducation program focused on sexual and internet self-regulation skills, healthy coping skills, and the harms caused by CSEM offending to children in the images. Adam was a quiet and mostly passive participant, but he completed the psychoeducation program satisfactorily and completed a subsequent period of probation without incident.

Bart (Higher Risk CSEM)

Bart served time in prison and participated in sexual offending treatment while in custody. He was assigned to a contact sexual offending stream because of his prior contact sexual offense. Though he initially appeared to be motivated to participate in treatment, Bart was not deemed to have made progress because he consistently minimized his responsibility and the seriousness of the sexual offense he committed as a juvenile, and he persistently claimed that CSEM offending was a victimless substitute for further sexual contact offending.

Sean (Sexual Solicitation)

Sean participated in treatment both in prison and the community, where his participation was described as acceptable in prison but unacceptable in the community. Sean had difficulties complying with the terms of his probation, including using the internet several times without prior approval, not maintaining his employment (he quit a job abruptly after an argument with a supervisor), and the suspicion he was not respecting his nighttime curfew. An updated dynamic risk assessment identified noncompliance with supervision as a new criminogenic need. The consensus among treatment providers and his probation officer was that Sean did better in custody than in the community, largely because there was more structure and a controlled environment in prison.

Elvis (Digital Exhibitionism)

Elvis received a probation order on conviction and completed treatment in a community sexual offending program. He struggled in the program because he was the only individual who had committed digital exhibitionism offenses, mostly against adults, and the treatment group mostly comprised individuals convicted of CSEM and/or sexual solicitation offending involving children. Elvis looked down on the other participants because he deemed them all to be "pedophiles." However, he was not disruptive and did not get into conflicts with other treatment participants. During treatment, Elvis acknowledged that he had significant social anxiety and a lack of positive people in his life; he had a relatively distant relationship with his younger brother and parents, and he had few friends.

Vince (Digital Voyeurism)

Vince had not been sentenced at the time of the evaluation, but the recommendation was sexual offending treatment in custody or the community, focusing on his sexual self-regulation skills and interpersonal functioning. Vince indicated that he would be willing to participate in treatment if it was required as part of his sentence. However, he did not volunteer for treatment.

Jack (Nonconsensual Sharing)

No treatment was recommended for Jack regarding his online sexual offending. However, he was offered and accepted counseling for his relationship functioning, focusing on his hostile attitudes toward women and his jealous and controlling behavior in past relationships. Jack was compliant with probation and completed his sentence without incident. He was deemed to have made satisfactory progress in counseling, especially in his attitudes about women. A pivotal moment for Jack was his recognition in counseling that his father, who left the family when Jack was 11, was similarly jealous and controlling toward Jack's mother during their relationship. Jack had almost no relationship with his father and was adamant that he did not want to turn out the same way.

Adrian (Technology-Facilitated Sexual Assault)

Adrian was reluctant to participate in sexual offending treatment, but he eventually agreed. His participation was deemed to be good because he was compliant and cooperative during the program, and he made some improvements in understanding the role of substance use and his hostile and adversarial beliefs about women in his sexual offending. However, the treating clinician doubted the sincerity of his change in beliefs about women. In contrast, Adrian appeared to be sincere in wishing to address his substance use, and he stated that the additional treatment he completed for substance abuse was much more helpful to him because he thought his offending risk would be addressed through the successful resolution of this problem.

Smith (Sexual Trafficking of Minors and Child Sexual Abuse Tourism)

Smith received a long prison sentence and refused to participate in treatment while he was in custody. He was placed in a protective custody unit for other individuals who had committed contact sexual offenses against children because of concerns he would be at risk of harm in the general prison population, given the nature of his offenses. Smith mostly kept to himself while in prison but did establish some casual friendships with several other men in his unit. Smith had received no institutional misconducts at this point in his sentence.

8

Prevention of Online Sexual Offenses

I added this new chapter (which is not in the first edition) to describe a public health framework for sexual abuse prevention, following the four steps set out by the Centers for Disease Control and Prevention (2024) in the United States regarding violence prevention:

1. Define and monitor the problem.
2. Identify risk and protective factors.
3. Develop and test prevention strategies.
4. Assure widespread adoption.

Earlier chapters have covered prevalence (Step 1), as well as risk and protective factors for online sexual offending (Chapter 5, in particular). In this chapter, I describe prevention approaches that have been developed and highlight the paths forward for identifying and disseminating the most promising approaches. Most of this chapter focuses on prevention approaches to prevent online sexual offending against minors because that has been the focus of prevention so far. I am enthusiastic about the potential for prevention approaches because they are proactive rather than reactive, take place before offenses take place, address a major gap in how we currently respond to the problems of online sexual offending, and are usually more cost-effective than treatment and other responses after crimes have occurred (see Letourneau et al., 2017, 2023).

In addition to child sexual exploitation material (CSEM) perpetration, we also want to prevent online sexual solicitation of children by older juveniles, which has only been recognized in the past 5 years as a concern after much policy, police, and practice focus on sexual solicitations from adults. Prevention of sexual assaults of adults should consider technology-facilitated sexual assaults. We also want to prevent image-based abuse, especially the sending of explicit images, nonconsensual resharing of explicit images, and sextortion. As I noted in Chapter 4, attitudes and norms were strong correlates of image-based behavior in young people, and the best way to shape those attitudes and norms is through early school-based and peer-based interventions.

In this chapter, I focus on primary and secondary prevention. Primary prevention approaches are designed to prevent the development of a public health problem and typically are delivered to a general audience. Examples of this include mandating seatbelts and airbags to prevent serious injury or death as a result of motor vehicle accidents and mandating childhood vaccinations to prevent serious illness outbreaks at school. In the context of online sexual offending, a primary prevention intervention could include setting and enforcing user age limits and policies to reduce stranger interactions between adults and children under a set age because these policies would affect all users and school-based interventions (described later) that are offered to all students in particular grades.

Secondary prevention approaches are designed to prevent the full emergence of a public health problem in people who are at risk or showing early signs of the problem. Examples of this approach include enhanced screenings for people at risk of cancer because of family history or evidence of genetic predispositions, diet and activity changes for people at risk of cardiovascular disease because of lifestyle or family history, and ergonomic interventions for people at risk of repetitive strain or other injuries. In the context of online sexual offending, a secondary prevention intervention might focus on individuals who are at risk of online sexual offending because they are sexually attracted to children. As we will see, most prevention efforts are secondary in nature and have focused on this particular at-risk group, with much less attention to other at-risk groups.

The logic of primary and secondary prevention is impeccable, in my opinion: It is better for the individuals involved and the rest of society to prevent online sexual offenses from taking place rather than responding only after harm has occurred. Tertiary prevention encompasses approaches designed to prevent the reoccurrence of a public health problem. Treatment in its various guises can be understood as tertiary prevention, where treatments (described in the previous chapter) are designed to prevent further offending among individuals who have been detected, whether through the criminal justice system (charged and convicted) or other means.

It is not only better for society and the individuals involved, but primary and secondary prevention can also be cost-effective because the interventions are relatively lighter in intensity—to be delivered at scale—and the costs associated with reacting to the problem can be high. It is hard to do this kind of economic analysis well because it relies on many assumptions and fuzzy estimates, but Letourneau et al. (2024) gave a shot at estimating the cost of incarceration in the United States for individuals convicted of sexual offenses. Using government sources of data, they estimated that the United States spends approximately

$5.5 billion a year to incarcerate adult perpetrators against children. State prison costs ($4.4 billion) account for most of this cost, given their greater number of cases, but federal and especially civil commitment costs are high per capita, given that federal and commitment sentences are much longer, and civil commitment, in particular, is over three times more expensive than prison. Conservatively, the United States spends billions on incarceration in responding to sexual offending, with some protection of children through incapacitation but with no impact or even a negative impact on recidivism due to incarceration on its own, without treatment. In contrast, Letourneau et al. pointed out that primary or secondary prevention gets almost no sustained government funding, and the investments are in the millions rather than billions.

The ReDirection survey results (Insoll et al., 2022) I have mentioned several times in this book suggest there are huge opportunities for prevention and early intervention by providing services to juveniles who are entering a developmental period where they become much more interested in sexuality, are likely to be exposed to pornography online, and may be exposed to CSEM as well, often by accident. This is also a developmental period when youths are online a lot, interacting with their peers and developing social connections and, hopefully, positive social supports. Remember that 70% of the ReDirection survey respondents said they first saw CSEM before age 18, 40% before age 13, and 51% said their first CSEM exposure was accidental.

I realize it is an uncomfortable and difficult idea for society and parents to contemplate, but this means we need to develop primary prevention interventions before age 13, which could be part of comprehensive sexual health education or other school-based interventions. We want to intervene before CSEM use becomes entrenched through habit; in the ReDirection survey, a majority said they had been viewing CSEM for less than 6 months, and a majority were viewing CSEM infrequently (Insoll et al., 2022). We simultaneously want to provide support to youths who may be discovering they may have pedohebephilia; we do not know what proportion of the ReDirection respondents might meet this criterion because the question was not asked. The fact that the most common category was girls ages 4 to 13 does suggest a high proportion might be pedohebephilic because, in many cases, this would not reflect youths seeking out peer-aged content.

PREVENTION FOR WHO?

Most prevention interventions have been designed for people who report concerns about sexual thoughts or behavior involving children (see Seto, Rodrigues, et al., 2023, for a review of existing perpetration prevention efforts; see also Stephens et al., 2022). These interventions include helplines, self-help sites, online interventions, and in-person interventions. Typically, these interventions are trying to reduce all sexual offending against children, which could include CSEM offending and online solicitation offending. In many cases, the content is clearly designed for individuals who are sexually attracted to children.

This is a major at-risk group for these kinds of behaviors, especially when they are also seeking help (Ingram et al., 2023), but there are other important at-risk groups as well, including some individuals who are excessively sexually preoccupied or highly antisocial and, thus, more likely to engage with CSEM or sexual solicitations of older adolescents, sexual assaults of adults, and image-based abuse of adults. The interventions for other at-risk groups would be at least somewhat different in content and approach than those for individuals who are sexually attracted to children; for example, both child-attracted persons and those who are sexually preoccupied might benefit from developing their sexual and internet self-regulation skills, but those who are sexually preoccupied might face less stigma and be higher in social functioning (see Chapter 6 and 7). For the highly antisocial at-risk group, general self-regulation, offense-permissive cognitions, and prosocial ties may be much more important than sexual or internet self-regulation, and sexual motivations might even be de-emphasized for some individuals who do not see themselves as sexually atypical.

Because almost all perpetration prevention has focused on individuals who are at risk because of sexual attraction to children, almost all perpetration prevention has focused on online sexual offending involving children, whether that is in the form of CSEM, sexual solicitations, trafficking, or tourism. There is an absence of perpetration prevention resources for individuals who are at risk of online sexual offending involving adults, particularly image-based abuse of adults through digital exhibitionism or voyeurism and technology-facilitated sexual assaults of adults.

In our Oak-funded review of available perpetration prevention interventions (Seto, Rodrigues, et al., 2023), we identified two large gaps in existing prevention interventions in terms of potential target groups. The first large gap was intrafamilial perpetration prevention, where pedohebephilia is uncommon in those who sexually offend intrafamilially, and intrafamilial offending can often better be explained as opportunistic offending by antisocial men in dysfunctional family situations where intimate partner violence or other child maltreatment may also occur (Pullman et al., 2017; Seto, Babchishin, et al., 2015). Stepfathers and older stepbrothers, in particular, account for a disproportionate amount of intrafamilial childhood sexual abuse (CSA), and this can include the production of CSEM, especially with younger children (Seto et al., 2016). Most step-relatives are caring or at least benign, but they statistically pose a greater risk than biological relatives (Daly & Wilson, 1999). Many persons at risk of online sexual offending involving related children may be reluctant to describe themselves as sexually attracted to children more generally and may find much of the existing content to be irrelevant. Hypothetically, at least, perpetration prevention might devote more attention to family factors, such as partner conflict, nonsexual child maltreatment, and family dynamics.

The second large gap we identified was perpetration prevention for juveniles. Almost all the interventions we identified in our review were targeted at adults (Seto et al., 2016), even though there are growing data suggesting older juveniles pose a risk to younger children in terms of nonconsensual resharing, sexual solicitation, and production of CSEM (either directly or through encouragement to self-generate; see Sutton & Finkelhor, 2023). In the general sexual offending literature, there are important differences between juvenile and adult perpetrators, and clinical and research knowledge about assessment, treatment, and prevention with adults may not apply to juveniles (Seto, 2018). In particular, paraphilic sexual interests play less of a role for juveniles who have sexually offended against children, whereas opportunism and developmentally linked poor impulse control play a bigger role (Seto et al., 2003; Seto & Lalumière, 2010). Prevention for intrafamilial and juvenile perpetration overlaps because many offenses committed by juveniles involve younger relatives, such as younger siblings, nieces or nephews, or cousins.

There are education campaigns (primary prevention) with no evaluation of outcomes to prevent image-based offending victimization. Henry et al. (2020) pointed out that education campaigns tend to focus on awareness and warn against sexting more generally, as opposed to focusing on nonconsensual sexting. I am not aware of any evidence that these kinds of education campaigns work. Other concerns are that antivictimization campaigns put the onus of prevention on potential targets, could contribute to victim blaming (e.g., "The person should have known better"), and still tend to focus on stranger danger instead of the risks posed by someone already known to the target. What could prevent image-based offending, such as nonconsensual resharing, digital exhibitionism, or voyeurism? For nonconsensual sharing, at least by juveniles, there is a lot of potential for interventions designed to influence offense-supportive attitudes and perceived norms (Seto et al., 2022).

Even among child-attracted persons, other factors are relevant besides sexual motivations. Stewart (2022) obtained online survey data from 609 men who reported attraction to children, as well as 224 men reporting other paraphilic interests. The mean age was 30 for the child-attracted men, 80% were White, half were from the United States (50%), and 4% reported prior sexual offending against children charges or convictions (others likely committed undetected sexual offenses and would have been unwilling to admit to them even in an anonymous survey). Most (90%) were attracted to girls under age 14, a majority (59%) were attracted to boys under age 14, and only 4% said they were exclusively attracted to children. Stewart administered 17 measures of adverse childhood experiences, attachment problems, impulsivity, offense-supportive cognitions, emotional congruence with children, sexual preoccupation, other paraphilic interests, mental health or personality problems, and loneliness. Latent cluster analysis of these data identified low ($n = 165$), moderate ($n = 270$), and high vulnerability ($n = 149$) groups for sexual offending involving children, reflecting their mean scores on the study measures (which may or may not predict sexual offending—e.g., depression). The high group had the highest means, and indeed, their group means exceeded suggested cutoff scores for adverse childhood experiences, sexual preoccupation, and mental health problems (particularly depression). Groups did not differ on variables related to pedohebephilia but did differ on their self-rated risk of sexually offending, though this was a small to medium effect. The strongest correlate of self-rated risk to sexually offend across all three vulnerability groups was offense-supportive cognitions; at the same time, the high vulnerability group did not strongly endorse offense-supportive cognitions, with a mean in the "neutral" range, whereas the low and moderate vulnerability groups disagreed with offense-supportive cognitions. Stewart found unexpectedly weak associations for established clinical risk factors, such as emotional congruence with children or sexual preoccupation, suggesting caution in extrapolating from clinical and forensic research to the community.

In comparing the child-attracted men and other paraphilic men in the Stewart (2022) study—keeping in mind the methodological confound that most child-attracted men were recruited from online forums, whereas most other paraphilic men were recruited from Amazon's Mechanical Turk (https://www.mturk.com), an online crowdsourcing platform that can be used to recruit for research studies—the child-attracted men had a younger age of first masturbation and first sexual contact but had fewer if any sexual partners. Child-attracted men were more likely to be single and had fewer interactions with children as parents, workers, or volunteers, which might suggest they coped with their sexual interest in children partly by reducing their contact with children. The low vulnerability group described earlier was similar to the other paraphilias group, whereas the small group of child-attracted men with detected sexual offending was more likely to be in the moderate or high vulnerability groups.

According to the risk–need–responsivity framework, Stewart's (2022) findings suggest that the low-vulnerability group was doing relatively well and unlikely to seek help. It follows that the moderate vulnerability group, the largest in number, might benefit from moderate-intensity interventions, including self-help websites and online clinician-guided treatment. The high-vulnerability group could benefit from higher intensity intervention, including in-person treatment. Given a high level of comorbidity and the possibility the person is resistant to the idea that they pose a risk to children (even if they do), treatment to address psychological vulnerabilities more generally could help prevent child sexual exploitation and abuse.

SELF-HELP RESOURCES

The earliest secondary perpetration prevention efforts involved establishing self-help resources through confidential helplines and/or webpages containing self-help information. Established examples of helplines and self-help websites include Stop It Now! USA (https://www.stopitnow.org), Stop It Now! UK & Ireland (https://www.stopitnow.org.uk), Troubled Desire (Germany; https://troubled-desire.com/en), ReDirection (Finland; https://www.suojellaanlapsia.fi/en/redirection), and Help Wanted (United States; https://www.helpwantedprevention.org/index.html). These interventions have not been rigorously evaluated to determine their impacts on proximal outcomes (dynamic risk factors such as sexual self-regulation skills) or behavioral outcomes in terms of perpetration. Some data from helplines or self-help sites have been presented or published, but they are mostly descriptions of users or methodologically weak evaluation data from small, self-selected surveys or qualitative interviews using pre–post designs without comparison groups or conditions. For example, a report by Newman et al. (2023) for the National Society for the Prevention of Cruelty to Children in the United Kingdom looked at campaign effects and self-reported change for Stop It Now! UK & Ireland and Don't Offend (a precursor to the Troubled Desire self-help site). Both self-help interventions showed evidence of increased engagement with media campaigns. Stop It Now! also had self-report data for a small sample of users that found a majority reported increased knowledge and awareness, and two thirds reported changes in their behavior, which might mean using CSEM less, using pornography less overall, or engaging in less risky behavior. A limitation of this evaluation is that the data are all self-reported, there were relatively few users, and the participants were almost surely highly selected because those who found the site unhelpful would be less likely to participate in the survey. These methodological issues are relevant to all self-help intervention evaluations in the absence of a control or comparison group or condition.

I will not describe each intervention in detail here; instead, I focus on the similarities across these interventions and highlight any available empirical data, especially if they involve any evaluation. One similarity across self-help interventions is a focus on people who are concerned about their sexual thoughts or behaviors toward children. This is not the same thing as pedohebephilia, but I suspect it is often read this way, especially given the common conflation of sexual interest and behavior and the assumption that only pedohebephilic individuals would have sexual thoughts or engage in behavior with children. This is incorrect, as I have mentioned more than once in this book. Some individuals who are sexually attracted to children might not acknowledge this attraction or do not see it as a concern because they prefer adults but are also attracted to children. Some at-risk family members may not agree they have sexual thoughts or behaviors toward children because their sexual thoughts might be about a specific child relative. There is another big gap between potential users and potential providers of these prevention services: Users might be more interested in their mental health and well-being (e.g., in learning how to more effectively and healthily cope with having sexual thoughts or feelings about children), whereas providers are more focused on the prevention of sexual offenses against children, where mental health effects of the intervention are seen as secondary to this primary goal.

Another similarity across interventions is an emphasis on providing anonymous and confidential help to increase recruitment and retention, given the stigma involved in identifying as someone with concerns about sexual thoughts or behaviors involving children or in seeking perpetration prevention help for other reasons. A third similarity is that self-help resources draw on a common body of knowledge regarding sexual and general self-regulation and other putative dynamic risk and protective factors to inform the intervention. As a result, there is a lot of overlap in their content and approaches. A lot of these resources focus on how to cope with sexual thoughts about children more effectively, to avoid risky situations where behavior could occur, and to improve social support and mental health to make the person more resilient.

The self-help site Troubled Desire is available in multiple languages. I mention this because many of the perpetration prevention resources identified by Seto, Rodrigues, et al. (2023) are in English only. Troubled Desire was first launched in 2017 in English, followed by German (2018), Spanish (2018), Portuguese (2019), French (2019), Hindi (2019), and Marathi (2018). The content of Troubled Desire is based on the Berlin Dissexuality Therapy Program (Beier, 2021), which is also the model behind the Dunkelfeld intervention (Beier et al., 2015) described in Chapter 7. Troubled Desire is psychoeducational, offering tips and exercises on how to exercise mindfulness, emotional regulation, and lifestyle management. According to Schuler et al. (2021), the Troubled Desire self-assessment was completed by 4,161 users (of 7,496 visitors who began the assessment) in the first 30 months, which averages to approximately 140 global visitors a month. This is an impressive sample size for research purposes but is small in terms of total reach, given the number of languages offered. Most users were men (91%), and 80% were under the age of 40, with the modal age category being 19 to 21 years old (so, the site is reaching young adults, which is encouraging from a prevention perspective). Most users (80%) reported pedophilic or hebephilic sexual interests. The majority said they were already committing CSEM offenses (73%), most of them undetected by police. Almost half (42%) also admitted to having sexual contact with one or more children. Offending reports were higher among those who admitted pedohebephilic interests than those who denied any such interests.

ReDirection (Insoll et al., 2022) is available in Spanish and, thus, can reach at-risk persons in Spain, Mexico, and other Global South countries in Central and South America. Similarly, Troubled Desire can reach at-risk persons in Brazil and India. Translation (such as into Arabic, French, Mandarin, and Russian) and cultural adaptation of self-help resources could greatly expand the reach of secondary prevention to other parts of the world.

I believe there is enormous potential for self-help helplines and websites because of their potential reach and cost-effectiveness. Even if their effects were only modest in scope, this could still mean a big difference in the perpetration of online sexual offending if these interventions could be delivered at scale. However, there are obstacles to delivering these services, and this is reflected in the relatively small numbers reported by most self-help sites when they report use information. Exceptions here are Stop It Now! UK & Ireland, which reports on its metrics regularly as part of its accountability to its funders, including the U.K. government. Unfortunately, the limited available data suggest most helplines and self-help websites have a limited reach (discussed later in this chapter), despite the anticipated demand for these services based on surveys and other sources suggesting a significant number of people have pedohebephilia, have viewed CSEM, or have engaged in sexual behavior toward children much younger than themselves, either as older juveniles or adults. Later in this chapter, I discuss the challenges for prevention recruitment and retention—including stigma, mistrust, anxiety about self-identification or detection, and confusion about mandatory reporting.

PEER SUPPORT

People concerned about their risk of online sexual offending involving children can find communities online. The potential contributions of online peer support forums are controversial because some people oppose the online congregation of people who are attracted to children, whether or not it has positive effects. Some of this opposition seems to involve stigma and antipathy toward the existence of people who might be interested in CSEM or online sexual solicitation involving children and youths. Some of the opposition may also be motivated by a concern that these online forums can have negative effects, such as facilitating offending (e.g., trading of CSEM) or sharing of tradecraft (Steel et al., 2022). Peer support could be beneficial in several ways: One is information sharing, including information about self-help resources, coping strategies that have been effective, and self-care. Another is through emotional social support, which could act as a protective factor by improving well-being and increasing resilience to the effects of risk factors such as negative mood or offense-supportive cognitions (see Chapters 5 and 6; see also Bekkers et al., 2024). Virtuous Pedophiles (https://virped.org) and B4U-ACT (https://www.b4uact.org) stand out as peer support groups online—Virtuous Pedophiles because it is explicitly against sexual contact with children and B4U-ACT because it explicitly endorses abiding by the law, whereas other forums have not taken an explicit stance or are supportive of adult–child sexuality.

A social support survey by Elchuk et al. (2022) of 202 child-attracted persons revealed expected associations between perceived lack of social support, internalized stigma, psychological distress, and suicidality. Moreover, loneliness partially mediated the association between stigma and psychological distress. Most of the respondents had disclosed their sexual attraction to children to someone in their lives, but this disclosure was not associated with mental health scores; instead, disclosure followed by social support was associated with less distress. Roche et al. (2022) looked at experiences of social support in another survey of 353 child-attracted persons (mean age 35, 81% men) recruited from forums and via Twitter. Most participants were current forum users, with an average of 6 years on forums. Participants reported their initial motivation to join forums was to feel less lonely.

As researchers predicted, emotional and informational support were the most common forms of support received, and tangible support was rare (Roche et al., 2022). Most participants (82%) also offered support, again, mostly emotional or informational. Contrary to the prediction that forum involvement reflected an absence of social support offline, a majority said they had disclosed their sexual attraction to children to someone in their offline lives. Those who visited more forums rated forums as less helpful, which may indicate forum shopping, where the person is looking for something they did not find. Participants found forums to be moderately helpful, on average. None of the study variables predicted the level of online support in a regression analysis. There was also a small group of 19 past users who indicated they left forums because they did not find them helpful, forums were badly managed, or they were concerned about legal or other consequences if their forum involvement was discovered.

Also relevant is a study by Jones et al. (2021) of 326 Virtuous Pedophile posts, looking at coping strategies shared online and identifying themes that were classified into three superordinate themes: (a) acceptance of pedophilia (or hebephilia), (b) strategies to stay safe, and (c) coping with sexual arousal toward children. The first theme is relevant to self-esteem, self-acceptance, and support or help seeking for individuals concerned they might use CSEM or sexually offend directly against children.

Peer support forums could have negative effects to the extent they share inaccurate information, endorse offense-supportive cognitions, or promote norms tolerant of online sexual offending. For example, some forums may regularly contain posts by users who believe that CSEM use is okay because it helps people avoid contact offending or may normalize sexual contact with children as beneficial to children or common historically or cross-culturally (Holt et al., 2010; Malesky & Ennis, 2004; O'Halloran & Quayle, 2010). I suspect a key factor in the valence of group influences is forum norms; one can contrast the potential effects of forums with anti-offending norms (like Virtuous Pedophiles) with other forums with norms that are more offense tolerant or even offense supportive.

ONLINE GUIDED INTERVENTION

Prevent It was piloted as a therapist-guided online treatment program designed to help adults reduce their CSEM use via cognitive-behavioral strategies (Lätth et al., 2022). Because participants were already using CSEM, we can think of Prevent It as a tertiary prevention program for mostly undetected CSEM perpetrators. The anonymous and confidential program involved a series of eight modules offered sequentially over 3 months, with completion of each module's assignments necessary to progress to the next module. Each module consisted of a short video (2–10 minutes long) with reading and exercises to work on throughout the week. Clinicians offered encouragement, feedback on the completed exercises, and answers to participant questions via encrypted text. Topics addressed in these modules included sexual preoccupation, coping with sexual interest in children, social support, and emotional well-being.

Prevent It is the only intervention I have found that has published outcome data on offending behavior (Lätth et al., 2022; also discussed later in this chapter).[1] Other strengths include online recruitment and participation strategies to protect the anonymity and security of participants, a randomized clinical trial design, preregistration, and evidence-based targets and techniques. An important limitation of the Prevent It trial was the high attrition rate, with

---

[1] Remember that I disclosed in the Preface that I am involved in an evaluation of a revised version of Prevent It in English (funded through the Oak Foundation) and in German, Swedish, and Portuguese (funded by the European Commission). I helped revise the Prevent It content for the current evaluations.

almost half the treatment group lost in the first or second session, whereas most of the placebo group stayed until the later modules. This differential attrition likely reflected a lack of motivational engagement, where the program assumed anyone signing up for treatment was motivated to change. It might also have reflected a need for a more gradual entry to the content and some rapport building within the constraints of a text-based, asynchronous service.

The results of the Lätth et al. (2022) evaluation, along with Prevent It user and clinician feedback, were used to revise the program—in particular, to increase motivational engagement and streamline the content so it could be provided in fewer modules. This revised version of the intervention, called Prevent It 2, is currently being evaluated in English, Swedish, Portuguese, and German (https://www.uke.de/english/landingpage/priority). These evaluations are using a wait-list control design, where potential participants concerned about their sexual urges toward children—recruited from darknet forums, social media, and other channels—will be randomly assigned to the intervention or wait-list. Prevent It 2 can be described as secondary and tertiary prevention because it is aimed at at-risk persons who might be using CSEM already.

IN-PERSON TREATMENT

Some in-person clinics provide perpetration prevention treatment. One of the best known internationally is the Dunkelfeld Project (Beier et al., 2015), which began as a pilot project in Berlin in 2004 and now comprises a network of 14 clinics across Germany, with expansion clinics in India and Switzerland. Dunkelfeld is a clinic-based intervention for men who are sexually attracted to prepubescent or pubescent children, whether or not they have offended against children. Dunkelfeld is a prevention intervention because individuals were eligible if they were concerned about their sexual urges toward children, whether or not they had acted on them. The name Dunkelfeld ("dark field") signifies that most, if not all, of these individuals were not known to the criminal justice system because they had either not offended or had committed undetected sexual offenses. Indeed, though most Dunkelfeld cases (72%) had viewed CSEM and a third (35%) had sexual contact with a child, most had never been detected by the criminal justice system. In other words, Dunkelfeld provided both secondary and tertiary prevention, where tertiary prevention includes treatment for undetected and detected perpetrators. The treatment consists of group therapy for 1 year, with individual therapy and medication as required.

A big advantage that Dunkelfeld has over in-person interventions in many other jurisdictions is the strong therapist–client confidentiality protection in Germany. Mandatory reporting is restricted to situations involving risk of death (e.g., someone makes a credible threat of homicide), so the Dunkelfeld clinicians could ask directly about sexual offending without the participants holding back because they feared self-incrimination and criminal prosecution. A disadvantage is the relative cost of the intervention over online or self-help options, given it runs over a year—or even longer—via small group or individual in-person therapy.

Another in-person intervention is Canada's Talking for Change (https://talkingforchange.ca), which provides a free, anonymous, and confidential helpline nationally and free and confidential (but not anonymous) virtual or in-person treatment in Ontario and Atlantic Canada. The developers presented some initial descriptive data at the 2021 national conference of the Association for the Treatment and Prevention of Sexual Abuse (Heasman, 2021). At that time, they had received 14 referrals between June and September 2021, with the majority (10 out of 14) being self-referrals. All were male and tended to be young (3/4 in their teens or 20s) and White (3/4). Half were unemployed, and half were single. Most (11 people) had a criminal history of some kind, including some who had committed CSEM or contact offenses. Only four participants met the diagnostic criteria for pedohebephilic disorder, and some participants had other paraphilic interests. Attendance and rated engagement were good, but it was too soon to tell if there were significant changes in putative dynamic risk factors. Importantly, the evaluation did not include a comparison or control condition, so it relies on a methodologically disadvantaged pre–post comparison, where changes could simply be a result of time or the selection effects of staying in treatment versus dropping out or being kicked out.

SCHOOL-BASED PREVENTION

Some prevention interventions are delivered in classrooms, so they can be considered primary prevention because they are available to all students, not only those who are identified as at risk (secondary prevention) or as already showing evidence of perpetration (tertiary). In this section, I discuss three examples of school-based prevention. There are multiple clinical trials demonstrating that Safe Dates (https://www.blueprintsprograms.org/programs/44999999/safe-dates/print) and Shifting Boundaries (https://crimesolutions.ojp.gov/ratedprograms/226), both teen violence prevention interventions, can also reduce peer-to-peer sexual violence (Foshee et al., 1998; Taylor et al., 2013). This could include technology-facilitated sexual violence against peers.

Safe Dates is a middle school and high school program to help prevent dating violence. It consists of nine classroom sessions and extracurricular activities (a play that teens perform and a poster contest; Foshee et al., 1998). It is available in English and Spanish and teaches youth about attitudes, gender roles, conflict resolution skills, and bystander intervention. Similarly, Shifting Boundaries is delivered in middle school and is another program designed to prevent dating and peer violence, including sexual harassment (Taylor et al., 2013). There are six classroom sessions and a school environment interaction (e.g., installing posters to increase awareness, identifying hot spots, changing school protocols).

Randomized controlled trials have found that both of these school-based interventions can reduce teen-on-teen sexual violence. It would be interesting to examine if these interventions can also reduce image-based abuse, such as the nonconsensual sharing of images by ex-partners or current partners. A positive feature of these school-based interventions is the emphasis on attitudes and norms, which we found to be significantly correlated with multiple image behaviors in an analysis of youth survey data, including nonconsensual sharing of images (Seto, Roche, Stroebel, et al., 2023).

Responsible Behavior with Younger Children (RBYC; Letourneau et al., 2024; Ruzicka et al., 2021) was specifically designed to reduce adolescent-perpetrated sexual offenses against younger children, and again, could have an impact on online behavior as well. RBYC is a school-based prevention program for sixth- and seventh-grade students, delivered in 10 45-minute sessions. Topics include education (developmental differences between teens and young children, prevention strategies, what child sexual abuse is), perspective taking, and how to prevent or intervene with CSA. The program is delivered by teachers or other youth-serving professionals. I discuss an early evaluation study of RBYC later in this chapter.

PREVENTION TECHNOLOGY

I have become more enthusiastic about environmental over personal prevention efforts because environmental interventions are more scalable. A change on a social app or platform can affect all users, whereas a person-based intervention can only reach some people and is also dependent on motivation to change and a valid model of behavior and mechanisms of change. However, environmental interventions are more likely to deter new or occasional users, who are not the most persistent and, thus, the greatest risk. Person-based interventions that target at-risk persons could address the most persistent and riskiest individuals, suggesting we need both ecosystem and individual interventions.

Just as the internet has facilitated online sexual offending through various affordances, such as anonymity and highly scaled social networks, technology also provides affordances for perpetration (and victimization) prevention. May-Chahal et al. (2022) conducted a review of technological tools for detecting or disrupting CSEM offending. These tech interventions can be organized into the following broad sets: (a) blocking the search for CSEM, (b) detecting CSEM or sexual solicitation activity, and (c) handling the reporting of incidents from users to prevent further incidents.

Most of these tech interventions focus on CSEM, which is a clear and present threat to tech companies with operations in the United States because American law requires them to report CSEM activity to the National Center for Missing and Exploited Children (NCMEC). Companies that provide services for minor users generally recognize that protecting users from CSEM activities—exposure to CSEM, being tricked or coerced into producing and sharing CSEM—and sexual solicitations by adults is good for user safety and public relations for their apps and platforms. Some platforms are beginning to address digital exhibitionism and image-based abuse as well. Omegle, a free web-based platform for random chats with strangers, shut down in November 2023 because a lawsuit alleged it was notorious for facilitating digital exhibitionism, including exhibitionism by adults toward minors (Tolentino & Tenbarge, 2023).

The first set of interventions attempts to reduce online CSEM offending by adding friction to search, especially for new users. An example is Google's search intervention, where searching for particular terms associated with CSEM produces a warning message and redirection to online resources (the Talking for Change hotline and therapy referral in Canada, Help Wanted self-help site in the United States). This creates friction for relatively new users who do not know where to look for CSEM in the clearnet or darknet. This can be contrasted with Yandex, a Russia-based search engine that does not restrict CSEM-related search terms. Another example is Facebook, where certain search terms associated with CSEM or online solicitations redirect users to online help resources. A third example is an intervention on Pornhub, which redirects Pornhub users using certain keywords suggesting an interest in CSEM to Stop It Now! UK & Ireland's self-help website. Scanlan et al. (2024) evaluated this intervention for a set of sessions in the United Kingdom between March 2022 and September 2023 and concluded that warning messages reduced searches using CSEM-suggestive keywords and directed some traffic to the Stop It Now! UK & Ireland helpline or self-help website.

The impact of these interventions is unknown because data are usually unavailable outside the tech companies. Some analogous data suggest that deterrence interventions can be effective: Prichard et al. (2022) conducted a proof-of-concept study by demonstrating that a warning box about possible legality for a fake "barely legal" pornography site reduced clicks, suggesting a similar kind of warning for pornography sites like Pornhub could make a difference. Prichard et al. randomly assigned 419 participants to one of five conditions: (a) 100 went directly to the landing page of the fake site, (b) 74 saw a warning message about potential harm to viewers, (c) 65 saw a warning message about potential harm to victims, (d) 81 were warned that police could track IP addresses, and (e) 99 were told the content might be illegal. (It is unclear why the conditions did not have equal group sizes in the study.) The attrition rates for the warnings ranged from 38% to 52%, compared with 27% who did not click through for the control group (first condition). The most effective were the warnings that IP addresses can be tracked ($OR = 2.64$) and that the content might be illegal ($OR = 2.99$).

An example of the second set of technology interventions is the use of PhotoDNA or other hash matching technology, which can identify known CSEM images and automatically trigger reports to NCMEC, as required by law in the United States, and further investigation by the tech company's trust and safety personnel. This can have a major impact if adopted by all major platforms where photo sharing can take place. In addition, some companies, such as Google, have developed machine-learning classifiers for detecting new suspected CSEM and have shared them with other companies (Todorovic & Chaudhuri, 2018). This technology could be used to detect previously unknown CSEM or CSEM-like content that can be flagged for human review.

A third set of technology interventions addresses reporting processes, including terms of service, how users can report concerns, and how reports of suspected CSEM or other illegal online behavior are investigated. The challenges of reporting have been amply described, and users can find it confusing, distressing, or frustrating. Reporting mechanisms are not always cleanly and clearly designed, and making these reports can be embarrassing and frightening if the user is directly involved (e.g., reporting they sent CSEM in response to an online sexual solicitation). Technology reporting, in general, can be quite frustrating because the investigation and decision-making processes are opaque, and even obvious violations of terms of service can result in no action taken, breeding cynicism. (I am no longer on Twitter/X, having made multiple complaints about violations of terms of service with no action taken.) Reporting mechanisms could be improved with more trained moderators and safeguards in place, but that adds significant costs that are sustainable only for larger tech companies.

The Thorn (2022) survey is particularly relevant when thinking about the limitations of blocking. Youths were asked about what they did when they experienced concerning online interactions. Youths preferred blocking the offending user first, then reporting, and then telling parents. Telling parents was probably the least preferred because of how embarrassing it would be to tell one's parents, especially with the realistic expectation that parents would blame the young person or take away devices or online access as a result (see the other Thorn survey regarding parent perceptions; Seto, Roche, Stroebel, et al., 2023).

An overview of what major tech companies are doing to promote minor user safety is available in a Technology Coalition Survey that was part of WeProtect Global Alliance's 2021 Global Threat Assessment. The survey asked 20 questions and got responses from 32 companies ranging in size from 250 employees to over 5,000 employees. Many companies who responded to the survey were engaged in some prevention work, but not all were. There is almost surely a selection bias in that companies who do not belong to the Coalition or did not respond to the survey are less likely to be actively intervening. Challenges identified in the survey included limits in staff time, money, and other resources. The largest companies can do the most, including developing machine learning tools to detect illegal online activity. In general, tech companies relied on user reporting, which is not scalable because of the number of staff required to respond to reports effectively and efficiently (going back to my Twitter/X experiences, the moderator likely had only seconds to review my complaints, look at the tweets or accounts involved, and make a decision). A large majority of companies use automated detection through hash matching, including PhotoDNA or similar tools for detecting known CSEM as well as machine learning classifiers for suspected CSEM; a slight majority of the companies also used text and video classifiers, and a third had created algorithms to flag potential online sexual solicitations. Sixty percent provide some deterrence messaging in their products, and about the same said they provide lists of help resources, such as the helplines and self-help sites mentioned earlier in this chapter.

What else can technology companies do? Following the same three types of technology interventions I have described, companies can further advance the friction for potential perpetrators. For example, Apple tried to introduce additional security options in 2021 for child accounts sending or receiving nude images but withdrew this after a public backlash expressing concerns about privacy and the unauthorized use of this technology (Nicas, 2021). More tech companies could use known and CSEM-detection classifiers and block search terms within their platforms and direct to resources, either voluntarily or as a result of government or industry regulation. Other technologies that have been developed could be used at wider scale. For example, the Canadian Centre for Child Protection created Project Arachnid (https://www.projectarachnid.ca/en), a web crawling software that can automatically scan accessible sites and identify known CSEM content. Detection of CSEM content can trigger a takedown notice, with the caveat that not all companies or all countries will comply with these notices.

Proactive Content Moderation

The major challenges of content moderation are increasingly recognized as we struggle with misinformation, hate speech, and trolling online. Machine learning algorithms can catch the most obvious infractions, such as flagging known CSEM, but there is an arms race because malicious actors try to beat the algorithms, there are asymmetric costs for false positives and false negatives in decision making, edge cases that require human moderation at a serious toll for moderators, and it is difficult to scale content moderation, given the sheer amount of content that is uploaded every minute. For example, hundreds of hours of video are uploaded to YouTube every minute, which precludes thorough content moderation (see M. Bergen's (2022) book *Like, Comment, Subscribe*).

Age Verification

I know age verification is anathema to some internet privacy absolutists because it would require some loss of user anonymity, but is there any other social space where age is not considered (as well as other demographic characteristics)? Would we accept much older adults attending elementary or high school to upgrade their education alongside children and underage teens? Do we allow children into adults-only bars and nightclubs? Age verification online makes sense, but there has been pushback regarding privacy concerns, technical challenges in doing age verification at scale in a robust and secure way, and other considerations, such as accessibility (many people do not trust or cannot access age verification services).

Cross-Platform Collaboration

An important avenue for further research and policy work is the use of multiple platforms for online sexual offending perpetration, as when an adult meets a minor on a gaming or other general multiuser platform, suggests connecting on a social network platform, and then uses direct messaging apps to facilitate CSEM and solicitation offenses. Each platform has only some relevant data on the interactions between this adult and minor, where no terms of service are violated on the initial platforms, and the messaging apps may become aware of violations of terms of service—through criminal behavior—but have no context for how the adult and minor met or how their interactions evolved. This impedes our ability to develop more effective prevention interventions. I recognize that there are legal, proprietary knowledge, and other challenges to multiplatform collaboration, but some multicompany collaboration is necessary for a more coherent and effective response to online perpetration. The Tech Coalition launched Lantern in 2023, a program for sharing key information across platforms about suspected perpetrators (Litton, 2023).

PREVENTION EVALUATIONS

There is limited evidence about the effects of perpetration prevention so far, with only a few studies, most relying on pre–post assessments or qualitative impressions of impact. I recognize that ultimate outcome data (the impact on sexual offenses involving children) are going to be hard to get with nonidentified participants, low base rates (e.g., for identified CSEM perpetrators), and therefore, the need for large follow-up studies with institutional data, not only self-report. These evaluations will likely rely on assessments of secondary outcomes, such as self-reported sexual urges toward CSEM or children, self-efficacy, and so on, corresponding to the risk and protective factors identified in Chapter 6. A systematic review (Seto, Rodrigues, et al., 2023) did not find good evidence for any prevention effort so far with regard to online sexual offending, except for the pilot study for Prevent It, which showed a significant reduction in CSEM use (Lätth et al., 2022).

ReDirection, the self-help site, got voluntary survey responses from 57 users (out of 70,000 website visits between September 2021 and February 2022; Suojellaan Lapsia, 2022); 75% of this small convenience sample said their CSEM use had decreased or stopped as a result of using the self-help resources, 71% said they found "reflecting on their own thoughts, feelings and behaviours" to be the most helpful ("Preliminary feedback from users of the ReDirection Self-Help Program" section), and 78% said they would not change anything about the content. That is an encouraging start, but obviously, 57 users out of 70,000 visits (which would likely involve multiple visits by some individuals, so fewer than 70,000 unique users) is a tiny and highly selected sample who were willing to complete the survey.

The Dunkelfeld intervention has been subject to one evaluation so far (Beier et al., 2015) that concluded the intervention had promise, comparing 53 individuals who completed treatment with 22 individuals who did not participate in treatment out of 319 child-attracted persons who were assessed, were eligible for treatment, and indicated they were interested in treatment between 2005 and 2011. There were significant pre–post changes in the treatment group on several self-report measures tapping into sexual self-regulation, offense-supportive cognitions, and emotional deficits, but there was no significant change in the comparison group. However, this analysis excluded treatment dropouts and was criticized by Mokros and Banse (2019), who reanalyzed the data and found no significant group-by-time interaction, thereby concluding that there was no significant effect of the Dunkelfeld intervention.

Whether one agrees with Mokros and Banse's (2019) criticisms, it is clear the evaluation by Beier et al. (2015) was underpowered and that treatment recruitment and retention have been challenging, given that only 53 of 319 eligible individuals (17%) completed the treatment over more than 5 years. Moreover, 319 individuals were assessed and eligible between 2005 and 2011, meaning fewer than 50 people could have entered treatment per year in a country with a population of over 80 million people.

Lätth et al. (2022) reported on the results of the pilot evaluation of Prevent It, which involved 160 English-speaking CSEM users recruited through advertisements on the darknet for people concerned about their use of CSEM. These participants were randomly assigned to the treatment versus a placebo condition where educational material was presented without homework exercises and clinician interactions. Using an intent-to-treat analysis, Lätth et al. found a significantly greater decrease in CSEM viewing time from pre- to posttreatment for individuals in the treatment group compared with the placebo condition. Indeed, approximately half the treatment participants reported no CSEM use in the prior week at posttreatment.

Ruzicka et al. (2021) described the results of a feasibility evaluation of RYBC, a school-based CSA primary prevention program, recognizing that there might be opposition to the program because of beliefs that CSA is not preventable; that the burden would be too high, given other nonacademic programs and demand; or because the content might be too sensitive or upsetting for children. The feasibility was evaluated by conducting focus groups with 18 educators, four parents, and 10 students at four urban middle schools in Maryland that were part of a pilot randomized clinical trial before the pilot trial began and then in interviews with seven educators who were part of the implementation. The results suggested there was support for primary prevention across the stakeholder groups, though this conclusion is limited by the fact that relatively few parents agreed to be part of the focus groups.

The pilot evaluation results were reported by Letourneau et al. (2024). The RBYC trial was conducted using a cohort wait-list design, where two schools were assigned to begin the program immediately and two schools were assigned to a waitlist for the program. A total of 160 students in Grades 6 or 7 were enrolled. The outcome measures were knowledge of developmental differences between adolescents and younger children, knowledge of CSA prevention strategies, knowledge of CSA law and related topics, and intentions to prevent or intervene with CSA against younger children. There were significant differences in knowledge of CSA law and related topics and intentions, but no significant difference in the knowledge of developmental differences or CSA prevention strategies.

INCLUDING PARENTS IN ONLINE SEXUAL OFFENDING PREVENTION

This book focuses on perpetration, reflecting what I focus on in my clinical and research activities. However, I have to include this section because parents are such an essential part of prevention when it comes to the online safety of minor users. A 2020 survey conducted in the European Union found that parents were the most common source of support for children who encountered problems online, with most children responding that they went to parents "sometimes" when they had online problems (Smahel et al., 2020, p. 48). Winters et al. (2023) surveyed CSA survivors and found that the survivors identified parent supervision as the best prevention response.

Parents are necessarily going to play a big role in protecting children, especially younger children. Parents can educate their kids about online safety practices, monitor their children's internet use, and support school-based prevention interventions such as RBYC. Parents can also manage the home environment to reduce risk by, for example, placing computers in a common area rather than in a bedroom, deciding whether or when their children should have access to smartphones or tablets, setting parental controls or restrictions on app and platform use (restrictive mediation), and engaging in open communication about online safety practices, expectations, and what to do if problems occur (active mediation). Parents can also be the ones children go to if something suspicious or potentially harmful has occurred. However, parents need more support because they do not feel prepared to handle some of these problems (Seto et al., 2022), and a third of the children in the European Union survey said their parents never or hardly talked to them about internet use (Smahel et al., 2020).

Wachs et al. (2020) conducted a large sample study about active versus restrictive parental mediation and found that active mediation was more effective than restrictive mediation. Corcoran et al.'s (2022) study of 306 parent–child dyads found that both active and restrictive mediation were associated with less sexually explicit image sending by children. Passive mediation (monitoring internet use only) was associated with more rather than less image sending, and technology controls specifically had no effect on sending images. Parental mediation appears to be moderated by child gender (more active mediation with girls than boys), age (more monitoring of younger children), and number of children (more restrictions on internet use in larger families; Sonck et al., 2013).

How else can parents protect their children? First, I discussed in Chapter 3 that the vulnerability factors for solicitation (and self-generating CSEM) are shared with other problematic experiences, so improving positive parenting practices and positive family environments can prevent online sexual offending, in addition to preventing other negative outcomes such as delinquency. CSA prevention education and communication in parents are associated with positive parenting practices and the estimated likelihood that their child is at risk (Rudolph et al., 2024). Parents were more likely to talk about bullying or drugs than CSA prevention, which, in turn, was more likely than talking about puberty, sex, and pornography. Rudolph et al. reported that most parents supported CSA prevention education, yet two thirds were also concerned this education could harm their children (e.g., make them anxious, scared, or upset), and two thirds already thought their kids could prevent sexual victimization. Seto et al. (2022) found that two thirds of parents who responded to an online survey had talked to their child about sexting, which is a start, but we do not know how effective these talks were. The same survey revealed that most parents did not feel prepared to handle the situation if their child's images were leaked. An interesting finding is that parents were more likely to expect their child had sexted than the base rates reported by children and youth in multiple studies would suggest (e.g., Madigan et al., 2018; Mori et al., 2019).

BYSTANDER INTERVENTIONS

Bystander interventions could also have a large impact on online sexual offending—for example, when friends observe or become aware that someone is engaging in risky online behavior. A systematic review by Jouriles et al. (2018) identified 24 studies and concluded there was evidence of significant positive effects on attitudes and beliefs about sexual violence and bystander behavior in college-based interventions. An example of bystander interventions to prevent CSA is provided by Darkness to Light (https://www.d2l.org), which has some empirical support (Letourneau et al., 2016). However, systematic reviews find mixed support for bystander interventions, with more evidence for shifts in attitudes and intentions and less evidence for shifts in behavior (Mujal et al., 2021). This evidence also suggests that the effects of bystander training fade over time, and studies have historically been methodologically weak, relying on pre–post comparisons but with a shift to more randomized trials or quasi-experimental designs more recently. Mainwaring et al. (2023) identified two moderators of bystander intervention effects: Women bystanders were more likely to intervene than men bystanders, and bystander intervention is more likely when the perceived norms support bystanders getting involved.

Bystander intervention is a potentially important option because bystanders can intervene when formal responses are not available. Results from a survey of 245 Australian residents (two thirds were female) ages 18 to 71 illustrate the potential for bystander intervention online (Flynn et al., 2022): 64% had observed image-based abuse, and 46% said or did something (a positive framing is that almost three quarters, 72%, of those who observed image-based abuse intervened in some way). Of these 46% who acted in some way, a little over half (56%) directly confronted the perpetrator; half told someone such as a friend, family member, or coworker; and 47% supported the victim. Consistent with other research, relatively few reported the perpetrator to the police or another authority (15%) or reported them to tech (7%).

Other studies suggest more of a gap: A Pew survey found that 66% of respondents reported witnessing online harassment, but less than half (30% of the respondents) had intervened as a bystander (Duggan, 2017). In an earlier study by eSafety (2017) of over 4,000 adults in Australia, 19% of the sample had witnessed image-based abuse, and of this subsample, 44% did not say or do anything, and another 7% said they did not know what to say or do. A. Powell et al. (2020) found a gap between witnessing abuse and intervening, as well as a gap between intentions to say or do something and actually saying or doing something. Women scored higher than men in both intentions and behavior (see Mainwaring et al., 2023).

A challenge for bystander intervention is that it is scary, and people often do not know what to do. Flynn et al. (2022) drew from their survey and 35 face-to-face groups with 219 participants to identify barriers and potential facilitators for bystander intervention. One barrier was that many did not realize that sharing personal sexual images without consent was against the law. Another barrier was offense-supportive attitudes and victim blaming, which was low overall but higher in men than women respondents. The relationship of the bystander to the victim and perpetrator, the risk of intervening, and estimates of whether other bystanders would be supportive were also seen as barriers. The relationship of the bystander to the victim and perpetrator—and whether other bystanders would be supportive—was also seen as relevant. Men were more likely to intervene than women, which is different from what has been found in prior research on bystander intervention (Banyard, 2011). Heterosexual participants were more likely to intervene than nonheterosexual participants. Directly confronting the perpetrator was seen as the most effective intervention.

CHALLENGES FOR PERPETRATION PREVENTION

In my review of perpetration prevention, several challenges are common across different initiatives. These challenges include recruitment and retention of participants, stigma, confusion about mandatory reporting requirements, and other potential barriers.

Recruitment and Retention

I think the biggest challenge for the prevention of online sexual offending will be recruitment and then retention of participants. There are multiple examples of the challenges for recruitment: Preventell (https://preventell.se/?lang=en) is a Swedish referral service that averaged 300 calls a year over 5 years in their first evaluation report in a country of over 10 million people (Adebahr et al., 2021). Stop It Now! UK & Ireland has solid numbers for their helpline and self-help website, but this can include English-speaking users from around the world, not only residents of the United Kingdom and Ireland. The Troubled Desire self-help site had 7,496 visitors from around the world in its first

30 months of operation, but the self-assessment was completed only by 4,161 users. This number of visitors averages approximately 140 users a month, which is an important accomplishment but a relatively small number considering how many languages the site was offered in and how many people it could, therefore, conceivably reach around the world.

Even with my enthusiasm for Prevent It's pilot results and personal involvement in the evaluation of a revised program, Prevent It 2, I am mindful that it took almost 3 years to recruit 160 CSEM users for the Prevent It pilot trial (Lätth et al., 2022). Dunkelfeld has treated a few hundred people over the years of operation but has evaluation data for less than 100 cases (Beier et al., 2015). A total of 144 referrals have been made to Talking for Change since 2021, with 85 assessments completed of 87 people referred for assessment and 37 program completions of 62 individuals recommended for treatment (with 16 individuals in treatment or on a wait-list at the time I received this update from Heasman, personal communication, November 17, 2023).

A total of 633 calls had been received by the Talking for Change helpline in the 3 years the helpline had been active (Heasman, personal communication, November 17, 2023). A slight majority (56%) of the calls were from individuals seeking help because of their concerns regarding sexual thoughts, feelings, or behavior involving children; most of these individuals were adults and self-identified as sexually attracted to children. Coleman (personal communication, March 6, 2022) shared an infographic about the launch of What's OK? (https://www.whatsok.org), a self-help resource designed for young people launched the previous year. The soft launch resulted in website visits from 2,270 users, where 38% said they had perpetrated or were at risk of perpetration. The live chat service had much less engagement, with 31 emails, seven texts, four chats, and zero phone calls. Similarly, in an evaluation of a pilot chat service for the ReDirection self-help site, there were only 16 users in a 10-month pilot period from November 2022 to August 2023 (Suojellaan Lapsia, 2023). Of these 16 users, 12 had already begun using ReDirection, two started both the same day, and only two started with the anonymous chat service. These individuals were motivated to change but had previous unsatisfactory help experiences and many espoused offense-supportive cognitions (Suojellaan Lapsia, 2023).

Measuring Outcomes

I believe the second biggest challenge in evaluating perpetration prevention is how to measure impact, given the reliance on self-report in mostly online, anonymous contexts. People may be reluctant to honestly answer questions about behavior due to concerns about self-incrimination, even with promises of anonymity and confidentiality. Changes in self-regulation, offense-supportive cognitions, or other dynamic risk factors are encouraging, but we do not yet have evidence that positive changes on these factors will then result in the reduction of online sexual offending compared with control groups or other benchmarks. Interventions that require ongoing contact have more opportunities to collect evaluation data. For example, online or in-person treatment programs (e.g., Prevent It, Talking for Change, Dunkelfeld) can include repeated assessments and, in the case of Prevent It, can have more rigorous evaluations through random assignment to conditions. This is much trickier for helplines or self-help sites, which may have only a short contact with anonymous users and may be unable to assign users randomly to different conditions.

Most, if not all, interventions are explicitly focused on reducing the risk of reoffending and that may antagonize some potential users. I have heard anecdotally that some child-attracted persons in online forums do not like the names of prevention efforts such as Stop It Now! and Prevent It because they focus on offending and are not perceived to be responding to the whole person. A different approach that emphasizes personal well-being as well as risk reduction could have broader appeal, thereby helping with recruitment and retention. Indeed, Lievesley et al. (2023) surveyed child-attracted persons and found they rated mental well-being and coping with stigma as higher treatment priorities than dealing with their sexual attraction to children. Integrating these different observations, I believe we need to develop a broader palette of interventions to address the myriad motivations for online sexual offending and different at-risk groups. For example, an online intervention advertised as focusing on emotional and internet self-regulation could have broader appeal and still have a positive impact on outcomes. I have already discussed how the current options are not designed for individuals who do not see themselves as being sexually attracted to children or for juveniles or family members. The intensity and "location" of these interventions depend on a better understanding of these forms of online sexual offending, including the risk to reoffend, dynamic risk and protective factors, and victim harms and other costs.

Other Barriers

A common objection to prevention is that dollars spent on prevention are somehow dollars taken away from law enforcement, support for victims, or other aspects of how we respond to the problem of online sexual offending. I understand this objection but disagree. Online sexual offending is a serious problem that warrants greater investment than it currently receives, especially as more of the world comes online. It does not have to be a zero-sum game in terms of spending.

There are multiple barriers facing potential users, potential providers, and perpetration prevention (see Austin & Salter, 2023). These additional barriers include stigma about sexual attraction to children (Jahnke, 2018b; Lievesley et al., 2023), confusion about mandatory reporting if a child is suspected to be at risk of abuse (Stephens et al., 2021), and access to trained, experienced, and willing service providers (Levenson & Grady, 2019). Stigma is a barrier because it can inhibit help seeking; indeed, stigma helps explain why prevention programs have struggled in terms of recruitment and then retention. Stigma may be greatest for individuals who acknowledge sexual attraction to children, but it could also affect individuals who do not believe they are sexually attracted to children but are seeking help (e.g., family members concerned they may pose a risk to children in their family). For mandatory reporting, some clinicians believe attraction to children is sufficient grounds to report someone as posing an imminent risk to children (Stephens et al., 2021). This confusion is problematic for potential service users, who worry they might somehow be identified or are concerned about what they can reveal if their identities are known. It is also confusing for intervention providers, who may avoid prevention work altogether or limit what they do because of confusion about their legal and regulatory obligations. Stigma, uncertainty about mandatory reporting, and training opportunities affect the number of potential service providers available. I address each of these barriers in more depth next.

Potential provider barriers include provider attitudes and beliefs about sexual attraction to children and sexual behavior targeting children, lack of formal training and supervision, and confusion about mandatory reporting when children might be at risk of abuse. Broader barriers to prevention include access to prevention resources; the belief that prevention does not work; the belief that sexual interest in children and sexual offending against children are synonymous; the belief that investment in perpetration prevention takes away resources from law enforcement, victims, or other equally important responses to the problem of online sexual offending; and the belief that the only response for sexual offending is more severe punishment.

Stigma

Stigma can include *self-stigma* (negative attitudes and beliefs the person holds about themselves because of a characteristic, such as sexual attraction to children), *public stigma* (negative attitudes and beliefs held by the general public), and *professional stigma* (negative attitudes and beliefs held by mental health and other professionals). Self-stigma is correlated with exposure to public stigma (Jahnke, 2018b; Shields et al., 2020) and may dramatically reduce well-being and increase the risk of sexually offending. Self-stigma is also associated with depression, low self-esteem, hopelessness, and suicidal ideation and behavior (see Chapter 6). Jahnke et al. (2015) proposed that stress and stigma led to worse emotional functioning, worse social functioning, and an increased endorsement of offense-supportive cognitions in reaction to that stress.

There is ample evidence of public stigma, where individuals with pedohebephilia, in general, but especially those who have sexually offended against children, are often viewed as the lowest of the low. Professionals are people too and may also hold stigmatizing views toward attraction to children and sexual offending involving children (e.g., Roche & Stephens, 2022; Stephens et al., 2021), which may help explain the willingness of professionals to make mandatory reports when the situation does not meet legal thresholds (Stephens et al., 2021). It is, therefore, understandable that many child-attracted persons are reluctant to seek mental health treatment, and those who do participate report disappointing experiences (B4U-ACT, 2011a, 2011b; Levenson & Grady, 2019).

Stigma is a major obstacle to recruiting people who are seeking help because of sexual urges toward children. Some secondary prevention interventions do not have to target people who self-identify as having sexual urges toward children. First, the skills they teach are generalizable; for example, someone might be willing to participate in prevention for "pornography addiction" or "compulsive pornography use," and the sexual self-regulation skills they learn in these programs would be helpful for those who have sexual urges toward children, as well as those who have a broader pattern of hypersexual urges. Second, a broader approach can be helpful because not all at-risk individuals specifically have sexual urges toward children, particularly those who target older adolescents or adults. Last, some individuals who are sexually attracted to children may not consider this attraction to be the top treatment priority (Lievesley et al., 2023).

Confusion About Mandatory Reporting
There is confusion about mandatory reporting in jurisdictions that oblige it, such as Canada and the United States. These mandatory reporting obligations vary from jurisdiction to jurisdiction regarding what is mandatory to report, who is mandated to report, and how reporting is done. I cannot cover all the different regulations, but many have the following elements in common: Mandated reporters—which almost always include health and social service professionals—are obliged to report to police or other authorities when an identifiable child is at risk of maltreatment. So, for example, an identified person who admitted to a clinician to sexually or nonsexually abusing a child could trigger an obligation to report this information to the police because an investigation could identify the child who is being harmed if there were sufficient details in the identified person's disclosure. Similarly, an identified person who admitted to having sexual fantasies about an identifiable child—for example, describing fantasies about their neighbor's child—could trigger this obligation because an investigation could find and protect the child at risk of being harmed. Even an anonymous intervention participant may report details that can identify a child at risk of harm, and this can trigger mandatory reporting. Mandatory reporting is not necessarily required if an identified person simply admits to having sexual urges about children without specifying which child and without any further identifying information.

Stephens et al. (2021) looked at mandatory reporting decisions for vignettes given to 309 registered clinicians or trainees in accredited programs. A decision to report was associated with greater participant stigma regarding sexual attraction to children. Deciding to report was also associated with the vignette conditions, which manipulated whether the person had used CSEM and whether the person had access to children. The decision to report was weakly related to or unrelated to demographic factors and professional experience, including years of experience, whether the clinicians or trainees had forensic training, and whether they had previously made a mandatory report. The three most commonly endorsed reasons for reporting were concern that children would be harmed if the report was not made (34%), concerns about professional liability (24%), and prior training (18%). Respondents thought that CSEM users had to be reported, perhaps because this could help identify and thus protect children who were depicted. The most common reasons given for not reporting were not believing the person was at risk for contact sexual offending (33%), concern for the client if the information was disclosed (26%), and prior training (25%). The fact that training is cited both as a reason to report and not to report implies that training parameters—the type of training and guidance provided on mandatory reporting—are key.

Limited Treatment Providers and Opportunities

The number of trained, experienced, and willing service providers is finite, and they are overrepresented in major urban centers and high-income areas, with much less access in more rural or impoverished areas. Moreover, even in wealthy geographies, there are often waiting lists for treatment spots, and therapy sessions are often unavailable in the evening or on weekends, which can conflict with work, school, or other weekday commitments. Because treatment is often offered in group format, in-person therapy also disadvantages those who cannot function in groups because of severe social anxiety or other issues.

One potential response to these geographic and economic constraints is teletherapy or hybrid intervention models. As the COVID-19 pandemic showed us, at an unexpected pace, teletherapy can work well, with both costs and benefits compared with in-person therapy. For example, the Fernandez et al. (2021) meta-analysis found a significant improvement as a result of live video psychotherapy (56 within-group comparison studies) and more improvement than the wait-list control in 47 between-group comparison studies, which were not different in effects from in-person psychotherapy. This suggests live video treatment could work for participants just as well as in-person treatment, with more convenience and access.

In line with more offerings of online-only or hybrid intervention is the @myTabu treatment protocol (Fromberger et al., 2021). This online clinician-guided intervention is for people who have been convicted of sexual offenses—including online sexual offenses—who are under community supervision. The aim of the @myTabu evaluation is to randomly assign 582 participants to treatment versus placebo conditions, with eight assessment points using self-reported scores on dynamic risk factors and, eventually, officially recorded recidivism. The treatment content involves psychoeducational text with images and videos, as well as self-guided exercises with automatic feedback and clinician-guided exercises with feedback. The placebo condition involves readings and other information but without active ingredients—the same mode, dose, and amount of support and attention by coaches, but topics include healthy living elements, such as nutrition, sleep, and exercise. An early evaluation from Schröder et al. (2023) of 113 participants in @myTabu found that they reported a high acceptance of online treatment, and this acceptance was associated with their attitudes about treatment and perceived norms (expectations of what close others would think). Interestingly, acceptance of @myTabu was not correlated with expectations regarding criminal justice agents, such as probation or parole officers.

There are multiple ways that online prevention services can be provided, including online screening or preparation for in-person services, online-only or hybrid services, or streaming lower risk individuals to online services and higher risk individuals to in-person services. Online interventions also allow for more creativity—for example, using virtual reality tools to test skills in a safe environment, such as practicing how to avoid risky situations with CSEM or children in vitro. I realize this is not a panacea because virtual care has accessibility challenges, such as having a suitable device, a reliable internet connection, and enough privacy to participate virtually. Also, even virtual intervention options can face challenges in terms of waiting lists, staff shortages, and funding.

HARM REDUCTION: ARE VIRTUAL CSEM AND CHILD SEX DOLLS SAFE AND EFFECTIVE?

Besides individual and technological prevention approaches, is there an opportunity for harm reduction? There is a great deal of controversy—with lots of opinions, despite no research—on whether access to virtual CSEM or child sex dolls (involving no real children; see Virtual CSEM and Child Sex Dolls section in Chapter 2) could be a safer substitute for pedohebephilic individuals who are committed to abstaining from sexually offending against children. I am specifically ruling out the use of deepfakes because they involve images of real persons and could have serious negative effects for those individuals. It is possible that virtual CSEM or child sex dolls could be part of a harm-reduction approach to CSEM offending because it can be sexually gratifying for at least some people who are interested in CSEM and does not involve the sexual exploitation and harm of a real child. A well-known harm-reduction example is the prescription of methadone for opioid addiction: Methadone is still addictive, but it can reduce the risk of a lethal overdose, associated crime, and unsafe use practices (e.g., sharing needles) compared with street-purchased opioids. In this context, a harm reduction approach would try to shift some CSEM perpetrators to virtual CSEM and other alternatives rather than expecting full abstinence, especially for the subset who are exclusively interested in children.

Whether a harm-reduction approach is viable in responding to CSEM offending requires determining whether access to virtual CSEM has an impact on the risk of sexually reoffending, including the future use of CSEM depicting real children or direct offenses against children. I have suggested in multiple media stories that access to virtual CSEM or child sex dolls may have both positive and negative effects, serving as a harm-reduction substitute for some CSEM users but inciting other CSEM users to further sexual offending, based on their risk and protective factors as outlined in Chapters 5 and 6 (Morin, 2016). I doubt whether this will ever be examined in research to inform policies and practices, but this research is needed. We have no evidence about the impact of virtual CSEM or child sex dolls because of public disgust at the idea and ethical objections (Appel, 2023).

At the same time, sex dolls are not a panacea. Zara et al. (2022) surveyed 100 individuals who had sexually offended and 244 nonoffending control respondents with similar socioeconomic statuses and found that those who had sexually offended (whether against children or adults) were less likely than controls to believe that sex robots or dolls would reduce their risk of sexually offending. In addition, offenders were less accepting and less willing to discuss having a relationship with a sex robot or doll. There was no nonsexually offending control group in this study, so we do not know if this difference reflects sexually offending specifically or criminal behavior more generally.

I have suggested in public media stories that the effects of virtual CSEM or child sex dolls likely depend on the person: Individuals who are at relatively low risk may benefit from a legal substitute sexual outlet because they are unlikely to act anyway, whereas those who are at a higher risk because they have self-regulation deficits, offense-supportive cognitions, and other factors described in Chapter 6 may experience stronger urges to sexually interact with children (e.g., Morin, 2016). I recognize that obstacles to considering these options include stigma, moral revulsion, and an unwillingness to empirically test these ideas because of legal, ethical, or public relations concerns. It is worth pointing out that a natural quasi-experiment is available because some countries do not criminalize virtual CSEM (United States), whereas others do (Canada and the United Kingdom). We could conceivably compare CSEM contact offending history and recidivism rates to see if there is a significant difference in outcomes in these countries after controlling for risk at a broad level (e.g., prior criminal history, including prior sexual offending).

It may be unrealistic to expect an adolescent or young adult who is exclusively interested in children to live the rest of their lives without any legal sexual expression (though they could still fantasize about and masturbate to legal child images). However, even if virtual CSEM or child sex dolls were allowed, uptake might be low for reasons such as squeamishness, concerns about legality or perceptions if discovered, or the belief it would not be satisfactory. Consistent with the possibility of poor uptake, Marečková et al. (2022) found that people who were sexually attracted to children ($n = 48$, 38%) were twice as likely to be willing to consider sex robots or dolls than the general community ($n = 806$, 18%), but this was still a minority of the respondents. A criticism of this survey is that the question was ambiguous because it was worded as "I desire sexual experience with a sex robot/doll." The question did not specify a child robot or doll, and desiring an experience is not the same as being willing to try something.

From a harm reduction point of view, someone viewing legal child content is less harmful than someone seeking illegal child content, where children were directly exploited to create the image. But there is revulsion and complicated legal and ethical issues around the depiction of real children, the use of these images for unintended purposes, and possible harm to children in knowing their images are being used for sexual purposes. These issues are, in turn, related to the even broader social dilemma of whether and how to regulate the use of personal likenesses online, such as the creation of deepfake pornography of adults without their consent. As I revise this text, there is a lot of press and public attention to the power of AI-driven text and image generators, which will only become more powerful and more pervasive over time.

SUMMARY

Prevention programs take a proactive rather than a reactive approach to the problem of online sexual offending. There has been a great deal of excitement about the potential for the prevention of online sexual offending, recognizing that the numbers of undetected perpetrators far exceed existing criminal justice and clinical resources. Most of the current programs focus on secondary prevention, targeting individuals at risk of online sexual offending, but school-based programs can provide primary prevention available to all students. I also see promise in prevention through parents and bystanders.

Most prevention efforts focus on adults at risk of online sexual offending because of sexual thoughts or behaviors involving children. Two major gaps in prevention are juveniles who engage in online sexual offending and individuals who do not see themselves as sexually interested in children. These prevention efforts may reach individuals engaging in CSEM offending, the sexual solicitation of younger adolescents and children, and the commercial sexual exploitation of children, but they will not seem relevant to individuals engaging in image-based abuse, such as digital exhibitionism, digital voyeurism, and the nonconsensual sharing of images or to individuals engaging in technology-facilitated sexual assaults against adults.

Limited evaluation data are available, and the only solid evidence for effectiveness comes from an online cognitive-behavioral intervention for undetected CSEM users. Strengths of this evaluation include the use of a randomized clinical trial design and the theoretical and empirical grounding of the program content. Limitations of this study include the reliance on self-report for the primary outcome of CSEM use and the relatively slow recruitment pace, highlighting one of the major barriers to advancing treatment for online sexual offending. Recruitment is likely to continue to be a challenge for prevention efforts until stigma, confusion about mandatory reporting, and accessibility are addressed.

In addition to prevention focusing on individuals, efforts to address the technological affordances that facilitate online sexual offending will play a critical role in prevention. This includes the widespread implementation of algorithms to detect known and suspected CSEM as well as suspected sexual solicitation through proactive content moderation, age verification to reduce suspicious interactions between adults and minors, and cross-platform information sharing to reduce perpetration that involves multiple apps or platforms.

RETURNING TO THE CASE EXAMPLES

The case examples I described in the earlier chapters highlight how online sexual offending prevention has mostly focused on individuals who are at risk because they have sexual urges regarding children. Of the different cases, only Bart (higher risk CSEM) and Smith (commercial sexual exploitation of children) would have been likely to consider the kinds of perpetration prevention programs that are currently offered. Even then, Smith refused to participate in treatment while in custody and may well have refused to seek out prevention help as well. Adam (lower risk CSEM) was concerned about his problematic and escalating pornography use but denied any specific sexual interest in children per se, and Sean (online sexual solicitation) admitted interest in adolescents around the age of consent, as well as adults, but not children. The others—Elvis (digital exhibitionism), Vince (digital voyeurism), Jack (image-based sexual abuse), and Adrian (technology-facilitated sexual assault)—reported being sexually attracted to adults only. Jack thought he could have benefited from education to understand the illegality and ramifications of sharing images of his ex-partner online and wished it was available through school as part of the standard sex education curriculum, which mostly focused on reproductive health information. Adrian had only a vague recall of a sexual assault prevention talk he had to attend as part of his college orientation week and wondered if it might have helped him if he had paid more attention.

9

Conclusions and Future Directions

Understanding and Preventing Online Sexual Offending

There has been tremendous progress in our understanding of online sexual offending, but this progress is uneven, with much more attention to child sexual exploitation material (CSEM) offending, progress on sexual solicitation offending, and more recognition and research regarding image-based offending, including digital exhibitionism and voyeurism. Much less research is available regarding technology-facilitated sexual assault of adults, sexual trafficking of children, and child sexual abuse tourism. Overall, we know much more about risk and needs assessment for online sexual offending than treatment or prevention.

We are still people when we are online, even if our behavior is affected by internet affordances, including online disinhibition effects. A lot of what we know about the psychology of sexual offending, in general, seems to apply to online sexual offending as well, which includes the relevance of the motivation–facilitation model of sexual offending (Seto, 2019), the kinds of psychologically meaningful risk factors associated with the onset or persistence of online offending, the relevance of the risk–need–responsivity framework in designing interventions, and the content and format of intervention approaches. This is good news because it suggests that many findings from the broader and more established sexual offending literature are useful starting points for online sexual offending.

https://doi.org/10.1037/0000428-010
Online Sexual Offending: Theory, Practice, and Policy, Second Edition, by M. C. Seto
Copyright © 2025 by the American Psychological Association. All rights reserved.

CSEM OFFENDING

The CSEM research literature has matured since the first edition of this book, with more studies of etiology, perpetrator characteristics, clinical and risk assessment methods, and intervention for this plurality of the online sexual offending population, at least as it comes to those who are seen in clinical and criminal justice settings. The available evidence indicates that most CSEM perpetrators are men who are predominantly motivated by sexual attraction to prepubescent or pubescent children. Even with this sexual attraction to prepubescent and pubescent children, however, a substantial minority have never committed contact sexual offenses, which can be explained by their lower levels of antisociality, as reflected in other criminal behavior; personality traits, such as impulsivity and callousness; offense-permissive cognitions; and unstable lifestyles in terms of employment, social connections, and substance use. Those who have committed both CSEM and contact offenses stand out as particularly likely to have pedophilia or hebephilia and a distinctly greater risk of sexual recidivism.

Detected CSEM offending fits well with the motivation–facilitation model (Seto, 2019), and what we have learned in the past few years about undetected CSEM offending seems to be fitting so far, though specifically pedohebephilia may play less of a role in studies of undetected CSEM users in the community. In more recent years, it has been recognized that these perpetrators may be a minority in a larger population that has committed CSEM offenses for other reasons. For example, there could be many adult CSEM users who are primarily interested in underage teens. This is socially prohibited and illegal, but it is unlikely to suggest paraphilia, and this CSEM use is unlikely to appear in criminal justice settings, given the uncertainty about the ages of depicted persons in content seized by police, and unlikely to appear in clinical settings unless the person is significantly distressed or impaired as a result.

The first peer-reviewed study describing the development of the Child Pornography Offender Risk Tool (CPORT) was published shortly after the first edition of this book (Seto & Eke, 2015). Since then, we have published a small validation study, and there have been several independent replications, albeit mostly with shortened versions because of the missing content items and sometimes a lack of information about stated sexual interests in children (Eke et al., 2019). Most of these replications have found evidence of significant predictive accuracy, with two exceptions: Pilon (2016), with a possibly overlapping sample in Ontario, found the CPORT predicted general but not sexual recidivism, and Soldino et al. (2021) did not find the CPORT was a significant predictor of sexual recidivism, though the Correlates of Admission of Sexual Interest in Children Scale did predict sexual recidivism. Cohen (2023) conducted the latest study of the CPORT and has the largest sample by far by following men on federal probation for CSEM offenses in the United States.

There has also been research examining other risk assessment tools, including the OASys Sexual Reoffending Predictor–Internet Version (Howard & Wakeling, 2021), which is based solely on criminal sanctions for sexual offending, including CSEM offending. There is evidence that the CPORT does better than the Risk Matrix 2000 (RM2000/S) and Static-99R in some respects (Helmus, Eke, Farmus, & Seto, 2024) and evidence the STABLE-2007 has predictive accuracy with adult male CSEM perpetrators, which provides an avenue for dynamic risk assessment to drive intervention planning and possibly the monitoring of changes in risk of sexually reoffending over time (e.g., as a result of treatment; Babchishin et al., 2023; Eke, 2022; Helmus, Eke, Farmus, & Seto, 2024).

There have been some advances in CSEM treatment, with the articulation of several evidence-based treatment models and a proliferation of treatment programs to address demand (see Table 7.1). Most interventions are adapted from existing treatment models in the criminogenic needs that are addressed, exercises, and other content. Because these models draw from the same literature, there is substantial similarity across interventions. There is unique content in the addition of intervention content regarding the self-regulation of internet use and conceptualizations of offending behavior (e.g., some individuals and some clinicians frame CSEM use in terms of pornography addiction). Unfortunately, there are still no evaluations of these CSEM interventions except for Prevent It, an online intervention for undetected CSEM users; the intervention produced significant reductions in self-reported CSEM use, albeit with high levels of attrition, especially in the first few sessions (Lätth et al., 2022). No evaluations demonstrating positive effects for detected CSEM perpetrators or relying on objective outcomes, such as criminal recidivism, have been reported yet in the peer-reviewed literature.

OTHER ONLINE SEXUAL OFFENDING

There has been more research on other forms of online sexual offending since the first edition of this book. This research includes more studies of solicitation perpetrators in terms of their demographic and psychological characteristics and tactics. Consistent with my earlier speculation, solicitation perpetrators are less likely to show evidence of pedophilia or hebephilia than CSEM perpetrators, and this group seems to be intermediate between CSEM and contact perpetrators on characteristics, such as criminal history and antisocial personality traits (cf. Seto et al., 2012). Sexual solicitation research has replicated an early distinction by Briggs et al. (2011) between fantasy- and contact-driven solicitations, with the additional complexity that individuals may engage in both forms of sexual solicitation (DeHart et al., 2017) and use a variety of different tactics, ranging from classical grooming to "blitz" requests for CSEM or sexual interactions. Solicitation perpetrators are an important population for further research on risk assessment, need assessment, and intervention, given that a study in Australia suggested they are at relatively higher risk of sexual recidivism than even contact perpetrators (Dowling et al., 2021).

I focused on CSEM and solicitation offending in the first edition as the two most common forms of online sexual offending detected by police or reported by minors. Image-based sexual offending is related to CSEM and online solicitation offending as well because self-generated CSEM can be used to blackmail or extort minors, or images sent to similar-aged peers can be nonconsensually reshared, especially by partners or ex-partners. The literature on image-based abuse by minors and adults has grown since the first edition. This literature reveals an important overlap with coercive control and intimate partner violence, suggesting commonalities in perpetrator characteristics, etiology, risk factors, and perhaps interventions as well. We do not know about the risk of recidivism for image-based sexual abuse or the important intervention needs.

There has been much less progress in online sexual offending against adults, however, particularly digital exhibitionism or voyeurism targeting adults and technology-facilitated sexual assault. There have been several reviews or studies about the role of dating apps in sexual assault, but we know little about perpetrator characteristics, assessment, and intervention. Similarly, there are relatively few studies on the sexual trafficking of children and child sexual abuse tourism, beyond the recognition that both forms of online sexual offending are more likely in lower income countries visited by individuals from relatively higher income countries (ECPAT, 2016b). I have suggested that existing risk assessment tools are suitable because individuals who engage in technology-facilitated sexual assault or commercial sexual exploitation of children through trafficking or tourism have committed contact sexual offenses. They might presumably also fit within existing treatment programs for individuals who have committed contact sexual offenses. However, there may be additional clinical considerations, and the generalizability of risk assessment, clinical assessment, and treatment knowledge need to be examined empirically.

ECOSYSTEMS

Online offending is driven by opportunity in terms of internet access over time and across space. Therefore, I expect a continuing trend toward more online sexual offending in underrepresented geographic regions as internet access continues to grow. Most online sexual offending is committed by men against women, children, and sometimes, other men (Babchishin et al., 2015; Henry et al., 2020; Karasavva & Forth, 2022). Much of it represents existing forms of sexual offending that have moved into the online space and, therefore, have been facilitated by digital affordances: digital CSEM instead of physical CSEM, online sexual solicitations instead of in-person solicitations, online sextortion instead of extortion with physical photographs or sexual messages, and digital instead of in-person exhibitionism and voyeurism. Sexual assaults, sexual trafficking, and child sexual abuse tourism occurred before the advent of online technologies, but all these forms of sexual offending can be facilitated by these technologies in terms of reach or frequency.

Ecosystem changes could make a big difference in the prevalence of online sexual offending, but decades into the internet era, we are still figuring out the legal, regulatory, and social considerations in regulating online spaces. The internet is not the Wild West anymore, not only for sexual offending but also for harassment, misinformation, political extremism, and many other serious problems we have discovered as internet use increases in scope and reach. It does not have to be this way. In addition to changing the technological ecosystem, we can do more to change the social ecosystem underpinning our use of technology. How have we grown to accept the levels and severity of online sexual harassment and abuse? How is it acceptable that receiving an unwanted sexual message or "dick pic" is just part of being online, especially in dating or social media apps or platforms?

It is an extremely uphill battle to counter these antisocial norms, but it is possible. For example, there was a time when smoking was popular and unquestioned, but this has changed over time, and smoking is now frowned on (even if it took decades, especially because of deliberate obfuscation by cigarette makers). More optimistically, over a shorter time, there have been significant shifts in norms regarding impaired driving or wearing seatbelts (Dinh-Zarr et al., 2001; Shults et al., 2001). We can and need to change internet behavior norms, not only for sexual interactions with minors by adults but also unwanted sexual solicitations or images sent to adults; the nonconsensual sharing of nudes or other sexual images, irrespective of age; and other problematic online behavior, including harassment, trolling, and bullying.

As a potential example of the importance of social and cultural contexts, the Disrupting Harm project by WeProtect produced individual country-level reports (https://www.end-violence.org/disrupting-harm#country-reports). As of September 2022, there were reports for Thailand, Vietnam, and the Philippines in Asia and Ethiopia, Uganda, Tanzania, and Kenya in Africa. Approximately 1,000 youths between the ages of 12 and 17 were recruited in each of these countries. There was significant variation in the proportions of these youths who had shared sexual images of themselves, from a low of 0.6% in Vietnam to a high of 10% in the Philippines. There was significant variation in the prevalence of seeking sexual content online as well, which suggests that social and cultural factors are relevant because all participating youths had access to the internet and were similar in age.

Though this is a book about applied psychology, written by a clinical and forensic psychologist and published by the American Psychological Association, we could do a lot to reduce online sexual offending by changing the technological and social environments without addressing individual psychologies directly. Individual assessment and intervention services are necessary, given the levels of distress that can be experienced by people seeking clinical help and given legal and other mandates for individuals who are detected for criminal behavior. But as I have stated multiple times in this book, the most scalable solution to the highly scaled-up problems of online sexual harassment, bullying, and offending requires changes in the platforms and their affordances, both as constraints against these problems and as nudges against individual perpetration. My primary examples are still the use of PhotoDNA and other hash matching technologies to flag known CSEM and new machine learning classifiers to flag suspected CSEM or sexual solicitation behavior. Other technological interventions show promise, such as warning messages when someone engages in suspicious behavior (Scanlan et al., 2024). I hope that some form of age verification will be legally mandated for some online spaces to reduce adult interactions with minors, especially younger minors.

FUTURE DIRECTIONS FOR RESEARCH

Most research on online sexual offending perpetration has been conducted on men from Western, educated, industrialized, rich, and democratic (WEIRD) societies, with much less known about men from non-WEIRD societies or women or juveniles anywhere. As the entire world goes online with the spread of reliable, high-speed internet access in the Global South, we cannot rely on WEIRD research, policy, and practices and assume these will apply as more of the world comes online. The Disrupting Harm surveys I mentioned indicate significant variations across countries in the prevalence of online behaviors, which may reflect both cultural and legal differences. I noted how Japan is quite different from many other countries in terms of tolerance for sexual content involving children and for the commercial sexual exploitation of teens. I am nonetheless confident that many, but not all, of the findings described in this book will be robust.

According to the limited international data available, I hypothesize that the associations between sexual attraction to children and different forms of online sexual offending will hold up, where a majority of those involved with CSEM are sexually attracted to prepubescent or pubescent children, in contrast to the majority of sexual solicitation perpetrators who are likely to be attracted to underage adolescents. We already know that prepubescent girls are the most popular CSEM age and gender category internationally because that is what is reported around the world to police repositories. I expect the large gender effect to persist, where men will be more likely to perpetrate than women, and girls will be more likely to be targeted than boys. I expect that both sexual motivations and antisociality will be involved in the onset and persistence of online sexual offending, where sexual motivations may also include excessive sexual preoccupation or paraphilic interests in exhibitionism, voyeurism, or coercive sex. However, there is already evidence of variation in the prevalence of online victimization, and this may be true as well for online perpetration, which suggests there is variation in vulnerability factors for victimization and perhaps risk factors for perpetration as well. Most risk research has focused on individual factors, even though social and systemic factors are also relevant.

What is less likely to be robust? I predict the demographic differences reported by Babchishin et al. (2011, 2015) about online CSEM perpetrators being more White and more educated than contact perpetrators will change as more of the world comes online and online technologies become easier to use (e.g., with even more intuitive user interfaces). I expect we will eventually see more women involved in online sexual offending, given evidence that the large gender discrepancy in clinical and correctional research on sexual offending against children is smaller when we look at self-report victimization data (see Cortoni, 2015). This has been interpreted as evidence of reporting and prosecution biases (e.g., women are less likely to be reported to police for criminal sexual behavior). To extrapolate from this, it may also be the case that online sexual offenses are less likely to be reported when a woman perpetrator is involved or when boys are targeted. Another demographic change I expect is more online perpetration by older juveniles against peers and younger juveniles (Sutton & Finkelhor, 2023).

There are still many questions that need to be addressed in future research. There is some evidence about the use of illegal pornography, such as depictions of sexual violence or bestiality, but what do we know beyond the likelihood that users are men and using a wide range of online pornography? The role of technology in offending against adults has not received as much attention as online sexual offending against minors, perhaps because it is seen as ancillary (happened to meet by dating app) rather than potentially integral as an affordance that increases the prevalence of this form of sexual offending. CSEM and sexual solicitation laws and policies specifically recognize the roles that online technologies play in facilitating these forms of sexual offending.

Almost all the assessment, treatment, and prevention chapter content was about CSEM and then sexual solicitation offending. We do not know what risk is posed by individuals who use technology to facilitate noncontact offending (digital exhibitionism or voyeurism) or sexual assaults of adults. They may be similar in risk to their noncontact or contact offending counterparts who do not use online technologies, but that is an empirical question. If I had to guess, I would say there are likely differences between digital exhibitionism and voyeurism and their counterparts because the latter group directly confronts a victim in physical space, just as I suspect there is a difference between fantasy- and contact-driven solicitation (again, fantasy driven involves no direct contact), and there is a big difference between those who view content depicting the sexual abuse of children (CSEM) and those who directly abuse children themselves. We do not know anything about the risk of future image-based sexual abuse, and because of that absence of knowledge about risk and needs, we do not know when and what interventions are required.

We need more research about the likelihood of sexual recidivism for sexual solicitation offending and other forms of online sexual offending other than CSEM offending. This includes probabilities of recidivism, the types of new sexual offenses, and whether there is evidence of escalation or de-escalation over time. It is likely that existing risk assessment tools can be adapted, but new items or new tools may be required. Even if sexual recidivism rates are quite low, there will be variation, and there is plausibly a relatively high-risk group that needs to be prioritized in terms of law enforcement and other responses. I confidently bet that any new risk assessment tools will include items about atypical sexuality—specifically paraphilias and sexual preoccupation as important motivations—and general criminality risk factors, such as age, criminal history, substance abuse, and antisocial personality traits and cognitions.

We also need more and better evaluations of current interventions to refine how we respond to the problem of online sexual offending, both reactively (treatment) and proactively (prevention). Given the many challenges in reaching at-risk people—including access, stigma, and confusion about mandatory reporting—I am more optimistic about technology interventions that change affordances and, thus, the ecosystems in which sexual offending can take place. These tech interventions can scale and are not reliant on individual motivation to change and, thus, recruitment and retention.

Like my previous books, I end with questions that I hope others will pursue as well. This includes further validation of the CPORT and validation of any new or adapted risk assessment tools suitable for CSEM offending to drive the risk principle of intervention for perpetration. Other risk tools can work for CSEM offending, including the RM2000/S, Static-99R, and general recidivism risk tools, such as the Offender Group Re-Conviction Scale Version 3 (Howard et al., 2009) or Post Conviction Risk Assessment (Johnson et al., 2011), though the CPORT has some advantages, especially for predicting CSEM recidivism. Existing tools can be applied to sexual solicitation offending involving attempted or completed meetings, but it would be valuable to confirm this in a study focusing on this offending population. We need to evaluate the predictive accuracy of existing or modified tools for other types of online sexual offending, especially fantasy-driven sexual solicitations and image-based sexual abuse. As discussed in Chapter 6, I believe the STABLE-2007 has clinical utility as a valid assessment tool for dynamic risk factors across types of online sexual offending, and the first study to look at this supports this idea for CSEM offending (Babchishin et al., 2023). An important next step would be demonstrating whether the STABLE-2007 or another dynamic risk assessment tool can complement static risk assessment tools such as the CPORT.

I would also like to see research to extend the use of clinical and risk assessment tools to women and juveniles who engage in CSEM or sexual solicitation offending. Again, I am less concerned about juveniles engaging in these behaviors with similar-aged peers, even if illegal, unless there is coercion. However, some adolescents will realize they are sexually interested in much younger children and may engage in CSEM or other online sexual offending—as well as contact offending—if they are at risk due to personality and other facilitation factors. We need investment in prevention and early intervention. Continuing on the theme of extending clinical and risk assessment, it would be important to identify valid tools for other forms of online sexual offending, including digital exhibitionism and voyeurism, image-based offending, and technology-facilitated contact offending against adults or children. These suggestions for further research focus on big practical gaps. I hope it is clear from the literature reviews in this book that we need more fundamental research on digital exhibitionism and voyeurism, sexual offending against adults, sexual trafficking, and sex tourism involving children.

Behavior and opportunity move faster than our psychology; our individual psychologies and social norms have not caught up with what technology enables. There have been successful public health and behavioral science campaigns to shift behavioral norms in many arenas, including smoking, seat belt wearing, and drinking and driving. Can we achieve similar results with regard to the nonconsensual sharing of sexual images and messages and other problematic online behavior?

I cannot predict how technology will evolve, but in the short term, deepfake technology will mean people can be extorted or manipulated without even self-generating content. I can easily imagine the technology will become good enough quite soon for personal users to create CSEM that cannot be easily distinguished from unaltered content depicting real children. What then? Will we learn to believe targets who deny being involved in CSEM? Will it affect outcomes for targets or perpetrators? Deepfake technology can also be used to harm adults through the generation and sharing of sexual images. For example, older users grew up without technology, whereas digital natives have grown up with technology. On the one hand, this means they are savvier (e.g., using encrypted messaging apps described in Seto, Roche, Stroebel, et al., 2023), but on the other, they have the means to self-generate, reshare, and possibly misuse nudes they are not developmentally ready for. (I am not sure about young adults either, but the law and social norms treat adults differently than juveniles.)

As more of our lives involve internet technologies, I suspect that some of the differences between online and offline offending will continue to blur to the extent that most offline (or traditional) sexual offending will involve internet technologies in some way. The distinction, then, will not be between online and offline offending per se but between offending that only occurs online or involves some kind of embodied interaction. Clearly, there is much more work required to improve research, policy, and practice when it comes to online sexual offending. I hope this book is a useful foundation for this necessary work.

APPENDIX

Child Pornography Offender Risk Tool (CPORT) and Correlates of Admission of Sexual Interest in Children Scale (CASIC) Scoring Guidelines

The development and validation of the Child Pornography Offender Risk Tool (CPORT) and Correlates of Admission of Sexual Interest in Children Scale (CASIC) were described in Chapter 6. This resource is intended to familiarize readers with the scoring and frequently asked questions about these tools. Readers who want more details can obtain the latest scoring guide and FAQ document directly from me (michael.seto@theroyal.ca).

Certification or formal training on the CPORT and CASIC are not required to use these tools. However, it is expected that users have the appropriate qualifications and experiences to conduct sexual recidivism risk assessments. This includes individuals with training in clinical or behavioral sciences, police investigation, and correctional supervision (probation or parole officers). It is the responsibility of the evaluator to remain current about research and practice in child sexual exploitation material (CSEM) offending and risk assessment.

The CPORT and CASIC are intended for men (age 18 or older) who have been convicted of one or more CSEM offenses. Because almost all charges for CSEM offenses result in conviction, men charged with a CSEM offense are eligible for scoring on the CPORT and CASIC, but this should be noted. The validity of the CPORT and CASIC is unknown for women or juveniles convicted of CSEM offenses. Evaluators must use their judgment if scoring the CPORT and CASIC outside jurisdictions where validation studies have been completed. Evaluators must also use their judgment when scoring these tools for specific racial, ethnic, or cultural groups because most men in the development and validation studies have been White men assessed in Canada, the United States, Australia, New Zealand, Iceland, Scotland, and Spain.

Both the CPORT and CASIC should be scored primarily from file information, ideally police file information. Additional clinical information or self-reports should be documented and acknowledged as deviations from the scoring procedures used in our development and validation research.

CHILD PORNOGRAPHY OFFENDER RISK TOOL (CPORT)

Our research on the CPORT was conducted using police investigation files, which are rich in some areas—police occurrence reports, criminal history, police interviews, and CSEM content—but were lacking in other areas, such as the results of clinical evaluations. Evaluators will likely have additional information beyond the police files, including correctional records from incarceration or probation or parole supervision, self-reported information from clinical interviews and questionnaires, and psychometric assessment tools. Some of this post-police involvement information is related to CPORT item content and may overlap in terms of psychological meaningfulness. For example, individuals assessed in a clinical setting or during a probation interview may disclose additional sexual or nonsexual offenses or may admit a sexual interest in children to the evaluator but not the police. As discussed in Chapter 6, evaluators must decide whether to include this information when scoring the CPORT and CASIC, using them as structured assessment tools, or note this information but score the tools "by the book."

CPORT items are scored as a yes (1; higher risk) or no (0; lower risk), with total scores ranging from 0 to 7. We recommend keeping notes about each scoring decision, which assists in the review of scoring and provides relevant information for case formulation and management. Exploring more complicated weightings in our development research did not remarkably increase predictive accuracy. Consistent with the larger sexual offending risk assessment literature, CPORT items appear to represent two risk dimensions reflecting motivations to sexually offend and factors that facilitate acting on these motivations (see Seto, 2019). The first three items capture antisociality reflecting facilitation (younger age, criminal history, conditional release failure), and the second group of items captures sexual interest in children as an important motivation for CSEM offending (admission of sexual interest in children, more boy than girl CSEM content, more boy than girl other child content). The item regarding contact sexual offending reflects both risk dimensions.

Each item is briefly described next, including frequently asked questions. The percentages in parentheses are the proportion of the combined sample in Eke et al. (2019) who scored positively on that item.

CPORT Item 1: Offender age at the time of the index investigation (53% yes)

This item is scored as yes if the individual was 35 or younger when the index police investigation began. In some cases, the initial investigation was for a different offense, but CSEM was discovered. The age of 35 was chosen because it was the median age of the sample in Seto and Eke (2015). Because age at the time of investigation is not always known, age at the time of criminal charges for CSEM offenses can be used when this age is known; this should be noted in the scoring.

CPORT Item 2: Any prior criminal history (41% yes)

This item is scored as yes if the individual had a juvenile or adult record for criminal charges. Self-reported offending is not counted, nor are violations of laws outside the criminal code. However, there are variations in laws, and Canadian criminal law should be used as a guide. For example, driving while impaired is not part of the criminal code in Australia but is in Canada and should be counted as prior criminal history.

CPORT Item 3: Any prior or index conditional release failure (bail, probation, parole, or other conditional release; 15% yes)

This item is scored as yes if the individual had any formal consequence for failing a condition of release on bail, probation, or parole, including the current CSEM charges. Self-reported failures or failures that did not result in a formal consequence, such as revocation of conditional release or new charges, are not counted. When failures of conditional release were known in the development sample described by Seto and Eke (2015), the most common reasons were using the internet when prohibited or being around children without a responsible adult when prohibited.

CPORT Item 4: Any prior or index contact sexual offense history (19% yes)

This item is scored as yes if the person had prior or concurrent criminal charges for a contact sexual offense. In most cases, the alleged victim was a child. In some cases, the concurrent charges resulted from an initial investigation for contact sexual offending, leading to the discovery of CSEM.

CPORT Item 5: Indication of pedophilic or hebephilic interests (37% yes)

This item is scored as yes if the person admitted to police that they had a sexual interest in prepubescent or pubescent children or were sexually aroused by CSEM depicting prepubescent or pubescent children. Admissions to others—for example, through statements made in an online forum—did not count. In some cases, pedophilic or hebephilic sexual interests were known to police because of a prior diagnosis of pedophilic disorder or hebephilic disorder.

CPORT Item 6: More boy than girl content (≥ 51%) in the child pornography content (16% yes)

This item is scored as yes if most CSEM content seized by police depicted boys. Depictions of men did not count. This could be determined by random sampling or qualitative review because it was rare that the count was close. On average, individuals who preferred boy CSEM content had collections in which three quarters were of boys.

CPORT Item 7: More boy than girl content (≥ 51%) in child nudity and other child content (17% yes)

This item is scored as yes if most other child content that did not meet the legal criteria for CSEM depicted boys. This included nudes that did not involve suggestive posing or explicit sexual activity, content depicting semiclothed children, and content depicting child models, child celebrities, or children known to the individual being assessed.

CORRELATES OF ADMISSION OF SEXUAL INTEREST IN CHILDREN SCALE (CASIC)

Admission of sexual interest in children is a risk factor for predicting any sexual recidivism on the CPORT (Item 5). This could be a problem item to score because of missing information, refusal to answer the question, or lying about sexual interest in children, especially in high-stakes situations, such as being prosecuted or sentenced for CSEM offenses. This led to our interest in developing the six-item scale we called the Correlates of Admission of Sexual Interest in Children Scale (CASIC; Seto & Eke, 2017) for use in conjunction with the CPORT.

A CASIC score of 3 or more is used to replace a missing CPORT Item 5, regardless of the number of CASIC items missing. However, we do not recommend scoring CPORT Item 5 as absent if the CASIC score is less than 3 when more than one CASIC item is missing because the missing CASIC items might be present and would have increased the CASIC score to 3 or more if known. Subsequent research has shown that CASIC scores are correlated with admissions of sexual interest in children to clinicians and with other pertinent variables (Azizian et al., in press; Hermann et al., 2024).

If an individual admitted their sexual interest in children to the police, we recommend that the CASIC still be scored and reported as a way of documenting and sharing more information about their CSEM and other relevant behavior. For example, information about the type of CSEM accessed by an individual or the time span of their CSEM activities may not always be consistently documented or shared.

The percentages are the proportion of the sample in Seto and Eke (2017) who scored yes on that CASIC item.

CASIC Item 1: Never married or lived common law (53% yes)
This item is scored as yes if the person had never legally married or lived common law. Common-law relationships were determined by evidence of long-term commitment rather than duration of co-residence. For example, individuals were deemed to have lived common law if they raised children together and/or shared finances or other assets.

CASIC Item 2: Possessed CSEM videos (65% yes)
This item is scored as yes if the individual possessed one or more CSEM videos of any length.

CASIC Item 3: Possessed CSEM stories or similar text (26% yes)
This item is scored as yes if the individual possessed stories that met the Canadian legal criteria for CSEM. Typically, these stories had explicit sexual content and described sexual interactions with children.

CASIC Item 4: CSEM activity spanned 2 years or more (51% yes)
This item is scored as yes if there is evidence the individual was involved with CSEM over 2 or more years. It was not necessary for this involvement to be continuous—for example, someone with evidence of CSEM activity 4 years

earlier and then again for the index CSEM investigation was deemed to be a yes, even if there was no evidence they had been involved in CSEM in the interim. Evidence includes statements made to the police or online, forensic evidence regarding CSEM files (e.g., time stamps spanning 2 or more years), or prior CSEM charges or convictions.

CASIC Item 5: Volunteering in a role with high access to children (9% yes)

This item is scored as yes if the person volunteered in a role with high access to children. This did not include employment because the activity had to be unpaid. In addition, volunteering where children might be present did not count. For example, volunteering as part of a church group where children might be incidentally present did not count, whereas volunteering for a children's group or Sunday School did.

CASIC Item 6: Engaging in online sexual communications with a minor or police officer posing as a minor (10% yes)

This item is scored as yes if the person engaged in online sexual communications with a minor or with a police officer posing as a minor. In many cases, the sexual communications involved CSEM or sexual solicitations.

REFERENCES

Adebahr, R., Söderström, E. Z., Arver, S., Jokinen, J., & Öberg, K. G. (2021). Reaching men and women at risk of committing sexual offences—Findings from the national Swedish telephone helpline PrevenTell. *Journal of Sexual Medicine, 18*(9), 1571–1581. https://doi.org/10.1016/j.jsxm.2021.06.008

Aebi, M., Plattner, B., Ernest, M., Kaszynski, K., & Bessler, C. (2014). Criminal history and future offending of juveniles convicted of the possession of child pornography. *Sexual Abuse, 26*(4), 375–390. https://doi.org/10.1177/1079063213492344

Ajzen, I., & Fishbein, M. (1980). *Understanding attitudes and predicting social behavior.* Prentice-Hall.

Allely, C. S., & Dubin, L. (2018). The contributory role of autism symptomology in child pornography offending: Why there is an urgent need for empirical research in this area. *Journal of Intellectual Disabilities and Offending Behaviour, 9*(4), 129–152. https://doi.org/10.1108/JIDOB-06-2018-0008

Allely, C. S., Kennedy, S., & Warren, I. (2019). A legal analysis of Australian criminal cases involving defendants with autism spectrum disorder charged with online sexual offending. *International Journal of Law and Psychiatry, 66,* Article 101456. https://doi.org/10.1016/j.ijlp.2019.101456

Allen, M., D'alessio, D. A. V. E., & Brezgel, K. (1995). A meta-analysis summarizing the effects of pornography II aggression after exposure. *Human Communication Research, 22*(2), 258–283. https://doi.org/10.1111/j.1468-2958.1995.tb00368.x

American Psychiatric Association. (2022). *Diagnostic and statistical manual of mental disorders* (5th ed., text rev.). https://doi.org/10.1176/appi.books.9780890425787

American Psychological Association. (2023). *Inclusive language guide* (2nd ed.). https://www.apa.org/about/apa/equity-diversity-inclusion/language-guidelines

Anderson, M., Vogels, E. A., & Turner, E. (2020). *The virtues and downsides of online dating.* Pew Research Center. https://www.pewresearch.org/internet/wp-content/uploads/sites/9/2020/02/PI_2020.02.06_online-dating_REPORT.pdf

Anzani, A., Di Sarno, M., & Prunas, A. (2018). Using smartphone apps to find sexual partners: A review of the literature. *Sexologies, 27*(3), e61–e65. https://doi.org/10.1016/j.sexol.2018.05.001

Appel, J. M. (2023). Unconventional harm reduction interventions for minor-attracted persons. *Clinical Ethics, 18*(2), 183–191. https://doi.org/10.1177/14777509221117981

Ashcroft v. Free Speech Coalition, 535 U.S. 234 (2002). https://supreme.justia.com/cases/federal/us/535/234/

Austin, K. M., & Salter, M. A. (2023). Policy barriers to child sexual abuse secondary prevention programs in Australia. *Journal of Sexual Aggression*. https://doi.org/10.1080/13552600.2023.2212001

Azizian, A., Eke, A. W., Farmus, L., Scott, S., & Seto, M. C. (in press). Convergent and divergent validity of the Child Pornography Offender Risk Tool (CPORT) in a clinical sample from California. *Sexual Abuse*.

B4U-ACT. (2011a). *Awareness of sexuality in youth, suicidality, and seeking mental health care*. https://www.b4uact.org/research/survey-results/youth-suicidality-and-seeking-care/

B4U-ACT. (2011b). *Experiences with mental health care and attitudes toward professional literature*. https://www.b4uact.org/research/survey-results/spring-2011-survey/

Babchishin, K. M., Dibayula, S., McCulloch, C., Hanson, R. K., & Helmus, L. M. (2023). ACUTE-2007 and STABLE-2007 predict recidivism for men adjudicated for child sexual exploitation material offending. *Law and Human Behavior, 47*(5), 606–618. https://doi.org/10.1037/lhb0000540

Babchishin, K. M., Hanson, R. K., & Hermann, C. A. (2011). The characteristics of online sex offenders: A meta-analysis. *Sexual Abuse, 23*(1), 92–123. https://doi.org/10.1177/1079063210370708

Babchishin, K. M., Hanson, R. K., & VanZuylen, H. (2015). Online child pornography offenders are different: A meta-analysis of the characteristics of online and offline sex offenders against children. *Archives of Sexual Behavior, 44*(1), 45–66. https://doi.org/10.1007/s10508-014-0270-x

Babchishin, K. M., Lee, S. C., Eke, A. W., & Seto, M. C. (2022). Temporal order of sexual offending is risk-relevant for individuals with Child Sexual Exploitation Materials offences. *Sexual Offending: Theory, Research, and Prevention, 17*, Article e7229. https://doi.org/10.5964/sotrap.7229

Babchishin, K. M., Merdian, H. L., Bartels, R. M., & Perkins, D. (2018). Child sexual exploitation materials offenders. *European Psychologist, 23*(2). https://doi.org/10.1027/1016-9040/a000326

Bailey, J. M., Bernhard, P. A., & Hsu, K. J. (2016). An internet study of men sexually attracted to children: Correlates of sexual offending against children. *Journal of Abnormal Psychology, 125*(7), 989–1000. https://doi.org/10.1037/abn0000213

Baird, K., & Connolly, J. (2023). Recruitment and entrapment pathways of minors into sex trafficking in Canada and the United States: A systematic review. *Trauma, Violence, & Abuse, 24*(1), 189–202. https://doi.org/10.1177/15248380211025241

Banyard, V. L. (2011). Who will help prevent sexual violence: Creating an ecological model of bystander intervention. *Psychology of Violence, 1*(3), 216–229. https://doi.org/10.1037/a0023739

Bártová, K., Androvičová, R., Krejčová, L., Weiss, P., & Klapilová, K. (2021). The prevalence of paraphilic interests in the Czech population: Preference, arousal, the use of pornography, fantasy, and behavior. *Journal of Sex Research*, *58*(1), 86–96. https://doi.org/10.1080/00224499.2019.1707468

Beier, K. M. (Ed.). (2021). *Pedophilia, hebephilia and sexual offending against children: The Berlin dissexuality therapy (BEDIT)*. Springer. https://doi.org/10.1007/978-3-030-61262-7

Beier, K. M., Grundmann, D., Kuhle, L. F., Scherner, G., Konrad, A., & Amelung, T. (2015). The German Dunkelfeld project: A pilot study to prevent child sexual abuse and the use of child abusive images. *Journal of Sexual Medicine*, *12*(2), 529–542. https://doi.org/10.1111/jsm.12785

Beier, K. M., Oezdemir, U. C., Schlinzig, E., Groll, A., Hupp, E., & Hellenschmidt, T. (2016). "Just dreaming of them": The Berlin project for primary prevention of child sexual abuse by Juveniles (PPJ). *Child Abuse & Neglect*, *52*, 1–10. https://doi.org/10.1016/j.chiabu.2015.12.009

Bekkers, L. M. J., Leukfeldt, E. R., & Holt, T. J. (2024). Online communities for child-attracted persons as informal mental health care: Exploring self-reported wellbeing outcomes. *Sexual Abuse*, *36*(2), 158–184. https://doi.org/10.1177/10790632231154882

Bell, A. (2020). *Measuring recidivism risk in child abuse material offenders using the CPORT-SV* [Unpublished master's thesis]. School of Psychology, University of New South Wales.

Bergen, E., Ahto, A., Schulz, A., Imhoff, R., Antfolk, J., Schuhmann, P., Alanko, K., Santtila, P., & Jern, P. (2015). Adult-adult and adult-child/adolescent online sexual interactions: An exploratory self-report study on the role of situational factors. *Journal of Sex Research*, *52*(9), 1006–1016. https://doi.org/10.1080/00224499.2014.914462

Bergen, E., Davidson, J., Schulz, A., Schuhmann, P., Johansson, A., Santtila, P., & Jern, P. (2014). The effects of using identity deception and suggesting secrecy on the outcomes of adult-adult and adult-child or -adolescent online sexual interactions. *Victims & Offenders*, *9*(3), 276–298. https://doi.org/10.1080/15564886.2013.873750

Bergen, M. (2022). *Like, comment, subscribe: Inside YouTube's chaotic rise to world domination*. Penguin.

Bergeron, A., Fortin, F., Charette, Y., Deslauriers-Varin, N., & Paquette, S. (2023). It's all about time: The influence of behaviour and timelines on suspect disclosure during investigative interviews. *Policing and Society*, *33*(7), 820–840. https://doi.org/10.1080/10439463.2023.2204234

Bickart, W., McLearen, A. M., Grady, M. D., & Stoler, K. (2019). A descriptive study of psychosocial characteristics and offense patterns in females with online child pornography offenses. *Psychiatry, Psychology and Law*, *26*(2), 295–311. https://doi.org/10.1080/13218719.2018.1506714

Black, C. (2018). *Predicting recidivism among an adult male child sexual abuse imagery offender population with the child pornography offender risk tool short version (CPORT-SV): A New Zealand validation study* [Unpublished master's thesis]. University of Canterbury Research Repository. https://doi.org/10.26021/6729

Blanchard, R., Kolla, N. J., Cantor, J. M., Klassen, P. E., Dickey, R., Kuban, M. E., & Blak, T. (2007). IQ, handedness, and pedophilia in adult male patients stratified by referral source. *Sexual Abuse*, *19*(3), 285–309. https://doi.org/10.1177/107906320701900307

Boer, D. P., Hart, S. D., Kropp, P. R., & Webster, C. D. (1997). *Manual for the Sexual Violence Risk-20: Professional guidelines for assessing risk of sexual violence*. Institute Against Family Violence.

Bonta, J., & Andrews, D. A. (2024). *The psychology of criminal conduct* (7th ed.). Routledge.

Bonta, J., Bourgon, G., Rugge, T., Pedneault, C. I., & Lee, S. C. (2021). A system-wide implementation and evaluation of the Strategic Training Initiative in Community Supervision (STICS). *Journal of Criminal Justice, 74*, Article 101816. https://doi.org/10.1016/j.jcrimjus.2021.101816

Bourget, D., & Bradford, J. (2018). 12. Current Ethics Dilemmas in the Assessment and Treatment of Sex Offenders. In E. Griffith (Ed.), *Ethics Challenges in Forensic Psychiatry and Psychology Practice* (pp. 190–207). New York Chichester, West Sussex: Columbia University Press. https://doi.org/10.7312/grif18330-013

Bourke, M. L., Fragomeli, L., Detar, P. J., Sullivan, M. A., Meyle, E., & O'Riordan, M. (2015). The use of tactical polygraph with sex offenders. *Journal of Sexual Aggression, 21*(3), 354–367. https://doi.org/10.1080/13552600.2014.886729

Bőthe, B., Bartók, R., Tóth-Király, I., Reid, R. C., Griffiths, M. D., Demetrovics, Z., & Orosz, G. (2018). Hypersexuality, gender, and sexual orientation: A large-scale psychometric survey study. *Archives of Sexual Behavior, 47*, 2265–2276. https://doi.org/10.1007/s10508-018-1201-z

Brankley, A. E., Babchishin, K. M., & Hanson, R. K. (2021). STABLE-2007 demonstrates predictive and incremental validity in assessing risk-relevant propensities for sexual offending: A meta-analysis. *Sexual Abuse, 33*(1), 34–62. https://doi.org/10.1177/1079063219871572

Briggs, P., Simon, W. T., & Simonsen, S. (2011). An exploratory study of internet-initiated sexual offenses and the chat room sex offender: Has the internet enabled a new typology of sex offender? *Sexual Abuse, 23*(1), 72–91. https://doi.org/10.1177/1079063210384275

Broome, L. J., Izura, C., & Davies, J. (2020). A psycho-linguistic profile of online grooming conversations: A comparative study of prison and police staff considerations. *Child Abuse & Neglect, 109*, Article 104647. https://doi.org/10.1016/j.chiabu.2020.104647

Broome, L. J., Izura, C., & Lorenzo-Dus, N. (2018). A systematic review of fantasy driven vs. contact driven internet-initiated sexual offences: Discrete or overlapping typologies? *Child Abuse & Neglect, 79*, 434–444. https://doi.org/10.1016/j.chiabu.2018.02.021

Brown, R., Napier, S., & Smith, R. (2020). Australians who view live streaming of child sexual abuse: An analysis of financial transactions (No. 589). *Trends & Issues in Crime and Criminal Justice*. Australian Institute of Criminology. https://doi.org/10.52922/ti04336

Brown, S. J. (2024). Assessing the risk of users of child sexual exploitation material committing further offences: A scoping review. *Journal of Sexual Aggression, 30*(1), 1–24. https://doi.org/10.1080/13552600.2022.2104394

Budin, L. E., & Johnson, C. F. (1989). Sex abuse prevention programs: Offenders' attitudes about their efficacy. *Child Abuse & Neglect, 13*(1), 77–87. https://doi.org/10.1016/0145-2134(89)90031-8

Burgess, A. W., Hartman, C. R., McCausland, M. P., & Powers, P. (1984). Response patterns in children and adolescents exploited through sex rings and pornography. *The American Journal of Psychiatry, 141*(5), 656–662. https://doi.org/10.1176/ajp.141.5.656

Bursztein, E., Clarke, E., DeLaune, M., Eliff, D. M., Hsu, N., Olson, L., Shehan, J., Thakur, M., Thomas, K., & Bright, T. (2019). Rethinking the detection of child sexual abuse imagery on the internet. In L. Liu & R. White (Eds.), *WWW '19: The World Wide Web conference* (pp. 2601–2607). ACM Digital Library. https://doi.org/10.1145/3308558.3313482

Calvete, E., Fernández-González, L., Royuela-Colomer, E., Morea, A., Larrucea-Iruretagoyena, M., Machimbarrena, J. M., Gónzalez-Cabrera, J., & Orue, I. (2021). Moderating factors of the association between being sexually solicited by adults and active online sexual behaviors in adolescents. *Computers in Human Behavior, 124*, 106935. https://doi.org/10.1016/j.chb.2021.106935

Campbell-Fuller, N., & Craig, L. A. (2009). The use of olfactory aversion and directed masturbation in modifying deviant sexual interest: A case study. *Journal of Sexual Aggression, 15*(2), 179–191. https://doi.org/10.1080/13552600902759556

Canadian Centre for Child Protection. (2017). *Survivors' survey: Full report 2017.* https://protectchildren.ca/pdfs/C3P_SurvivorsSurveyFullReport2017.pdf

Carey, E. G., Ridler, I., Ford, T. J., & Stringaris, A. (2023). Editorial perspective: When is a 'small effect' actually large and impactful? *Journal of Child Psychology and Psychiatry, 64*(11), 1643–1647. https://doi.org/10.1111/jcpp.13817

Centers for Disease Control and Prevention. (2024, April 9). *About The Public Health Approach to Violence Prevention.* https://www.cdc.gov/violence-prevention/about/about-the-public-health-approach-to-violence-prevention.html

Chiu, M. M., Seigfried-Spellar, K. C., & Ringenberg, T. R. (2018). Exploring detection of contact vs. fantasy online sexual offenders in chats with minors: Statistical discourse analysis of self-disclosure and emotion words. *Child Abuse & Neglect, 81*, 128–138. https://doi.org/10.1016/j.chiabu.2018.04.004

Chopin, J., Paquette, S., & Fortin, F. (2023). Geeks and newbies: Investigating the criminal expertise of online sex offenders. *Deviant Behavior, 44*(4), 493–509. https://doi.org/10.1080/01639625.2022.2059417

Christensen, L. S., & Tsagaris, G. S. (2020). Offenders convicted of child sexual exploitation material offences: Characteristics of offenders and an exploration of judicial censure. *Psychiatry, Psychology and Law, 27*(4), 647–664. https://doi.org/10.1080/13218719.2020.1742240

Ciani, A. S. C., Scarpazza, C., Covelli, V., & Battaglia, U. (2019). Profiling acquired pedophilic behavior: Retrospective analysis of 66 Italian forensic cases of pedophilia. *International Journal of Law and Psychiatry, 67*, Article 101508. https://doi.org/10.1016/j.ijlp.2019.101508

Clancy, E. M., Klettke, B., & Hallford, D. J. (2019). The dark side of sexting—Factors predicting the dissemination of sexts. *Computers in Human Behavior, 92*, 266–272. https://doi.org/10.1016/j.chb.2018.11.023

Cockbain, E., & Olver, K. (2019). Child trafficking: characteristics, complexities, and challenges. In I. Bryce, Y. Robinson, & W. Petherick (Eds.), *Child Abuse and Neglect* (pp. 95–116). Academic Press. https://doi.org/10.1016/B978-0-12-815344-4.00006-4

Cohen, T. H. (2023). Building a risk tool for persons placed on federal post-conviction supervision for child sexual exploitation material offenses: Documenting the federal system's past, current, and future efforts. *Federal Probation, 87*(1), 19–31.

Colburn, D. A., Finkelhor, D., & Turner, H. A. (2023). Help-seeking from websites and police in the aftermath of technology-facilitated victimization. *Journal of Interpersonal Violence, 38*(21–22), 11642–11665. https://doi.org/10.1177/08862605231186156

Conte, J. R., Wolf, S., & Smith, T. (1989). What sexual offenders tell us about prevention strategies. *Child Abuse & Neglect, 13*(2), 293–301. https://doi.org/10.1016/0145-2134(89)90016-1

Cooper, A. (1998). Sexuality and the internet: Surfing into the new millennium. *CyberPsychology & Behavior, 1*(2), 187–193. https://doi.org/10.1089/cpb.1998.1.187

Corcoran, E., Doty, J., Wisniewski, P., & Gabrielli, J. (2022). Youth sexting and associations with parental media mediation. *Computers in Human Behavior, 132*, 107263. https://doi.org/10.1016/j.chb.2022.107263

Cording, J. R., & Beggs Christofferson, S. M. (2017). Theoretical and practical issues for the measurement of protective factors. *Aggression and Violent Behavior, 32*, 45–54. https://doi.org/10.1016/j.avb.2016.12.007

Cortoni, F. (2015). What is so special about female sexual offenders? Introduction to the special issue on female sexual offenders. *Sexual Abuse, 27*(3), 232–234. https://doi.org/10.1177/1079063214564392

Cortoni, F., Babchishin, K. M., & Rat, C. (2016). The proportion of sexual offenders who are female is higher than thought: A meta-analysis. *Criminal Justice and Behavior, 44*(2), 145–162. https://doi.org/10.1177/0093854816658923

Cortoni, F., Babchishin, K. M., & Rat, C. (2017). The proportion of sexual offenders who are female is higher than thought: A meta-analysis. *Criminal Justice and Behavior, 44*(2), 145–162. https://doi.org/10.1177/0093854816658923

Cortoni, F., Hanson, R. K., & Coache, M. È. (2010). The recidivism rates of female sexual offenders are low: A meta-analysis. *Sexual Abuse, 22*(4), 387–401. https://doi.org/10.1177/1079063210372142

Craven, S., Brown, S., & Gilchrist, E. (2006). Sexual grooming of children: Review of literature and theoretical considerations. *Journal of Sexual Aggression, 12*(3), 287–299. https://doi.org/10.1080/13552600601069414

Cubitt, T. I. C., Napier, S., & Brown, R. (2023). Understanding the offline criminal behavior of individuals who live stream child sexual abuse. *Journal of Interpersonal Violence, 38*(9–10), 6624–6649. https://doi.org/10.1177/08862605221137712

Dalley, M. (2010). *Hidden abuse—Hidden crime. The domestic trafficking of children and youth in Canada: The relationship to sexual exploitation, running away and children at risk of harm*. Canadian Police Centre for Missing and Exploited Children. https://www.publicsafety.gc.ca/lbrr/archives/cnmcs-plcng/cn30898-eng.pdf

Daly, M., & Wilson, M. (1999). *The truth about Cinderella: A Darwinian view of parental love*. Yale University Press.

Dardis, C. M., & Richards, E. C. (2022). Nonconsensual distribution of sexually explicit images within a context of coercive control: Frequency, characteristics, and associations with other forms of victimization. *Violence Against Women, 28*(15–16), 3933–3954. https://doi.org/10.1177/10778012221077126

Davis, J. D., Glotfelty, E., & Miles, G. (2017). "No other choice": A baseline study on the vulnerabilities of males in the sex trade in Chiang Mai, Thailand. *Dignity, 2*(4), 10. https://doi.org/10.23860/dignity.2017.02.04.10

Davis, N., Lennings, C., & Green, T. (2018). Improving practice in child sexual abuse image investigations through identification of offender characteristics. *Sexual Abuse in Australia and New Zealand*, e73.

DeHart, D., Dwyer, G., Seto, M. C., Moran, R., Letourneau, E., & Schwarz-Watts, D. (2017). Internet sexual solicitation of children: A proposed typology of offenders based on their chats, e-mails, and social network posts. *Journal of Sexual Aggression, 23*(1), 77–89. https://doi.org/10.1080/13552600.2016.1241309

Department of Justice Canada. (2022). *Overrepresentation of Black people in the Canadian criminal justice system: Fact sheet.* https://www.justice.gc.ca/eng/rp-pr/jr/obpccjs-spnsjpc/pdf/RSD_JF2022_Black_Overrepresentation_in_CJS_EN.pdf

De Roos, M. D. R. (2017). *Mimicry deception theory applied to grooming behaviors of child sexual abuse* [Unpublished master's thesis]. University of Texas at El Paso.

Dervley, R., Perkins, D., Whitehead, H., Bailey, A., Gillespie, S., & Squire, T. (2017). Themes in participant feedback on a risk reduction programme for child sexual exploitation material offenders. *Journal of Sexual Aggression, 23*(1), 46–61. https://doi.org/10.1080/13552600.2016.1269958

de Santisteban, P., & Gámez-Guadix, M. (2018). Prevalence and risk factors among minors for online sexual solicitations and interactions with adults. *Journal of Sex Research, 55*(7), 939–950. https://doi.org/10.1080/00224499.2017.1386763

Desjardins, V. (2021). *Do they all act the same? Identification of the strategies associated with different types of online sex solicitors' discourses* [Unpublished master's thesis]. Université de Montréal. https://papyrus.bib.umontreal.ca/xmlui/bitstream/handle/1866/25447/Desjardins_Vicky_2020_Memoire.pdf?sequence=2&isAllowed=y

de Vogel, V., de Vries Robbé, M., de Ruiter, C., & Bouman, Y. H. A. (2011). Assessing protective factors in forensic psychiatric practice: Introducing the SAPROF. *International Journal of Forensic Mental Health, 10*(3), 171–177. https://doi.org/10.1080/14999013.2011.600230

de Vries Robbé, M., Mann, R. E., Maruna, S., & Thornton, D. (2015). An exploration of protective factors supporting desistance from sexual offending. *Sexual Abuse, 27*(1), 16–33. https://doi.org/10.1177/1079063214547582

Dietzel, C. (2021). The three dimensions of unsolicited dick pics: Men who have sex with men's experiences of sending and receiving unsolicited dick pics on dating apps. *Sexuality & Culture, 26*(3), 834–852. https://doi.org/10.1007/s12119-021-09920-y

Dinh-Zarr, T. B., Sleet, D. A., Shults, R. A., Zaza, S., Elder, R. W., Nichols, J. L., Thompson, R. S., Sosin, D. M., & the Task Force on Community Preventive Services. (2001). Reviews of evidence regarding interventions to increase the use of safety belts. *American Journal of Preventive Medicine, 21*(4), 48–65. https://doi.org/10.1016/S0749-3797(01)00378-6

Dodge, A. (2021). Trading nudes like hockey cards: Exploring the diversity of 'revenge porn' cases responded to in law. *Social & Legal Studies, 30*(3), 448–468. https://doi.org/10.1177/0964663920935155

Dodge, A., & Spencer, D. C. (2018). Online sexual violence, child pornography or something else entirely? Police responses to non-consensual intimate image sharing among youth. *Social & Legal Studies, 27*(5), 636–657. https://doi.org/10.1177/0964663917724866

Dowling, C., Morgan, A., & Pooley, K. (2021). Reoffending among child sexual offenders (No. 628). *Trends and Issues in Crime and Criminal Justice.* Australian Institute of Criminology. https://doi.org/10.52922/ti78085

Duggan, M. (2017). *Online harassment 2017.* Pew Research Center. https://www.pewresearch.org/internet/wp-content/uploads/sites/9/2017/07/PI_2017.07.11_Online-Harassment_FINAL.pdf

Echevarria, S. G., Peterson, R., & Woerner, J. (2023). College students' experiences of dating app facilitated sexual violence and associations with mental health symptoms and well-being. *Journal of Sex Research, 60*(8), 1193–1205. https://doi.org/10.1080/00224499.2022.2130858

ECPAT. (2016a). *Travelling child sex offenders in Cambodia.* https://ecpat.org/wp-content/uploads/2021/08/Action-Pour-Les-Enfants-APLE-Travelling-Child-Sex-Offenders-in-Cambodia.pdf

ECPAT. (2016b). *Offenders on the move: Global study of sexual exploitation of children in travel and tourism.* https://ecpat.org/wp-content/uploads/2021/08/Global-Report-Offenders-on-the-Move.pdf

Eelmaa, S. (2022). Sexualization of children in deepfakes and hentai: Examining Reddit user views. *Trames, 26*(2), 229–248. https://doi.org/10.3176/tr.2022.2.07

Eher, R., Hofer, S., Buchgeher, A., Domany, S., Turner, D., & Olver, M. E. (2020, January 7). The predictive properties of psychiatric diagnoses, dynamic risk and dynamic risk change assessed by the VRS-SO in forensically admitted and released sexual offenders. *Frontiers in Psychiatry, 10,* Article 922. https://doi.org/10.3389/fpsyt.2019.00922

Eher, R., Matthes, A., Schilling, F., Haubner-Maclean, T., & Rettenberger, M. (2012). Dynamic risk assessment in sexual offenders using STABLE-2000 and the STABLE-2007: An investigation of predictive and incremental validity. *Sexual Abuse, 24*(1), 5–28. https://doi.org/10.1177/1079063211403164

Eke, A. W. (2022, October 7). *Predictive accuracy of the Static-99R in two samples of men adjudicated for child sexual exploitation material offending* [Paper presentation]. Association for the Treatment and Prevention of Sexual Abuse Conference, Los Angeles, CA, United States.

Eke, A. W., Helmus, L. M., & Seto, M. C. (2019). A validation study of the Child Pornography Offender Risk Tool (CPORT). *Sexual Abuse, 31*(4), 456–476. https://doi.org/10.1177/1079063218762434

Eke, A. W., & Seto, M. C. (2023). Correspondence of child age and gender distribution in child sexual exploitation material and other child content with age and gender of child sexual assault victims. *Sexual Abuse, 35*(3), 375–397. https://doi.org/10.1177/10790632221108951

Eke, A. W., Seto, M. C., & Williams, J. (2011). Examining the criminal history and future offending of child pornography offenders: An extended prospective follow-up study. *Law and Human Behavior, 35*(6), 466–478. https://doi.org/10.1007/s10979-010-9252-2

Elchuk, D. L., McPhail, I. V., & Olver, M. E. (2022). Stigma-related stress, complex correlates of disclosure, mental health, and loneliness in minor-attracted people. *Stigma and Health, 7*(1), 100–112. https://doi.org/10.1037/sah0000317

Elliot, I., & Hambly, O. (2023). *Horizon and iHorizon: An uncontrolled before–after study of clinical outcomes.* United Kingdom Ministry of Justice. https://assets.publishing.service.gov.uk/government/uploads/system/uploads/attachment_data/file/1137650/horizon-iHorizon-uncontrolled-study.pdf

Elliott, M., Browne, K., & Kilcoyne, J. (1995). Child sexual abuse prevention: What offenders tell us. *Child Abuse & Neglect, 19*(5), 579–594. https://doi.org/10.1016/0145-2134(95)00017-3

Erkan, V., Schröder, J., Briken, P., & Tozdan, S. (2023). Factors associated with contact sexual offending among a non-forensic sample of women with sexual interest in children—Results from an anonymous online survey. *Sexual Abuse, 36*(4). Advance online publication. https://doi.org/10.1177/10790632231159076

eSafety. (2017). *Image-based abuse.* https://www.esafety.gov.au/about-us/research/image-based-abuse

Fairlie, R. W. (2017). Have we finally bridged the digital divide? Smart phone and internet use patterns by race and ethnicity. *First Monday, 22*(9). Advance online publication. https://doi.org/10.5210/fm.v22i9.7919

Faitakis, M., Stephens, S., & Seto, M. C. (2023). The predictive validity of the Revised Screening Scale for Pedophilic Interests (SSPI-2). *Sexual Abuse, 35*(5), 649–663. https://doi.org/10.1177/10790632221149696

Farmer, M., Beech, A. R., & Ward, T. (2012). Assessing desistance in child molesters: A qualitative analysis. *Journal of Interpersonal Violence, 27*(5), 930–950. https://doi.org/10.1177/0886260511423255

Farrington, P. (2015). *Circles of support and accountability: The role of social support in preventing sexual offender recidivism* [Doctoral dissertation]. University of Birmingham. https://etheses.bham.ac.uk/id/eprint/5785

Fazel, S., Ramesh, T., & Hawton, K. (2017). Suicide in prisons: An international study of prevalence and contributory factors. *The Lancet Psychiatry, 4*(12), 946–952. https://doi.org/10.1016/S2215-0366(17)30430-3

Federal Trade Commission. (2022, August). *What to know about romance scams.* https://consumer.ftc.gov/articles/what-know-about-romance-scams

Fernandez, E., Woldgabreal, Y., Day, A., Pham, T., Gleich, B., & Aboujaoude, E. (2021). Live psychotherapy by video versus in-person: A meta-analysis of efficacy and its relationship to types and targets of treatment. *Clinical Psychology & Psychotherapy, 28*(6), 1535–1549. https://doi.org/10.1002/cpp.2594

Fido, D., Harper, C. A., Duff, S., & Page, T. E. (2023). *Understanding social judgments of, and proclivities to commit upskirting.* PsyArXiv. https://doi.org/10.31234/osf.io/yvsxz

Fido, D., Rao, J., & Harper, C. A. (2022). Celebrity status, sex, and variation in psychopathy predicts judgements of and proclivity to generate and distribute deepfake pornography. *Computers in Human Behavior, 129*, Article 107141. https://doi.org/10.1016/j.chb.2021.107141

Filice, E., Abeywickrama, K. D., Parry, D. C., & Johnson, C. W. (2022). Sexual violence and abuse in online dating: A scoping review. *Aggression and Violent Behavior, 67*, Article 101781. https://doi.org/10.1016/j.avb.2022.101781

Finkelhor, D., Turner, H., & Colburn, D. (2022). Prevalence of online sexual offenses against children in the US. *JAMA Network Open, 5*(10), e2234471. https://doi.org/10.1001/jamanetworkopen.2022.34471

Finkelhor, D., Turner, H., & Colburn, D. (2023). Which dynamics make online child sexual abuse and cyberstalking more emotionally impactful: Perpetrator identity and images? *Child Abuse & Neglect, 137*, Article 106020. https://doi.org/10.1016/j.chiabu.2023.106020

Flynn, A., Cama, E., & Scott, A. J. (2022). *Preventing image-based cybercrime in Australia: The role of bystanders.* Australian Criminology Research Council.

Fortin, F., Paquette, S., & Leclerc, C. (2019). The effect of child sexual exploitation images collection size on offender sentencing. *International Review of Law Computers & Technology, 33*(3), 330–348. https://doi.org/10.1080/13600869.2018.1560553

Fortin, F., & Proulx, J. (2019). Sexual interests of child sexual exploitation material (CSEM) consumers: Four patterns of severity over time. *International Journal of Offender Therapy and Comparative Criminology, 63*(1), 55–76. https://doi.org/10.1177/0306624X18794135

Foshee, V. A., Bauman, K. E., Arriaga, X. B., Helms, R. W., Koch, G. G., & Linder, G. F. (1998). An evaluation of Safe Dates, an adolescent dating violence prevention program. *American Journal of Public Health, 88*(1), 45–50. https://doi.org/10.2105/AJPH.88.1.45

Franchino-Olsen, H. (2021). Vulnerabilities relevant for commercial sexual exploitation of children/domestic minor sex trafficking: A systematic review of risk factors. *Trauma, Violence, & Abuse, 22*(1), 99–111. https://doi.org/10.1177/1524838018821956

Fraser, J. M., Babchishin, K. M., & Helmus, L. M. (2023). Emotional congruence with children: An empirical examination of different models in men with a history of sexually offending against children. *Sexual Abuse, 36*(5). Advance online publication. https://doi.org/10.1177/10790632231172160

Fredlund, C., Dahlström, Ö., Svedin, C. G., Wadsby, M., Jonsson, L. S., & Priebe, G. (2018). Adolescents' motives for selling sex in a welfare state—A Swedish national study. *Child Abuse & Neglect, 81*, 286–295. https://doi.org/10.1016/j.chiabu.2018.04.030

Frei, A., Erenay, N., Dittmann, V., & Graf, M. (2005). Paedophilia on the internet—A study of 33 convicted offenders in the Canton of Lucerne. *Swiss Medical Weekly, 135*(33–34), 488–494. https://doi.org/10.4414/smw.2005.11095

Freund, K., Watson, R., & Rienzo, D. (1988). The value of self-reports in the study of voyeurism and exhibitionism. *Annals of Sex Research, 1*(2), 243–262. https://doi.org/10.1007/BF00852800

Fromberger, P., Schröder, S., Bauer, L., Siegel, B., Tozdan, S., Briken, P., Buntrock, C., Etzler, S., Rettenberger, M., Leha, A., & Müller, J. L. (2021, January 7). @myTabu—A placebo controlled randomized trial of a guided web-based intervention for individuals who sexually abused children and individuals who consumed child sexual exploitation material: A clinical study protocol. *Frontiers in Psychiatry, 11*, Article 575464. https://doi.org/10.3389/fpsyt.2020.575464

Gámez-Guadix, M., Almendros, C., Calvete, E., & de Santisteban, P. (2018). Persuasion strategies and sexual solicitations and interactions in online sexual grooming of adolescents: Modeling direct and indirect pathways. *Journal of Adolescence, 63*(1), 11–18. https://doi.org/10.1016/j.adolescence.2017.12.002

Gámez-Guadix, M., & Mateos-Pérez, E. (2019). Longitudinal and reciprocal relationships between sexting, online sexual solicitations, and cyberbullying among minors. *Computers in Human Behavior, 94*, 70–76. https://doi.org/10.1016/j.chb.2019.01.004

Gannon, T. A., Olver, M. E., Mallion, J. S., & James, M. (2019). Does specialized psychological treatment for offending reduce recidivism? A meta-analysis examining staff and program variables as predictors of treatment effectiveness. *Clinical Psychology Review, 73*, 101752. https://doi.org/10.1016/j.cpr.2019.101752

Gassó, A. M., Forero, C. G., Piqueras, J., & Gómez-Durán, E. L. (2022, September 28). Psychopathological aspects of sexting and IBSA perpetrators: A brief research report. *Frontiers in Psychiatry, 13*, Article 983881. https://doi.org/10.3389/fpsyt.2022.983881

Gearing, R. E., El-Bassel, N., Ghesquiere, A., Baldwin, S., Gillies, J., & Ngeow, E. (2011). Major ingredients of fidelity: A review and scientific guide to improving quality of intervention research implementation. *Clinical Psychology Review, 31*(1), 79–88. https://doi.org/10.1016/j.cpr.2010.09.007

Gewirtz-Meydan, A., Volman-Pampanel, D., Opuda, E., & Tarshish, N. (2024). Dating apps: A new emerging platform for sexual harassment? A scoping review. *Trauma, Violence, & Abuse*, 25(1), 752–763. https://doi.org/10.1177/15248380231162969

Gewirtz-Meydan, A., Walsh, W., Wolak, J., & Finkelhor, D. (2018). The complex experience of child pornography survivors. *Child Abuse & Neglect*, 80, 238–248. https://doi.org/10.1016/j.chiabu.2018.03.031

Gezinski, L. B., & Gonzalez-Pons, K. M. (2022). Sex trafficking and technology: A systematic review of recruitment and exploitation. *Journal of Human Trafficking*, 10(3). https://doi.org/10.1080/23322705.2022.2034378

Gigerenzer, G., & Gaissmaier, W. (2011). Heuristic decision making. *Annual Review of Psychology*, 62(1), 451–482. https://doi.org/10.1146/annurev-psych-120709-145346

Gillespie, S. M., Bailey, A., Squire, T., Carey, M. L., Eldridge, H. J., & Beech, A. R. (2018). An evaluation of a community-based psycho-educational program for users of child sexual exploitation material. *Sexual Abuse*, 30(2), 169–191. https://doi.org/10.1177/1079063216639591

Gledhill, J. (2016). *Grooming child victims in an online environment* [Unpublished doctoral dissertation]. Purdue University. https://docs.lib.purdue.edu/dissertations/AAI1489663/

Goller, A., Jones, R., Dittmann, V., Taylor, P., & Graf, M. (2016). Criminal recidivism of illegal pornography offenders in the overall population—A national cohort study of 4612 offenders in Switzerland. *Advances in Applied Sociology*, 6(2), 48–56. https://doi.org/10.4236/aasoci.2016.62005

Gottfredson, M. R., & Hirschi, T. (1990). *A general theory of crime*. Stanford University Press. https://doi.org/10.1515/9781503621794

Gouveia, C. P. F. (2024). *A prevalência de pedófilos entre os abusadores sexuais de crianças: validação da SSPI-2* [The prevalence of pedophilia in child sexual abusers: Validation of SSPI-2; unpublished doctoral dissertation]. Universidade do Minho, Portugal.

Graham, N. (2019). *Examining the use of hebephilia and paraphilia non-consent in sexually violent predator (SVP) evaluations* [Unpublished doctoral dissertation]. City University of New York.

Grannò, S., Mosca, A., & Walravens-Evans, J. (2020). *Denouncing child manipulation to produce sexualised imagery on YouTube*. PsyArXiv. https://doi.org/10.31235/osf.io/cyq4r

Gray, S. R., Abel, G. G., Jordan, A., Garby, T., Wiegel, M., & Harlow, N. (2015). Visual Reaction Time™ as a predictor of sexual offense recidivism. *Sexual Abuse*, 27(2), 173–188. https://doi.org/10.1177/1079063213502680

Gress, C. L., Anderson, J. O., & Laws, D. R. (2013). Delays in attentional processing when viewing sexual imagery: The development and comparison of two measures. *Legal and Criminological Psychology*, 18(1), 66–82. https://doi.org/10.1111/j.2044-8333.2011.02032.x

Grubbs, J. B., Perry, S. L., Wilt, J. A., & Reid, R. C. (2019). Pornography problems due to moral incongruence: An integrative model with a systematic review and meta-analysis. *Archives of Sexual Behavior*, 48(2), 397–415. https://doi.org/10.1007/s10508-018-1248-x

Grubin, D., Joyce, A., & Holden, E. J. (2014). Polygraph testing of "low risk" offenders arrested for downloading indecent images of children. *Sexual Offender Treatment*, 9(1).

Gunnarsdóttir, H. Ó. (2019). *Risk assessment of convicted child pornography offenders in Iceland 2000–2017* [Unpublished doctoral dissertation]. Reykjavík University.

Hamilton-Giachritsis, C., Hanson, E., Whittle, H., Alves-Costa, F., & Beech, A. (2020). Technology assisted child sexual abuse in the UK: Young people's views on the impact of online sexual abuse. *Children and Youth Services Review, 119*, Article 105451. https://doi.org/10.1016/j.childyouth.2020.105451

Hanson, R. K. (2022). *Prediction statistics for psychological assessment*. American Psychological Association. https://doi.org/10.1037/0000275-000

Hanson, R. K., Bourgon, G., Helmus, L., & Hodgson, S. (2009). The principles of effective correctional treatment also apply to sexual offenders: A meta-analysis. *Criminal Justice and Behavior, 36*(9), 865–891. https://doi.org/10.1177/0093854809338545

Hanson, R. K., & Bussière, M. T. (1998). Predicting relapse: A meta-analysis of sexual offender recidivism studies. *Journal of Consulting and Clinical Psychology, 66*(2), 348–362. https://doi.org/10.1037/0022-006X.66.2.348

Hanson, R. K., Harris, A. J., Letourneau, E., Helmus, L. M., & Thornton, D. (2018). Reductions in risk based on time offense-free in the community: Once a sexual offender, not always a sexual offender. *Psychology, Public Policy, and Law, 24*(1), 48–63. https://doi.org/10.1037/law0000135

Hanson, R. K., Harris, A. J., Scott, T. L., & Helmus, L. (2007). *Assessing the risk of sexual offenders on community supervision: The Dynamic Supervision Project*. Public Safety Canada.

Hanson, R. K., & Morton-Bourgon, K. E. (2005). The characteristics of persistent sexual offenders: A meta-analysis of recidivism studies. *Journal of Consulting and Clinical Psychology, 73*(6), 1154–1163. https://doi.org/10.1037/0022-006X.73.6.1154

Hanson, R. K., & Morton-Bourgon, K. E. (2009). The accuracy of recidivism risk assessments for sexual offenders: A meta-analysis of 118 prediction studies. *Psychological Assessment, 21*(1), 1–21. https://doi.org/10.1037/a0014421

Hanson, R. K., & Thornton, D. (1999). *Static-99: Improving actuarial risk assessments for sex offenders* (User Report 99-02). Department of the Solicitor General of Canada.

Harkins, L., & Beech, A. R. (2007). A review of the factors that can influence the effectiveness of sexual offender treatment: Risk, need, responsivity, and process issues. *Aggression and Violent Behavior, 12*(6), 615–627. https://doi.org/10.1016/j.avb.2006.10.006

Harris, G. T., Lalumière, M. L., Seto, M. C., Rice, M. E., & Chaplin, T. C. (2012). Explaining the erectile responses of rapists to rape stories: The contributions of sexual activity, non-consent, and violence with injury. *Archives of Sexual Behavior, 41*, 221–229. https://doi.org/10.1007/s10508-012-9940-8

Harris, G. T., Rice, M. E., Quinsey, V. L., & Cormier, C. A. (2015). *Violent offenders: Appraising and managing risk* (3rd ed.). American Psychological Association. https://doi.org/10.1037/14572-000

Hartley, R. D., Testa, A., & Martinez, E. (2021). Race, ethnicity, and punishment for federal sex offenses: Changing composition in child pornography and sex abuse cases and temporal disparity in sentencing over time. *Sexual Abuse, 33*(8), 891–922. https://doi.org/10.1177/1079063220981062

Heasman, A. (2021, October 1). *Development & evaluation of anonymous & non-Anonymous secondary prevention services in Canada*. Virtual national conference of the Association for the Treatment of Sexual Abuse.

Helmus, L. M. (2023). Recidivism rates of men charged/convicted of child pornography offences. *The Forum Newsletter*, *35*(2). http://newsmanager.commpartners.com/atsa/issues/2023-03-15/2.html

Helmus, L. M., Eke, A. W., Farmus, L., & Seto, M. C. (2024). The CPORT and Risk Matrix 2000 for men convicted of child sexual exploitation material (CSEM) offenses: A predictive accuracy comparison and meta-analysis. *Criminal Justice and Behavior*, *51*(1), 3–23. https://doi.org/10.1177/00938548231208194

Helmus, L. M., Eke, A. W., & Seto, M. (2024). What risk assessment tools can be used with men convicted of Child Sexual Exploitation Material (CSEM) offenses? Recommendations from a review of current research. *CrimRxiv*. https://doi.org/10.21428/cb6ab371.76d0bec4

Helmus, L., Hanson, R. K., Babchishin, K. M., & Mann, R. E. (2013). Attitudes supportive of sexual offending predict recidivism: A meta-analysis. *Trauma, Violence, & Abuse*, *14*(1), 34–53. https://doi.org/10.1177/1524838012462244

Hendrickson, J. (2024, January 8). *How to detect hidden surveillance cameras with your phone*. How-To Geek. https://www.howtogeek.com/411095/how-to-detect-hidden-surveillance-cameras-with-your-phone/

Henek, M., & Bartels, R. (2020). Adult-as-schoolgirl sexual fantasies: Investigating their relationship with sexual interest in children within a male sample. *Sexual Offending: Theory, Research, and Prevention*, *15*(1), 1–14. https://doi.org/10.5964/sotrap.3069

Henrich, J., Heine, S. J., & Norenzayan, A. (2010). The weirdest people in the world? *Behavioral and Brain Sciences*, *33*(2–3), 61–83. https://doi.org/10.1017/S0140525X0999152X

Henry, N., McGlynn, C., Flynn, A., Johnson, K., Powell, A., & Scott, A. J. (2020). *Image-based sexual abuse: A study on the causes and consequences of non-consensual nude or sexual imagery*. Routledge. https://doi.org/10.4324/9781351135153

Henshaw, M., Arnold, C., Darjee, R., Ogloff, J., & Clough, J. (2020). Enhancing evidence-based treatment of child sexual abuse material offenders: The development of the CEM-COPE Program (No. 607). *Trends and Issues in Crime and Criminal Justice*. Australian Institute of Criminology. https://doi.org/10.52922/ti04787

Henshaw, M., Ogloff, J. R., & Clough, J. A. (2017). Looking beyond the screen: A critical review of the literature on the online child pornography offender. *Sexual Abuse*, *29*(5), 416–445. https://doi.org/10.1177/1079063215603690

Henshaw, M., Ogloff, J. R. P., & Clough, J. A. (2018). Demographic, mental health, and offending characteristics of online child exploitation material offenders: A comparison with contact-only and dual sexual offenders. *Behavioral Sciences & the Law*, *36*(2), 198–215. https://doi.org/10.1002/bsl.2337

Hermann, C. A., Fernane, S., Eke, A. W., & Seto, M. C. (2024). *Validity of the Child Pornography Offender Risk Tool and the Correlates of Admitted Sexual Interest in Children in a sample of men serving community supervision sentences for child sexual exploitation material offenses* [Manuscript in preparation]. Ontario Ministry of the Solicitor General.

Hermann, C. A., McPhail, I. V., Helmus, L. M., & Hanson, R. K. (2017). Emotional congruence with children is associated with sexual deviancy in sexual offenders against children. *International Journal of Offender Therapy and Comparative Criminology*, *61*(12), 1311–1334. https://doi.org/10.1177/0306624X15620830

Holt, T. J., Blevins, K. R., & Burkert, N. (2010). Considering the pedophile subculture online. *Sexual Abuse*, *22*(1), 3–24. https://doi.org/10.1177/1079063209344979

Howard, P., Francis, B., Soothill, K., & Humphreys, L. (2009). *OGRS 3: The revised Offender Group Reconviction Scale*. Ministry of Justice. https://core.ac.uk/reader/1556521

Howard, P., & Wakeling, H. (2021). *Comparing two predictors of sexual recidivism: The Risk Matrix 2000 and the OASys Sexual Reoffending Predictor*. HM Prison and Probation Service. https://assets.publishing.service.gov.uk/media/600eaacfd3bf7f05c06dfc48/comparing-2-predictors-sexual-recidivism.pdf

Howitt, D. (1995). Pornography and the paedophile: Is it criminogenic? *British Journal of Medical Psychology, 68*(1), 15–27. https://doi.org/10.1111/j.2044-8341.1995.tb01810.x

Hu, Y., Clancy, E. M., & Klettke, B. (2023). Longitudinal sexting research: A systematic review. *Psych, 5*(2), 526–544. https://doi.org/10.3390/psych5020035

Ibrahim, D. (2023). *Online child sexual exploitation and abuse in Canada: A statistical profile of police-reported incidents and court charges, 2014 to 2020*. Statistics Canada. https://publications.gc.ca/collections/collection_2023/statcan/85-005-x/CS85-005-2023-1-eng.pdf

Ingram, M., Thorne, E., Klag, M. J., Letourneau, E. J., & Seto, M. C. (2023). *Self-reported perpetration of online child sexual exploitation and abuse: A systematic review* [Manuscript submitted for publication]. Department of Mental Health, Johns Hopkins Bloomberg School of Public Health.

Insoll, T., Díaz Bethencourt, E., Ovaska, A., & Vaaranen-Valkonen, N. (2024). *Multilingual perspectives on child sexual abuse material offenders: Insights from English, Russian, Portuguese and Spanish-speaking offenders*. Suojellaan Lapsia. https://www.suojellaanlapsia.fi/en/post/2know-language-focused-report

Insoll, T., Ovaska, A. K., Nurmi, J., Aaltonen, M., & Vaaranen-Valkonen, N. (2022). Risk factors for child sexual abuse material users contacting children online: Results of an anonymous multilingual survey on the dark web. *Journal of Online Trust & Safety, 1*(2). Advance online publication. https://doi.org/10.54501/jots.v1i2.29

Instagram. (2021, March 17). *Continuing to make Instagram safer for the youngest members of our community*. https://about.instagram.com/blog/announcements/continuing-to-make-instagram-safer-for-the-youngest-members-of-our-community

International Center for Missing and Exploited Children. (2017). *Online grooming of children for sexual purposes: Model legislation & global review*. https://www.icmec.org/online-grooming-of-children-for-sexual-purposes-model-legislation-global-review/

International Center for Missing and Exploited Children. (2018). *Studies in child protection: Sexual extortion and nonconsensual pornography*. https://www.icmec.org/wp-content/uploads/2018/10/Sexual-Extortion_Nonconsensual-Pornography_final_10-26-18.pdf

International Center for Missing and Exploited Children. (2023). *Child sexual abuse material: Model legislation & global review* (10th ed.). https://www.icmec.org/csam-model-legislation_10th_ed_oct_2023/

International Justice Mission. (2013). *Commercial sexual exploitation of children in Cambodia*. https://ijmstoragelive.blob.core.windows.net/ijmna/documents/studies/Commercial-Sexual-Exploitation-of-Children-in-Cambodia.pdf

International Justice Mission. (2014). *Online sexual exploitation of children in the Philippines: Analysis and recommendations for governments, industry, and civil society*.

https://ijmstoragelive.blob.core.windows.net/ijmna/documents/studies/Final-Public-Full-Report-5_20_2020.pdf

International Justice Mission. (2015). *Results summary*. https://ijmstoragelive.blob.core.windows.net/ijmna/documents/IJM-Cambodia-2015-CSEC-Prevalence-Study-Results-Summary.pdf

Internet Watch Foundation. (2018). *Trends in online child sexual exploitation: Examining the distribution of captures of live-streamed child sexual abuse.* https://www.iwf.org.uk/media/23jj3nc2/distribution-of-captures-of-live-streamed-child-sexual-abuse-final.pdf

Internet Watch Foundation. (2023). *How AI is being abused to create child sexual abuse imagery.* https://www.iwf.org.uk/media/q4zll2ya/iwf-ai-csam-report_public-oct23v1.pdf

Jahnke, S. (2018a). Emotions and cognitions associated with the stigma of non-offending pedophilia: A vignette experiment. *Archives of Sexual Behavior, 47*(2), 363–373. https://doi.org/10.1007/s10508-017-1073-7

Jahnke, S. (2018b). The stigma of pedophilia: Clinical and forensic implications. *European Psychologist, 23*(2), 144–153. https://doi.org/10.1027/1016-9040/a000325

Jahnke, S., Schmidt, A. F., Geradt, M., & Hoyer, J. (2015). Stigma-related stress and its correlates among men with pedophilic sexual interests. *Archives of Sexual Behavior, 44*(8), 2173–2187. https://doi.org/10.1007/s10508-015-0503-7

Janssen, E., & Bancroft, J. (2007). The dual control model: The role of sexual inhibition and excitation in sexual arousal and behavior. In E. Janssen (Ed.), *The psychophysiology of sex* (pp. 197–222). Indiana University Press.

Jeglic, E. L., & Winters, G. M. (2023). The role of technology in the perpetration of childhood sexual abuse: The importance of considering both in-person and online interactions. *Children, 10*(8), 1306. https://doi.org/10.3390/children10081306

Jenkins, P. (2001). *Beyond tolerance: Child pornography on the internet*. NYU Press.

Jespersen, A. F., Lalumière, M. L., & Seto, M. C. (2009). Sexual abuse history among adult sex offenders and non-sex offenders: A meta-analysis. *Child Abuse & Neglect, 33*(3), 179–192. https://doi.org/10.1016/j.chiabu.2008.07.004

Johnson, J. L., Lowenkamp, C. T., VanBenschoten, S. W., & Robinson, C. R. (2011). The construction and validation of the federal Post Conviction Risk Assessment (PCRA). *Federal Probation, 75*(2), 16–29.

Joleby, M., Lunde, C., Landström, S., & Jonsson, L. S. (2020, December 6). "All of me is completely different": Experiences and consequences among victims of technology-assisted child sexual abuse. *Frontiers in Psychology, 11*, Article 606218. https://doi.org/10.3389/fpsyg.2020.606218

Joleby, M., Lunde, C., Landström, S., & Jonsson, L. S. (2021). Offender strategies for engaging children in online sexual activity. *Child Abuse & Neglect, 120*, Article 105214. https://doi.org/10.1016/j.chiabu.2021.105214

Jones, S. J., Ó Ciardha, C., & Elliott, I. A. (2021). Identifying the coping strategies of nonoffending pedophilic and hebephilic individuals from their online forum posts. *Sexual Abuse, 33*(7), 793–815. https://doi.org/10.1177/1079063220965953

Jouriles, E. N., Krauss, A., Vu, N. L., Banyard, V. L., & McDonald, R. (2018). Bystander programs addressing sexual violence on college campuses: A systematic review and meta-analysis of program outcomes and delivery methods. *Journal of American College Health, 66*(6), 457–466. https://doi.org/10.1080/07448481.2018.1431906

Joyal, C. C., & Carpentier, J. (2022). Concordance and discordance between paraphilic interests and behaviors: A follow-up study. *Journal of Sex Research*, 59(3), 385–390. https://doi.org/10.1080/00224499.2021.1986801

Kahneman, D., & Tversky, A. (1977). *Intuitive prediction: Biases and corrective procedures*. Decision Research, Perceptronics.

Karasavva, V. (2020). *iPredator: Image-based sexual abuse risk factors and motivators* [Unpublished doctoral dissertation]. Carleton University.

Karasavva, V., Brunet, L., Smodis, A., Swanek, J., & Forth, A. (2023). Putting the Y in cyberflashing: Exploring the prevalence and predictors of the reasons for sending unsolicited nude or sexual images. *Computers in Human Behavior*, 140, Article 107593. https://doi.org/10.1016/j.chb.2022.107593

Karasavva, V., & Forth, A. (2022). Personality, attitudinal, and demographic predictors of non-consensual dissemination of intimate images. *Journal of Interpersonal Violence*, 37(21–22), NP19265–NP19289. https://doi.org/10.1177/08862605211043586

Karlsson, J., & Josephson, S. (2021). *"Everything that is not a yes is a no": A report about children's everyday exposure to sexual crimes and their protective strategies*. ECPAT Sweden. https://ecpat.se/wp-content/uploads/2020/12/ECPAT-Report-2021_Everything-that-is-not-a-yes-is-a-no.pdf

Kaufman, K. L., Holmberg, J. K., Orts, K. A., McCrady, F. E., Rotzien, A. L., Daleiden, E. L., & Hilliker, D. R. (1998). Factors influencing sexual offenders' modus operandi: An examination of victim-offender relatedness and age. *Child Maltreatment*, 3(4), 349–361. https://doi.org/10.1177/1077559598003004007

Kelley, S. M., Ambroziak, G., Thornton, D., & Barahal, R. M. (2020). How do professionals assess sexual recidivism risk? An updated survey of practices. *Sexual Abuse*, 32(1), 3–29. https://doi.org/10.1177/1079063218800474

Kettleborough, D. G., & Merdian, H. L. (2017). Gateway to offending behaviour: Permission-giving thoughts of online users of child sexual exploitation material. *Journal of Sexual Aggression*, 23(1), 19–32. https://doi.org/10.1080/13552600.2016.1231852

Key, R., Underwood, A., Farnham, F., Marzano, L., & Hawton, K. (2021). Suicidal behavior in individuals accused or convicted of child sex abuse or indecent image offenses: Systematic review of prevalence and risk factors. *Suicide and Life-Threatening Behavior*, 51(4), 715–728. https://doi.org/10.1111/sltb.12749

Kleijn, M., & Bogaerts, S. (2021). Sexual offending pathways and chat conversations in an online environment. *Sexual Abuse*, 33(8), 871–890. https://doi.org/10.1177/1079063220981061

Klein, V., Schmidt, A. F., Turner, D., & Briken, P. (2015). Are sex drive and hypersexuality associated with pedophilic interest and child sexual abuse in a male community sample? *PLOS ONE*, 10(7), e0129730. https://doi.org/10.1371/journal.pone.0129730

Kliethermes, B. C. (2021). *The effect of child sexual exploitation material offender age, motivation for use, and treatment interest on public perceptions of offense and treatment* [Unpublished doctoral dissertation]. The University of North Dakota.

Kloess, J. A., Hamilton-Giachritsis, C. E., & Beech, A. R. (2019). Offense processes of online sexual grooming and abuse of children via internet communication platforms. *Sexual Abuse*, 31(1), 73–96. https://doi.org/10.1177/1079063217720927

Kloess, J. A., & van der Bruggen, M. (2023). Trust and relationship development among users in Dark Web child sexual exploitation and abuse networks:

A literature review from a psychological and criminological perspective. *Trauma, Violence, & Abuse, 24*(3), 1220–1237. https://doi.org/10.1177/15248380211057274

Koops, T., Turner, D., Neutze, J., & Briken, P. (2017). Child sex tourism—Prevalence of and risk factors for its use in a German community sample. *BMC Public Health, 17*(1), 344. https://doi.org/10.1186/s12889-017-4270-3

Korchia, T., Boyer, L., Deneuville, M., Etchecopar-Etchart, D., Lancon, C., & Fond, G. (2022). ADHD prevalence in patients with hypersexuality and paraphilic disorders: A systematic review and meta-analysis. *European Archives of Psychiatry and Clinical Neuroscience, 272*(8), 1413–1420. https://doi.org/10.1007/s00406-022-01421-9

Kozar, C. J., & Day, A. (2012). The therapeutic alliance in offending behavior programs: A necessary and sufficient condition for change? *Aggression and Violent Behavior, 17*(5), 482–487. https://doi.org/10.1016/j.avb.2012.07.004

Krone, T., & Smith, R. G. (2017). Trajectories in online child sexual exploitation offending in Australia (No. 524). *Trends and Issues in Crime and Criminal Justice*. Australian Institute of Criminology. https://doi.org/10.52922/ti137144

Krone, T., Smith, R. G., Cartwright, J., Hutchings, A., Tomison, A., & Napier, S. (2017). *Online child sexual exploitation offenders: A study of Australian law enforcement data*. Criminology Research Grants. https://www.aic.gov.au/sites/default/files/2020-05/58-1213-FinalReport.pdf

Kuhle, L. F., Schlinzig, E., Kaiser, G., Amelung, T., Konrad, A., Röhle, R., & Beier, K. M. (2017). The association of sexual preference and dynamic risk factors with undetected child pornography offending. *Journal of Sexual Aggression, 23*(1), 3–18. https://doi.org/10.1080/13552600.2016.1201157

Lalumière, M. L., & Quinsey, V. L. (1994). The discriminability of rapists from non-sex offenders using phallometric measures: A meta-analysis. *Criminal Justice and Behavior, 21*(1), 150–175. https://doi.org/10.1177/0093854894021001010

Lalumière, M. L., & Quinsey, V. L. (1996). Sexual deviance, antisociality, mating effort, and the use of sexually coercive behaviors. *Personality and Individual Differences, 21*(1), 33–48. https://doi.org/10.1016/0191-8869(96)00059-1

Lam, A., Mitchell, J., & Seto, M. C. (2010). Lay perceptions of child pornography offenders. *Canadian Journal of Criminology and Criminal Justice, 52*(2), 173–201. https://doi.org/10.3138/cjccj.52.2.173

Lampalzer, U., Tozdan, S., von Franqué, F., & Briken, P. (2021). Referral for group or individual treatment? Factors for consideration in the case of self-referred individuals with a sexual interest in minors. *International Journal of Impotence Research, 33*(3), 348–363. https://doi.org/10.1038/s41443-020-0296-7

Landripet, I., Buško, V., & Štulhofer, A. (2019). Testing the content progression thesis: A longitudinal assessment of pornography use and preference for coercive and violent content among male adolescents. *Social Science Research, 81*, 32–41. https://doi.org/10.1016/j.ssresearch.2019.03.003

Lang, R. A., & Frenzel, R. R. (1988). How sex offenders lure children. *Annals of Sex Research, 1*(2), 303–317. https://doi.org/10.1007/BF00852802

Långström, N., & Seto, M. C. (2006). Exhibitionistic and voyeuristic behavior in a Swedish national population survey. *Archives of Sexual Behavior, 35*(4), 427–435. https://doi.org/10.1007/s10508-006-9042-6

Lapowsky, I. (2023, June 24). The race to prevent 'the worst case scenario for machine learning.' *The New York Times*. https://www.nytimes.com/2023/06/24/business/ai-generated-explicit-images.html

Lasher, M. P., & McGrath, R. J. (2017). Desistance from sexual and other violent offending among child sexual abusers: Observations using the Sex Offender Treatment Intervention and Progress Scale. *Criminal Justice and Behavior*, *44*(3), 416–431. https://doi.org/10.1177/0093854816670194

Lätth, J., Landgren, V., McMahan, A., Sparre, C., Eriksson, J., Malki, K., Söderquist, E., Öberg, K. G., Rozental, A., Andersson, G., Kaldo, V., Långström, N., & Rahm, C. (2022). Effects of internet-delivered cognitive behavioral therapy on use of child sexual abuse material: A randomized placebo-controlled trial on the Darknet. *Internet Interventions*, *30*, Article 100590. https://doi.org/10.1016/j.invent.2022.100590

Laub, J. H., & Sampson, R. J. (2009). *Shared beginnings, divergent lives: Delinquent boys to age 70*. Harvard University Press. https://doi.org/10.2307/j.ctv1q3z28f

Lee, A. F., Li, N.-C., Lamade, R., Schuler, A., & Prentky, R. A. (2012). Predicting hands-on child sexual offenses among possessors of internet child pornography. *Psychology, Public Policy, and Law*, *18*(4), 644–672. https://doi.org/10.1037/a0027517

Lee, S. C., Babchishin, K. M., Mularczyk, K. P., & Hanson, R. K. (2024). Dynamic risk scales degrade over time: Evidence for reassessments. *Assessment*, *31*(3), 698–714. https://doi.org/10.1177/10731911231177227

Letourneau, E. J., Henggeler, S. W., McCart, M. R., Borduin, C. M., Schewe, P. A., & Armstrong, K. S. (2013). Two-year follow-up of a randomized effectiveness trial evaluating MST for juveniles who sexually offend. *Journal of Family Psychology*, *27*(6), 978–985. https://doi.org/10.1037/a0034710

Letourneau, E. J., Nietert, P. J., & Rheingold, A. A. (2016). Initial assessment of stewards of children program effects on child sexual abuse reporting rates in selected South Carolina counties. *Child Maltreatment*, *21*(1), 74–79. https://doi.org/10.1177/1077559515615232

Letourneau, E. J., Roberts, T. W. M., Malone, L., & Sun, Y. (2023). No check we won't write: A report on the high cost of sex offender incarceration. *Sexual Abuse*, *35*(1), 54–82. https://doi.org/10.1177/10790632221078305

Letourneau, E. J., Schaeffer, C. M., Bradshaw, C. P., & Feder, K. A. (2017). Preventing the onset of child sexual abuse by targeting young adolescents with universal prevention programming. *Child Maltreatment*, *22*(2), 100–111. https://doi.org/10.1177/1077559517692439

Letourneau, E. J., Schaeffer, C. M., Bradshaw, C. P., Ruzicka, A. E., Assini-Meytin, L. C., Nair, R., & Thorne, E. (2024). Responsible behavior with younger children: Results from a pilot randomized evaluation of a school-based child sexual abuse perpetration prevention program. *Child Maltreatment*, *29*(1), 129–141. https://doi.org/10.1177/10775595221130737

Levenson, J. S. (2011). "But I didn't do it!": Ethical treatment of sex offenders in denial. *Sexual Abuse*, *23*(3), 346–364. https://doi.org/10.1177/1079063210382048

Levenson, J. S., & Grady, M. D. (2019). Preventing sexual abuse: Perspectives of minor-attracted persons about seeking help. *Sexual Abuse*, *31*(8), 991–1013. https://doi.org/10.1177/1079063218797713

Levenson, J. S., & Macgowan, M. J. (2004). Engagement, denial, and treatment progress among sex offenders in group therapy. *Sexual Abuse*, *16*(1), 49–63. https://doi.org/10.1177/107906320401600104

Lewis, R., & Anitha, S. (2023). Upskirting: A systematic literature review. *Trauma, Violence, & Abuse*, *24*(3), 2003–2018. https://doi.org/10.1177/15248380221082091

Lievesley, R., Harper, C. A., Swaby, H., & Woodward, E. (2023). Identifying and working with appropriate treatment targets with people who are sexually attracted to children. *Journal of Sex & Marital Therapy*, *49*(5), 497–516. https://doi.org/10.1080/0092623X.2022.2149437

Litton, S. (2023, November 7). *Announcing Lantern: The first child safety cross-platform signal sharing program*. Tech Coalition. https://www.technologycoalition.org/newsroom/announcing-lantern

Liu, Y. (2022). Peeping Wang: A bird's eye view on video voyeurism among Chinese men attracted to men. *Journal of Sex Research*, *60*(4), 574–583. https://doi.org/10.1080/00224499.2021.2022589

Long, M., Alison, L., Tejeiro, R., Hendricks, E., & Giles, S. (2016). KIRAT: Law enforcement's prioritization tool for investigating indecent image offenders. *Psychology, Public Policy, and Law*, *22*(1), 12–21. https://doi.org/10.1037/law0000069

Lykins, A. D., Cantor, J. M., Kuban, M. E., Blak, T., Dickey, R., Klassen, P. E., & Blanchard, R. (2010). The relation between peak response magnitudes and agreement in diagnoses obtained from two different phallometric tests for pedophilia. *Sexual Abuse*, *22*(1), 42–57. https://doi.org/10.1177/1079063209352094

Maas, M. K., Cary, K. M., Clancy, E. M., Klettke, B., McCauley, H. L., & Temple, J. R. (2021). Slutpage use among U.S. college students: The secret and social platforms of image-based sexual abuse. *Archives of Sexual Behavior*, *50*(5), 2203–2214. https://doi.org/10.1007/s10508-021-01920-1

Madigan, S., Ly, A., Rash, C. L., Van Ouytsel, J., & Temple, J. R. (2018). Prevalence of multiple forms of sexting behavior among youth: A systematic review and meta-analysis. *JAMA Pediatrics*, *172*(4), 327–335. https://doi.org/10.1001/jamapediatrics.2017.5314

Madill, A., & Zhao, Y. (2022). Are female paraphilias hiding in plain sight? Risqué male–male erotica for women in Sinophone and Anglophone regions. *Archives of Sexual Behavior*, *51*(2), 897–910. https://doi.org/10.1007/s10508-021-02107-4

Mainwaring, C., Gabbert, F., & Scott, A. J. (2023). A systematic review exploring variables related to bystander intervention in sexual violence contexts. *Trauma, Violence, & Abuse*, *24*(3), 1727–1742. https://doi.org/10.1177/15248380221079660

Malamuth, N. M., Lamade, R. V., Koss, M. P., Lopez, E., Seaman, C., & Prentky, R. (2021). Factors predictive of sexual violence: Testing the four pillars of the Confluence Model in a large diverse sample of college men. *Aggressive Behavior*, *47*(4), 405–420. https://doi.org/10.1002/ab.21960

Malamuth, N. M., Linz, D., Heavey, C. L., Barnes, G., & Acker, M. (1995). Using the confluence model of sexual aggression to predict men's conflict with women: A 10-year follow-up study. *Journal of Personality and Social Psychology*, *69*(2), 353–369. https://doi.org/10.1037/0022-3514.69.2.353

Malesky, L. A., Jr. (2007). Predatory online behavior: Modus operandi of convicted sex offenders in identifying potential victims and contacting minors over the internet. *Journal of Child Sexual Abuse*, *16*(2), 23–32. https://doi.org/10.1300/J070v16n02_02

Malesky, L. A., Jr., & Ennis, L. (2004). Supportive distortions: An analysis of posts on a pedophile internet message board. *Journal of Addictions & Offender Counseling*, *24*(2), 92–100. https://doi.org/10.1002/j.2161-1874.2004.tb00185.x

Mandau, M. B. H. (2020). 'Directly in your face': A qualitative study on the sending and receiving of unsolicited 'dick pics' among young adults. *Sexuality & Culture*, *24*(1), 72–93. https://doi.org/10.1007/s12119-019-09626-2

Mann, R. E., Hanson, R. K., & Thornton, D. (2010). Assessing risk for sexual recidivism: Some proposals on the nature of psychologically meaningful risk factors. *Sexual Abuse, 22*(2), 191–217. https://doi.org/10.1177/1079063210366039

March, E., & Wagstaff, D. L. (2017, December 17). Sending nudes: Sex, self-rated mate value, and trait Machiavellianism predict sending unsolicited explicit images. *Frontiers in Psychology, 8*, Article 2210. https://doi.org/10.3389/fpsyg.2017.02210

Marcus, D. K., O'Connell, D., Norris, A. L., & Sawaqdeh, A. (2014). Is the Dodo bird endangered in the 21st century? A meta-analysis of treatment comparison studies. *Clinical Psychology Review, 34*(7), 519–530. https://doi.org/10.1016/j.cpr.2014.08.001

Marečková, A., Androvičová, R., Bártová, K., Krejčová, L., & Klapilová, K. (2022). Men with paraphilic interests and their desire to interact with a sex robot. *Journal of Future Robot Life, 3*(1), 39–48. https://doi.org/10.3233/FRL-210010

Marshall, L. E., O'Brien, M. D., Marshall, W. L., Booth, B., & Davis, A. (2012). Obsessive-compulsive disorder, social phobia, and loneliness in incarcerated internet child pornography offenders. *Sexual Addiction & Compulsivity, 19*(1–2), 41–52. https://doi.org/10.1080/10720162.2012.665291

Marshall, W. L., Serran, G. A., Fernandez, Y. M., Mulloy, R., Mann, R., & Thornton, D. (2003). Therapist characteristics in the treatment of sexual offenders: Tentative data on their relationship with indices of behaviour change. *Journal of Sexual Aggression, 9*(1), 25–30. https://doi.org/10.1080/355260031000137940

Martijn, F. M., Babchishin, K. M., Pullman, L. E., & Seto, M. C. (2020). Sexual attraction and falling in love in persons with pedohebephilia. *Archives of Sexual Behavior, 49*(4), 1305–1318. https://doi.org/10.1007/s10508-019-01579-9

Marx, C. M., Müller, K. W., & Beutel, M. E. (2021). Adverse childhood experiences in persons with excessive and destructive online behaviour. *Cyberpsychology: Journal of Psychosocial Research of Cyberspace, 15*(3), Article 5. https://doi.org/10.5817/CP2021-3-5

May-Chahal, C., Peersman, C., Rashid, A., Brennan, M., Mills, E., Mei, P., & Barbrook, J. (2022). *A rapid evidence assessment of technical tools for the detection and disruption of Child Sexual Abuse Media (CSAM) and CSAM offenders in the ASEAN region* [Technical report]. Lancaster University & University of Bristol. https://research-information.bris.ac.uk/ws/portalfiles/portal/360349691/REA_Draft_Final2.pdf

McCarthy, J. A. (2010). Internet sexual activity: A comparison between contact and non-contact child pornography offenders. *Journal of Sexual Aggression, 16*(2), 181–195. https://doi.org/10.1080/13552601003760006

McGlynn, C., & Bows, H. (2019). Possessing extreme pornography: Policing, prosecutions and the need for reform. *Journal of Criminal Law, 83*(6), 473–488. https://doi.org/10.1177/0022018319877783

McGlynn, C., Rackley, E., & Houghton, R. (2017). Beyond 'revenge porn': The continuum of image-based sexual abuse. *Feminist Legal Studies, 25*(1), 25–46. https://doi.org/10.1007/s10691-017-9343-2

McMahan, A., Roche, K., Dreyhaupt, R., Seto, M. C., & Rahm, C. (2023). Changes in sexual thoughts and behaviors in a clinical sample of child sexual abuse material users under the COVID-19 pandemic. *Sexual and Relationship Therapy*. https://doi.org/10.1080/14681994.2023.2215710

McManus, M. A., Long, M. L., Alison, L., & Almond, L. (2015). Factors associated with contact child sexual abuse in a sample of indecent image offenders. *Journal *of Sexual Aggression, 21*(3), 368–384. https://doi.org/10.1080/13552600.2014.927009

McMurran, M. (2004). Assessing and changing motivation to offend. In W. Miles Cox & Eric Klinger (Eds.), *Handbook of motivational counseling: Concepts, approaches, and assessment* (pp. 319–334). Wiley.

McMurran, M. (2009). Motivational interviewing with offenders: A systematic review. *Legal and Criminological Psychology, 14*(1), 83–100. https://doi.org/10.1348/135532508X278326

McMurran, M., & Ward, T. (2010). Treatment readiness, treatment engagement and behaviour change. *Criminal Behaviour and Mental Health, 20*(2), 75–85. https://doi.org/10.1002/cbm.762

McPhail, I. V., Hermann, C. A., & Fernandez, Y. M. (2014). Correlates of emotional congruence with children in sexual offenders against children: A test of theoretical models in an incarcerated sample. *Child Abuse & Neglect, 38*(2), 336–346. https://doi.org/10.1016/j.chiabu.2013.10.002

McPhail, I. V., Hermann, C. A., & Nunes, K. L. (2013). Emotional congruence with children and sexual offending against children: A meta-analytic review. *Journal of Consulting and Clinical Psychology, 81*(4), 737–749. https://doi.org/10.1037/a0033248

McPhail, I. V., Olver, M. E., Brouillette-Alarie, S., & Looman, J. (2018). Taxometric analysis of the latent structure of pedophilic interest. *Archives of Sexual Behavior, 47*, 2223–2240. https://doi.org/10.1007/s10508-018-1225-4

McPhail, I. V., Olver, M. E., Nicholaichuk, T. P., & Haynes, A. (2021). Convergent and predictive associations of three measures of pedophilic interest. *Sexual Abuse, 33*(7), 816–838. https://doi.org/10.1177/1079063220968042

Merdian, H. L., Moghaddam, N., Boer, D. P., Wilson, N., Thakker, J., Curtis, C., & Dawson, D. (2018). Fantasy-driven versus contact-driven users of child sexual exploitation material: Offender classification and implications for their risk assessment. *Sexual Abuse, 30*(3), 230–253. https://doi.org/10.1177/1079063216641109

Merdian, H. L., Perkins, D. E., Dustagheer, E., & Glorney, E. (2020). Development of a case formulation model for individuals who have viewed, distributed, and/or shared child sexual exploitation material. *International Journal of Offender Therapy and Comparative Criminology, 64*(10–11), 1055–1073. https://doi.org/10.1177/0306624X17748067

Merdian, H. L., Perkins, D. E., McCashin, D., & Stevanovic, J. (2021). Integrating structured individual offending pathway analysis into group treatment for individuals who have accessed, shared, and/or distributed child sexual exploitation material: A feasibility study and preliminary outcome evaluation. *Psychology, Crime & Law, 27*(6), 579–605. https://doi.org/10.1080/1068316X.2020.1849690

Merdian, H. L., Perkins, D. E., Webster, S. D., & McCashin, D. (2019). Transnational child sexual abuse: Outcomes from a roundtable discussion. *International Journal of Environmental Research and Public Health, 16*(2), 243. https://doi.org/10.3390/ijerph16020243

Merdian, H. L., Wilson, N., Thakker, J., Curtis, C., & Boer, D. P. (2013). "So why did you do it?": Explanations provided by child pornography offenders. *Sexual Offender Treatment, 8*(1), 1–19.

Meta. (2022, November 21). *Protecting teens and their privacy on Facebook and Instagram*. https://about.fb.com/news/2022/11/protecting-teens-and-their-privacy-on-facebook-and-instagram/

Mews, A., Di Bella, L., & Purver, M. (2017). *Impact evaluation of the prison-based Core Sex Offender Treatment Programme*. United Kingdom Ministry of Justice. https://assets.publishing.service.gov.uk/media/5a82a191ed915d74e3402c41/sotp-report-print.pdf

Mgbako, C. A. (2020). The mainstreaming of sex workers' rights as human rights. *Harvard Journal of Law & Gender, 43*, 91–136.

Middleton, D., Mandeville-Norden, R., & Hayes, E. (2009). Does treatment work with internet sex offenders? Emerging findings from the Internet Sex Offender Treatment Programme (i-SOTP). *Journal of Sexual Aggression, 15*(1), 5–19. https://doi.org/10.1080/13552600802673444

Mills, J. F., & Kroner, D. G. (2005). An investigation into the relationship between socially desirable responding and offender self-report. *Psychological Services, 2*(1), 70–80. https://doi.org/10.1037/1541-1559.2.1.70

Mills, J. F., Kroner, D. G., & Forth, A. E. (2002). Measures of Criminal Attitudes and Associates (MCAA) development, factor structure, reliability, and validity. *Assessment, 9*(3), 240–253. https://doi.org/10.1177/1073191102009003003

Mitchell, K. J., Finkelhor, D., & Wolak, J. (2007). Online requests for sexual pictures from youth: Risk factors and incident characteristics. *Journal of Adolescent Health, 41*(2), 196–203. https://doi.org/10.1016/j.jadohealth.2007.03.013

Mokros, A., & Banse, R. (2019). The "Dunkelfeld" project for self-identified pedophiles: A reappraisal of its effectiveness. *Journal of Sexual Medicine, 16*(5), 609–613. https://doi.org/10.1016/j.jsxm.2019.02.009

Monahan, J. (1981). *Predicting violent behavior: An assessment of clinical techniques*. Sage.

Moncher, F. J., & Prinz, R. J. (1991). Treatment fidelity in outcome studies. *Clinical Psychology Review, 11*(3), 247–266. https://doi.org/10.1016/0272-7358(91)90103-2

Morgan, S. (2015). *Understanding individuals who access sexualised images of children* [Doctoral dissertation]. The University of Auckland. https://researchspace.auckland.ac.nz/handle/2292/26647

Mori, C., Cooke, J. E., Temple, J. R., Ly, A., Lu, Y., Anderson, N., Rash, C., & Madigan, S. (2020). The prevalence of sexting behaviors among emerging adults: A meta-analysis. *Archives of Sexual Behavior, 49*, 1103–1119. https://doi.org/10.1007/s10508-020-01656-4

Mori, C., Temple, J. R., Browne, D., & Madigan, S. (2019). Association of sexting with sexual behaviors and mental health among adolescents: A systematic review and meta-analysis. *JAMA Pediatrics, 173*(8), 770–779. https://doi.org/10.1001/jamapediatrics.2019.1658

Morin, R. (2016, January 11). Can child dolls keep pedophiles from offending? *The Atlantic*. https://www.theatlantic.com/health/archive/2016/01/can-child-dolls-keep-pedophiles-from-offending/423324/

Mujal, G. N., Taylor, M. E., Fry, J. L., Gochez-Kerr, T. H., & Weaver, N. L. (2021). A systematic review of bystander interventions for the prevention of sexual violence. *Trauma, Violence, & Abuse, 22*(2), 381–396. https://doi.org/10.1177/1524838019849587

Najdowski, C. J. (2017). Legal responses to non-consensual pornography: Current policy in the United States and future directions for research. *Psychology, Public Policy, and Law, 23*(2), 154–165. https://doi.org/10.1037/law0000123

Nardett, G., Simonet, R., & Findlater, D. (2021). *An initial analysis of the impact of the coronavirus pandemic on callers to the Stop It Now! UK and Ireland helpline*. Lucy Faithfull Foundation. https://www.stopitnow.org.uk/wp-content/uploads/

2021/08/Covid_19_insights_from_the_Stop_It_Now_helpline_summary_April-September_2020.pdf

National Center for Missing and Exploited Children. (2017). *The online enticement of children: An in-depth analysis of CyberTipline reports*. https://www.missingkids.org/content/dam/missingkids/pdfs/ncmec-analysis/Online%20Enticement%20Pre-Travel1.pdf

National Conference of State Legislatures. (2022). *Racial and ethnic disparities in the justice system*. https://documents.ncsl.org/wwwncsl/Criminal-Justice/Racial-and-Ethnic-Disparities-in-the-Justice-System_v03.pdf

National Institute of Mental Health. (2024). *Suicide*. https://www.nimh.nih.gov/health/statistics/suicide

Neutze, J., Seto, M. C., Schaefer, G. A., Mundt, I. A., & Beier, K. M. (2011). Predictors of child pornography offenses and child sexual abuse in a community sample of pedophiles and hebephiles. *Sexual Abuse, 23*(2), 212–242. https://doi.org/10.1177/1079063210382043

Newman, E. F., Efthymiadou, E., Quayle, E., Squire, T., Denis, D., Wortley, R., Beier, K. M., & Koukopoulos, N. (2023). The impact of a public health campaign to deter viewing of child sexual abuse images online: A case study of the UK Stop It Now! Campaign. *Sexual Abuse*. Advance online publication. https://doi.org/10.1177/10790632231205784

Nicas, J. (2021, August 18). Are Apple's tools against child abuse bad for your privacy? *New York Times*. Retrieved on September 13, 2024, from https://www.nytimes.com/2021/08/18/technology/apple-child-abuse-tech-privacy.html

Nicol, S. J., Harris, D. A., Kebbell, M. R., & Ogilvie, J. (2021). Online child sexual exploitation material: A comparison from police data on men charged with child sexual exploitation material exclusively and men charged with contact child sexual abuse exclusively. *Sexual Offending: Theory, Research, and Prevention, 16*, 1–18. https://doi.org/10.5964/sotrap.4301

Nielssen, O., O'Dea, J., Sullivan, D., Rodriguez, M., Bourget, D., & Large, M. (2011). Child pornography offenders detected by surveillance of the internet and by other methods. *Criminal Behaviour and Mental Health, 21*(3), 215–224. https://doi.org/10.1002/cbm.809

Nolan, T., Willis, G. M., Thornton, D., Kelley, S. M., & Christofferson, S. B. (2023). Attending to the positive: A retrospective validation of the Structured Assessment of Protective Factors–Sexual Offence Version. *Sexual Abuse, 35*(2), 241–260. https://doi.org/10.1177/10790632221098354

Noll, J. G., Haag, A. C., Shenk, C. E., Wright, M. F., Barnes, J. E., Kohram, M., Malgaroli, M., Foley, D. J., Kouril, M., & Bonanno, G. A. (2022). An observational study of internet behaviours for adolescent females following sexual abuse. *Nature Human Behaviour, 6*(1), 74–87. https://doi.org/10.1038/s41562-021-01187-5

Nunes, K. L., Hanson, R. K., Firestone, P., Moulden, H. M., Greenberg, D. M., & Bradford, J. M. (2007). Denial predicts recidivism for some sexual offenders. *Sexual Abuse, 19*(2), 91–105. https://doi.org/10.1177/107906320701900202

Nunes, K. L., Hermann, C. A., Maimone, S., & Woods, M. (2015). Thinking clearly about violent cognitions: Attitudes may be distinct from other cognitions. *Journal of Interpersonal Violence, 30*(8), 1322–1347. https://doi.org/10.1177/0886260514540329

Nuotte, M., & Sivonen, R. (2023). *Factors associated with suicidal ideation and behaviour among Finnish speaking CSAM users* [Unpublished master's thesis]. University of Eastern Finland.

O'Brien, J. E., & Li, W. (2020). The role of the internet in the grooming, exploitation, and exit of United States domestic minor sex trafficking victims. *Journal of Children and Media, 14*(2), 187–203. https://doi.org/10.1080/17482798.2019.1688668

O'Connor, J., Smith, L., Woerner, J., & Khan, A. (2024). Protective factors for sexual violence perpetration among high school and college students: A systematic review. *Trauma, Violence, & Abuse, 25*(2), 1073–1087. https://doi.org/10.1177/15248380231171189

Office for National Statistics. (2021). *Ethnic group, England and Wales: Census 2021*. https://www.ons.gov.uk/peoplepopulationandcommunity/culturalidentity/ethnicity/bulletins/ethnicgroupenglandandwales/census2021

Ogaki, M. (2018). Theoretical explanations of Jyoshi Kousei Business ("JK Business") in Japan. *Dignity, 3*(1), 11. https://doi.org/10.23860/dignity.2018.03.01.11

Ogas, O., & Gaddam, S. (2011). *A billion wicked thoughts: What the world's largest experiment reveals about human desire*. Dutton.

O'Halloran, E., & Quayle, E. (2010). A content analysis of a "boy love" support forum: Revisiting Durkin and Bryant. *Journal of Sexual Aggression, 16*(1), 71–85. https://doi.org/10.1080/13552600903395319

Olver, M. (2003). *The development and validation of the Violence Risk Scale: Sexual Offender Version (VRS: SO) and its relationship to psychopathy and treatment attrition* [Doctoral dissertation]. University of Saskatchewan. https://harvest.usask.ca/items/6d66d493-fd07-4056-9c57-d576e40d91cd

Olver, M. E., Kelley, S. M., Kingston, D. A., Beggs Christofferson, S. M., Thornton, D., & Wong, S. C. (2021). Incremental contributions of static and dynamic sexual violence risk assessment: Integrating Static-99R and VRS-SO common language risk levels. *Criminal Justice and Behavior, 48*(8), 1091–1110. https://doi.org/10.1177/0093854820974400

Olver, M. E., Kingston, D. A., Laverty, E. K., & Seto, M. C. (2022). Psychometric properties of common measures of hypersexuality in an online Canadian sample. *Journal of Sexual Medicine, 19*(2), 331–346. https://doi.org/10.1016/j.jsxm.2021.12.002

Olver, M. E., Nicholaichuk, T. P., Kingston, D. A., & Wong, S. C. P. (2020). A prospective multisite examination of dynamic sexual violence risk: Extension and update to Olver, Nicholaichuk, Kingston, and Wong (2014). *Journal of Consulting and Clinical Psychology, 88*(4), 362–371. https://doi.org/10.1037/ccp0000478

Olver, M. E., Sowden, J. N., Kingston, D. A., Nicholaichuk, T. P., Gordon, A., Beggs Christofferson, S. M., & Wong, S. C. (2018). Predictive accuracy of violence risk scale–sexual offender version risk and change scores in treated Canadian Aboriginal and non-Aboriginal sexual offenders. *Sexual Abuse, 30*(3), 254–275. https://doi.org/10.1177/1079063216649594

Olver, M. E., & Wong, S. (2011). Predictors of sex offender treatment dropout: Psychopathy, sex offender risk, and responsivity implications. *Psychology, Crime & Law, 17*(5), 457–471. https://doi.org/10.1080/10683160903318876

O'Malley, R. L., & Holt, K. M. (2022). Cyber sextortion: An exploratory analysis of different perpetrators engaging in a similar crime. *Journal of Interpersonal Violence, 37*(1–2), 258–283. https://doi.org/10.1177/0886260520909186

Oswald, F., Lopes, A., Skoda, K., Hesse, C. L., & Pedersen, C. L. (2020). I'll show you mine so you'll show me yours: Motivations and personality variables in photographic exhibitionism. *Journal of Sex Research, 57*(5), 597–609. https://doi.org/10.1080/00224499.2019.1639036

Otterman, S. (2018, November 30). Sending lewd nudes to strangers could mean a year in jail. *The New York Times*. https://www.nytimes.com/2018/11/30/nyregion/airdrop-sexual-harassment.html

Otto, R. K., & Douglas, K. S. (Eds.). (2011). *Handbook of violence risk assessment*. Routledge. https://doi.org/10.4324/9780203843666

Our World in Data. (2022). *Number of people using the internet*. https://ourworldindata.org/grapher/number-of-internet-users

Our World in Data. (2023). *Share of the population using the internet*. https://ourworldindata.org/grapher/share-of-individuals-using-the-internet

Owens, J. N., Eakin, J. D., Hoffer, T., Muirhead, Y., & Shelton, J. L. E. (2016). Investigative aspects of crossover offending from a sample of FBI online child sexual exploitation cases. *Aggression and Violent Behavior*, 30, 3–14. https://doi.org/10.1016/j.avb.2016.07.001

Pacheco, E., Melhuish, N., & Fiske, J. (2019). *Image-based sexual abuse: A snapshot of New Zealand adults' experiences*. Netsafe. https://osf.io/preprints/socarxiv/hwjqk/download

Paden, S. G., Azizian, A., Sreenivasan, S., McGuire, J., Brooks Holliday, S., & Seto, M. C. (2021). A comparison of risk factors among discharged military veterans and civilians involuntarily hospitalized under California's sexually violent predator act. *Sexual Abuse*, 33(6), 678–697. https://doi.org/10.1177/1079063220940305

Paquette, S., & Cortoni, F. (2020). The development and validation of the Cognitions of Internet Sexual Offending (C-ISO) Scale. *Sexual Abuse*, 32(8), 907–930. https://doi.org/10.1177/1079063219862281

Paquette, S., & Cortoni, F. (2021). Offence-supportive cognitions, atypical sexuality, problematic self-regulation, and perceived anonymity among online and contact sexual offenders against children. *Archives of Sexual Behavior*, 50(5), 2173–2187. https://doi.org/10.1007/s10508-020-01863-z

Paquette, S., & Fortin, F. (2021). A peek into their mind? An exploration of links between offense-supportive statements and behaviors among men who sexually exploit children and adolescents online. *CrimRxiv*. https://doi.org/10.21428/cb6ab371.d8f418c2

Paquette, S., & McPhail, I. V. (2020). Construction and preliminary validation of the Cognitive and Emotional Congruence with Children (C-ECWC) Scale. *Psychological Assessment*, 32(8), 739–751. https://doi.org/10.1037/pas0000832

Parhar, K. K., Wormith, J. S., Derkzen, D. M., & Beauregard, A. M. (2008). Offender coercion in treatment: A meta-analysis of effectiveness. *Criminal Justice and Behavior*, 35(9), 1109–1135. https://doi.org/10.1177/0093854808320169

Parker, C. (Host). (2021, June 16). Stalkerware with Eva Galperin (No. 68) [Audio podcast episode]. In *The Easy Prey Podcast*. Easy Prey. https://whatismyipaddress.com/stalkerware-with-eva-galperin

Patel, U., & Roesch, R. (2022). The prevalence of technology-facilitated sexual violence: A meta-analysis and systematic review. *Trauma, Violence, & Abuse*, 23(2), 428–443. https://doi.org/10.1177/1524838020958057

Paul, B., & Linz, D. G. (2008). The effects of exposure to virtual child pornography on viewer cognitions and attitudes toward deviant sexual behavior. *Communication Research*, 35(1), 3–38. https://doi.org/10.1177/0093650207309359

Pedersen, W., Bakken, A., Stefansen, K., & von Soest, T. (2023). Sexual victimization in the digital age: A population-based study of physical and image-based sexual abuse among adolescents. *Archives of Sexual Behavior, 52*(1), 399–410. https://doi.org/10.1007/s10508-021-02200-8

Perillo, A. D., Calkins, C., & Jeglic, E. L. (2021). Evaluating selection for sexually violent predator (SVP) commitment: A comparison of those committed, not committed, and nearly committed. *Psychology, Public Policy, and Law, 27*(1), 98–111. https://doi.org/10.1037/law0000283

Peters, E. M., Morrison, T., McDermott, D. T., Bishop, C. J., & Kiss, M. (2014). Age is in the eye of the beholder: Examining the cues employed to construct the illusion of youth in teen pornography. *Sexuality & Culture, 18*(3), 527–546. https://doi.org/10.1007/s12119-013-9210-5

Phan, A., Seigfried-Spellar, K., & Choo, K. K. R. (2021). Threaten me softly: A review of potential dating app risks. *Computers in Human Behavior Reports, 3*, 100055. https://doi.org/10.1016/j.chbr.2021.100055

Piché, L., & Schweighofer, A. (2023). *Working with offenders who view online child sexual exploitation material*. Routledge. https://doi.org/10.4324/9781003388142

Pilon, A. (2016). *The predictive validity of general and offence-specific risk assessment tools for child pornography offenders' reoffending* [Unpublished doctoral dissertation]. University of Saskatchewan.

Polaris Project. (2016). *More than drinks for sale: Exposing sex trafficking in cantinas and bars in the U.S.* https://polarisproject.org/wp-content/uploads/2019/09/MoreThanDrinksForSale_FINAL.pdf

Pooley, K., & Boxall, H. (2020). Mobile dating applications and sexual and violent offending (No. 612). *Trends and Issues in Crime and Criminal Justice.* Australian Institute of Criminology. https://www.aic.gov.au/publications/tandi/tandi612

Powell, A., & Henry, N. (2019). Technology-facilitated sexual violence victimization: Results from an online survey of Australian adults. *Journal of Interpersonal Violence, 34*(17), 3637–3665. https://doi.org/10.1177/0886260516672055

Powell, A., Henry, N., Flynn, A., & Scott, A. J. (2019). Image-based sexual abuse: The extent, nature, and predictors of perpetration in a community sample of Australian residents. *Computers in Human Behavior, 92*, 393–402. https://doi.org/10.1016/j.chb.2018.11.009

Powell, A., Scott, A. J., Flynn, A., & Henry, N. (2020). *Image-based sexual abuse: An international study of victims and perpetrators*. Royal Melbourne Institute of Technology. https://researchmgt.monash.edu/ws/portalfiles/portal/319918063/ImageBasedSexualAbuseReport_170220_WEB_2.pdf

Powell, M. B., Casey, S., & Rouse, J. (2021). Online child sexual offenders' language use in real-time chats (No. 643). *Trends and Issues in Crime and Criminal Justice.* Australian Institute of Criminology. https://www.aic.gov.au/publications/tandi/tandi643

Prat, S., Bertsch, I., Chudzik, L., & Réveillère, Ch. (2014). Women convicted of a sexual offence, including child pornography production: Two case reports. *Journal of Forensic and Legal Medicine, 23*, 22–24. https://doi.org/10.1016/j.jflm.2014.01.002

Prichard, J., Wortley, R., Watters, P. A., Spiranovic, C., Hunn, C., & Krone, T. (2022). Effects of automated messages on internet users attempting to access "barely legal" pornography. *Sexual Abuse, 34*(1), 106–124. https://doi.org/10.1177/10790632211013809

Pullman, L. E., Sawatsky, M. L., Babchishin, K. M., McPhail, I. V., & Seto, M. C. (2017). Differences between biological and sociolegal incest offenders: A meta-analysis.

Aggression and Violent Behavior, 34, 228–237. https://doi.org/10.1016/j.avb.2017.01.003

Qu, J., Shen, S., Sun, I. Y., Farmer, A. K., & Xue, J. (2022). Sexting victimization among dating app users: A comparison of U.S. and Chinese college students. *Journal of Interpersonal Violence, 37*(19–20), NP17109–NP17132. https://doi.org/10.1177/08862605211028281

Quayle, E. (2021). Affordances, social media and the criminogenic nature of the internet: Technology-mediated child sexual abuse. In E. Caffo (Ed.), *Online child sexual exploitation: Treatment and prevention of abuse in a digital world* (pp. 33–48). Springer. https://doi.org/10.1007/978-3-030-66654-5_4

Quayle, E., Jonsson, L. S., Cooper, K., Traynor, J., & Svedin, C. G. (2018). Children in identified sexual images—Who are they? Self- and non-self-taken images in the International Child Sexual Exploitation Image Database, 2006–2015. *Child Abuse Review, 27*(3), 223–238. https://doi.org/10.1002/car.2507

Reavis, J., Eke, A. W., Farmus, L., & Seto, M. C. (2023). *Personality and psychopathology of individuals with online child sexual exploitation offenses* [Manuscript submitted for publication]. Intrapsychic.

Reid, J. A., Huard, J., & Haskell, R. A. (2015). Family-facilitated juvenile sex trafficking. *Journal of Crime and Justice, 38*(3), 361–376. https://doi.org/10.1080/0735648X.2014.967965

Reijnen, L., Bulten, E., & Nijman, H. (2009). Demographic and personality characteristics of internet child pornography downloaders in comparison to other offenders. *Journal of Child Sexual Abuse, 18*(6), 611–622. https://doi.org/10.1080/10538710903317232

Rheingold, H. (2000). *The virtual community, revised edition: Homesteading on the electronic frontier.* MIT Press.

Rimer, J. R. (2019). "In the street they're real, in a picture they're not": Constructions of children and childhood among users of online child sexual exploitation material. *Child Abuse & Neglect, 90,* 160–173. https://doi.org/10.1016/j.chiabu.2018.12.008

Rimer, J. R., & Holt, K. (2023). "It was in control of me": Notions of addiction and online child sexual exploitation material offending. *Sexual Abuse, 35*(1), 3–30. https://doi.org/10.1177/10790632211070797

Ringenberg, T. R., Seigfried-Spellar, K. C., Rayz, J. M., & Rogers, M. K. (2022). A scoping review of child grooming strategies: Pre- and post-internet. *Child Abuse & Neglect, 123,* Article 105392. https://doi.org/10.1016/j.chiabu.2021.105392

Ringrose, J., Regehr, K., & Whitehead, S. (2021). Teen girls' experiences negotiating the ubiquitous dick pic: Sexual double standards and the normalization of image based sexual harassment. *Sex Roles, 85*(9–10), 558–576. https://doi.org/10.1007/s11199-021-01236-3

Roche, K., & Stephens, S. (2022). Clinician stigma and willingness to treat those with sexual interest in children. *Sexual Offending: Theory, Research, and Prevention, 17,* 1–13. https://doi.org/10.5964/sotrap.5463

Roche, K., Stephens, S., Moss, S., & Seto, M. C. (2022). Online forum use in child attracted persons. *Canadian Journal of Human Sexuality, 31*(3), 409–421. https://doi.org/10.3138/cjhs.2022-0007

Romano, M., & Peters, L. (2015). Evaluating the mechanisms of change in motivational interviewing in the treatment of mental health problems: A review and meta-analysis. *Clinical Psychology Review, 38,* 1–12. https://doi.org/10.1016/j.cpr.2015.02.008

Rosenbloom, A. L. (2013). Inaccuracy of age assessment from images of post-pubescent subjects in cases of alleged child pornography. *International Journal of Legal Medicine, 127*(2), 467–471. https://doi.org/10.1007/s00414-012-0765-8

Rowse, J., Bolt, C., & Gaya, S. (2020). Swipe right: The emergence of dating-app facilitated sexual assault. A descriptive retrospective audit of forensic examination caseload in an Australian metropolitan service. *Forensic Science, Medicine and Pathology, 16,* 71–77. https://doi.org/10.1007/s12024-019-00201-7

Rudolph, J. I., van Berkel, S. R., Zimmer-Gembeck, M. J., Walsh, K., Straker, D., & Campbell, T. (2024). Parental involvement in programs to prevent child sexual abuse: A systematic review of four decades of research. *Trauma, Violence, & Abuse, 25*(1), 560–576. https://doi.org/10.1177/15248380231156408

Ruzicka, A. E., Assini-Meytin, L. C., Schaeffer, C. M., Bradshaw, C. P., & Letourneau, E. J. (2021). Responsible behavior with younger children: Examining the feasibility of a classroom-based program to prevent child sexual abuse perpetration by adolescents. *Journal of Child Sexual Abuse, 30*(4), 461–481. https://doi.org/10.1080/10538712.2021.1881858

Ryan, C. L. (2017). *Computer and internet use in the United States: 2016.* U.S. Department of Commerce, Economics and Statistics Administration, U.S. Census Bureau. https://www.census.gov/content/dam/Census/library/publications/2018/acs/ACS-39.pdf

Salter, M., & Whitten, T. (2022). A comparative content analysis of pre-internet and contemporary child sexual abuse material. *Deviant Behavior, 43*(9), 1120–1134. https://doi.org/10.1080/01639625.2021.1967707

Salter, M., & Wong, T. (2023). Parental production of child sexual abuse material: A critical review. *Trauma, Violence, & Abuse, 25*(3). Advance online publication. https://doi.org/10.1177/15248380231195891

Salter, M., Wong, W. K. T., Breckenridge, K., Scott, S., Cooper, S., & Peleg, N. (2021). Production and distribution of child sexual abuse material by parental figures (No. 616). *Trends & Issues in Crime and Criminal Justice.* Australian Institute of Criminology. https://doi.org/10.52922/ti04916

Sarkar, S. (2015). Use of technology in human trafficking networks and sexual exploitation: A cross-sectional multi-country study. *Transnational Social Review, 5*(1), 55–68. https://doi.org/10.1080/21931674.2014.991184

Savage, L. (2024). *Online child sexual exploitation: A statistical profile of police-reported incidents in Canada, 2014 to 2022.* Statistics Canada. https://www150.statcan.gc.ca/n1/en/pub/85-002-x/2024001/article/00003-eng.pdf?st=u4n1cRdS

Save the Children Finland. (2021). *Grooming in the eyes of a child—A report on the experiences of children on online grooming.* https://pelastakaalapset.s3.eu-west-1.amazonaws.com/main/2021/08/03151159/grooming_in_the_eyes_of_a_child_2021.pdf

Savoie, V., Quayle, E., Flynn, E., & O'Rourke, S. (2022). Predicting risk of reoffending in persons with child sexual exploitation material offense histories: The use of child pornography offender risk tool in a Scottish population. *Sexual Abuse, 34*(5), 568–596. https://doi.org/10.1177/10790632211047190

Scanlan, J., Prichard, J., Hall, L. C., Watters, P., & Wortley, R. (2024). *reThink Chatbot Evaluation.* https://www.iwf.org.uk/media/pvvnnjvf/rethink-chatbot-evaluation-report.pdf

Schaaf, S. (2022). *Heterogeneity in offenders who sexually exploit children online: A comparison of online child sexual exploitation material users* [Unpublished doctoral dissertation]. Fairleigh Dickinson University.

Schippers, E. E., Smid, W. J., Hoogsteder, L. M., Planting, C. H., & de Vogel, V. (2023). Pedophilia is associated with lower sexual interest in adults: Meta-analyses and a systematic review with men who had sexually offended against children. *Aggression and Violent Behavior, 69,* Article 101813. https://doi.org/10.1016/j.avb.2022.101813

Schmucker, M., & Lösel, F. (2015). The effects of sexual offender treatment on recidivism: An international meta-analysis of sound quality evaluations. *Journal of Experimental Criminology, 11*(4), 597–630. https://doi.org/10.1007/s11292-015-9241-z

Schneevogt, D., Chiang, E., & Grant, T. (2018). Do Perverted Justice chat logs contain examples of overt persuasion and sexual extortion? A research note responding to Chiang and Grant (2017, 2018). *Language and Law, 5*(1), 97–102.

Schröder, S., Bauer, L., Müller, J. L., Briken, P., Fromberger, P., & Tozdan, S. (2023). Web-based interventions for individuals who committed sexual offenses against children: Development, evaluation, and implementation. *Criminal Justice and Behavior, 50*(2), 235–251. https://doi.org/10.1177/00938548221140351

Schuler, M., Gieseler, H., Schweder, K. W., von Heyden, M., & Beier, K. M. (2021). Characteristics of the users of Troubled Desire, a web-based self-management app for individuals with sexual interest in children: Descriptive analysis of self-assessment data. *JMIR Mental Health, 8*(2), Article e22277. https://doi.org/10.2196/22277

Schulz, A., Bergen, E., Schuhmann, P., Hoyer, J., & Santtila, P. (2016). Online sexual solicitation of minors: How often and between whom does it occur? *Journal of Research in Crime and Delinquency, 53*(2), 165–188. https://doi.org/10.1177/0022427815599426

Scurich, N., & Gongola, J. (2021). Prevalence of polymorphism ("crossover") among sexual offenders. *Journal of Criminal Justice, 77,* 101853. https://doi.org/10.1016/j.jcrimjus.2021.101853

Scurich, N., & Krauss, D. A. (2023). Risk assessment of child-pornography-exclusive offenders. *Law and Human Behavior, 47*(4), 499–509. https://doi.org/10.1037/lhb0000537

Seigfried-Spellar, K. C., & Rogers, M. K. (2013). Does deviant pornography use follow a Guttman-like progression? *Computers in Human Behavior, 29*(5), 1997–2003. https://doi.org/10.1016/j.chb.2013.04.018

Seiser, A., Eher, R., Turner, D., & Rettenberger, M. (2023). The prevalence of mental disorders among incarcerated adult men convicted of child sexual exploitation material offences. *CNS Spectrums, 28*(6), 719–725. https://doi.org/10.1017/S1092852923002262

Seto, M. C. (2008). *Pedophilia and sexual offending against children: Theory, assessment, and intervention.* American Psychological Association. https://doi.org/10.1037/11639-000

Seto, M. C. (2012). Is pedophilia a sexual orientation? *Archives of Sexual Behavior, 41*(1), 231–236. https://doi.org/10.1007/s10508-011-9882-6

Seto, M. C. (2013). *Internet sex offenders.* American Psychological Association. https://doi.org/10.1037/14191-000

Seto, M. C. (2017a). The motivation–facilitation model of sexual offending. *Sexual Abuse.* Advance online publication.

Seto, M. C. (2017b). The puzzle of male chronophilias. *Archives of Sexual Behavior*, *46*(1), 3–22. https://doi.org/10.1007/s10508-016-0799-y

Seto, M. C. (2018). *Pedophilia and sexual offending against children: Theory, assessment, and intervention* (2nd ed.). American Psychological Association. https://doi.org/10.1037/0000107-000

Seto, M. C. (2019). The motivation–facilitation model of sexual offending. *Sexual Abuse*, *31*(1), 3–24. https://doi.org/10.1177/1079063217720919

Seto, M. C. (2022). Clinical and conceptual problems with pedophilic disorder in the *DSM-5-TR* [Commentary]. *Archives of Sexual Behavior*, *51*(4), 1833–1837. https://doi.org/10.1007/s10508-022-02336-1

Seto, M. C., Augustyn, C., Roche, K., & Hilkes, G. (2023). Empirically-based dynamic risk and protective factors for sexual offending. *Clinical Psychology Review, 102355*. https://doi.org/10.1016/j.cpr.2023.102355

Seto, M. C., Babchishin, K. M., Pullman, L. E., & McPhail, I. V. (2015). The puzzle of intrafamilial child sexual abuse: A meta-analysis comparing intrafamilial and extrafamilial offenders with child victims. *Clinical Psychology Review*, *39*, 42–57. https://doi.org/10.1016/j.cpr.2015.04.001

Seto, M. C., Buckman, C., Dwyer, R. G., & Quayle, E. (2018). *Production and active trading of child sexual exploitation images depicting identified victims*. NCMEC/Thorn. https://www.missingkids.org/content/dam/missingkids/pdfs/ncmec-analysis/Production%20and%20Active%20Trading%20of%20CSAM_FullReport_FINAL.pdf

Seto, M. C., Cantor, J. M., & Blanchard, R. (2006). Child pornography offenses are a valid diagnostic indicator of pedophilia. *Journal of Abnormal Psychology*, *115*(3), 610–615. https://doi.org/10.1037/0021-843X.115.3.610

Seto, M. C., Curry, S., Dawson, S. J., Bradford, J. M. W., & Chivers, M. L. (2021). Concordance of paraphilic interests and behaviors. *Journal of Sex Research*, *58*(4), 424–437. https://doi.org/10.1080/00224499.2020.1830018

Seto, M. C., & Eke, A. W. (2005). The criminal histories and later offending of child pornography offenders. *Sexual Abuse*, *17*(2), 201–210. https://doi.org/10.1177/107906320501700209

Seto, M. C., & Eke, A. W. (2015). Predicting recidivism among adult male child pornography offenders: Development of the Child Pornography Offender Risk Tool (CPORT). *Law and Human Behavior*, *39*(4), 416–429. https://doi.org/10.1037/lhb0000128

Seto, M. C., & Eke, A. W. (2017). Correlates of admitted sexual interest in children among individuals convicted of child pornography offenses. *Law and Human Behavior*, *41*(3), 305–313. https://doi.org/10.1037/lhb0000240

Seto, M. C., & Eke, A. W. (in press). Child sexual exploitation material offenses: Differences in individual and case characteristics based on how they came to attention of police. *Police Practice and Research*. https://doi.org/10.1080/15614263.2024.2342782

Seto, M. C., Fedoroff, J. P., Bradford, J. M., Knack, N., Rodrigues, N. C., Curry, S., Booth, B., Gray, J., Cameron, C., Bourget, D., Messina, S., James, E., Watson, D., Gulati, S., Balmaceda, R., & Ahmed, A. G. (2016). Reliability and validity of the *DSM-IV-TR* and proposed *DSM-5* criteria for pedophilia: Implications for the *ICD-11* and the next *DSM*. *International Journal of Law and Psychiatry*, *49*(Pt. A), 98–106. https://doi.org/10.1016/j.ijlp.2016.08.002

Seto, M. C., Hanson, R. K., & Babchishin, K. M. (2011). Contact sexual offending by men with online sexual offenses. *Sexual Abuse*, *23*(1), 124–145. https://doi.org/10.1177/1079063210369013

Seto, M. C., Hermann, C. A., Kjellgren, C., Priebe, G., Svedin, C. G., & Långström, N. (2015). Viewing child pornography: Prevalence and correlates in a representative community sample of young Swedish men. *Archives of Sexual Behavior, 44*(1), 67–79. https://doi.org/10.1007/s10508-013-0244-4

Seto, M. C., & Lalumière, M. L. (2001). A brief screening scale to identify pedophilic interests among child molesters. *Sexual Abuse, 13*(1), 15–25. https://doi.org/10.1177/107906320101300103

Seto, M. C., & Lalumière, M. L. (2010). What is so special about male adolescent sexual offending? A review and test of explanations through meta-analysis. *Psychological Bulletin, 136*(4), 526–575. https://doi.org/10.1037/a0019700

Seto, M. C., Murphy, W. D., Page, J., & Ennis, L. (2003). Detecting anomalous sexual interests in juvenile sex offenders. *Annals of the New York Academy of Sciences, 989*(1), 118–130. https://doi.org/10.1111/j.1749-6632.2003.tb07298.x

Seto, M. C., Reeves, L., & Jung, S. (2010). Explanations given by child pornography offenders for their crimes. *Journal of Sexual Aggression, 16*(2), 169–180. https://doi.org/10.1080/13552600903572396

Seto, M. C., Roche, K. M., Coleman, J., Findlater, D., & Letourneau, E. J. (2023). *Child sexual abuse prevention: Self-help seeking during the COVID-19 pandemic* [Manuscript submitted for publication]. Royal Ottawa Health Care Group.

Seto, M. C., Roche, K., Goharian, A., & Stroebel, M. (2022). American parents' perceptions of child explicit image sharing. *Journal of Online Trust & Safety, 1*(4). Advance online publication. https://doi.org/10.54501/jots.v1i4.75

Seto, M. C., Roche, K., Stroebel, M., Gonzalez-Pons, K., & Goharian, A. (2023). Sending, receiving, and nonconsensually sharing nude or near nude images by youth. *Journal of Adolescence, 95*(4), 672–685. https://doi.org/10.1002/jad.12143

Seto, M. C., Rodrigues, N., Roche, K., Curry, S., & Letourneau, E. J. (2023). *Evaluating child sexual abuse perpetration prevention efforts: A systematic and scoping review* [Manuscript submitted for publication]. Royal Ottawa Health Care Group.

Seto, M. C., Sandler, J. C., & Freeman, N. J. (2017). The revised Screening Scale for Pedophilic Interests: Predictive and concurrent validity. *Sexual Abuse, 29*(7), 636–657. https://doi.org/10.1177/1079063215618375

Seto, M. C., Stephens, S., Lalumière, M. L., & Cantor, J. M. (2017). The revised Screening Scale for Pedophilic Interests (SSPI-2): Development and criterion-related validation. *Sexual Abuse, 29*(7), 619–635. https://doi.org/10.1177/1079063215612444

Seto, M. C., Wood, J. M., Babchishin, K. M., & Flynn, S. (2012). Online solicitation offenders are different from child pornography offenders and lower risk contact sexual offenders. *Law and Human Behavior, 36*(4), 320–330. https://doi.org/10.1037/h0093925

Sheehan, V., & Sullivan, J. (2010). A qualitative analysis of child sex offenders involved in the manufacture of indecent images of children. *Journal of Sexual Aggression, 16*(2), 143–167. https://doi.org/10.1080/13552601003698644

Sheikh, M. M. R., & Rogers, M. M. (2024). Technology-facilitated sexual violence and abuse in low and middle-income countries: A scoping review. *Trauma, Violence, & Abuse, 25*(2), 1614–1629. https://doi.org/10.1177/15248380231191189

Shelton, J., Eakin, J., Hoffer, T., Muirhead, Y., & Owens, J. (2016). Online child sexual exploitation: An investigative analysis of offender characteristics and offending behavior. *Aggression and Violent Behavior, 30*, 15–23. https://doi.org/10.1016/j.avb.2016.07.002

Shields, R. T., Murray, S. M., Ruzicka, A. E., Buckman, C., Kahn, G., Benelmouffok, A., & Letourneau, E. J. (2020). Help wanted: Lessons on prevention from young adults with a sexual interest in prepubescent children. *Child Abuse & Neglect, 105*, Article 104416. https://doi.org/10.1016/j.chiabu.2020.104416

Shults, R. A., Elder, R. W., Sleet, D. A., Nichols, J. L., Alao, M. O., Carande-Kulis, V. G., Zaza, S., Sosin, D. M., Thompson, R. S., & the Task Force on Community Preventive Services. (2001). Reviews of evidence regarding interventions to reduce alcohol-impaired driving. *American Journal of Preventive Medicine, 21*(4, Suppl. 1), 66–88. https://doi.org/10.1016/S0749-3797(01)00381-6

Simonovska, T., Sinclair, R., & Duval, K. (2023, May 18). International health and wellness of online child sexual exploitation police personnel: Individual, management, and organizational realms of responsibility. *Frontiers in Psychology, 14*, Article 1155733. https://doi.org/10.3389/fpsyg.2023.1155733

Simpson, J. A., & Gangestad, S. W. (1991). Individual differences in sociosexuality: Evidence for convergent and discriminant validity. *Journal of Personality and Social Psychology, 60*(6), 870–883. https://doi.org/10.1037/0022-3514.60.6.870

Singh, J. P., Grann, M., & Fazel, S. (2011). A comparative study of violence risk assessment tools: A systematic review and metaregression analysis of 68 studies involving 25,980 participants. *Clinical Psychology Review, 31*(3), 499–513. https://doi.org/10.1016/j.cpr.2010.11.009

Smahel, D., Machackova, H., Mascheroni, G., Dedkova, L., Staksrud, E., Ólafsson, K., Livingstone, S., & Hasebrink, U. (2020). *EU Kids Online 2020: Survey results from 19 countries*. LSE Research Online. https://doi.org/10.21953/lse.47fdeqj01ofo

Soldino, V., Carbonell-Vayá, E. J., & Seigfried-Spellar, K. C. (2021). Spanish validation of the Child Pornography Offender Risk Tool. *Sexual Abuse, 33*(5), 503–528. https://doi.org/10.1177/1079063220928958

Soldino, V., & Seigfried-Spellar, K. C. (2024). Criminological differences between contact-driven and online-focused suspects in online child sexual grooming police reports. *Child Abuse & Neglect, 149*, Article 106696. https://doi.org/10.1016/j.chiabu.2024.106696

Sonck, N., Nikken, P., & De Haan, J. (2013). Determinants of internet mediation: A comparison of the reports by Dutch parents and children. *Journal of Children and Media, 7*(1), 96–113. https://doi.org/10.1080/17482798.2012.739806

Sparks, B., Stephens, S., & Trendell, S. (2023). Image-based sexual abuse: Victim-perpetrator overlap and risk-related correlates of coerced sexting, non-consensual dissemination of intimate images, and cyberflashing. *Computers in Human Behavior, 148*, Article 107879. https://doi.org/10.1016/j.chb.2023.107879

Spence, R., Harrison, A., Bradbury, P., Bleakley, P., Martellozzo, E., & DeMarco, J. (2023). Content moderators' strategies for coping with the stress of moderating content online. *Journal of Online Trust & Safety, 1*(5). Advance online publication. https://doi.org/10.54501/jots.v1i5.91

Steel, C. M., Newman, E., O'Rourke, S., & Quayle, E. (2020a). An integrative review of historical technology and countermeasure usage trends in online child sexual exploitation material offenders. *Forensic Science International: Digital Investigation, 33*, Article 300971. https://doi.org/10.1016/j.fsidi.2020.300971

Steel, C. M., Newman, E., O'Rourke, S., & Quayle, E. (2020b). A systematic review of cognitive distortions in online child sexual exploitation material offenders. *Aggression and Violent Behavior, 51*, Article 101375. https://doi.org/10.1016/j.avb.2020.101375

Steel, C., Newman, E., O'Rourke, S., & Quayle, E. (2022). Technical behaviours of child sexual exploitation material offenders. *Journal of Digital Forensics, Security and Law, 17*, Article 2. https://doi.org/10.15394/jdfsl.2022.1794

Steel, C. M., Newman, E., O'Rourke, S., & Quayle, E. (2023). Self perceptions and cognitions of child sexual exploitation material offenders. *International Journal of Offender Therapy and Comparative Criminology, 67*(10–11), 1017–1036. https://doi.org/10.1177/0306624X211062161

Steely, M., Ten Bensel, T., Bratton, T., & Lytle, R. (2018). All part of the process? A qualitative examination of change in online child pornography behaviors. *Criminal justice Studies, 31*(3), 279–296. https://doi.org/10.1080/1478601X.2018.1492389

Stein, D. M., & Lambert, M. J. (1984). On the relationship between therapist experience and psychotherapy outcome. *Clinical Psychology Review, 4*(2), 127–142. https://doi.org/10.1016/0272-7358(84)90025-4

Stephens, S., Elchuk, D., Davidson, M., & Williams, S. (2022). A review of childhood sexual abuse perpetration prevention programs. *Current Psychiatry Reports, 24*(11), 679–685. https://doi.org/10.1007/s11920-022-01375-8

Stephens, S., & McPhail, I. V. (2021). A preliminary examination of sexual interest in children in a non-representative community sample of females. *Journal of Sex & Marital Therapy, 47*(6), 591–604. https://doi.org/10.1080/0092623X.2021.1928804

Stephens, S., McPhail, I. V., Heasman, A., & Moss, S. (2021). Mandatory reporting and clinician decision-making when a client discloses sexual interest in children. *Canadian Journal of Behavioural Science/Revue canadienne des sciences du comportement, 53*(3), 263–273. https://doi.org/10.1037/cbs0000247

Stephens, S., Seto, M. C., Cantor, J. M., & Lalumière, M. L. (2019). The Revised Screening Scale for Pedophilic Interests (SSPI-2) may be a measure of pedohebephilia. *Journal of Sexual Medicine, 16*(10), 1655–1663. https://doi.org/10.1016/j.jsxm.2019.07.015

Stewart, H. (2022). *Characteristics of minor attracted persons in the community: Developing a biopsychosocial-sexual typology of men with sexual interests in children* [Unpublished doctoral dissertation]. University of New Brunswick.

Sturgess, D., Woodhams, J., & Tonkin, M. (2016). Treatment engagement from the perspective of the offender: Reasons for noncompletion and completion of treatment—A systematic review. *International Journal of Offender Therapy and Comparative Criminology, 60*(16), 1873–1896. https://doi.org/10.1177/0306624X15586038

Suler, J. (2004). The online disinhibition effect. *CyberPsychology & Behavior, 7*(3), 321–326. https://doi.org/10.1089/1094931041291295

Suojellaan Lapsia. (2022, December 13). *Feedback from users suggests that ReDirection self-help program successfully decreases CSAM use.* https://www.suojellaanlapsia.fi/en/post/feedback-from-users-suggests-that-redirection-self-help-program-successfully-decreases-csam-use

Suojellaan Lapsia. (2023, September 4). *'Chat to a specialist': Evaluation of an anonymous chat function of the ReDirection program.* https://www.suojellaanlapsia.fi/post/rdchat-evaluation-report-2

Surjadi, B., Bullens, R., van Horn, J., & Bogaerts, S. (2010). Internet offending: Sexual and non-sexual functions within a Dutch sample. *Journal of Sexual Aggression, 16*(1), 47–58. https://doi.org/10.1080/13552600903470054

Sutton, S., & Finkelhor, D. (2023). Perpetrators' identity in online crimes against children: A meta-analysis. *Trauma, Violence, & Abuse, 25*(3). Advance online publication. https://doi.org/10.1177/15248380231194072

Svedin, C. G., Back, K., & Barnen, R. (1996). *Children who don't speak out: About children being used in child pornography*. Radda Baren.

Taylor, B. G., Stein, N. D., Mumford, E. A., & Woods, D. (2013). Shifting Boundaries: An experimental evaluation of a dating violence prevention program in middle schools. *Prevention Science, 14*(1), 64–76. https://doi.org/10.1007/s11121-012-0293-2

Taylor-Smith, J. S. (2021). Public perceptions of indecent image offenders. *The Plymouth Student Scientist, 14*(2), 636–650.

Teunissen, C., Boxall, H., Napier, S., & Brown, R. (2022). The sexual exploitation of Australian children on dating apps and websites (No. 658). *Trends and Issues in Crime and Criminal Justice*. Australian Institute of Criminology. https://doi.org/10.52922/ti78757

Thibodeau, M., Laplante, E., Carpentier, J., Spearson Goulet, J.-A., & Le Lagedec, A. (2023, September 28–October 1). *What about the specific responsivity factors of child sexual exploitation material (CSEM) consumers?* [Paper presentation]. Association for the Treatment and Prevention of Sexual Abuse Conference, Aurora, CO, United States.

Thompson, C. (2019). *Everyday misogyny: On 'upskirting' as image-based sexual abuse* [Unpublished doctoral dissertation]. University of Melbourne.

Thompson, M. P., & Morrison, D. J. (2013). Prospective predictors of technology-based sexual coercion by college males. *Psychology of Violence, 3*(3), 233–246. https://doi.org/10.1037/a0030904

Thorn. (2021). *Responding to online threats: Minors' perspectives on disclosing, reporting, and blocking. Findings from 2020 quantitative research among 9–17 year olds*. https://info.thorn.org/hubfs/Research/Responding%20to%20Online%20Threats_2021-Full-Report.pdf

Thorn. (2022). *Online grooming: Examining risky encounters amid everyday digital socialization. Findings from 2021 qualitative and quantitative research among 9–17-year-olds*. https://info.thorn.org/hubfs/Research/2022_Online_Grooming_Report.pdf

Thorn. (2023). *Responding to online threats: Minors' perspectives on disclosing, reporting, and blocking in 2021. Findings from 2021 quantitative research among 9–17-year-olds*. https://info.thorn.org/hubfs/Research/Thorn_ROT_Monitoring_2021.pdf

Thorne, J. R. (2020). *Exploring the link between sexual thoughts of children and sexual offending against children* [Unpublished doctoral dissertation]. Johns Hopkins University.

Thornton, D., Mann, R., Webster, S., Blud, L., Travers, R., Friendship, C., & Erikson, M. (2003). Distinguishing between and combining risks for sexual and violent recidivism. In R. Prentky, E. Janus, & M. C. Seto (Eds.), *Understanding and managing sexually coercive behavior. Annals of the New York Academy of Sciences, 989*(1), 225–235. https://doi.org/10.1111/j.1749-6632.2003.tb07308.x

Todorovic, N., & Chaudhuri, A. (2018, September 3). *Using AI to help organizations detect and report child sexual abuse material online*. Google. https://blog.google/around-the-globe/google-europe/using-ai-help-organizations-detect-and-report-child-sexual-abuse-material-online/

Tolentino, D., & Tenbarge, K. (2023, November 4). *Omegle, the anonymous video chat site, shuts down after 14 years*. NBC News. https://www.nbcnews.com/tech/

social-media/omegle-shut-down-did-why-leif-k-brooks-shutdown-alternatives-rcna124393

Turner-Moore, T., & Waterman, M. (2017). Men presenting with sexual thoughts of children or coercion: Flights of fancy or plans for crime? *Journal of Sexual Medicine*, *14*(1), 113–124. https://doi.org/10.1016/j.jsxm.2016.11.003

UNICEF. (n.d.). *Ending online child sexual exploitation and abuse*. https://www.unicef.org/documents/ending-online-child-sexual-exploitation-and-abuse

United States Sentencing Commission. (2021). *Federal sentencing of child pornography: Production offenses*. https://www.ussc.gov/sites/default/files/pdf/research-and-publications/research-publications/2021/20211013_Production-CP.pdf

van den Berg, J. W., Smid, W., Schepers, K., Wever, E., van Beek, D., Janssen, E., & Gijs, L. (2018). The predictive properties of dynamic sex offender risk assessment instruments: A meta-analysis. *Psychological Assessment*, *30*(2), 179–191. https://doi.org/10.1037/pas0000454

van der Bruggen, M., & Blokland, A. (2022). Profiling darkweb child sexual exploitation material forum members using longitudinal posting history data. *Social Science Computer Review*, *40*(4), 865–891. https://doi.org/10.1177/0894439321994894

van Gijn-Grosvenor, E. L., & Lamb, M. E. (2016). Behavioural differences between online sexual groomers approaching boys and girls. *Journal of Child Sexual Abuse*, *25*(5), 577–596. https://doi.org/10.1080/10538712.2016.1189473

van Wijk, A., & van Esseveldt, J. (2021). Criminal careers of extrajudicial child sexual exploitation material users; a longitudinal and comparative study. *Journal of Crime and Criminal Behavior*, *1*(1), 53–68.

van Wijk, A., Vermeiren, R., Loeber, R., Hart-Kerkhoffs, L., Doreleijers, T., & Bullens, R. (2006). Juvenile sex offenders compared to non-sex offenders: A review of the literature 1995–2005. *Trauma, Violence, & Abuse*, *7*(4), 227–243. https://doi.org/10.1177/1524838006292519

Viljoen, J. L., Vargen, L. M., Cochrane, D. M., Jonnson, M. R., Goossens, I., & Monjazeb, S. (2021). Do structured risk assessments predict violent, any, and sexual offending better than unstructured judgment? An umbrella review. *Psychology, Public Policy, and Law*, *27*(1), 79–97. https://doi.org/10.1037/law0000299

Wachs, S., Michelsen, A., Wright, M. F., Gámez-Guadix, M., Almendros, C., Kwon, Y., Na, E.-Y., Sittichai, R., Singh, R., Biswal, R., Görzig, A., & Yanagida, T. (2020). A routine activity approach to understand cybergrooming victimization among adolescents from six countries. *Cyberpsychology, Behavior, and Social Networking*, *23*(4), 218–224. https://doi.org/10.1089/cyber.2019.0426

Wager, N., Gallagher, B., Armitage, R., Rogerson, M., Christmann, K., Parkinson, S., Reeves, C., Ioannou, M., & Synnott, J. (2018). *Rapid evidence assessment: Quantifying online facilitated child sexual abuse: Report for the Independent Inquiry into Child Sexual Abuse*. Home Office.

Wakeling, H. C., Howard, P., & Barnett, G. (2011). Comparing the validity of the RM2000 scales and OGRS3 for predicting recidivism by internet sexual offenders. *Sexual Abuse*, *23*(1), 146–168. https://doi.org/10.1177/1079063210375974

Walker, A., Kazemian, L., Lussier, P., & Na, C. (2020). The role of family support in the explanation of patterns of desistance among individuals convicted of a sexual offense. *Journal of Interpersonal Violence*, *35*(17–18), 3643–3665. https://doi.org/10.1177/0886260517712273

Walker, A., Makin, D. A., & Morczek, A. L. (2016). Finding Lolita: A comparative analysis of interest in youth-oriented pornography. *Sexuality & Culture, 20*(3), 657–683. https://doi.org/10.1007/s12119-016-9355-0

Walker, K., & Sleath, E. (2017). A systematic review of the current knowledge regarding revenge pornography and non-consensual sharing of sexually explicit media. *Aggression and Violent Behavior, 36*, 9–24. https://doi.org/10.1016/j.avb.2017.06.010

Wampold, B. E., Mondin, G. W., Moody, M., Stich, F., Benson, K., & Ahn, H. N. (1997). A meta-analysis of outcome studies comparing bona fide psychotherapies: Empirically, "all must have prizes." *Psychological Bulletin, 122*(3), 203–215. https://doi.org/10.1037/0033-2909.122.3.203

Ward, T. (2002). The management of risk and the design of good lives. *Australian Psychologist, 37*(3), 172–179. https://doi.org/10.1080/00050060210001706846

Ward, T., & Hudson, S. M. (1998). A model of the relapse process in sexual offenders. *Journal of Interpersonal Violence, 13*(6), 700–725. https://doi.org/10.1177/088626098013006003

Warnica, R. (2019, May 8). Child sex dolls are definitely 'icky' but should the law criminalize these coping behaviours? *National Post*. https://nationalpost.com/news/canada/its-definitely-icky-but-should-it-be-a-crime

Webb, L., Craissati, J., & Keen, S. (2007). Characteristics of internet child pornography offenders: A comparison with child molesters. *Sexual Abuse, 19*(4), 449–465. https://doi.org/10.1177/107906320701900408

Webster, S., Davidson, J., Bifulco, A., Gottschalk, P., Caretti, V., Pham, T., Grove-Hills, J., Turley, C., Tompkins, C., Ciulla, S., Milazzo, V., Schimmenti, A., & Craparo, G. (2012). *European Online Grooming Project: Final report*. https://europeanonlinegroomingproject.com/wp-content/file-uploads/European-Online-Grooming-Project-Final-Report.pdf

WeProtect Global Alliance. (2021). *Global threat assessment 2021: Working together to end the sexual abuse of children online*. https://www.weprotect.org/wp-content/plugins/pdfjs-viewer-shortcode/pdfjs/web/viewer.php?file=/wp-content/uploads/Global-Threat-Assessment-2021.pdf

WeProtect Global Alliance. (2023). *Global threat assessment 2023: Assessing the scale and scope of child sexual exploitation and abuse online, to transform the response*. https://www.weprotect.org/wp-content/uploads/Global-Threat-Assessment-2023-English.pdf

WeProtect Global Alliance and ECPAT. (2022). *Child sexual exploitation and abuse online: Survivors' perspectives*. https://www.weprotect.org/wp-content/uploads/05-01-2022_Project-Report_EN_FINAL.pdf

Wertz, M., Schobel, S., Schiltz, K., & Rettenberger, M. (2023). A comparison of the predictive accuracy of structured and unstructured risk assessment methods for the prediction of recidivism in individuals convicted of sexual and violent offense. *Psychological Assessment, 35*(2), 152–164. https://doi.org/10.1037/pas0001192

Whitaker, D. J., Le, B., Hanson, R. K., Baker, C. K., McMahon, P. M., Ryan, G., Klein, A., & Rice, D. D. (2008). Risk factors for the perpetration of child sexual abuse: A review and meta-analysis. *Child Abuse & Neglect, 32*(5), 529–548. https://doi.org/10.1016/j.chiabu.2007.08.005

Whittle, H., Hamilton-Giachritsis, C., Beech, A., & Collings, G. (2013). A review of online grooming: Characteristics and concerns. *Aggression and Violent Behavior, 18*(1), 62–70. https://doi.org/10.1016/j.avb.2012.09.003

Wild, T. S. N., Müller, I., Fromberger, P., Jordan, K., Klein, L., & Müller, J. L. (2020, March 2). Prevention of sexual child abuse: Preliminary results from an outpatient therapy program. *Frontiers in Psychiatry, 11*, Article 88. https://doi.org/10.3389/fpsyt.2020.00088

Willis, G. M., & Letourneau, E. J. (2018). Promoting accurate and respectful language to describe individuals and groups. *Sexual Abuse, 30*(5), 480–483. https://doi.org/10.1177/1079063218783799

Willis, G. M., Thornton, D., Kelley, S. M., & de Vries Robbé, M. (2021). *Structured Assessment of Protective Factors for Violence Risk–Sex Offense Version (SAPROF-SO) pilot manual* [Unpublished manuscript]. Department of Psychology, University of Auckland.

Wilpert, J., & Janssen, E. (2020). Characteristics of offending and non-offending CSA helpline users explored. *Journal of Forensic Practice, 22*(3), 173–183. https://doi.org/10.1108/JFP-03-2020-0011

Wilson, G., & Cox, D. (1983). *The child lovers: A study of paedophiles in society*. Peter Owen.

Wilson, R. J. (1999). Emotional congruence in sexual offenders against children. *Sexual Abuse, 11*(1), 33–47. https://doi.org/10.1177/107906329901100104

Winters, G. M., Colombino, N., Schaaf, S., Calkins, C., & Jeglic, E. L. (2023). Survivor perspectives of preventing child sexual abuse: A multi-level approach. *Victims & Offenders*, 1–23. https://doi.org/10.1080/15564886.2023.2174231

Wolak, J., & Finkelhor, D. (2013). Are crimes by online predators different from crimes by sex offenders who know youth in-person? *Journal of Adolescent Health, 53*(6), 736–741. https://doi.org/10.1016/j.jadohealth.2013.06.010

Wolak, J., Finkelhor, D., & Mitchell, K. (2011). Child pornography possessors: Trends in offender and case characteristics. *Sexual Abuse, 23*(1), 22–42. https://doi.org/10.1177/1079063210372143

Wolak, J., Finkelhor, D., & Mitchell, K. J. (2012). *Trends in arrests for child pornography possession: The Third National Juvenile Online Victimization Study (NJOV-3)*. https://scholars.unh.edu/ccrc/46/

Wolak, J., Finkelhor, D., Mitchell, K. J., & Jones, L. M. (2011). Arrests for child pornography production: Data at two time points from a national sample of U.S. law enforcement agencies. *Child Maltreatment, 16*(3), 184–195. https://doi.org/10.1177/1077559511415837

Wolak, J., Finkelhor, D., Mitchell, K. J., & Ybarra, M. L. (2008). Online "predators" and their victims: Myths, realities, and implications for prevention and treatment. *American Psychologist, 63*(2), 111–128. https://doi.org/10.1037/0003-066X.63.2.111

Wolak, J., Finkelhor, D., Walsh, W., & Treitman, L. (2018). Sextortion of minors: Characteristics and dynamics. *Journal of Adolescent Health, 62*(1), 72–79. https://doi.org/10.1016/j.jadohealth.2017.08.014

Woodhams, J., Kloess, J. A., Jose, B., & Hamilton-Giachritsis, C. E. (2021, April 8). Characteristics and behaviors of anonymous users of dark web platforms suspected of child sexual offenses. *Frontiers in Psychology, 12*, Article 623668. https://doi.org/10.3389/fpsyg.2021.623668

World Health Organization. (1994). *International statistical classification of diseases and related health problems* (10th ed.). https://icd.who.int/browse10/2019/en

World Health Organization. (2019). *International statistical classification of diseases and related health problems* (11th ed.). https://icd.who.int

Wortley, R., & Smallbone, S. (Eds.). (2006). *Situational prevention of sexual offenses against children*. Willan.

Wright, P. J., Tokunaga, R. S., & Kraus, A. (2016). A meta-analysis of pornography consumption and actual acts of sexual aggression in general population studies. *Journal of Communication*, 66(1), 183–205. https://doi.org/10.1111/jcom.12201

Yamaguchi, M. (2023, June 16). *Japan raises the age of sexual consent to 16 from 13, which was among the world's lowest*. PBS Newshour. https://www.pbs.org/newshour/world/japan-raises-the-age-of-sexual-consent-to-16-from-13-which-was-among-the-worlds-lowest

Young, S. (1997). The use of normalization as a strategy in the sexual exploitation of children by adult offenders. *The Canadian Journal of Human Sexuality*, 6(4), 285–296.

Zara, G., Veggi, S., & Farrington, D. P. (2022). Sexbots as synthetic companions: Comparing attitudes of official sex offenders and non-offenders. *International Journal of Social Robotics*, 14(2), 479–498. https://doi.org/10.1007/s12369-021-00797-3

INDEX

A

Actuarial measures, 139–140
ACUTE-2007, 150–151
Adults
   online sexual harassment of, 67
   sexual trafficking of, 101
   technology-facilitated sexual assault of, 9, 97–100, 118–119
Affordances, technological, 25–28
Age verification, 218
AI (artificial intelligence), 54
Anitha, S., 92
Antisociality, 126–127, 171
Antisocial peers, 169–170
Artificial intelligence (AI), 54
Autism spectrum conditions, 174–175
Azizian, A., 24

B

Babchishin, K. M., 38–39, 57
Bailey, J. M., 115
Bartels, R., 59
Beier, K. M., 190
Bell, A. 154–155
Bergen, E., 118
Bergeron, A., 177
Bestiality, 59–60
Biastophilia, 10
Bickart, W., 48
Blockage hypothesis, 165
Bogaerts, S., 52
Bows, H., 60

Boxall, H., 98
Broome, L. J., 78–79, 83
Brown, R., 52–53
Budin, L. E., 74

C

Cambodia, 103
Canadian Centre for Child Protection, 16–18, 46
Case formulation model, 121–122
CASIC (Correlates of Admission of Sexual Interest in Children Scale), 243, 246–247
CEM-COPE (Coping With Child Exploitation Material Use), 190–191
Centers for Disease Control and Prevention, 203
Changes over time
   in child sexual exploitation material (CSEM), 41–43
   in online sexual offending, 19–20
Child Pornography Offender Risk Tool (CPORT), 138, 151–153, 161, 234, 243–245
Child sex dolls, 54–55, 229–230
Child sexual abuse tourism, 9, 103–104, 119
Child sexual exploitation material (CSEM), 31–66
   case examples, 65–66
   changes over time, 41–43

Child sexual exploitation material (CSEM) (*continued*)
  content of, 35–38
  deepfakes, 55–56
  ecosystems of, 60–65
  as gateway offense, 130–132
  legal definitions, 31–32
  live streaming, 51–54
  offending, 116–117
  other illegal pornography, 56–60
  pathways, 120–128
  perpetrator characteristics, 38–41
  perpetrator countermeasures, 43–44
  prevalence of, 32–35
  production of, 44–48
  self-generated CSEM and sexting, 48–51
  virtual CSEM and child sex dolls, 54–55
Chopin, J., 43–44
Clearnet, 15
Clinical assessment topics, 172–178
Cockbain, E., 102
Coercive sexual sadism disorder, 10
Cognitions, offense-supportive, 166–168
Cognitions of Internet Sexual Offending (C-ISO), 168
Cognitive and Emotional Congruence with Children scale, 165–166
Commercial sexual exploitation of minors, 9
Community data, 147
Contact-driven solicitations, of minors, 77–80
Conte, J. R., 74
Coping, sexualized, 111, 118
Coping With Child Exploitation Material Use (CEM-COPE), 190–191
Correlates of Admission of Sexual Interest in Children Scale (CASIC), 154–158, 243, 246–247
Cortoni, F., 116, 168
CPORT. *See* Child Pornography Offender Risk Tool
Crime, self-control theory of, 114–115
Criminogenic needs assessment, 160–162
Cross-platform collaboration, 218–219
CSAM (child sexual abuse material). *See* CSEM (child sexual exploitation material)
CSEM. *See* Child sexual exploitation material
CSEM-adjacent content, 57–58
Cubitt, T. I. C., 53
Cultural environments, 64

D

Darknet, 15, 19
Davis, J. D., 103
Deepfakes, 8, 54–56
Denial of responsibility, 177–178
Desjardins, V., 78
"Dick pics," 89–91

Digital exhibitionism, 8, 89–93
Digital voyeurism, 8
Diversion, 197–198
Dodge, A., 197
Dual control model, of sexual arousal, 114
Dual perpetrators, 146
Dunkelfeld Prevention Project, 189–190, 194–195, 213–214, 219
Dynamic risk factors, 140–142

E

Echevarria, S. G., 98
Ecosystem changes, 236–237
ECPAT. *See* End Child Prostitution and Trafficking
Eke, A. W., 59, 131
Emotional congruence with children, 164–166
End Child Prostitution and Trafficking (ECPAT), 16, 18, 72
Engage Plus program, 189
Ethnicity, 23–24
Etiology, 109–112
European Online Grooming Project, 78–79
Excrement, 59–60
Exhibitionism, 8, 10, 89–93

F

Facilitation factors, 126–128
Fantasy-driven solicitations, of minors, 77–80
Filice, E., 98
Finkelhor, D., 34
Finland, 76, 84–85
Fortin, F., 37, 111
Fredlund, C., 53

G

Galperin, Eva, 100
Gámez-Guadix, M., 73, 85, 95
Gender differences, in sexual exploitation, 21–23
Gender preferences, of perpetrators, 36–37
Gewirtz-Meydan, A., 16–18, 99, 116
Gledhill, J., 69
Goller, A., 60
Gongola, J., 37
Grooming, 72–75
Group therapy, 196
Grubbs, J. B., 128

H

Hanson, R. K., 115, 152, 192
Harm reduction, 229–231
Hebephilia, 10, 122–124. *See also* Pedohebephilia
Helmus, L. M., 167

Helplines, 210
Henek, M., 59
Henry, N., 93–94, 97–98
"High school girls" businesses, 63
Holt, K. M., 97, 112
Horizon program, 188
Hybrid intervention models, 228
Hypersexuality, 10, 124–125, 164
Hypersexual solicitations, 79

I

Ibrahim, D., 69–70
iHorizon program, 188–189
Image-based offending, 93–95, 118
Image-based sexual abuse, 8
Immaturity hypothesis, 165
Individual therapy, 196
Inform Plus program, 189
In-person treatment, 213–214
Insoll, T., 130
Intense mating effort, 125
International Center for Missing and Exploited Children, 62
International Justice Mission, 103
Internet self-regulation deficits, 194
Internet Sex Offender Treatment Programme (i-SOTP), 187–188
Internet technologies, 13–15
Internet use, problematic, 127–128, 171–172
Internet Watch Foundation, 51, 54
Interventions, delivery of, 195–196
Intimacy-seeking solicitations, 79
Intrafamilial perpetration prevention, 206
i-SOTP (Internet Sex Offender Treatment Programme), 187–188

J

Japan, 63–64
Jeglic, E. L., 34–35
Johnson, C. F., 74
Joleby, M., 76–77
Josephson, S., 53–54
Juveniles, 194–195, 206–207
Jyoshi kousei ("high school girls") businesses, 63

K

Karasavva, V., 91, 92
Karlsson, J., 53–54
Kent Internet Risk Assessment Tool–Version 2 (KIRAT-2), 148–149
KIRAT-2 (Kent Internet Risk Assessment Tool–Version 2), 148–149
Kleijn, M., 52
Klein, V., 115
Kliethermes, B. C., 111

Koops, T., 104
Krauss, D. A., 156

L

Lam, A., 37–38
Lätth, J., 220
Laws, 31–32, 62–64
Lee, A. F., 172
Lewis, R., 92
Liu, Y., 93
Live streaming, 51–54
Loneliness, 169

M

Maas, M. K., 95
Madigan, S., 49
Madill, A., 23
Malesky, L. A., Jr., 75–76
Mandatory reporting, 227–228
Mann, R. E., 160
March, E., 90
Mateos-Pérez, E., 85
McGlynn, C., 60
McPhail, I. V., 165
Merdian, H. L., 81, 120–122
Middleton, D., 187
Minimization of responsibility, 177–178
Morgan, S., 116
Mori, C., 49
Morrison, D. J., 99
Motivation–facilitation model, 112–136
    application of, 116–119
    case examples, 132–136
    CSEM as gateway offense, 130–132
    CSEM pathways, 120–128
    limitations of, 119–120
    methodological issues, 128–130
Motivation to change, 192–193
Multiplied sextortion, 9

N

Najdowski, C. J., 56–57
National Center for Missing and Exploited Children (NCMEC), 47, 76, 82, 96
National Juvenile Online Victimization (NJOV), 42, 47, 70–71
Need principle, 137, 160
Nonconsensual sharing, 8, 49, 50

O

OASys Sexual Reoffending Predictor–Internet Version (OSP/I), 149–150, 156–157, 234–235
Offense-specific tools, 146–147
Offense-supportive cognitions, 166–168

Olver, K., 102
Olver, M. E., 141, 161, 164, 167, 184, 189
O'Malley, R. L., 97
Online guided intervention, 212–213
OSP/I. *See* OASys Sexual Reoffending Predictor–Internet Version
Oswald, F., 90–91
Outcome measures, 224–225

P

Paden, S. G., 24
Paquette, S., 116, 165, 168
Paraphilias, 9–10
Paraphilic disorder diagnoses, 173
Parents, 221–222
Patel, U., 34
Pedersen, W., 95
Pedohebephilia, 10, 163
Pedophilia, 10, 122–124, 162–164. *See also* Pedohebephilia
Peer support, 210–211
Perpetration prevention for juveniles, 206–207
Perpetrator(s). *See also* Treatment of perpetrators
  characteristics of, 38–41
  countermeasures for, 43–44
  detection of, 41, 44, 128
  dual, 146
  explanations of, 110–112
  gender preferences of, 36–37
Piché and Schweighofer's Treatment Model, 191
Polaris Project, 102
Police, undercover, 129–130
Policy environments, 62–64
Pooley, K., 98
Pornography, 56–60, 111, 124–125, 127–128, 131, 164
Post Conviction Risk Assessment, 156
Powell, A., 19, 97–98
Powell, M. B., 74–75
Prevention of online sexual offenses, 203–232
  and bystander interventions, 222–223
  case examples, 232
  challenges for, 223–229
  evaluations of, 219–220
  harm reduction, 229–231
  including parent in, 221–222
  in-person treatment, 213–214
  online guided intervention, 212–213
  and peer support, 210–211
  school-based, 214–215
  targets of prevention efforts, 205–208
  technology for, 215–219
Prevention programs
  barriers to, 225–226
  recruitment and retention for, 223–224

Prevent It program, 212–213
Prioritization tools, for risk, 147–150
Proactive content moderation, 218
Professional stigma, 226
PROTECT Act (US), 103
Protective factors, 119–120, 141, 143
Proulx, J., 37, 111
Pseudo-recidivism, 144–145
Public stigma, 226

Q

Quayle, E., 42

R

Race, 23–24
Reavis, J., 81
Recidivism rates, 143–146
Recruitment and retention, for prevention programs, 223–224
ReDirection survey, 41, 51
Reid, J. A., 101
Research, future directions for, 238–241
Responsibility, denial or minimization of, 177–178
Responsivity principle, 138, 172–173
Rimer, J. R., 112
Ringrose, J., 95
Risk, 137–172
  accumulating risk knowledge, 143–147
  assessing dynamic risk factors, 162–172
  assessment of, 138–143
  case examples, 179–182
  Child Pornography Offender Risk Tool (CPORT), 151–153
  Correlates of Admission of Sexual Interest in Children Scale (CASIC), 154–158
  criminogenic needs assessment, 160–162
  principle of, 137
  prioritization tools, 147–150
  Screening Scale for Pedophilic Interests (SSPI-2), 158–160
  of self-harm, 176
Risk assessment, structured, 139
Risk factors, 140–142, 145–146
Risk Matrix 2000 (RM2000/S), 148, 157
Risk–Need–Responsivity Framework, 137, 191–192
RM2000/S (Risk Matrix 2000), 148, 157
Roesch, R., 34
Rogers, M. K., 111
Rogers, M. M., 25
Ruzicka, A. E., 220

S

Safe Dates, 214
Salter, M., 46

Save the Children Finland, 84–85
Savoie, V., 156
Schaaf, S., 82
School-based prevention of online sexual offenses, 214–215
Schultz, A., 69
Screening Scale for Pedophilic Interests (SSPI-2), 158–160
Scurich, N., 37, 156
Seigfried-Spellar, K. C., 77–78, 111
Self-control theory of crime, 114–115
Self-harm risk, 176
Self-help resources, 208–210
Self-stigma, 226
Seto, M. C., 57, 59
Sex dolls, 54–55, 229–230
Sexting, 48–51
Sextortion, 8–9, 96–97
Sexual arousal, dual control model of, 114
Sexual disorder comorbidity, 174
Sexual exploitation
  commercial, 9
  gender differences in, 21–23
Sexual harm, prevalence and impact of, 16–19
Sexuality hypothesis, 165
Sexualized coping, 111, 118
Sexual motivations, 122
Sexual orientation, 23
Sexual recidivism rates, 143–146
Sexual sadism, 10
Sexual self-regulation, 193
Sexual solicitation of minors, 67–87
  case examples, 86–87
  comparisons with other perpetrator groups, 80–83
  fantasy- vs. contact-driven solicitations, 77–80
  methodological considerations, 83–84
  online solicitations compared with grooming, 72–75
  online solicitation tactics, 75–77
  perpetrator characteristics, 70–72
  prevalence of, 68–70
  target vulnerabilities, 84–85
Sexual trafficking, 9, 100–102, 119
Sexual violence, 56, 59–60
Sharing, nonconsensual. *See* Nonconsensual sharing
Sheikh, M. M. R., 25
Shifting Boundaries, 214
Situational factors, 114, 127
Social functioning, 194
Social isolation, 169
Social support, positive, 170–171
Sociosexuality, 125
Soldino, V., 77–78
Solicitations, 77–80, 117–118. *See also* Sexual solicitation of minors

Sparks, B., 94
Spencer, D. C., 197
SSPI-2 (Screening Scale for Pedophilic Interests-2), 158–160
STABLE-2007, 150–151, 160–162
Stalkerware, 100
State facilitation factors, 114
Static-99R (risk tool), 81, 150, 157–158
Static risk factors, 140–142
Steel, C. M., 20
Steely, M., 110
Stephens, S., 227
Stephens and McPhail, 22
Stewart, H., 207–208
Stigma, 226–227
Stop It Now!, 169, 170, 208–210, 216
Suicide risk, 176
Surjadi, B., 110
Sutton, S., 34

T

Talking for Change, 214
Taylor-Smith, J. S., 38
Technological affordances, 25–28
Technology, deepfake, 8, 54–56
Technology, for prevention of online sexual offenses, 215–219
Technology environments, 61–62
Technology-facilitated sexual assault of adults, 9, 97–100, 118–119
Teen pornography, 58
Telephone therapy, 228
Terminology, 6–10
Teunissen, C., 98
Thailand, 103
Therapy, individual vs. group, 196
Thibodeau, M., 175
Thompson, M. P., 99
Thorn, J. R., 34–35
Thorn Foundation, 49, 68, 84, 217
Tourism, child sexual abuse, 119
Trait facilitation factors, 113
Transnational child sexual abuse, 9
Treatment of perpetrators, 183–202
  case examples, 200–202
  common questions about, 198–199
  delivery of interventions, 195–196
  diversion, 197–198
  evidence-based recommendations for, 191–195
  models of, 185–191
Troubled Desire, 208–210, 223
Turner-Moore, T., 58–59

U

United States Sentencing Commission, 40, 45–46, 51
Unstructured risk assessment, 138–139

V

van Esseveldt, J., 197
van Gijn-Grosvenor and Lamb, 83
van Wijk, A., 197
Verification, of age, 218
Virtual CSEM, 229
Voyeurism, 8, 10

W

Wager, N., 68
Wagstaff, D. L., 90
Walker, A., 58
Waterman, M., 58–59

Websites, self-help, 210
WEIRD biases in research, 21, 24–25
WeProtect Alliance, 63, 72
WeProtect Global Alliance, 16, 18, 50, 217
Wild, T. S. N., 190
Winters, G. M., 34–35
Wolak, J., 71, 83, 96
Women, 194
Wong, T., 46
Woodhams, J., 61

Z

Zhao, Y., 23

ABOUT THE AUTHOR

Michael C. Seto, PhD, received his doctorate in psychology in 1997 from Queen's University in Kingston, Canada. He is a registered clinical forensic psychologist and a forensic research director with the Royal Ottawa Health Care Group. He is a professor of psychiatry at the University of Ottawa, with cross-appointments to the University of Toronto and Carleton University. Dr. Seto has published extensively on pedophilia, online sexual offending, sexual offending against children, violence risk assessment, and offenders with mental disorders, and he regularly presents at scientific meetings and professional workshops on these topics. The first edition of this book was published in 2013 by the American Psychological Association, which also published his book *Pedophilia and Sexual Offending Against Children, Second Edition,* in 2018. Further professional information is available from Dr. Seto's LinkedIn profile: https://ca.linkedin.com/in/mcseto. Information about his research—including scoring guides for the SSPI-2, CPORT, and CASIC; conference handouts; and access to peer-reviewed papers—is available through his ResearchGate profile (https://www.researchgate.net/profile/Michael_Seto).